HMS FEARLESS

HMS FEARLESS

THE MIGHTY LION

1965–2002

A Biography of a Warship and Her Ship's Company

by

EWEN SOUTHBY-TAILYOUR

Foreword by

The Lord Carrington, KG

Pen & Sword
MARITIME

First published in Great Britain in 2006 and reprinted in this format in 2013 by

PEN & SWORD MARITIME
an imprint of
Pen & Sword Books Ltd
47 Church Street, Barnsley
South Yorkshire, S70 2AS

ISBN: 1-84415-054-2
ISBN: 978-1-84415-054-0
ISBN: 978-1-78159-364-6

A CIP catalogue record for this book
is available from the British Library.

Typeset in 10/12pt Palatino by
Concept, Huddersfield, West Yorkshire

Printed and bound in India by
Replika Press Pvt. Ltd.

For a complete list of Pen & Sword titles please contact
PEN & SWORD BOOKS LIMITED
47 Church Street, Barnsley, South Yorkshire, S70 2AS, England
E-mail: enquiries@pen-and-sword.co.uk
Website: www.pen-and-sword.co.uk

Also by Ewen Southby-Tailyour

Falkland Islands Shores.
Reasons in Writing: A Commandos View of the Falklands War.
Amphibious Assault Falklands: The Battle for San Carlos.
Blondie: A Life of Lieutenant-Colonel HG Hasler, DSO, OBE, RM.
The Next Moon: A British Agent Behind the Lines in Wartime France.
Jane's Special Forces Recognition Guide. (Editor)
Jane's Amphibious and Special Forces. (Editor)

Contents

HMS *Fearless*

Motto

Explicit Nomen

Pennant number

L 10

(Previously L 3004)

Call sign

GKYQ

Seventh ship of the Royal Navy to bear the name

Battle Honours
Heligoland 1914, Jutland 1916, Norway 1940, Atlantic 1941, Malta Convoys 1941,
Mediterranean 1941, Falkland Islands 1982.

If I want a thing done well in a distant part of the world
I always send a Captain of the Royal Navy

Lord Palmerston

Commanding Officers

Captain H. A. Corbett DSO DSC RN   30 June 1965
Captain M. W. B. Kerr DSC RN   29 May 1967
Captain J. R. S. Gerard-Pearse RN   3 April 1969
Captain B. J. Straker OBE RN   20 October 1970
Captain S. A. C. Cassels RN   22 March 1972
Captain J. B. Rumble RN   18 June 1973
Captain L. A. Bird MVO RN   13 August 1975
Captain W. R. S. Thomas OBE RN   24 August 1977
Captain E. S. J. Larken RN   4 May 1981
Captain R. Trussell RN   4 March 1983
Captain P. G. J. Murison RN   11 December 1985
Captain S. R. Meyer RN   6 February 1990
Captain S. Moore RN   18 December 1991
Captain A. J. S. Taylor RN   30 July 1993
Captain R. A. I. McLean OBE RN   4 April 1995
Captain M. S. Williams RN   10 December 1996
Captain J. R. Fanshawe RN   28 August 1998
Captain C. J. Parry RN   7 December 1999
Captain T. A. Cunningham RN   4 April 2001
Commander B. H. Warren OBE RN   12 May 2002

Summary of Operations

Operations in support of ground forces – Ras al Ara, Aden 1966
Operation FATE – Hauf, Western Aden Protectorate 1966
Operations in support of the Radfan Campaign, South Arabia 1966
Operations to support withdrawal of British troops from Durban, South Africa 1966
Operation MAGISTER – withdrawal from Aden 1967
Operation DIOGENES – Gibraltar 1968
Operation ESTIMATE – Lagos 1969
Operation MOTORMAN/GLASSCUTTER/CARCAN – Northern Ireland 1972
Stood by for operations off Grenada 1974
Stood by for operations in Cyprus 1974
Operation CORPORATE/SUTTON – Falkland Islands 1982
Operation OFFCUT – Lebanon 1983
Stood by for Operation GRANBY – Iraq 1990
Operation SUMMER BREEZE – drug interdiction off Puerto Rico 1991
Operation SILKMAN – Sierra Leone (cancelled due to engine room fire) 2000
Stood by, offshore, during handover of Hong Kong 1997
Operation ORACLE – Afghanistan 2001
Operation VERITAS – Afghanistan 2002

... and at the last count, 138 major, national and international exercises plus at least as many 'in-house' amphibious landings and civilian aid projects.

Dedicated to

The Crew of *Foxtrot Four*

Choiseul Sound
8 June 1982

Colour Sergeant B. R. Johnston QGM Royal Marines
Sergeant R. J. Rotherham Royal Marines
LME(M) D. Miller Royal Navy
Marine A. J. Rundle
Marine R. D. Griffin
MEA(P) A. S. James Royal Navy

Supplement to the *London Gazette*, 8 October 1982:

The Queen has been graciously pleased to approve the Posthumous award of the Queen's Gallantry Medal to the undermentioned in recognition of gallantry during the operations in the South Atlantic.

Colour-Sergeant Brian Johnston, coxswain of LCU F4, was working in the vicinity of HMS Antelope when her unexploded bomb detonated, starting an immediate fire which caused her crew, already at emergency stations, to be ordered to abandon ship. Without hesitation Colour-Sergeant Johnston laid his craft alongside the Antelope and began to fight the fire and take off survivors. At approximately 2200Z he was ordered to stay clear of the ship because of the severity of the fire and the presence of a second unexploded bomb. Colour-Sergeant Johnston remained alongside until his load was complete. In all LCU F4 rescued over 100 survivors from the Antelope.

On 8th June, LCU F4 was attacked by enemy aircraft in Choiseul Sound. During this action Colour-Sergeant Johnston and five of his crew were killed. Colour-Sergeant Johnston's selfless bravery in the face of extreme danger was in the highest traditions of the Corps.

Remembering also Petty Officer ACM Ben Casey and Corporal 'Doc' Love, DSM, who were lost in an aircraft accident while serving with 846 NAS in HMS Fearless during the Falklands War.

Remembering, too, those who died while serving on board in peacetime.

Previous Royal Navy ships named *Fearless*

First:
A Gunboat of 149 tons launched at Gravesend in 1794. Carried 12 cannon and a complement of 50. Foundered in Cawsand Bay, Plymouth, in January 1804 – where she still lies.

Second:
Gun-brig of 180 tons launched in 1804. 12 cannon. Bombarded Copenhagen in 1807 as part of the Fleet under Admiral James Gambier. Wrecked near Cadiz in 1812.

Third:
Wooden, steam paddle tender of 165 tons launched in 1831. Ex-GPO vessel, the *Flamer*. Renamed *Fearless* in 1837 when the Admiralty took over the Packet Service. Served until 1875 then broken up on Admiralty orders.

Fourth:
3rd Class Torpedo Cruiser of 1,430 tons built by Vickers. Laid down in 1886 and launched in 1888. Armed with four 5-inch guns and three torpedo tubes. Commissioned at Portsmouth and served mainly in the Mediterranean but also saw service at the Cape of Good Hope in 1899. Paid off in 1900 and recommissioned for China in 1901. Finally sold in 1905.

The fourth HMS *Fearless*.

The fifth HMS *Fearless*.

Fifth:
Active Class Light Scout Cruiser of 3,440 tons launched in 1912. Both oil and coal fired. Carried ten 4-inch guns, four 3-pounder guns and two 21-inch torpedo tubes. Battle honours 1914 – Heligoland, 1916 – Jutland. Rammed and sank British submarine *K.17* on 31 January 1918. Served with the Home Fleet between 1913–14, seeing action off the Dutch coast on 18 August 1914 with the German light cruiser *Rostock*. Ten days later off Heligoland, she was present at the sinking of the German destroyer *V-187*. Two years later she was at the Battle of Jutland; subsequently attached to the 12th Submarine Flotilla. Present at the Battle of May Island in the Firth of Forth in 1915. Sold in November 1921.

A drifter named *Fearless* took part, in company with many Royal Navy ships, against a German destroyer raid in the Dover Strait on 15 February 1918. A spurious claim perhaps as she was not 'commissioned'.

Sixth:
F Class Destroyer of 1,375 tons. Launched in Birkenhead in 1934. Four 4.7-inch guns and eight 21-inch torpedo tubes. Involved in the Spanish Civil War in 1937. In Vaagsfjord on 15 April 1940 sank *U.49* in company with HMS *Brazen*. In 1940 she attacked French ships off Mers el Kebir as part of Force H under Vice Admiral Sir James Somerville. On 9 February 1941 she bombarded Genoa as part of Force H. On 18 June 1941 she sank *U.38* off Cadiz in company with HMSs

The sixth HMS *Fearless*

Faulkner, Foresight, Forester and *Foxhound*. Member of Force H escorting a convoy from Gibraltar to Malta when, on 23 July 1941 she was damaged by Italian torpedo aircraft while screening HMS *Ark Royal* off Galita island during Operation SUBSTANCE. Too damaged to be taken in tow she was sunk north of Bone by HMS *Forester* that same day.

Foreword

by

The Lord Carrington, KG.

First Lord of the Admiralty: 1959–1963
Secretary of State for Defence: 1970–1974
Secretary of State for Foreign and Commonwealth Affairs: 1979–1982

Ewen Southby-Tailyour, with the help of her Commanding Officers, has written a splendid biography of HMS *Fearless*: her ups, her downs, the excitements and the boredom, coupled with trenchant comments from successive Ships Companies.

It so happens, that when the idea of an Assault Ship of the type of *Fearless* and *Intrepid* was being considered, I happened to be First Lord of the Admiralty and I remember well the discussions which led to the eventual commissioning of *Fearless*. By the late 50s, the Landing Ship Tanks, which were used during the Second World War, were out of date and obsolete and, incidentally, exceedingly uncomfortable, as I remember when crossing the Channel in June 1944. From this discussion came *Fearless* and *Intrepid*. I have to say that those of us who looked at the drawings, did not think that they were likely to be very beautiful ships, nor were they. Looking back, it is astonishing to realize that the cost of the ship was only £8 million. A small yacht is as much as we could expect today, though at that time, their Lordships were aghast at the price.

Fearless never took part in a major war, thanks to the deterrent which NATO posed during the Cold War years but as you will read, there was a good deal of incident in her thirty-seven years,

Lord Carrington and Chief Cook Chow Tan BEM. Commander (S) Norman in the centre.

not least, of course, the battle for the Falkland Islands. At the same time, she was the venue for a number of interesting meetings. The most significant being to host the Prime Minister, Harold Wilson, together with his entourage, during one of the endless discussions with Ian Smith. The entourage, as you will discover, provided some hilarious moments.

Colonel Southby-Tailyour writes with first-hand knowledge. This is a fascinating and enjoyable book and more importantly, a valuable piece of Naval history.

Glossary

This is an at-a-glance check list of the most used acronyms: fuller details will be found within the text.

2IC	Second in Command
AB	Able Seaman
ABU	Amphibious Beach Unit
ACC	Army Catering Corps
AGI	Russian intelligence gathering vessel
AMP	Assisted Maintenance Period
AOA	Amphibious Objective Area
AOO	Amphibious Operations Officer
AOR	Amphibious Operations Room
ASRM	Assault Squadron Royal Marines
ASW	Anti-Submarine Warfare
ATF	Amphibious Task Force
ATG	Amphibious Task Group
ATTURM	Amphibious Trials and Training Unit Royal Marines (Instow, North Devon)
AVCAT	Aviation Fuel (kerosene based)
AVGAS	Aviation Fuel (petrol)
AVO	Aviation Officer
AVRE	Armoured Vehicle Royal Engineers
BAOR	British Army of the Rhine
BARV	Beach Armoured Recovery Vehicle
Bde	Brigade
BFG	British Forces (Persian) Gulf
Bn	Battalion (infantry)
BNA	British Naval Attaché
BOST	Basic Operational Sea Training
Bty	Battery (artillery)
C2	Command and Control
C3I	Command, Control, Communications and Intelligence
C4I	Command, Control, Communications, Computers and Intelligence
CAP	Combat Air Patrol
CBG	Carrier Battle Group
Cdo	Commando
CDS	Chief of the Defence Staff
CGRM	Commandant General Royal Marines
Chaff	Small strips of metal foil fired into the air to confuse enemy radar-guided missiles

C-in-C	Commander-in-Chief
CIWS	Close-in Weapon System (ship defence weapon)
CLF	Commander, Landing Force
CND	Campaign for Nuclear Disarmament
CO	Commanding Officer
COIN	Counter Insurgency
COMAF	Commodore Amphibious Forces (later COMAW then COMATG)
COMATG	Commodore Amphibious Task Group
COMAW	Commodore Amphibious Warfare
COMINT	Communications Intelligence
COMUKMARFOR	Commander United Kingdom Maritime Force
COMUKAMPHIBFOR	Commander United Kingdom Amphibious Force (CGRM)
Coy	Company (Royal Marines and infantry)
CPO	Chief Petty Officer
CPX	Command Post Exercise
C/Sgt	Colour Sergeant
CTCRM	Commando Training Centre Royal Marines (Lympstone, south Devon)
CTP	Cocktail Party
CVS	Light aircraft carrier
DA	Defence Attaché
DAMP	Dockyard Assisted Maintenance Period
DCO	Duty Commanding Officer
DGS	Director General Ships
DLF	Dhofar Liberation Front (later PFLOAG)
DLG	Guided Missile Destroyer
Dogwatches	Between 1600 and 2000 hours
DSM	Detachment Sergeant Major
DTS	Dartmouth Training Squadron (Ship)
DUKW	Second World War wheeled amphibious truck
EAP	Eastern Aden Protectorate
ECM	Electronic Counter Measures
EMF	Embarked Military Force
Eng	Engineer
EOKA	Greek-Cypriot liberation movement
EW	Electronic Warfare
FAA	Fleet Air Arm
FC	Fleet Chief
FCMAA	Fleet Chief Master at Arms
Fd Arty	Field Artillery
FEARSOS	Fearless Standing Orders
FEARTEM	Fearless Temporary Memorandum
FEF	Far East Fleet
FFO	Furnace Fuel Oil
Flyco	Flying Command

FOB	Forward Operating Base (landing craft/helicopters)
FOCAS	Flag Officer Carriers and Amphibious Ships (later FOF3)
FOF1 (2 and 3)	Flag Officer First Flotilla (Second and Third Flotillas)
FOSNI	Flag Officer Scotland and Northern Ireland
FOST	Flag Officer Sea Training (Portland, now Plymouth)
FRA	Federal Regular Army (Aden)
Gp	Group
GPS	Global Positioning System
HATS	Harbour Acceptance Trials
Helo	Helicopter
HF	High Frequency
HMG	Heavy Machine Gun (0.5 inch)
HODS	Heads of Department
HQ1	Ship's damage control centre
IFF	Identification Friend or Foe
IRC	Inflatable Raiding Craft (Gemini)
ISD	In Service Date
JMC	Joint Maritime Course
JNCO	Junior Non Commissioned Officer
JR	Junior Rates
LCA	Landing Craft Assault (later known as an LCVP)
LCM	Landing Craft Mechanised (later known as an LCU)
LCT	Landing Craft Tank
LCU	Landing Craft Utility
LCVP	Landing Craft Vehicle and Personnel
LMA	Leading Medical Attendant
LMEM	Leading Marine Engineering Mechanic
LOA	Local Overseas Allowance
Logs	Logistics
LPD	Landing Platform Dock (Assault Ship)
LPH	Landing Platform Helicopter
LS	Leading Seaman
LSA	Landing Ship Assault
LSD	Landing Ship Dock
LSL	Landing Ship Logistic
LST	Landing Ship Tank
MA	Medical Attendant
MAA	Master At Arms (senior NCO of the ship's company)
MACC	Military Aid to the Civil Community
MCM	Mine Counter Measures
MCT	Maritime Counter Terrorism
ME	Mechanical Engineer

MEF	Middle East Fleet
MEM	Marine Engineer Mechanic
MEO	Marine Engineer Officer (senior engineer in a ship)
Mexeflote	Sectioned-raft powered by huge outboard engines. Carried on the sides of LSLs for the landing of heavy equipment. Can be split into different lengths
MGRM	Major General Royal Marines
MLC	Minor Landing Craft (LCU, LCM, LCVP, IRC, RRC, RIB etc)
MSR	Main Supply Route
MT 80 MOGAS	Vehicle Fuel
MV	Motor Vessel
NA	Naval Attaché
NAS	Naval Air Squadron
NGS	Naval Gunfire Support
OCAD	Officer Commanding Amphibious Detachment (later OCAS)
OCAS	Officer Commanding Amphibious Squadron
OOW	Officer of the Watch
OPLAN	Operational Plan
ORBAT	Order of Battle
OS	Ordinary Seaman
OUT	Officer Under Training
PFLOAG	People's Front for the Liberation of the Arabian Gulf
PJHQ	Permanent Joint Headquarters
PMO	Principal Medical Officer
PNG	Passive night goggles
PO	Petty Officer
POME	Petty Officer Marine Engineer
PPS	Parliamentary Private Secretary
PWO	Principal Warfare Officer
PXD	Post Exercise Discussion
QMS	Quartermaster Sergeant
RA	Royal Artillery
RAPC	Royal Army Pay Corps
RAS(L)(S)	Replenishment At Sea (liquids) (solids)
RASC	Royal Army Service Corps
RCT	Royal Corps of Transport
RE	Royal Engineers
REME	Royal Electrical and Mechanical Engineers
RFA	Royal Fleet Auxiliary
RIB	Rigid Inflatable Boat
RLC	Royal Logistics Corps
RNLMC	Royal Netherlands Marine Corps
ROE	Rules of Engagement

ROP	Report of Proceedings
RPL	Ramped Powered Lighter
RRC	Rigid Raiding Craft
RS	Royal Signals
RSM	Regimental Sergeant Major
RTR	Royal Tank Regiment
SACEUR	Supreme Allied Commander Europe
SACLANT	Supreme Allied Commander Atlantic
SAF	Sultan of Oman's Armed Forces
SAS	Special Air Service
SATS	Sea Acceptance Trials
SBD	Special Boat Detachment (SBS)
SBS	Special Boat Squadron (now Service)
SDV	Swimmer Delivery Vehicle
Seacat	Short range surface to air missile
SEAL	Sea Air Land (US special forces)
SHAR	Sea Harrier vertical take off/landing fighter
SHP	Shaft Horse Power
SIGINT	Signals Intelligence
SNCO	Senior Non Commissioned Officer
SOR	Ships Operations Room
SR	Senior Rates
SSN	Nuclear Powered Submarine
STUFT	Ship(s) Taken Up From Trade
TLC	Tank Landing Craft (later LCT)
TMMATLM	Those Magnificent Men and their Landing Machines
UHF	Ultra High Freqency
VHF	Very High Frequency
WAP	Western Aden Protectorate
WEO	Weapons Electrical Officer
WO	Warrant Officer
WRNS	Womens Royal Naval Service – Wrens
XO	Executive Officer
YO	Young Officer (under training)

Introduction

In writing this biography I am mindful that *Fearless* was a twin and that her younger sister, *Intrepid*, could just as easily have been the subject of a similar work. That having been said, some have expressed a personal view that the elder sibling was the more 'chummy' ship but any comparison would be wrong as Captain Sym Taylor, Executive Officer of one and Commanding Officer of the other, has written:[1]

> *In their earlier days there was a friendly but quite definite rivalry between the Ships' Companies of both* Intrepid *and* Fearless. *In later years, with only one ship in commission at any time, this rivalry was replaced with a feeling of real pride in serving in the Amphibious Flagship and taking part in something that was completely different from the rest of the Navy. Over many years a deep-rooted LPD family spirit was established, which was readily obvious in both ships.*
>
> *In my time, going from* Intrepid *to* Fearless *with a gap of five years, it was reassuring to be able to serve again with more than half of the ship's company. Serving in these ships became much requested as many of the ship's company went from one LPD to a shore billet, then to the other ship, and then back again and so on for years: this led to a professional, experienced and happy ship's company that maintained unique skills.*

Thus, in general terms, whenever someone – for instance, Rear Admiral Burnell-Nugent[2] from the Gulf in August 2001 – praises the flexibility of *Fearless* he could easily have been doing so for *Intrepid* had she too (or instead) been under his command. General descriptions apply to both ships while individual comments, rightly, highlight any differences.

It would be easy simply to chronicle the life of HMS *Fearless* in an endless description of Portland work-ups, inspections, exercises, dockyard maintenance periods, long sea passages and visits, so I have tended to home-in on those occasions that were significant in some manner. This is not a blow-by-blow chronicle of her deeds, many of which have been merely footnoted or even left out altogether, but is more in the nature of an anthology of those deeds. The choice of inclusion has been mine: others, no doubt, would have chosen different examples of how the ship operated.

My primary aim has been to give an overall impression of what life was like in the last third of the twentieth century (and for two years of this century) in the Royal Navy in general but in this extraordinary class of ship in particular. Of course, any anthology is only as good as the stories sent for possible use and while I have tried to include everyone's offering, no matter how small, there will be huge gaps and those simply because no one has felt strongly enough to fill them. It is certainly not my job to re-invent stories even if I know of their existence but not of their detail, although the temptation to do so was almost unbearable!

Despite the wealth of material received, I am sad that the well of information began to dry up the closer we came towards the end of *Fearless*'s life. This may have been because many of her ship's company were still serving and the Official Secrets Act was exerting more of a malign influence on a desire to help, or it may have been because time spent in *Fearless* had yet to be seen in relation to an individual's wider experience of life. Nevertheless, I had hoped for a greater proportion of lower deck to wardroom offerings.

To the non-cognoscenti it might appear that life was one long run ashore or maintenance period, interspersed occasionally by inspections and exercises and only too rarely, by operations.

Much of *Fearless's* life was spent during the Cold War when the deployments, exercises and demonstrations – often, and on purpose, in full view of shadowing Soviet bloc ships – were part of that 'war'. She was on duty then as much as she was when taking part in Operations FATE, MOTORMAN, CORPORATE or ORACLE. The Cold War was also 'fought' through showing the flag in non-aligned countries where standards of seamanship and behaviour ashore, as well as impressive on board entertainment for military, diplomatic, civil and political dignitaries were, each one, a small battle for the hearts and diplomatic minds of 'wobbly' states or even potential enemy states.

There were, of course, boring periods and sometimes a boring sameness between one NATO exercise and the next and even, sometimes, between one Dartmouth Training Cruise and the next.

Those who know the Royal Navy will also know that periods of tedium make up a ship's life: months in dockyard hands, weeks at sea on passage (although few find this boring for the ship at last and, perhaps all too briefly, can settle into a steady routine and 'do her own thing') and long, hard hours of inspections, trials and training. It is the runs ashore – seeing the world – that encourage Jack and Royal to join in the first place while, to many, operations are the icing on the cake; but too much icing can be (so I am told) just as tedious as too much cake.

One should be pleased that the number of operations were few, for war indicates a collapse of diplomacy and political expediency but, along with 'paid travel', it is another reason why many join the armed forces. The scarcity of major operations was, perhaps, indicative of the successful part played by the Royal Navy in the Cold War. It was suggested by Admiral of the Fleet Lord Lewin[3] that the satisfactory conclusion of the Falklands campaign in the United Kingdom's favour helped the Cold War to end – and *Fearless* was absolutely central to that 'conflict'.

Fearless was a 'flag ship' and so had more than her fair share of high level visits and visitors and with those came the parties. While, to the outsider, these may have seemed fun and almost extravagant they are part of a major warship's life. They are, of course, not so amusing for the gangway staff stifling or freezing in their best uniforms, or for the engineering department struggling with the air conditioning or the landing craft crews if the ship is anchored offshore, nor, especially, for the supply department personnel working long hours in preparation, serving and clearing up. Neither was it entirely unknown for the hosts, once the last guest had departed, to collapse with a not-so-quiet-comment of, 'Thank God that's all over!' for not every official party list – whether it be in the wardroom or the Warrant Officers' and CPOs' Mess – hinted, in advance, of a wild evening with long-haired, long-limbed, Foreign Office Third Secretaries or millionaire, teenage daughters of the local rum-distillery's owner: some (of the parties) were very hard going indeed.

Fearless was fortunate too, for while her *raison d'être* was to command, transport, land, support and recover a landing force, when that force needed training it was often in colourful places, for her work was inshore off beaches or up fjords and not on anti-submarine patrols in the north Atlantic wastes nor under the Arctic icecap. *Fearless's* duties required her almost anywhere from Norway to the West Indies, from the Gulf to the Far East – not forgetting the occasional visit to Florida, South Africa, the Black Sea, Hong Kong, Australia or the South Atlantic.

Exercises also brought briefings and post exercise discussions – PXDs or 'wash-ups' – and these tended to be held in such tourist traps as Tromso, Naples, Athens, San Juan, Bahrain, Singapore or Malta, and while the captains and colonels, commodores, brigadiers, admirals and generals deliberated, those members of the ship's company and embarked military force not involved could make the most of these exotic surroundings – and they did, and that too is part of the *Fearless* story. When not employed on amphibious duties the needs of midshipmen and apprentices to gain sea time in the Arctic, Mediterranean and the West Indies also provided interesting visits and experiences.

Because of her ability to carry almost anything on wheels or tracks or that floated or flew and that could fit, and because she had a suite of quarters designed for the purpose, more than once was *Fearless* the preferred venue for diplomatic discussions, trade fairs and the like. She was used around the globe by ambassadors, consuls, captains of industry and Secretaries of State – even Prime Ministers – to entertain their counterparts: sometimes with rather ulterior motives.

In short she was more than the sum of the parts that make up a warship; she was unique and, as a steamship, became more unique with age. Serving in her was also an unusual experience which is why many who did so would return, willingly, in anticipation of more variety to come.

Her first commission began with operations in the Middle East and her last, thirty-seven years later, concluded with operations in the Middle East. In between there were some tragedies and much fun but throughout the good times and the bad there was an overriding professionalism that kept her name in the public eye through four decades and I have tried to show why, while at the same time skipping over the bits that were, frankly, not significant to that success. By and large she was an efficient ship – mostly a supremely efficient ship – but there were cock-ups and mistakes and these must, too, be recognized for if something has gone well but by default, it might not go so well next time. Success should be analysed equally as carefully as failure.

At the outset I was determined that each Commanding Officer should introduce his own chapter – indeed stamp his mark on 'his' chapter much as he stamped his mark on 'his' time in command: I would then merely add in the linking narratives. It has almost worked out like that with each Commanding Officer setting the scene. Those that asked to see what others had written were refused – that way there would have been too much uniformity – for, surely, no Commanding Officer had ever asked, in advance, how his predecessor had commanded *Fearless*? For my part, I have made no serious comment on *Fearless*'s 'characters' at any level but have, only occasionally, done so on outsiders and events.

If there has to be a secondary aim, mine has been quite simple: I have wanted to explain how the ship worked, how she was manned and for what purpose. In doing so I hope to have shown how much fun life in *Fearless* could often be and how stimulating and challenging it certainly was – and, thus, how professionally rewarding.

At the end I was struck by how frequently industrial relations impacted on *Fearless*'s life and yet she had a proud record of – almost always – putting to sea on time; but it remains a sad indictment of the manner in which the country faced the Cold War against Communism – especially at home – that its armed forces were dogged by delays, inefficient workmanship and an increasingly restrictive – and sometimes spurious – application of 'health and safety' issues. I was also surprised at how often HM Customs and Excise operated in a manner unworthy of a uniformed organization.

A factor that cropped up regularly was *Fearless*'s mechanical state, for it does seem that she was remarkably prone to mechanical defects – from quite an early age – yet Tom Cunningham made his view well known, 'Don't take things to bits to see why they are working'.

Opinions on three other aspects were almost equally prevalent, summed up best by Captain Simon Cassels when describing a Mediterranean deployment in the autumn of 1972. It may seem odd to bring up such points so early on but they were features of design that were to dog *Fearless* and *Intrepid* throughout their lives and to cause them embarrassment, with increasing fervour, as the world tries to become a 'greener' place:

Gash disposal ... the problems of gash disposal were highlighted yet again ... in the Norwegian Fjords. A ship of this size with an embarked force can only store a maximum of three days of garbage before conditions become unacceptable both from the point of view of hygiene and space taken up . . . . Since the LPD's main task is to work on the flanks of NATO either in Norwegian waters or the tideless Eastern Mediterranean it . . . is imperative that the problems of disposal of packaging and tin cans in particular be solved . . . . More recently the problem of gash disposal has been exacerbated by the continual failure of the gash disposal units. On arrival in Malta both units in the dining halls were unserviceable and the spare unit provided from the UK was of the wrong pattern.

Soot blowing (every four hours) . . . Local pollution regulations in Volos places severe restrictions on soot blowing. This is another problem which will be increased as anti-pollution laws become more stringently enforced.

Heads discharges . . . . In Gibraltar, Malta and Volos the ship was acutely aware of the unsightly pollution of heads discharges. At Volos the harbourmaster was too kind to comment verbally but, by his expression, his sentiments were clear. At Dhekelia ships may only anchor in certain positions for fear of fouling the bathing beaches during the on shore breeze. In short, unless settling tanks are fitted in large HM Ships it will not be long before they are unwelcome in several ports in the Mediterranean.

While on that subject, it is said that of all the senses, smell brings back the most distant and vivid memories so it is odd, perhaps, that no one has recalled *Fearless's* distinct aromas: the acrid funnel smoke mixed with the deep-frying fumes that pervaded the after Seacat deck; burnt aviation fuel across the flight deck and, the most noisome and the most idiosyncratic of all, the blue haze and choking atmosphere of the dock when eight, 600-hp LCM diesel engines were 'flashed up' before the stern gate was lowered. More modern memories will include the heady scent that wafted along the passageways and flats from the Wren's 4L1 mess deck prior to a run ashore or an up-channel-night party. Memories indeed!

Although much of *Fearless's* history glows with good deeds and good people with few willing to admit they did not enjoy life on board, this is, of course, a nonsense. For instance there was at least one known, attempted suicide; although evidence might have suggested that it was a form of self-gratification that went wrong. Nor, by a long way, was everyone who served in her beyond reproach: there was a chaplain who enjoyed living among men just a little too much – he had to go quickly; an amphibious operations officer who chose quite the wrong moment to have one drink too many – he was not promoted; a commanding officer who might have been relieved of his command but for the loyalty of his executive officer who refused to do an admiral's dirty work[4] – neither were promoted, although the commander should have been, and there was yet another AOO described in a letter to the author by his ex-commanding officer as 'thoroughly charming – utterly useless!'

Not everyone in the twenty-first century enjoyed serving in a ship conceived in the 1940s, designed in the 1950s and built in the 1960s as just eleven out of the 500 or so people who have placed comments on Colin Waite's *Fearless* and *Intrepid* website[5] testify. In toto, these 'discontents' have complained:

I never forget the day I walked off the Fat Fearless Freddie *for the last time . . . it was the happiest day of my life!! what a truly god awful draft, that cockroach-infested lump of rust you all seem so misty eyed about should have been the major player in a SINKEX about 20 years ago, preferably starring as the target!!*

When we came back from the Windies they thought all the seaman's mess were drug smugglers, remember that L/REG Jones? Save the Fearless*? Nah, don't think so!*

Worst ship of my entire 23 years service.

Would be happy to pull the plug and send her to the bottom.

Worst draft of my life. Happy to see her made into razor blades, just like Albion, *another rust bucket.*

Sink it! It's a tub.

Truly awful ship. Cramped rust bucket, long past her sell by date. Melt her down for scrap and use the money to buy hats. That's if you can actually melt down rust.

Heap of rusting scrap. Will be glad to see the day the breakers get the gas cutters on the old heap.

Served 78–80 very unhappily.

Worst draft in 27 years. Would like to think I will be shaving with bits of her. Drop the nostalgia trip guys its only a lump of rusting tin.

Accommodation dreadful, nothing worked, chronic chain of command, some extremely spiteful individuals in positions of authority. When it goes to the bottom, I shall be extremely glad indeed.

It is probably more instructive, though, to read just a fraction of the 500 or so e-mails that offer an opposing view – all from the lower deck:

She was one hell of a ship, just like a small village, very friendly and lots of pubs.

Had a rough few nights sleeping on the tank deck while Royal Marines Embarked Force, but would definitely do it all again. If you want anybody over the side chipping (if she has a civilian future) give us a shout.

Served as a Royal Marines landing craft crewman ... Falklands .... An amazing place to live, I can remember there were about 30 of us in 2C2 mess and we had some really wild 'up channel' nights. Favourite memories: The solitude of the starboard quarterdeck in the middle of the night when lifebuoy ghost (I calculated on leaving the ship that I spent about two and a half days of my life on duty there!). The tremendous village fayres *we had mid ocean. The beauty of the ship when she was being fully doused with water in the NBC state (a perk of being in an LCVP at the time). Tremendous banyans in the West Indies. The sheer terror of hooking up to davits on an LCVP in a force 6. The really nice ice creams that a couple of enterprising Petty Officers sold from the NAAFI deck, even in the Falklands. Hands to bathe with the stern ramp down in the Adriatic, we weren't so much scared of the possibility of sharks, it was the matelot with the rifle in case of sharks who gave us bootnecks the most concern.*

No place like home for Brandy Sours.

Corporal Landing Craft coxswain. Served in Intrepid *as well. Some good runs ashore especially the Military Hospital at Dhekelia Cyprus with Red Caps chasing naked bootnecks through the entrance of the hospital, don't ask how!!* Fearless *must be saved at least for our grandchildren.*

As a retired Primary School Head Teacher I believe children should learn about their history and visiting a ship such as HMS Fearless *will bring history to life for them. It is NOT jingoistic, but patriotic. God Save the Queen, Rule Britannia!*

Special Operations, Royal Signals. Only did 10 days on Fearless *when we were pulled out of Swaziland and shipped from Durban to Aden in 1966. They only let us polish the brass, but I enjoyed the trip and grog ration.*

Who remembers the REM that set light to the FMAA's guests Minimoke and got caught? Great times.

Fearless and Intrepid *are familiar ships here in Malta and I was very happy to pilot the* Fearless *in and out of Grand Harbour. I therefore wish you every success with your project and hope that you succeed in saving this grand old lady which has contributed so much to Britain's naval heritage.*

A Dutch Marine's salute to all my fellow Marines and to L10!! Qua Patet Orbis!!

Best ship I ever served in!! Six years of my life, and one husband gained!!!

Been the best draft so far (for this Wren)! There were some good times down our mess – and other messes come to think of it!!

Remember the gay chef incident, the Algiers dog shoot, the marines cockerel kidnapping, Lebanon, New Year in Limassol, the MV Gerhardt *and of course the Marines Gronks Board.*

3P2 was THE PARTY mess.

My boyfriend (ex now!!) was on Fearless *1990. Went on many a Families Day to* Fearless. *Miss her, not him!!*

Served, drank and was disciplined in the old girl between 1981–83 as part of 4th Assault Squadron. Fond memories working with the Senior Service, not something you hear a bootie say very often.

Best I've ever been on. More trouble and women than I could shake a big stick at.

Served on her 1st Commission. EM. Part of Ships Group. 3J2 Mess. Great Ship, Great Crew. Had a fantastic time. Well done on the web site.

Ex Naafi staff 96 to 02. Big hello to the Corporals from 4J2, thanks for all the social invites!

Bloody good trips, never want to paint that mast again. Spent more time on a plank stage than I did on the flight deck. Good ship though.

I can remember my little sister saying when we went to meet (my father) home from one of his 'trips' away: 'No wonder dad's been away for so long if that little thing's been pulling them!' She was referring to the tug!

I received shelter and TLC on the 23rd May 1982, much appreciated. From an ex Antelope.

To end on another up-beat note – literally: a golden theme that ran through *Fearless*'s life was the presence on board of a band, whether for operations, training or just sheer enjoyment and no matter from which of the three services. On those few occasions when musicians were not embarked a vital dimension to life was missing.

It only remains for me on behalf of the ship's companies of *Fearless* and *Intrepid* to wish *Albion* and *Bulwark* all best wishes for their futures in the sure knowledge that the trend set by their immediate predecessors will continue to bear fruit over the next thirty or so years. Hardly surprisingly, these sentiments were also made by many contributors to this book, from Able Seaman to Admiral and from Royal Marine to General.

No biography – and certainly no anthology – can be complete so I trust that the events and stories recounted here are representative of *Fearless*'s long life but, of equal importance, I hope that they also trigger many more personal memories than could possibly be contained between these covers.

Ewen Southby-Tailyour
South Devon, Spring 2006

Acknowledgements

There is no doubt where my thanks must start and Commodore Tom Cunningham, the last sea-going Commanding Officer of HMS *Fearless*, heads the list along with his Executive Officer, Captain Brian Warren and his Operations Officer, Lieutenant Commander Rob Wilson. The summons to help prepare HMS *Fearless*'s biography came from Brian on 2 December 2001 and preceded a flight to Barcelona in March for a meeting with the team, homeward-bound from operations off Afghanistan. Over an introductory lunch ashore, Rob outlined the proposal before I was briefed in detail by Tom and Brian.

At the time the plan was to organize a final paying-off dance in Portsmouth at the end of 2002 to coincide with the sale of a heavily illustrated book covering *Fearless*'s long life and not just her final commission. Time was short – nine months from gestation to publication – but it became impossibly shorter with the Labour Government's sudden parsimonious decision to bring her demise forward by six or so months: news that reached the ship during her final foreign port visit. Unhappily, unexpectedly but conveniently, we then had more time to publish a comprehensive tribute to the longest serving Royal Navy ship of her era – *pace* HMS *Victory*. It crossed my mind to reproduce here the picture of the inaugural re-planning meeting, held in a Barcelona restaurant, but an unusual sense of propriety has overcome me!

The following three-day passage to Gibraltar is worthy of a small tome in itself, 'sponsored' as it was, by a well-known purveyor of fine port and accompanied by dozens upon dozens of well-remembered stories representing almost every rank and skill on board. These anecdotes covered a good part of the ship's thirty-plus years, such was the depth of almost continuous experience still contained among that final ship's company. Thus my second tranche of thanks goes to the members of the last wardroom, Detachment Sergeant Majors' mess, POME's Mess, Corporals' Mess and, for the night before I was poured into the sea-boat outside territorial waters – somewhere off Gibraltar at 0300 – to members of the Royal Marines 'Barracks'. I remember, too, the encouragement given to me in those heady days by Lieutenant Colonel Steve Bruce, the ship's last AOO.

With guidance from Rob Wilson, the general form of the 'new' book became clear and with the unstinting help of all the surviving Commanding Officers it began to take on the shape I wanted. It would be repetitive to name them here for they head each chapter but my thanks are due to every one of them for this book is, in so many ways, their story as spokesmen for their individual ship's company. Three Commanding Officers, very sadly, were not alive to introduce their own chapters so Commander John Lock has done so for his Captain, John Rumble while Rear Admiral Mark Kerr was closely involved with his father's contribution. My most sincere thanks are due to them both for undertaking this difficult task. Captain Richard Thomas left copies of his Reports of Proceedings from which I have gleaned enough of his views on commanding the ship to allow me, as it were, to speak for him. Surprisingly I could find no photographs from either his time in command or from his subsequent sojourn with the House of Lords but I am indebted to his eldest daughter, Victoria Owen, for her help and especially for the charming photograph of her, her mother and siblings which heads her father's chapter.

Every Commanding Officer responded willingly to my requests although some did take a little longer than others: nevertheless I am most grateful for the total enthusiasm and absolute desire to help. Wing Commander Clare Walton deserves special thanks for her tenacity and patience in this respect: she will know why! Some Commanding Officers went further and prodded ex members of their ship's company to respond and many did, much to the benefit of the book as a whole. Invidious though it may appear, I must single out the ship's very first Commanding Officer, Captain Hugh Corbett, who did more than anyone to encourage me and to canvass the surviving members of his team for details of those vital, early, influential days of this 'new' concept. Among those willingly coerced were Commander Peter Shevlin; Commander Peter Baseby; Lieutenant Commander Ken Trace; Commander Tony Smith; Major 'Tiny' Whitworth; Major Jim Carman; Captain Michael Walker, Royal Signals: Sergeant Tom Potts; Colour Sergeant Petterson; Lieutenant Commander John Nichol; the family of the late Chief Shipwright Artificer Reg Eccles; Lieutenant Commander Mike Walton; Captain C D Wareham, RE; Lieutenant Commander Richard Perceval Maxwell; Lieutenant Colonel Robin Bullock-Webster, (Regimental Adjutant of the Irish Guards who helped trace military details of the Hauf Raid); Colour Sergeant 'Styx' Westacott and Sergeant Terry Radley.

Others who have helped throughout the book include Rear Admiral Peter Marsden; Rear Admiral John Carlill; Sir Keith Speed; the late Lieutenant General Sir John Richards; Commander Colin Robinson; Captain Jeremy Ledger; Major Jimmy Nobbs, RE; Major Ian Lamb; Brigadier Roger Dillon; Warrant Officer Moss Pearson (whose address book proved particularly invaluable); Captain Ron Wheeler; CMEM Mick Ahern; Warrant Officer Sammy Carlisle; Warrant Officer Geoff Haywood; Surgeon Captain Douglas Whyte; Commodore Simon Thornewill; RSM Jim Quigley; Miss Kate Adie; Lieutenant Commander Alan George; Lieutenant Nicky Cullen (the only lady officer bold enough to contribute – and a most worthy, interesting account it is); Councillor Tony Randerson and Alderman Ted Agar of Scarborough City Council; Lieutenant Bob Lane (Disposal and Reserve Organization) and CCMEA (ML) Tim Slann

Putting aside operational demands on his time, Rear Admiral (then) James Burnell-Nugent rallied to the call with a 'two-star' perspective of having *Fearless* under command during operations in 2001. Although she had never been under direct 'two-star' operational command – in theatre – in 1982 I had hoped for a similar comment about her performance in the South Atlantic but my request was peremptorily refused. Despite receiving international praise, not everyone held *Fearless*'s successful, amphibious command team during the Falklands War in the same high regard, although this is believed to be the only example of such criticism throughout her life.

Requests through all the obvious media outlets produced more stories and brief memories: all those correspondents that are not mentioned above but who have been quoted in the text will find due acknowledgements as they occur, yet, as I say in the Introduction, I had hoped for more offerings from the lower deck. Rear Admiral Jeremy Larken sent his precious Order Books – prime research documents – that until now had not been seen by the public and all should be grateful for that personal insight into a ship in battle. Commodore James Fanshawe lent all manner of diaries and personal memorabilia which, too, helped to add colour to the overall narrative.

My thanks must include John Ambler and Matthew Little of the Royal Marines Museum and, in particular, Lieutenant General Sir Henry Beverley for releasing, exceptionally, the Wardroom Line Books, allowing me to study them in the peace of my own studio. As a prime research source they were more helpful than most official archives which are subjected to the thirty-year rule: a rule that casts too long and unnecessary a shadow, even over unclassified material. These magnificent volumes are not just the pictorial and cartoon history of the officers' activities but are a sometimes irreverent, often satirical, occasionally truthful insight into the life of the ship as a whole. Anyone wishing for such an interpretation of events at every level could do no better than spend a week studying their pages. While the level of cartoon or caricature was, generally, of a high standard I chose to home in on just one artist as a sample: Lieutenant Commander PAF (Paf) Grant's likenesses of his chosen subjects are near perfect. Those reproduced within these covers are the best of his excellent collection.

Captain Christopher Page, the Royal Navy Historian, opened his archives to me for which I am more than appreciative while Major Mark Bentinck, the Royal Marines Historian, offered the expected, useful advice on sources of information. The National Archives at Kew were, unusually in my experience, of little use other than to allow me to study the ship's logs up to the early 1970s.

The series of Annexes add depth to the overall story and while some, being ship's appointments, could have been in their correct chronological position, I felt that these appointments should stand apart from the main text as single examples of the various duties. Likewise, the embarked force appointments add to the sum of the whole and if these are a little oriented towards the military that is hardly surprising. Conversely, the 'jungly' pilot's view could have been Annexed but David Lord's extensive comments from the Falklands era – and the journey home – have been placed where they are properly relevant. I really am most grateful to him and all authors of the Annexes.

My trawl for information introduced me to the Internet at its most provocative and, sometimes, at its most obtuse. Numerous snippets were sent but not all came with a contributor's name or if they did it was lost through my inability to grasp the nuances of modern communications.

Now to photographs: with copyright and identification problems they have produced their normal confusions. Everyone was willing to raid their albums and in some cases lend me complete volumes and even send them in the post – an act of faith in the Royal Mail and my honesty that was, perhaps, rather touching. Some removed photographs from pristine pages in order that *Fearless*'s photographic history could be as complete and as all-embracing as possible. The chapters in which they have been placed will, by and large, indicate where credit is due.

Every illustration between these covers has come from a private collection yet, quite clearly, many of these originated from official sources. Surprisingly some pictures came via the Internet, also without credits, and I even received a number of photographs in the post with no covering letter and thus no return address. Sadly, therefore, it has not been possible to credit many photographs but if this can be corrected in a second edition I will be delighted to oblige. I have tried to cover the whole range of activities and, to save on the limited number allowed by the publisher, I have preferred 'action' shots of Commanding Officers rather than the standard 'mug shot'. As I was limited to 150 illustrations covering thirty-seven busy years I had to be more selective than I would have liked. The omissions are obvious: for instance no one sent a photograph of that amazing complex of engineering workshops on 1 Deck forward of the Flight Deck and there are none of the Junior Rates Dining Hall at meal times: apart from the vehicle decks and flight deck it was the largest gathering place for briefings, assault stations, films and so on.

For the perspective of the two embarked 'one stars' during exercise and operations – the Commodore and Brigadier – Commodore Jamie Miller found time to send opinions that have earned a worthy place in the ship's history. Unable to persuade a brigadier (also from the twenty-first century) to offer a more modern perspective, Major General Julian Thompson kindly, and with little notice, added his 1982 thoughts to those of a brigade major from almost exactly a decade earlier.

As always, Robin Wade, my long-suffering agent and retired Gordon Highlander, guided this biography through its gestation and in doing so acted as that essential, professional buffer between anxious publisher and laid back author. My continued thanks to him for his wisdom – and well-needed humour. Susan Econicoff's editing has been masterly and for that I am also grateful.

Finally I – we all – must thank Lord Carrington for so enthusiastically endorsing this unashamed eulogy to a fine old lady. After much thought and some trepidation I decided that there could be no better choice for this important task and so I was thrilled when he accepted my invitation. Perhaps even wider thanks are due for it was Lord Carrington's signature on the procurement document when he was First Lord of the Admiralty that gave the United Kingdom two ships that were, without doubt and despite no major wars, of 'the utmost utility to the Nation' for over a third of a century.

Amphibious Warfare and the LPD Concept

If amphibious warfare had not been a facet of some post-war British defence policies there would have been no need for LPDs, LPHs or LSLs.

While that, in its broadest sense, is true, it is also true that a ship – an LPD – that is part dock, part airfield, part barracks, part stores ship, part hospital, part maintenance and repair workshop and part command and control headquarters will always be useful, in peace and conventional warfare.

Over 70 per cent of the world's population, 80 per cent of countries and almost all centres of international trade and military power lie within the littoral regions of the world. Trade routes and most oil, gas and mineral reserves tend to be found in the adjacent waters.

Thus, governments with maritime and amphibious forces have a unique political, diplomatic and strategic tool that can be brought to bear close to the bulk of the world's population. A maritime force can sail, project influence ashore without landing, withdraw and re-deploy by exercising freedom of navigation in adjacent international waters; all without loss of face on either side.

An amphibious operation projects power, support or medical and humanitarian relief inland from the sea, rivers or lakes without, necessarily, using formal ports, slipways, ro-ro terminals, beaching sites or airfields. It can be militarily offensive or defensive, be conducted by search and rescue organizations, customs or drug enforcement or by disaster relief agencies.

At one extreme, an amphibious operation is concerned with the littoral in its fullest depth (600 nautical miles in the case of US forces) while at the other extreme it may be two men inserted covertly from a submarine or canoe – or even the repositioning of a flock of sheep.

Although separated by time and sophistication of equipment, a number of quotes offer similar views. For instance the Duke of Wellington said of his land successes in the Peninsula War at the beginning of the nineteenth century:

> *If anyone wishes to know the history of this war, I will tell them that it is our maritime superiority gives me the power of maintaining my army while the enemy are unable to do so.*

... while Admiral Sir Bertram Ramsay (General Eisenhower's naval commander for Operation OVERLORD – Normandy, 6 June, 1944) wrote:

> *A combined operation is but the opening under particular circumstances of a purely army battle. It is the function of the navy and the air to help the army establish a base, or bases, on the hostile coast, from which the military plan to gain an objective must be developed. It is upon the army to plan for the fulfilment of its objective that the combined plan must depend. . . . Once the army have decided how they wish to fight the land battle, it is necessary to examine how the troops can be put ashore to give effect to the army plan. In general, it is the responsibility of the navy to land the army as they require but, as the plan develops, naval considerations will arise which must be discussed and agreed upon.*

Admiral of the Fleet Lord Fisher delivered the same message but more succinctly:

> *The British Army should be a projectile to be fired by the Navy!*

With the post Cold War philosophy of expeditionary warfare exercising the principles of Ship to Objective Manoeuvre (STOM) and Operational Manoeuvre from the Sea (OMTS) these views now stand as strong as ever, although in this politically-craven era, it might also be well to remember another of Admiral Fisher's dicta:

> *The essence of war is violence and moderation in war is imbecility.*

Violence to ensure success implies risk-taking; a course of action well known to successful navies as Captain Kit Layman[6] commented at the end of the amphibious landings at San Carlos during the opening stages of the amphibious operations of the Falklands War in 1982.[7] The message being, that if neither politicians nor military commanders are prepared to use violence (implying a risk of losses and casualties to achieve the aim) then no phase of war, and especially not an amphibious phase, should be entered into. The opening phases of peacekeeping operations may, under certain circumstances, be an exception to this unwritten principle of war.

Marines, sea soldiers or naval infantry, trained in the tactics of assault landings have a long history in amphibious raiding, boarding at sea or establishing footholds ashore for future land-based operations. The earliest account of this comes from 1000 BC when Egyptian 'sea peoples' fought in ship-to-ship actions. The first recorded amphibious operations were the Persian landings at Marathon in 490 BC, followed by the Romans who employed amphibious tactics to build their Empire in the Mediterranean and then in England in 55 BC.

The specialist role of the 'sea soldier' was given a more modern impetus when Spain formed her Marine Infantry in 1537; but some things never change for in 1905 the military author and tactician, Colonel C.E. Callwell, wrote during an age when steam power was thought by some to have solved the landing problem, that:

> *The actual landing of troops and stores from transport is, unless the disembarkation takes place in some well-sheltered harbour, just as liable to interruption by bad weather as it was in the sailing era. The beaching of boats is as difficult and dangerous nowadays if the sea gets up, as it ever was.*

... as General Eisenhower discovered thirty-nine years later at Normandy.

The Greeks and Romans recognized the difficulties of putting men and equipment ashore, as did the Spanish in 1558, the French in 1805, the Allies at Gallipoli in 1915 and the Germans in 1940. Nor were the US-sponsored landings in Cuba's Bay of Pigs and the USMC's landings on Somalia's beaches unqualified successes, although in these last instances, faulty intelligence and public opinion coupled with a sceptical press corps were also to blame.

The British expedition against the French coastal town of Rochefort in 1757 is an example of a breakdown in control (if not of command) where the admiral, Sir Edward Hawke (Commanding the Fleet), did everything in his power to aid the general, Sir John Mordaunt (Commanding the Landing Force). There was no absence of cooperation but the resolute Admiral had little sympathy with, as he viewed it, the indecision and lack of enterprise displayed by the Army under conditions which were difficult. At Mordaunt's court martial Hawke is quoted as saying,

> *I always looked upon it as my duty to convey the troops to the road of Basque and there, if possible, to find out a landing place for them and in the case of their landing to give them all assistance in my power for that purpose, but with respect to the question: 'Whither should they land or not?' I thought it was the part of the Generals to determine that question by themselves. I considered it a matter of judgement which merely related to them and that the sea had nothing to do with it.*

By modern convention it was the Admiral who might now be considered to have been at fault yet good lessons were learned from that expedition for at the end of the Seven Years War (1756–63) the historian John MacIntire, was able to report that once the decision to land had been made and the landing points chosen:

> *The whole command of the army is (now) given to a sea officer who conducts them to the place of landing. The (military) officer has little to do until the men are out of the boats for then is the time for him to show his judgement.*

Therein lies the basic maxim which, with some streamlining, exists today, although it would be a foolish naval officer who chose a landing place without military (and now, political) approval.

Nevertheless, throughout history there has been a tendency on the part of ground troops to misunderstand the difficulties of naval forces and, of course, vice versa. Not so the Duke of Wellington who, when summing up his Peninsula Campaign successes, paid tribute to the part played by the Royal Navy and which is quoted earlier. A fact that moved Colonel Calwell to write before the First World War:

> *In all disembarkation, whether they are opposed or not, naval assistance is indispensable. That is a principle which is universally accepted in the British service. Where landings have to take place on slippery rocks, where in fact the process of getting out of the boats on to the shore presents special difficulties, it is preferable to detail naval personnel to gain a footing on land to start with and prior to the troops approaching. The soldier is not best at this sort of work. The bluejacket and marine are accustomed to it, and they are not prone to the perils and confusions of landing at an awkward place under fire, by falling into the water out of sheer clumsiness. Naval history provides a number of instances of small landing parties despatched from ships of war performing brilliant exploits on shore. Undertakings of this class are scarcely the soldiers' business.*

History is also littered with examples when armies have not wanted to be part of amphibious campaigns. The second Battle of Narvik in Norway in 1941 is one where the admiral and rather more junior general disagreed on almost every point. The general was relieved of his command, yet still no British infantry took part in the assault on that city, a task left to the French Foreign Legion, once they and their armour had been put ashore by British landing craft commanded and manned by Royal Marines and sailors.

The British Army was also reluctant to help Admiral Nelson in his ill-fated expedition to capture Santa Cruz on Tenerife in 1797 and as recently as 1982, the British Army and Air Force Chiefs of Staff were hesitant to commit their forces to what they were certain would be a humiliating defeat for the Royal Navy in the South Atlantic.

Few military campaigns have not involved an amphibious operation across a beach or through a captured port, whether it be the prelude to a major land operation, an exploratory raid to test enemy morale, to rehearse command procedures or to test equipment and gain experience for a larger enterprise in the future. The final destruction of the Nazi regime began with a series of amphibious operations in the Mediterranean and the English Channel. After the Normandy landings of June 1944, the combined Allied armies had to be supplied by sea. As they advanced eastwards they continued to be supported by amphibious operations that turned the enemy's sea flank; one of the most useful was that at Walcheren in November 1944. Even in 2002 the capture of Iraq's Al Faw peninsula was a classic of modern amphibious, joint warfare – across and above beaches – that paved the way for the capture of Basra.

'Amphibious operations,' said Winston Churchill, 'have to fit together like a jewelled bracelet' and that includes preparation, planning and making allowances for weather and surf conditions. Little has changed in this respect for exposed beaches are still expanses across which men may have to fight while struggling with heavy equipment, probably soft sand and with no natural cover from fire. Beach gradients and the necessary draught of troop-carrying vessels still ensure a wade, as they have done since man first began his territorial expansion via the sea. There is nothing new in this despite helicopters and hovercraft now being part of the amphibious equation.

Beaches and ports may be mere stepping stones, conduits to greater things, but they are often the most difficult targets to capture. An amphibious battle, by sea and air, to secure a beachhead may be a minor opening phase of a land war but it can be the most bloody, the most vital to win and deserves the utmost attention to detail.

Unlike 1918 when it all but died, in 1945 the art of amphibious warfare was kept alive in the Royal Navy by the elderly, slow, over-worked LST(A)s and LCTs of the Amphibious Warfare Squadron. These ships could do many things except operate helicopters, indeed they had one advantage over their successors, they could land heavy armour directly onto the beach.

The 6 June 1944, is arguably where the seeds for modern amphibious warfare were sown although remarkable leaps had been made prior to the Normandy landings and not all in the United Kingdom and the United States. Germany had shown a sophisticated understanding of the practicalities of the problems during the First World War as anyone who has read Erskine Childers's *The Riddle of the Sands* will have discovered. By the early stages of the Second World War that sophistication had increased and was coupled to a surprising ingenuity that produced plans, techniques and equipment that, quite simply, were far ahead of their time, pre-dating many ideas that would not find their way into modern amphibious warfare for some years. Those wishing to study German supremacy in the amphibious art at this time should read Peter Schenk's *Invasion of England 1940*.[8] Japan, too and uniquely, had already designed a mother ship for landing operations and built the *Shinshu Maru* in 1934–35: she also possessed aircraft carriers which the Germans never did.

For her part, the United Kingdom at the beginning of the Second World War, was ill-equipped to carry out any serious amphibious assault and the United States – yet to be involved – was equally backward. After the First World War combined operations (thanks to the Gallipoli campaign) suffering from a bad press, had been pushed, understandably, into the background of naval aspirations. Approaching a defended beach in ships' boats, the only craft available, was regarded as suicide. Further, the awful prospect of having to get out of these open boats to land on an enfiladed beach was not considered, quite rightly, to be a sensible operation of war.

Since 1921 combined operations had been studied at the three services' staff colleges where, if not in practice then at least in educated theory, some of the principles were kept alive. In 1936 the Director of the Royal Navy's Staff College at Greenwich wrote to the Admiral President of the War College:[9]

> The Staff College fully realizes the importance of the part the navy will play in any amphibious expedition and ... as a sea power, the predominant partner in any operation will be the navy. As such the navy should take the initiative for the design and provision of craft, in the organization required for mounting an overseas expedition and in the supply of any special equipment required.

The Admiral forwarded the letter with a recommendation that 'a permanent committee be established to consider the subject and that a small training and development establishment of the three services should lead to real and rapid progress'.[10]

Consequently a Combined Operations Sub-Committee was established and agreement reached for an Inter-Services Training and Development Centre (ISTDC) to be formed on 2 May 1938, at Fort Cumberland, Eastney, under the command of a naval captain. Work began in June with the first exercise held that summer by a cruiser squadron landing soldiers from open boats propelled by muffled oars onto Slapton Sands in south Devon so 'no progress in technique had taken place since the Crimea'.[11]

In 1924 the Madden Committee proposed that the Royal Marines should raise independent companies to form the landing force for expeditions This came to naught although a few brigade-strength landing exercises were carried out. Gallipoli cast a long shadow.

In practice the Royal Marines and Royal Navy came close with the establishment of the Mobile Naval Base Defence Organizations and the Royal Marines Fortress Unit whose task it was to carry out opposed landings under the Unit's rather junior Landing Officer. At Narvik in 1940 for example, amphibious operations were conducted by men of the RMFU who landed and recovered troops and tanks of the French Foreign Legion.

Eventually combined operations were to receive the necessary momentum under the leadership first of General Bourne,[12] secondly, Admiral of the Fleet Lord Keyes and finally under Commodore (to begin with) Lord Mountbatten.

After the defeat of the Allied armies in France and the Low Countries in May 1940, the only way of returning to the offensive, other than through bombing, was by conducting amphibious raids onto the occupied coasts with the aim of causing the enemy to disperse his forces and equipment uneconomically. Further, the successful execution of a raid was considered excellent for morale at a time when the country was, strategically, on the defensive.[13]

On 14 June 1940, the Adjutant General of the Royal Marines, Lieutenant General A.G.B. Bourne, CB, DSO, MVO, was appointed by the three Chiefs of Staff to be Commander of Raiding Operations (originally, Offensive Operations). Additionally he was to act as Adviser to the Chiefs of Staff on Combined Operations and remain Adjutant General of the Royal Marines. General Bourne's remit from the Chiefs of Staff Committee was:[14]

> ... to harass the enemy (by raiding operations) and cause him to disperse his forces and to create material damage particularly on the coastline from Northern Norway to the western limit of German-occupied France ... You are to keep the Chiefs of Staff informed of any operations you propose to carry out.

Despite good intentions at the latter end of the 1930s General Bourne had taken over an operational concept that, in the words of the Deputy Chiefs of Staff,[15] did not seem to be progressing:

> With the material at present available it is impossible to stage any landing operation on a hostile shore with a force of a brigade or more sooner than six months from the time that order is given.

The Inter-Services Training and Development Centre was then brought under General Bourne's command and with it the following instruction:

> In addition we wish you to press on with the development and production of special landing craft and equipment and to advise us when the occasion arises, as to its allotment.

By mid-1940 General Bourne, now Director of Combined Operations, was not considered senior enough for the task, so the following letter was sent by Mr Churchill on 17 July 1940:

> Prime Minister to General Ismay and Sir Edward Bridges.
>
> I have appointed Admiral of the Fleet Sir Roger Keyes as Director of Combined Operations ... General Bourne should be informed that ... it is essential to have an officer of higher rank in charge ... and in any case the Royal Marines must play a leading part in this organization ...

No new directive was issued to Admiral Keyes who, by the end of July 1940, had under command about 500 men in commandos, 740 men in Independent Companies, 15 Assault Landing craft and 4 Minor Landing Craft. The Admiral of the Fleet did not last long for he disagreed with the Chiefs of Staff over the conduct of Exercise LEAPFROG in Scapa Flow and, among other factors, with a recommendation of his that a properly equipped headquarters ship was vital to success. Mr Churchill replaced him with Lord Louis Mountbatten as Adviser on Combined Operations. In December 1943 the Commodore was further promoted with a final title change to Chief of Combined Operations.

Churchill required Mountbatten to 'mount a programme of raids of ever-increasing intensity with the invasion of France the main object' and for this overriding priority he was 'to create the machine, devise the appliances, find the bases, create the training areas and select the site for the assault'.

Landing craft at that time were still primitive; for instance one of only two craft available for the amphibious landings at Narvik in May 1940, and capable of landing a French Foreign Legion tank, was water-jet propelled with a top speed – on the rare occasion that the inlets were free of weed – of four knots. The second was a slightly faster, twin screwed, shallower draught craft.

Flight deck of HMS *Theseus* on 6 November 1956. 45 Commando, Royal Marines, deploying ashore.

Matters improved by June 1944 but by the 1960s the ships were becoming elderly. The Royal Navy's Amphibious Warfare Squadron, originally based in Malta and subsequently in Bahrain, consisted, between 1963 and 1964 when under the command of the Captain Amphibious Warfare, Mark Kerr – a future Commanding Officer of HMS *Fearless* – of the River class frigate HMS *Meon*, and a matrix of the LST(A)s HMSs *Anzio*, *Striker* and *Messina* and three LCTs, *Bastion*, *Redoubt* and *Parapet*. A motor launch, HMS *Ickford*, commanded by a Royal Marine lieutenant, had not made the move to the Gulf. The Squadron seldom carried infantry as most accommodation was taken up by the men of the Seaborne Tank Force which, during that period, came from the Royal Scots Greys and the Queen's Royal Lancers although in practice each LST could land an assualt wave of 208 infantry in her eight LCAs. Other units of the Amphibious Warfare Squadron were the Naval Beach Unit, the Army Beach Unit of Royal Engineers, 601 Signal Troop, Royal Signals and No. 3 Special Boat Detachment, Royal Marines.

Whatever else may be said of Suez in 1956 – an amphibious success but a diplomatic disaster – it saved the day for the Royal Marines in particular and amphibious warfare in general. As a direct result of the successful use of HMS *Meon* as the Headquarters ship (and vectoring ship for the Minor Landing Craft) and the use of HMSs *Ocean* and *Theseus* as makeshift LPHs, the Admiralty was forced to look again at the value of a modern amphibious fleet.

HMS *Bulwark* with her nine helicopter spots.

HMS *Meon* in the Persian Gulf in the early 1960s.

Helicopters had been used in action before Suez by the Americans (Korea) and the French (North Africa) but neither country had used them for an opposed assault from the sea. The British had used helicopters to ferry Royal Marines ashore in Malaya in 1953 and by the time the Suez crisis occurred a study was under way in the Admiralty looking at some form of helicopter

HMS Anzio entering Grand Harbour.

HMS *Bastion* **in the Persian Gulf in the early 1960s.**

carrier. The United Sates was, though, the first to commission a specialist helicopter-capable ship with the conversion of the carrier USS *Thetis Bay* into a Landing Platform Helicopter alongside an intensive period of building which included the 'new' concept of a Landing Platform Dock. In fact the idea was not 'new' as preliminary designs had been drawn up by the British prior to 1944 but had never reached beyond concept stage.[16,17]

HMS *Messina* **with naval lighterage pontoon.**

HMS *Anzio* entering the short cut into the Persian Gulf.

Now with the conversion, post Suez, of first *Bulwark* then *Albion*[18] and with Major General J.L. Moulton[19] – a Royal Marine – as Chief of Amphibious Warfare, answerable direct to the Chief of Defence Staff, the requirement for a dedicated, purpose built headquarters ship was identified, as was the continuing need to land heavy armour and artillery.

General Moulton did not find his task as Chief of Amphibious Warfare easy for the three single-service headquarters were very independent, and not at all interested in Amphibious Warfare as will be seen from this passage in Julian Thompon's book *The Royal Marines. From Sea Soldiers to a Special Force*[20] where he quotes General Moulton:

> The Army had two jobs: post-colonial and the British Army of the Rhine (BAOR). The former took priority in their affections; they clung to the garrisons and bases tenaciously. The Amphibious Warfare concept and carrier task forces were rivals and a threat to the Army's aspirations to hang on to these garrisons. The Director Royal Armoured Corps was only interested in BAOR.
>
> Several views prevailed in the Royal Navy. The overwhelming majority were preoccupied with anti-submarine warfare in the North Atlantic. The LPH was irrelevant in this context. The politicians on the other hand viewed the Royal Navy as useful for policing the withdrawal from Empire, which was popular with the Fleet Air Arm, but not with the ASW fraternity.
>
> The RAF had the deterrent, the V Bombers, which were viewed by them as a continuation of the Trenchard strategic bombing vision. The RAF also took the line that any small-scale intervention would be by air.

However, and almost entirely due to General Moulton's persistence, six LSLs and two LPDs were to be procured and so it was into this complicated world that HMS *Fearless*, the Royal Navy's first Landing Platform Dock, was launched on 19 December 1963.

Chapter One

Staff Requirements and Specifications

HMS *Fearless*'s family tree can be traced to a British Second World War design for a dock ship which the US Navy took up with success towards the end of the war in the Pacific. In 1947 a further British design for a Landing Ship Dock (LSD) of about 4,500 tons was cancelled as the threat was then perceived to have moved to the Atlantic and underwater. In 1952 a larger LSD design was mooted but it was not until August 1959 that the Admiralty, with Lord Carrington as its First Lord, issued a staff requirement for two ships to replace the LST(A)s of the Amphibious Warfare Squadron.

In the Navy Estimates of 1961–1962, £8 million were requested for the build of the first assault ship and an Invitation to Tender issued.[21] Only Harland and Wolff of Belfast submitted a bid lower than the limit and their price of £7,925,575 was accepted. Other bidders were Swan Hunters, Cammal Laird, John Brown and Hawthorn Leslie with the most expensive at over £8.5 million from Fairfield Shipbuilding and Engineering. Blessed with full order books, Scotts Shipbuilding and Vickers Armstrong made no offer.

So what, precisely, was required? Certainly tanks needed to be put ashore in an assault pasture: during the war, the 5,000 ton (fully laden) LSTs[22] and the 1,000 ton LCTs had been developed to land tanks directly onto a beach but they had limited room for troops other than those required to man and maintain the embarked vehicles and, being flat bottomed for beaching, were not good sea-boats. They were used over long distances but rolled like pigs which is not only uncomfortable but dangerous should cargo or vehicles break loose – as they often did. The new ship had still to place tanks ashore but not 'itself' beach and so the dock configuration had been drawn up. The Americans had taken this initially-British concept and developed it into the first of their Amphibious Transport Docks.

To study the conception of the British LPD it is necessary to have a flashback to February 1942 when British thoughts were turning to the ships needed to put Allied troops back into Europe. On 27 October 1942 the first Naval Staff Requirement – TSD 1346/42 – was drafted for a mother ship that would land main battle tanks via smaller Tank Landing Craft (TLC) carried in a floodable dock. The preamble reads:

- Requirement is to carry 2 × TLC with tanks embarked on an ocean passage... .
- The carrier should, by means of flooding, be able to embark and float out TLC. The form of the stern to be such that a tank or motor transport can run out from the ship into a floating TLC over the TLC ramp.
- It is not a requirement that this ship should be able to beach.
- The ship should have a designed speed of 'X' knots.[23] This should give a speed of 14 knots in tropical waters after 6 months out of dock and in normal load conditions.
- 5,000 miles at 14 knots
- 4 × 2 pdrs
- 8 Oerlikans
- Gyro compass
- Habitability: Suitable for both tropical and arctic conditions. Accommodation required for the crews of 24 tanks and HQ personnel and for 2 × TLC crews with their maintenance

personnel. This will be Navy: 5 officers and 24 ratings and, Military: 24 officers and 220 other ranks. Hammocks and pipe cot bunks.

'Amendment Number Three', dated January 1944, asked for smoke-making apparatus for self protection. It will be noted that no account was made for embarked infantry nor any command and control: it was not until after Suez that the same file was dusted off and the following inserted:

> *Revised Draft Requirements for Landing Transport Dock.*
>
> *Main Features: To embark, transport on ocean passage and discharge over beaches assault elements of a Brigade Group.*

The speed of this newer concept was to be not less than 20 knots with the same endurance of 5,000 nautical miles.

It was now decided that assault ships should also perform the function of amphibious or tri-service command; a task that would, for the whole of their lives, sit uneasily with that of heavy lift assault ships able to launch troops and equipment into an opposed landing if necessary. From the beginning the command would wish to be as far removed from immediate danger as possible – this had nothing to do with personal safety but common sense – while the assaulting troops with their supporting armour, artillery and logistic support needed as short a watergap as possible. Of course the positive side to this dual purpose, and one that was to be fully exercised, was that the LPDs could operate independently if necessary, adding to their flexibility in all manner of unforeseen operations.

Thus the shape of the ships[24] became clear, a factor that was, to some extent, to be dictated by the dimensions of the British Army's 3-ton lorries which, in turn decided the size of the LCMs.[25]

Then at last a brief Admiralty News Release[26] was issued, purposefully giving no idea of the complexity and, indeed, the flexibility, of this addition to the United Kingdom's defence capability. Much of that would have to wait until her commissioning before becoming 'public knowledge'.

In the meantime it will be useful to quote from a document which was jointly issued by the Navy Department[27] and the Joint Warfare Staff giving the final specification of the LPD. It is undated but almost certainly written in late 1964 or early 1965 and was never released to the public.

The Assault Ship

1. The Assault Ships (LSA)[28], *Fearless* and *Intrepid* are planned to commission in November 1965 and Autumn 1966 respectively and to become operational in the Autumn of 1966 and at the end of 1968 respectively. The following is a summary of their capabilities.

Drawing showing internal vehicle decks.

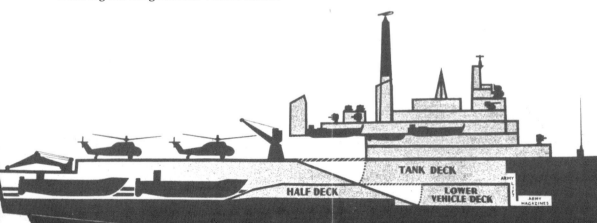

Characteristics

2. The 12,000 tons, 20 knot Assault Ship, with her 5,000 miles range at this speed, is the m versatile ship for amphibious warfare built for the Royal Navy. Each ship has:

   a. A specially designed Assault Operations Room for joint use by a Naval Amphibio Group Commander, a Landing Force Commander and their staffs and incorporating Supporting Arms Coordination Centre.

   b. An integrated Communications System providing 13 HF and 9 UHF lines.

   c. Accommodation at ship's company standards for a military force of about 400, which could spend several weeks on board.

   d. Accommodation for short periods for a military force of about 750, the increase over the numbers in c. being taken up on camp-beds. (Accommodation figures have yet to be confirmed by trial).

   e. A landing craft squadron consisting of four LCM(9)s (carried in the dock) and four LCA(2)s (carried at davits). SRN5 Hovercraft could be carried in the dock in lieu of two LCM(9)s.

   f. 15,560 sq. ft. of enclosed deck space specifically designed for the carriage of military vehicles, weapons and stores.

   g. A Flight Deck fully equipped for day and night flying, with Flying Control position, two landing spots and associated fuelling arrangements and power supplies. Reduced helicopter flying is possible with the forward part of the Flight Deck being used for vehicle stowage.

   h. Three Magazines, served by a platform lift, to carry 50 tons of Army ammunition or stores.

Early model. Note early Flyco position, a deck-level cubby hole.

Operational Concept

3. The basic concept for the Assault Ship is that she will form part of an Amphibious Group, whose main component will be a Commando Ship or Ships, and carry the Force Headquarters, armour, artillery, heavy vehicles, equipment and stores, plus additional infantry if required, The Assault Ship's LCM(9)s can each carry two tanks or up to 100 ton loads from the ship to the landing beach, while the infantry can be landed by LCA(2)s, DUKW[29] or by helicopter.

4. The Assault Ship has been designed as the Command Ship for the Naval Amphibious Group Commander and the Landing Force Commander, replacing HMS *Meon* in this role. The senior Royal Marines officer's staff function will be as Amphibious Operations Officer, responsible for the overall control of loading and unloading the ship.

5. The ship's characteristics fit her for a wide range of roles. In addition to the conventional assault (whether seaborne, or combined seaborne/airborne), she could act in support of an airborne intervention, provide, in the peacekeeping role, an impressive show of force, or act in the supply and transport roles, in particular for heavy equipment and helicopter. Her dock and workshops will enable her to provide maintenance support for small craft.

Method of Operating The Assault Ship

6. The Assault Ship can carry vehicles in four spaces – the Tank Deck (3 Deck), the Half Deck (4 Deck), the Lower Vehicle Deck (5 Deck) and on the forward half of the Flight Deck.[30] All these spaces are interconnected by 20° ramps. The Tank Deck has an apron at the after end which leads down into the Dock, and this apron forms the loading point for the LCM(9)s or alternatively acts as ramp into the dock when it is dried out. The dock is closed at the after end by a hydraulically-operated gate hinged at the bottom.

7. The four LCA(2)s are carried at power-operated gravity davits and the four LCM(9)s carried in the dock. Each LCA(2) is capable of carrying 26 fully equipped troops and each LCM(9) as previously mentioned can carry two Centurion tanks or a combination of other vehicles. By filling water ballast tanks, the draught of the ship is increased, flooding the dock to a sufficient depth to float a fully laden LCM(9). These craft can then operate under their own power from the apron at the fore end of the dock. Ballasting and the operation of the stern gate is controlled from the Ballast Control Position.

8. The ship can also carry up to four[31] DUKWs on the dock apron without affecting the number of other vehicles that can be carried. Each DUKW can carry 25 men or 2½ tons of stores. However their presence on the apron prevents the LCM(9)s being loaded.[32]

9. The discharge of all vehicles from the ship from a distance of eight miles offshore might take not less than fourteen hours.

10. The use of helicopters, either from a Commando Ship or the RAF's Theatre Short Range Transport Force, will further and very significantly reduce the time taken to unload men, light vehicles and stores.

The Ship's Military Load

11. Subject to her physical capacity, and to seamanlike safety precautions, the Assault Ship must carry the numbers and types of weapons, vehicles and troops that the Military Commander states he requires to accomplish the particular task allotted to him ashore.

12. For a purely Internal Security operation, the principal need might be for helicopters, scout cars and vehicles. A Middle-East contingency plan might require tanks, artillery and vehicles, while a South East Asian operation might call for infantry and artillery to be landed by helicopter. Therefore all that can be usefully stated here is the space available for vehicle stowage with any limitations. These are:

	Area (sq ft)	Height Limit (feet)	Vehicle Wt limit (tons)	Specimen Load
a. Tank Deck (3 Deck):	7,280	15	50	10 × tanks 1 × ARV 1 × Dozer
b. Half Deck (4 Deck)	4,460	8	15	6 × 105 mm guns 18 × ¼ ton vehicles plus trailers
c. Lower Vehicle Deck (5 Deck)	3,320	12	15	7 × 3 ton vehicles
d. Flight Deck (1 Deck) 50 m × 23 m	6,200	11½	8½	12 × 3 ton vehicles 5 × Unit Light Helicopters
e. LCMs				2 × Main Battle Tanks (each)

13. Access from Half Deck to Lower Vehicle Deck is by means of two fixed ramps.

The Size of The Vehicle Load

14. Although loading the Tank Deck and LCM(9)s to capacity will enable the Military Commander to have the maximum number of tracks, wheels and guns for his operation, at the same time it robs him of any flexibility in choice as to the sequence in which he requires different loads to be landed. The ship becomes irrevocably committed to off-loading the majority of the vehicles according to one pre-arranged plan. Where the Military Commander needs to retain the ability to react in more than one way as to what he will land first, then the LCM(9)s must be left empty and the after end of the Tank Deck left clear. If armour is carried, this means reducing the Assault Ship's load from a complete squadron to a half squadron of eight or nine tanks.

Helicopter Operations

15. The Flight Deck has facilities for AVCAT pressure refuelling and external power supplies. This fully equipped Flight Deck and the trained FAA complement provide the Assault Ship with a good helicopter operating capability both by day and night for the following possible roles:
    a. To disembark or embark personnel, stores and light vehicles by means of helicopters of the Commando Ship or the RAF.
    b. An initial base for any service helicopters.
    c. A spare deck.

16. With appropriate increases of the FAA complement the ship would be able to operate four Wessex V helicopters for up to four weeks and six to eight Wessex V helicopters for shorter periods. When working with Wessex helicopters, provided that the Flight Deck is clear of vehicles, there is sufficient space for two spots to be operated simultaneously and for two more aircraft to be kept ready on deck with rotors folded.

17. As there are no bulk stowage facilities for AVGAS, embarked units will be required to provide their own pre-packed fuel together with first line maintenance facilities for their light helicopters.

Logistics

18. The following facilities are provided for the Embarked Military Force:

   a. 40 tons of MT 80 vehicle fuel is carried, which can be pumped to flight deck filling positions.

   b. Approximately 160 tons of fresh water, in excess of that required for domestic purpose, can be distilled daily.

   c. Three inter-connected Army magazines with a total capacity of 50 tons are located forward of the Lower Vehicle Deck. A stores lift is fitted between the Tank and Lower Vehicle Deck which serves these Army stores, and overhead travelling cranes connect the top of the lift and the dock. Four powered forklift trucks are carried for moving stores about the ship, particularly bringing loads up the ramps to the Flight Deck for helicopter off-loading.

Safety Arrangements in Vehicle Spaces

19. In order that vehicles may be stowed on board, loaded with both fuel and ammunition the vehicle decks are fitted with :

   a. Water Spray Systems

   b. Foam Drenching

   c. A Fire Curtain at the after end of the Tank Deck

   d. Approaches through air locks

20. Ventilation and exhaust systems are provided so that a proportion of vehicles can run their engines for maintenance or movement.

Ship's Data

21. Dimensions, Speed and Endurance:

Length overall	521 ft 6 ins
Breadth extreme	80 ft
Deep condition	
Displacement	12,100 tons
Draught forward	20 ft 6 ins
Draught aft	20 ft 6 ins
Ballasted condition (dock flooded)	
Displacement	16,850 tons
Draught forward	23 ft
Draught aft	32 ft
Endurance/Speed	5,000 nautical miles at 20 m knots

Ship's Complement

22.

	Officers	Seniors	Juniors	Total
a. Ships Staff (including Canteen staff)	27	107	271	405
b. RM Assault Detachment (including LME mechanics for LCM(9)	3	7	43	53
c. Amphibious Beach Unit (including DUKW Section)	2	7	50	59
d. Ship Signal Troop	1	1	14	16
TOTAL:	33	122	378	533
e. Commodore's Staff	4	3	6	13
TOTAL:	37	125	384	546
Embarked Military Force (at Ship's Company standards)	30	41	323	394
Combined TOTAL:	67	166	707	940

Note: The above figures have yet to be finalised.

Additional Troop Capacity

23. For short periods only the ship has the following additional austerity troop-carrying capacity:

Officers	Seniors	Rank and File	Total
25	40	295	360

which would give a total embarked force of approximately:

55	81	617	753

Notes:
a. The above figures can only be an approximation at this stage.
b. Ranks of the military force in excess of the numbers catered for at ship's company standards will sleep on camp beds and share dining hall, heads and bathroom facilities with the remainder of the embarked military force.

Specialists Units

24. In addition to the normal naval departments, the following are permanently embarked as members of the ship's company.
   a. Royal Marines Assault Squadrons comprising the Officers Commanding and the crews of the LCM(9) and LCA(2) squadrons.
   b. Ships Signal Troop; a Royal Signals unit with the task of manning certain support and non-naval radio links operated from the Assault Operations Room. Their shore going capability is limited to the provision of certain man-pack radios.

    c. Amphibious Beach Unit consisting of various Royal Marines and Army specialists and commanded by a Captain RM with the task of marking, developing and controlling a selected landing beach so as to facilitate the beaching and unloading of craft and the subsequent moving of their loads inland.

    d. DUKW Detachment. When required, a RASC detachment of four[33] DUKW wheeled amphibians will be provided from theatre resources to augment the permanently embarked Amphibious Beach Unit.

Office Accommodation for Embarked Force

25. Offices will include:

    a. Military Staff Office (adjoining the office of the Staff of the Commodore Amphibious Warfare).

    b. Military Commander's Office and Suite (adjoining those of COMAF).[34]

    c. Intelligence Office.

    d. Administrative Office.

Machinery Installation

26. The main machinery is arranged in two self-contained units each driving one shaft. The units are separated as far as possible to reduce the risk of both being damaged by one underwater explosion. Each unit contains one boxed boiler supplying steam to a main turbine rated to generate continuously 11,000 SHP at 210 rpm and for auxiliary services. Each unit is controlled throughout the whole power range from its own self-contained machinery control room. The machinery has been arranged so that as a normal duty, one unit can supply the harbour domestic load, thus allowing the other unit to be shut down and isolated for maintenance. Limited cross connections of services are provided to enable the machinery of one unit to be steamed from the boiler in the other unit.[35]

Fuel

27. Stowage is provided for 2,000 tons of FFO, 140 tons of DIESO, 25 tons of AVCAT, and 40 tons of MT 80 MOGAS.

Electric Power

28. Electric power is generated at 440 volts, 3 phase, 60 cycles per second and is provided by the following generators:

    a. 4 – 1,000 Kw Steam Turbo-Generators, two in each machinery space.

    b. 2 – 450 Kw Diesel Generators, one on No. 4 Deck forward and one on No. 8 Deck starboard aft.

Armament

29. Four Seacat launchers are fitted, two on No. 01 Deck forward and two on No. 03 Deck amidships. Each launcher is controlled by a GWS director Mark 20. All four systems are directed by a GDS 5 system.

30. Two Mark VII 40 mm single mountings are fitted on No. 04 Deck abreast the compass platform, each mounting being served from its own 04 Deck magazine.

Sonar and Echo Sounding Equipment

31. The ship is fitted with Echo Sounder Type 765 AK. It is intended to fit Type 182 Towed Decoy Equipment.

HMS *Fearless* before the addition of Portakabins and the extension to 02 Deck.

Communications

32. The Integrated Communications System fitted is highly flexible and provides Rear Link Assault Tactical Channels. The 13 HF lines available can be varied in power output up to 1 Kw. Double, Single and Independent Side Band modes can be used.
33. 9 UHF Channels are available: 3-693, 3-692, 3-691. No Radar Intercept ECM or HF DF equipment is fitted, but there is a Standard Search Bay Radio Intercept capability.

Radar

34. The following are fitted:
    a. Type 993 with TIU 5   Type 978 with true motion
    b. IFF 10 with SIF   Ship–ship transponder

Landing Craft and Amphibians

35. LCM(9). Each craft is capable of carrying two Centurion or main battle tanks or four 3 ton vehicles and land them on to a beach with gradient of 1 in 100 into the following depths of water:[36]
    a. Tanks – 4 ft. 6 ins.
    b. Wheeled vehicles, less ¼-tonners, 8 ft.
    c. ¼-ton vehicles 2 ft. 6 ins.

19

36. The LCM(9) has an endurance of 600 miles at 10 knots and is fitted with un-stabilised Type 975 Radar to provide for accurate navigation to the beach. It has a crew of seven and accommodation at austere scales is provided to allow these craft to operate independently.

37. LCA(2). Four LCA(2) will be carried at power-operated davits. Each craft has a crew of three and is capable of carrying 36 fully-equipped troops or a ¼ ton vehicle and trailer. The LCA(2) has an endurance of 160 miles at 9 knots.[37]

38. DUKW. These six-wheeled amphibians have a maximum speed of 5 knots in water and 46 mph on road. They are capable of crossing soft sand or mud by automatically reducing tyre pressure, and can carry 2½ tons of cargo.

More detail for the LCMs may be of interest. The first prototype, L3507, was laid down at Vospers Yard, Southampton in April 1962 and accepted on 19 March 1963 while the second, L3508, was laid down in May 1962 and handed over, appropriately, on 6 June 1963. Both were trialled by the Amphibious Trials and Training Unit[38] at Instow in north Devon and also by the 10th Landing Craft Training Squadron at Poole. *Fearless*'s landing craft (numbers L700-L703)[39] were built by Brook Marine of Lowestoft. In all fourteen LCMs were built including the four for HMS *Intrepid* and 'spare craft' for training, trials and replacements. Other constructors included Richard Dunstan Ltd. and J. Bolson and Sons Ltd.

The design was described in *Jane's Fighting Ships* of the time as 'having been evolved as the result of the most exhaustive tanks trials ever carried out on a landing craft. Scale models were made and operated by remote control in the Admiralty Experiment Works test tank at Haslar using simulated wave conditions to prove the design in the roughest possible sea conditions resulting in a design incorporating new standards of landing craft stability'. The LCM's dimensions were:

Displacement:	75 tons light, 176 tons loaded
Length overall:	85 feet
Breadth:	21.5 feet
Draught (aft):	5.5 feet

Propulsion was by courtesy of twin Davey Paxman diesels of the A6YHXAM type (624 bhp) via a 'V' drive to two propellers encased in Kort Nozzles; this allowed the engines to be placed as far aft as possible thus increasing well-deck space. With no rudders these nozzles gave more precise control when entering or leaving the dock as well as providing protection when beaching. Top speed was 9.5 knots although 10 knots was claimed by the builders. Hydraulic power operated the ramp, the vehicle and ramp recovery winch and the kedge anchor winch.

Rudimentary accommodation arrangements were fitted between the well deck and the machinery space with six bunks for the seven crew and a marine 'heads'. The crew consisted of a Royal Marines Colour Sergeant (coxswain), a Royal Marines Corporal (second coxswain), four Royal Marines (three deckhands and one signaller) and one Leading Mechanician (E) (engineer).

The LCA/LCVP Mk 2s were driven by twin Foden FD6 diesels of 200 bhp giving a claimed top speed of 10 knots. The LCVP Mk2's dimensions were:

Displacement:	11.5 tons light, 16 tons full load
Length:	43 feet
Breadth:	10 feet
Draught (aft):	2.5 feet

Their hulls were constructed of marine ply with, above the waterline, an outside cladding of steel. They had no hydraulics with the ramps and kedge anchor being operated by hand. The crew consisted of a Corporal (coxswain and signaller) and two Royal Marines as deckhands. The initial build was by the Dorset Yacht Company at Poole.

The equipment of the Amphibious Beach Unit bears a mention. Two Michigan 75 'tractors' with buckets for preparing a beach and the ability to unroll (and roll up) 120 feet rolls of Class 30 aluminium beach trackway were also part of the ABU.[40] A Royal Engineer Diving Section assisted in the recovery of drowned vehicles and a Communications Section was needed for controlling vessels approaching the beach and for liaising with the ground troops inland and the ships – not always just the LPD – offloading from offshore.

To establish, run and control a beach required a range of equipment much of which would be pre-loaded into two LCMs for the first wave of an unopposed landing. An opposed landing might require the first wave of four LCMs to be pre-loaded with main battle tanks in concert with LCAs laden with infantry before the ABU could be landed to prepare the beach to accept soft-skinned, wheeled vehicles – but the permutations were endless. Nevertheless the equipment required included two Land Rovers, one 3-ton lorry (containing food, tents, rubber 'S' tanks for storing fresh water on the beach ready for distribution inland, the beach limits and transit signs and two Gemini inflatable raiding craft each powered by a 40 hp outboard), one Beach Armoured Recovery Vehicle (BARV) and the two Michigan 75 'tractors', one with a bulldozer blade or bucket and the other with an 'A' frame for lifting and laying the six spools of trackway.

The personnel to run this unique unit were divided into a Signals Section, a Control Section, an Engineer Section, a Plant Section, a Recovery Section and a Royal Corps of Transport Section (who also were the Vehicle Decks party for marshalling vehicles when on board but who could augment the ABU once the ship was empty).

The Centurion BARV was a fascinating beast weighing approximately 40 tons which could achieve speeds on dry land in excess of 30 mph. Interestingly, the milometer 'un-wound' when reversing. It could wade into 9 feet 4 inches of flat calm water and was powered by a Rolls Royce Merlin engine which, when started up in the pre-dawn light, would bring tears of nostalgia to those who could recall the aircraft engines of the Second World War. Among very many uses the BARV was employed for recovering tanks or for pushing grounded landing craft into deeper water. It was, notoriously, used as a run-ashore vehicle in Greece and as the beachmaster's transport to a Brigade Orders Group in the jungle.

Chapter Two

Commander P.J. Shevlin, Royal Navy

First Senior Officer and Commissioning Commander
First Executive Officer
Later, Commodore, AM, Royal Australian Navy

Build, launch, fitting-out and organization

On 1 December 1961, the Admiralty under its First Lord, Lord Carrington,[41] placed an order with Harland and Wolff of Belfast for the first of two assault ships at a revised, estimated coast of £10m: an order for the second of class was placed with John Brown of Clydebank on 1 May 1962. On 25 July 1962 the Admiralty issued the News Release mentioned earlier which read in full:

The keel of the first of a new type of Assault Ship will be layed at the Belfast shipyard of Harland and Wolff Ltd, today, Wednesday 25th July. When it is subsequently launched the ship will be named Fearless. *Besides constructing the hull, Messrs. Harland and Wolff will also be the main machinery contractors. Assault Ships are a new design for the Royal Navy and will displace between 10,000 and 15,000 tons. They will operate with a Royal Marine Commando, launching landing craft through a special flooded compartment in the open stern. They will have a large flat deck space which will be used to accommodate military transport and to operate helicopters. The* Fearless *is expected to join the fleet in 1965.*

The first MAA L D Tuffnell BEM and the first Executive Officer, Commander Peter Shevlin.

The keel of LSA 01 – yard number 1651 – was laid as ordained by the News Release: work then continued much as scheduled until the launch date of 19 December 1963.

Once the build was under way, the first of a number of specialists began to work on the developing hull, among whom was Lieutenant (E) Ken Trace[42] the Ballast Control Officer and Dockmaster. He was appointed early so that ballasting – one of the most unique aspects of LSA 01 – could be studied. Ken Trace's other task was to write the definitive operating manual and for this he was given assistance by the manufacturers, Boulton Paul of Wolverhampton.

Building.

He was surprised by other design arrangements and cites the stern gate as a prime example. This structure was being built on huge racks alongside the position it would eventually take, with the engineers keen to impress how the tolerances were to the nearest 1,000th of an inch, but Ken Trace was less impressed with the 'rather agricultural' nature of the massive horizontal hinges with no access for lubrication. As it was to become increasingly difficult to move the gate over the years, a basic oiling routine would be adopted requiring huge doses of lubricating oil after each de-ballasting.

From the start the British Army embraced the LPD concept and even if they were not a charge to the Army vote – as the Landing Ships Logistic (LSLs)[43] had been – the military would use them and so it was fitting that the wife of the Chief of the General Staff should, in due course, name and launch the vessel.[44] The Royal Marines, after all, had their LPHs.

Decking.

More decking.

Guests to witness Lady Hull perform the ceremony on 19 December 1963 were invited by Harland and Wolff's chairman, Mr John S. Baillie, to be at No. 1 Slipway, Queen's Shipyard, no later than 12.10 p.m. ready for the launch at 12.30 followed by luncheon at 1.00 p.m. The official guest list numbered 171 with General Sir Richard Hull the principal military and the Prime Minister of Northern Ireland, Captain the Rt. Hon. Terence O'Neill, the principal political VIPs.

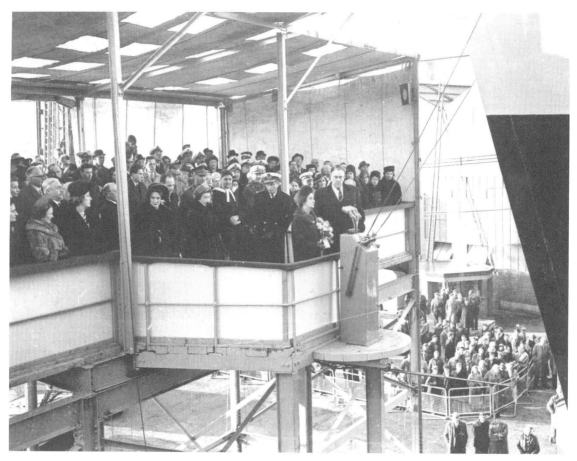

The launch party.

Vice Admiral J.B. Frewen, Vice Chief of the Naval Staff, represented the Royal Navy while Lieutenant General Sir Malcom Cartwright-Taylor, Commandant General, Royal Marines, and Major General R.D. Houghton, represented the Corps.

Inevitably there was the usual crop of bizarre incidents that attend such occasions; one concerned the media which had been ordered not to photograph, nor describe, the stern of the ship. They behaved well, only to be up-staged by a Russian merchant ship which, fortuitously, was moored to an adjacent jetty. The crew, no doubt including for the occasion – and probably for much of the build – a good proportion of KGB 'seamen', cheered lustily as *Fearless*'s secret stern gate shouldered aside the muddy waters of Lough Belfast.

Commander Peter Shevlin, the first Senior Officer appointed to this new ship – indeed this new concept – takes up the story:

I had arrived in the Harland and Wolff Shipyard on 11 August 1964 as Senior Officer of the stand-by party of officers and senior ratings supervising and advising on the fitting-out of the ship and had two hours before Admiral Sir Michael Le Fanu[45], the Controller of the Navy, arrived for an inspection!

Having survived that hurdle, I was pleasantly surprised to find that the Directors of Harland and Wolff invited me to lunch each day. A very pleasant social occasion and a useful way of getting decisions made.

Launch.

HMS *Fearless*'s stern configuration that was of such interest to the USSR at her launch. A later photograph.

The first major decision was the selection of colours for the ship's internal compartments. Having embarked Army personnel in a frigate, I thought it would be helpful for port side mess decks and passages to have red colours and starboard side to have green so that embarked troops knew where they were.

I was concerned that the Navy's practice of working out complements by the numbers needed to fight the ship was quite inappropriate for Fearless. *The crews required for two single 40 mm, power operated, gun mountings, four Seacat Missile launchers, and Operations Room and Wheelhouse crews was ludicrous to maintain the standards expected of a 12,000-ton warship so, on 9 September I submitted proposals for a more realistic complement.*

On 14 September I flew over to the USA, leading a small team for a two week visit to the US Navy's Atlantic Fleet, Amphibious Force Base at Little Creek, Norfolk, Virginia to determine whether the RN design was better or worse in any aspect. We spent two days in USS Raleigh,[46] *three days in the Little Creek Amphibious School and four days at sea in the USS* La Salle *which was exercising her helicopter and landing craft and procedures. Our first day in* Raleigh *was embarrassing. The Executive Officer had told us that lunch in the wardroom was from 1200 to 1300. I decided that a polite time for visitors to arrive, not appearing too greedy, would be 1210 but, to our horror, we found the entire complement of officers standing to attention behind their seats waiting for the British! I apologized profusely for not having checked that the USN did not follow RN Mess procedures at lunchtime.[47]*

Comparing Fearless's *General Arrangement Drawings, which I had brought with me, with what I found in the USN ships convinced me that our design was deficient in three important aspects:*

a. Fearless's *Flying Control Position was planned more like a 1950's era destroyer's Gun Direction Position. An open, uncovered space with minimum communications. The USS* La Salle's *arrangements seemed a model to aim for, enclosed, air conditioned, with TV to the Compass Platform and comprehensive internal and external communications.*

b. *The wooden barrier that divided the landing craft dock in the USN ships stretched further aft than in* Fearless *and the coxswains of the US craft said they liked the way their barrier rollers guided them into the correct bay.*

c. *The walkways along the docksides for landing craft line handlers stretched further aft than in* Fearless *and thus enabled lines to be passed to incoming craft earlier than would be possible with our current design.*

On return to Belfast in October my report was forwarded to the Director of Naval Equipment, Captain J.A.R. Troup,[48] so on 2 November I was invited to Bath to explain the reasons for my recommended changes. I had been Captain Troup's assistant when he was Commander of HMS Victorious *and now he was Commanding Officer (designate) of HMS* Intrepid. *He supported my recommendations – against opposition from the Director General of Ship Design.*

November saw the issue of a more realistic Scheme of Complement but the increased numbers raised new problems, the planned accommodation was now inadequate: back to Bath for more discussions with Captain Troup and DG Ships.

In 1965, interest in the ship widened. The Queen's Dragoon Guards, based in Northern Ireland, provided armoured cars to test the vehicle decks and ramps. The Devon and Dorset Regiment, one of the resident infantry regiments, provided troops and weapons to try out embarked force facilities. Then the death of Sir Winston Churchill on 24 January led to proposals to rename the lead ship HMS Churchill *and to abandon the 'Assault Ship' description in favour of the US Navy's much less bellicose, Landing Platform Dock. Thankfully, those proposals came to nothing.*

Over the next three months I visited Flag Officer Naval Air Command at RNAS Yeovilton to discuss the ship's helicopter operating potential and training required for the ship's small FAA complement and the Flag Officer Sea Training, Rear Admiral Bayly,[49] whose Staff Gunnery Officer I had been, to brief him and his staff on Assault Ship work-up requirements.

The Queen's Dragoon Guards arranged for me to visit the Royal Armoured Corps Training Centre at Bovington as I felt that Fearless's *Executive Officer (designate) ought to have some feel for manoeuvering a tank on the Tank Deck. On St Patrick's Day this visitor from Ireland was provided with a forenoon of Centurion driving experience. I soon felt I had got the hang of steering by track levers and so accepted an invitation to take my tank round a circuit. When a pond appeared I carried out the drill that my instructor had given me but, either I had misunderstood him, or his directions had not been intended as helpful, for a moment later, my tank stalled in the middle of the pond. Seemingly from nowhere a team of camera-wielding Armoured Corps officers appeared to photograph what looked surprisingly like a surrendering U-Boat captain! They made amends with an excellent lunch.*

On 29 April I led a second overseas reconnaissance party; this time to France to inspect the French Navy's new amphibious ship, the FS Ouragon,[50] *to see if we could learn anything useful from their design. Liaison officers met us and showed us the tourist sites of Paris before flying us to Brest the next day where a very good luncheon preceded an extensive tour of* Ouragon. *We were intrigued by the 'Wine Line' which ran to every Mess and Mess-deck, to provide each man with his daily ration of vino. Sadly and correctly, I did not think there was any possibility of getting a similar facility built into* Fearless!

On 23 June we received the first of the ship's Assault Landing Craft[51] and tested it at its davits. Then it was over to England again to give a presentation on the ship's capabilities to Headquarters 3 Division and the Brigade Commanders of 2 and 3 Brigades.

In due course Peter Shevlin would become the Executive Officer and while the following résumé was written some years later it is just as relevant for 1965:

The XO was responsible for the organization, administration and training of all onboard. In this role he was assisted by the First Lieutenant, Damage Control Officer, Warrant Officer Master at Arms and Ship's Physical Training Instructor and their respective teams.

The key Executive Department function was whole ship coordination which ensured that the multitude of onboard activities were de-conflicted and correctly manned.

One of the Department's other functions was to provide the Regulating Branch of service policemen.

Although Commander Shevlin was the first 'Senior Officer' of the ship, the honour of being the first commander to join was the Commander (E), A.J.R. (Tony) Smith in March 1964.

'Do you like Guinness?' my Appointer asked me, 'Because I have your name down to join HMS Fearless.'

I devoted some time getting to know as much as possible about the design of the ship and the scope of my responsibilities as her Marine Engineer Officer. Visits to the Design Section at Bath and to the shipyard disabused me of the Appointer's claim that it was very simple – 'just two sets of destroyer's engines with a few extra bits'. To a chap like me who had served in frigates and destroyers, the size of the hull, albeit only a keel and a few of the lower strakes of hull plating at the time, was pretty awesome and the novel design of those 'extra bits' needed to sustain a large complement of naval and army personnel and to operate a floating dock, large landing craft of about 200 tonnes [sic] displacement each, tanks, guns and beach assault vehicles, together with 4 helicopters made me realise that I would have my hands full.

On arrival Tony Smith was met by 'Paddy', the Admiralty Overseeing Engineer who enjoyed great fame having served with distinction throughout the war in submarines:

The going to work was alright but the coming back revealed that there were more hazards to road travel than the absence of any Driving Test in Northern Ireland at that time. These could be summarised as the County Down Station Bar, the wardroom of the Naval Air Station at Sydenham, Gerry's Bar at Holywood, The Widow Murphy's (alias the Imperial Hotel at Bangor), the Canberra Bar (alias The Coalheavers) and the Crawfordsburn Hotel. This gave Paddy a number of options for our route home and he always selected an interesting permutation. I learned to like Guinness very much!

Harland and Wolff treated us with typical Ulster hospitality: the Directors' dining room was under the charge of Robert the butler, a man of imposing stature. As an experiment, haggis was put on Friday's menus and, observing that most on our table enjoyed the new dish, it became a permanent feature. Robert, wishing that all the conventions should be observed, always came round with a generous libation of Scotch. Terrifying!

I attended the offices and ship each day, seeing the boilers and machinery set in place and, as steam and electrical power became available, witnessing the trials of the auxiliary machinery. Being the first of a new class, the ship was subjected to a number of additional trials, including a Heeling Trial, which lingers in the memory perhaps because I felt that there were many nicer ways to spend a Saturday (fishing day) than watching the slow and painstaking procedure of loading weights onto the deck edges and measuring the degree of list that the ship took on. The trial had to take place on a Saturday because there had to be no disturbance by work in or around the ship, and for the same reason, the ship had to have the gangways removed and be hauled out into the channel. The ship was then listed 15° either way and, whilst readings were being taken, everyone had to stay still, not an easy job when you were perched on a slope of nearly 1 in 4.

Captain Hugh Corbett joined rather earlier than he would normally have done: his reputation had preceded him and it was soon apparent that he was going to live up to it, spraying out questions and ideas and wanting answers in an instant. The Heads of Department, preoccupied with the preparations for taking responsibility from the shipbuilders, felt that the heat was on them! Not much chance for many Guinnesses then.

The following was written some years after commissioning and explains, simply, what the Marine Engineering Department did:

The Department provided a vast range of services to enable the ship to operate effectively. Main propulsion, electricity generation, fresh water, sewerage, air conditioning, refrigeration, heating, lighting, the constant preservation and repair of the ship's structure. 170 people worked within the Marine Engineering Department, ranging from the Marine Engineering Officer (MEO), known as Commander (E), through the trade sections to Junior Marine Engineering Mechanics.

Among the other officers who joined before Commandeer Shevlin was the ship's first Amphibious Operations Officer or AOO, Major L.S. 'Tiny' Whitworth. Although Major Whitworth, who arrived in April 1964, did not command the Amphibious Detachment he was the senior Royal Marines officer embarked whose task, prior to commissioning, was formulating the internal and external communications systems and establishing the assault routes within the ship from mess decks to assembly points. Men proceeding ashore in an assault configuration had a choice of three routes to their point of disembarkation and not every one from the same mess deck would have the same destination: the flight deck for those going by helicopter; the waist decks either side for those travelling in one of the four LCAs or the tank deck for those travelling by LCM.

The Officer Commanding the Amphibious Detachment (OCAD)[52] – with the appropriate powers of punishment – was a Royal Marines captain but the first officer to hold this post was replaced early by a second Royal Marines Major – Jim Carman – supported by a Detachment Sergeant Major and HQ team. Beneath them the Amphibious Detachment was split three ways: the Landing Craft Squadron with the OCAD in command and a Royal Marine Lieutenant, David Minords,[53] as his Second in Command, ran the four LCMs and four LCAs.

The second sub-unit was the Amphibious Beach Unit commanded, initially, by the beachmaster – the vastly experienced Captain George Wheatley, Royal Marines.[54] His Second in Command was a Royal Engineers Captain, L.H. Jamieson, but this appointment was soon altered to that for a Royal Corps of Transport officer as the Vehicle Decks Officer.[55] The ABU's task was to advise on the suitability of beaches, in conjunction with those responsible for carrying out reconnaissance; establishing the appropriate command and control facilities; setting up beach transits for landing craft; laying trackway where necessary; running a salvage team for drowned vehicles or broached craft using the Beach Armoured Recovery Vehicle, manned by four Royal Engineers' personnel, one of whom was a diver; storing and distributing bulk fuel and water and generally being the physical link between the shipping and the shore – an all purpose conduit for the safe transit of men, vehicles and stores across the watergap. As the BARV could wade into 9 feet of calm water it was also useful as a temporary mooring point for landing craft.

The third sub-unit within the Amphibious Detachment was 621 Signals Troop, commanded by a Royal Signals captain, Captain M.J.P. Vann. The second officer to command this troop was Captain Michael Walker[56] who explains:[57]

621 Signals Troop provided communications for the Brigade HQ to command and control fighting and front line units ashore while the headquarters was landing and establishing itself securely. The Troop operators were fully integrated into the Ship's Communications Department. The Ship's Communications Officer was in overall control; OC 621 became Deputy Communications Officer and the RN SD Lieutenant became the Assistant Communications Officer.

Major Whitworth, who had recently been the Staff Operations Officer of 42 Commando in the Far East during the time of HMS *Bulwark*'s first commission as a Helicopter Carrier (later LPH) brought with him Corporal (shortly to be promoted to Sergeant) A.F. (Tony) Coppard and his MOA, or batman in Army parlance. Tony Coppard had also accrued invaluable experience as an 'amphibious' clerk when serving in the Amphibious Warfare Squadron's headquarters ship, the River class frigate HMS *Meon*. These three lived in digs spread across Belfast (including the Shankill Road) and commuted to work in uniform, often on public transport.

Yet another of the advance party and an equally vital member, was the Amphibious Detachment's Signals Sergeant, Tom Potts.[58] He and his Royal Marines signallers manned the communications in the LCMs and the Amphibious Beach Unit, and were responsible for those in the LCAs. He and the OCAD operated all the ship's amphibious communications from a corner of the Ship's Operations Room.

Fitting out. Note open cubby hole for Flyco.

Although Tom Potts had had experience with the Amphibious Warfare Squadron in the Persian Gulf most of his young signallers knew only the Unit Command Net of a Royal Marines Commando. Significantly, the Royal Navy communications equipment was equally unknown and so Tom Potts spent many of his early days introducing his men to the UHF A43 and the HF A13 sets as well as the Landing Craft Primary and Landing Craft Secondary wireless nets.

Tom Potts's secondary duty was as a guide to men as they arrived on board which meant getting to know the ship and its compartments intimately and quickly. He also began a tradition, initially frowned upon by the senior ship's officers as there were adequate Chiefs' and POs' messes, of establishing a small bar in the RM SNCOs' mess deck. Stocking this with the necessary beer pumps while seeking an unofficial stowage space for the beer kegs was not easy. Passing the Commanding Officer and the Commander on the Flight Deck, with a barrel of beer balanced on his shoulder, he was close enough to hear one remark to the other that the Royal Marines Detachment had its priorities all wrong! Some may prefer the opposing view.

When the Detachment moved on board, the duty SNCO for that first night was Colour Sergeant Patterson the Quartermaster Sergeant (QMS) who had arrived direct from the Royal Marines' Depot at Deal in Kent where he had been used to recruits. He was nonplussed when, on asking a 'high spirited naval Killick' to keep quiet for rounds, he was forced to point out that he was a Colour Sergeant of the Royal Marines, only to receive the reply, 'I don't care what colour you are. . . .'

It became a well-used cliché for some months but which, too, highlighted that it was not only the Army that was new to the Navy; very few naval hands had served with the Royal Marines and were thus unused to military rank structures.

In those early days the military element was joined by a Royal Artillery Lieutenant Colonel, Freddie Newall, as the Army trials officer, who is remembered as much for his love of, and demand for, curries, as for his wise counsel and experience. He was to be indispensable as the link between the ship and her potential customers.

Another early joiner was the Deputy Supply Officer, Lieutenant Commander John Nichol:

> The ship was storing when I joined with everything coming from England in huge wooden containers known as Chacons. I remember one labelled 'Urgent' being brought alongside by horse and cart!
>
> As well as being in charge of Naval Stores and Wardroom Staff, I was Divisional Officer for the Supply Department of some 80 ratings including two soldiers – an Army Catering Corps Cook Sergeant and a Pay Corps Corporal – and therefore, somewhat unsurprisingly, a regular figure at Commander's Requestmen and Defaulters!
>
> The large size of the Supply Department was dictated by the fact that the ship was in effect a 'floating hotel' with the number of 'guests' fluctuating wildly from day to day. An embarked force could well double the numbers to be catered for. Under Charles Denman's wise leadership the Department was soon running smoothly and ready to cope with any eventuality.

The Commander (S) – Charles Denman[59] – had for many years been secretary to Admiral Le Fanu and recalled little of standing by the ship except, in agreement with the Commander:

> The weather and the food. Those lunches every day in the Harland and Wolff Director's Dining Room – no wonder shipbuilding was so expensive and took so long!

There were a number of other departments whose functions need explaining at this early stage. Though these notes were written after new systems had been added, they still give a flavour of the basics:

The small Weapons Engineering Department was responsible for the maintenance of all weapons, computers, radars, communications and navigation systems. The ship had a number of radars used for surveillance or for navigation in poor weather.

The Warfare and Executive Department was headed by the Executive Officer and divided into several sub-departments: Navigation, Seamanship, Above Water Warfare, Radar, Communications, Damage Control and Executive functions. Fearless was the last ship to employ ratings exclusively from the old Operations Branch specializations. This resulted in a higher average age than could be expected in most warships; the average age of the Able Seamen, for example, was 25: borne out by the large number of Good Conduct badges and Long Service and Good Conduct medals seen onboard.

Air Department. The ability to move men and equipment by helicopter offered a fast, flexible and effective response to a crisis.

Medical Department. The Sickbay provided a range of services similar to those of a general medical and dental practice. The medical team consisted of a doctor, a dentist, two Senior Medical Branch Ratings and five Junior Medical Branch Ratings. Areas of particular activity were preventive dentistry, health promotion and first aid training.

Lieutenant Ken Trace and CPO Reg Eccles at the ballast control panel.

The last word from this period goes to Ken Trace and his Ballast Control Team. The first use of the ballast system was not in docking-down but to carry out a 'tilt-test' alongside the jetty. The contractors insisted that this would be conducted by their own team, led by a bowler-hatted gentlemen in a white boiler suit.

This test checked that the ballast pumps worked correctly and that various items of equipment functioned at different angles of heel. To begin with all went well with the free-flooding of the tanks until a 2° angle was achieved. Ken Trace and his two chief petty officers were allowed to watch but 'in no way were they to interfere'. All remained well as the slow heeling continued towards 3° when there was an unexpected loss of main power. The control consul operator, looking most assured, switched to the battery back-up system and started to shut off the valves but the heeling continued past 3° at which point the operator began a 'controlled panic'. The two chiefs, bursting to tell 'the bowler hat' what the matter was, were motioned by Ken Trace to keep quiet.

As the ship reached 4°, and with no sign of slowing, the operator turned in desperation and asked if Ken Trace could 'fix it'. The two chief petty officers were dispatched to the two valve compartments, forward and aft as, unknown to the Harland and Wolff operator, they had all assisted the Boulton and Paul engineers in setting up the controls when the ballasting system had been originally fitted. Within a few minutes the ship stopped heeling. Ken Trace then explained that the battery back-up system merely provided light to indicate the position of the tanks valves – open or shut – and the amount of water in each tank. To operate the valves by power from the control console required the ship's full 330 volt system.

Main machinery control panel.

As a direct result the contractors accepted that the ship's staff were fully conversant with the operating procedures and, in due course, asked them to carry out the Contractors Sea Trials on their behalf – but with Harland and Wolff accepting full responsibility. One of the team was Chief Shipwright Artificer Reg Eccles[60] whose privilege it was to be, in due course, the first shipwright to operate the ballast control in its proper function and who would eventually control the forward and aft valves while Ken Trace himself, as dockmaster, would control the main pumps. In those early days, the team often ended up de-ballasting with one pump; requiring them to remain closed-up in the Ballast Control Room for up to ten hours at a time.

And so the ship's company slowly came together.

Chapter Three

Captain H.A. Corbett, DSO, DSC, Royal Navy

First Commanding Officer
1965–1967
Later, CBE

Commissioning and Trials.
Home Waters, Middle East, South Africa, Far East

Captain Hugh Corbett served mostly in destroyers from 1936 to 1945, including command of HMS *Wheatland* (in which he was awarded the DSO for operations in the Adriatic having won the DSC as First Lieutenant of HMS *Lookout* during the North Africa campaign). Later he commanded HMSs *Charity*, *Cockade* and *Caesar*. In 1940 he was Mentioned in Dispatches serving in HMS *Brazen* off Norway while in company with the previous HMS *Fearless*. He retired in 1969 as Head of the Naval Manpower Future Policy Division. Hugh Corbett writes:

Captain Hugh Corbett, DSO, DSC, RN.

> Fearless, *with her younger sister,* Intrepid, *was designed to deploy the amphibious assault element – including main battle tanks – of an army Brigade Group with Joint Headquarters and communications. Indeed, her initial complement reflected this with the inclusion of forty army personnel mainly from the Royal Signals, Royal Corps of Transport and Royal Engineers. The Royal Marines, without heavy armour, and more dependent on helicopters and swift ship to shore flexibility relied, then, on the Commando Carriers,* Bulwark *and* Albion.
>
> *The official title for this new style of amphibious vessel was Assault Ship but this was later changed – much to my Commander's disapproval – for Landing Platform Dock (LPD) to fit in with NATO (in reality – American) terminology.*
>
> *I joined the ship in Belfast on 5 July 1965 allowing Commander Shevlin to revert from Senior Officer to Executive Officer. Just over four months later the ship was commissioned and, two days after that, she sailed – although not wholly complete – in order to meet our long-standing date for tuning the communications systems, both military and naval, into Plymouth Command.*
>
> *Then, between December 1965 and February 1966 the first-of-class trials began. In addition to Royal Navy, Royal Marines and official civilian visitors, the ship's company's senior army officer, Lieutenant Colonel A.F. Newall, Royal Artillery arranged visits for army commanders wherever the ship went as*

well as giving conducted tours for officers and units and embarking the weirdest of vehicles to see if their sizes, shapes and weights would fit.

The first commission of the first of a new class of ship is a unique experience. One young man, an Ordinary Seaman, remarked three months after we commissioned, 'Every day we do something that's never been done before'. Trials in the Solent with hovercraft and a Press Open day followed and all this before I took the ship to Portland on 4 March for the official work-up under the critical and helpful eyes of the Flag Officer Sea Training and his staff. Frigates would arrive at Portland fearful but **Fearless** welcomed all the expertise that the experienced staff could give her while the lack of visitors, for the first time, allowed us to 'find ourselves'.

Fearless had been lucky: we had always been up with, or ahead of, our trials programme, and we were grateful to Messrs Harland and Wolff for getting us to sea within two weeks of the planned date, despite delays in supply of equipment. This prompt start was made at a price, in the number of loose ends we had to pick up in the early days, but it paid off. The men who weathered those stormy early months of amphibious trials, testing and tuning will remember that we surprised Portland by arriving there, not in trepidation at the tough prospect of work-up, but thanking God that their strong team of experts could help us solve our problems. One solution was an increase of over 50 in our complement, and I was glad of the opportunity to thank all the original ship's company; the senior members who bore the brunt of our shortages by doing the work of two or three men when we were all hard pressed learning our jobs, and the young men who shouldered much responsibility before they were trained. We came out of the aptly named 'trials period' toughened into a resolute and united team. We even began to hone our sports teams with matches against the local Borstal before returning to Belfast for completion in mid-February. This proved necessary, for numerous small alterations were highlighted in the short but bad weather passage.

The first-of-class trials were completed in July – August with noise-ranging experiments involving visits to the western Mediterranean and subsequent modification of the propellers; to Loch Fyne for machinery noise ranging and finally to Portland for the sound and degaussing ranges and thence to Portsmouth for Navy Days and 42,000 visitors in three days – no problem!

The stream of experts and units who visited or embarked in the Assault Ship placed a great strain upon her ship's company: we were constantly under inspection, continually 'open to visitors'. We learnt a great deal from our Embarked Forces, and took much pride in the many corps, regiments and units that became associated with us. Some came to us uncertain, or openly doubtful of our usefulness: their reaction to the experience was surprise at our potential and versatility.

Fearless sailed from Portsmouth on 13 September 1966 calling at Gibraltar and Malta (visitors galore) to arrive in Aden on 29 September where the Middle East Command under Admiral Le Fanu, set the ship to work at once. Visitors from all three services began this period with minor exercises then on 11 October a troop of Scout cars were embarked and landed in the Western Protectorate to surprise rebel tribesmen inland. On 24 October a battalion of Irish Guards and five RAF helicopters under Brigadier Bremner were embarked to assault a base on the Omani border to the east.[61] This village complex was unassailable by land and used by a terrorist group who were harassing Muscat and Oman. At one stage **Fearless** anchored only for the Engineer Officer to appear on the bridge clutching a bucket of jelly fish and the warning that the condenser inlets would be fully blocked unless the ship weighed promptly. She did and the unforeseen attack by Portuguese-men-of-war was averted.

Next a visit to Mombasa for minor exercises and a return to Aden prior to a pre-planned exercise in the Persian Gulf but instead we sailed for Durban where we arrived on the 25 November. We were required to evacuate a battalion of the Royal Irish Fusiliers from Swaziland as trouble in Southern Rhodesia was preventing them from being flown north. **Fearless** returned them to Aden with their band playing on the flight deck. The ship had been welcomed in Durban despite the tension at the time.

Fearless's experience in the Middle East Command had established her potential and she sailed on 11 December for Singapore.

The Far East Station was less action-packed though the visitor invasion remained intense wherever the ship went. In March 1967 a fleet amphibious exercise off Penang with Bulwark *also taking part was the ship's biggest yet and at the end of the month we sailed for Okinawa, Japan and Korea enjoying generous hospitality and returning the many kindnesses with conducted tours for local services and*

Pre-wetting trials. June 1966.

offering help to numerous charitable projects ashore. We returned to Singapore in April for a six weeks' maintenance period where the opportunity was taken by the Chaplain to organise a team for the refurbishment of a Salvation Army Children's Home.

At this stage the Amphibious Detachment had handled well over a thousand tanks and vehicles and more than five hundred trailers without mishap. There had been over a thousand deck landings from all three services and thus the ship had developed into a truly triphibious Assault Ship. Within a year of commissioning, we also had a couple of small but significant operations and a military evacuation under our belt, operations which could not have been done so swiftly or effectively by any other ship.

In my forward to the ship's First Commission Book I could not end without mention of sport: it was a splendid parting present when under the floodlights in Singapore, our rugger team won and our soccer team retained the Big Ships' challenge trophies. Our teams of sailors, Royal Marines and soldiers understandably caused mutterings about 'Combined Service' from ships with bigger but less widely talented complements. I ended with the words: 'I hope that this book will convey to those who read it some of the excitement, stimulus and pride in achievement that we who have lived its story have enjoyed. It seems almost incredible to me that we came together as strangers so short a while ago at the end of 1965 to an uncompleted ship. To live through this period of such rapid progress is a stirring experience. Rarely can a new concept have proved itself so quickly. We can now say with confidence the words which we spoke in faith at our commissioning ceremony: We are **Fearless***, we fear nothing!'*

I should like to repeat what I wrote at the end of my Report of Proceedings after our cruise to Japan and Korea: 'I felt proud, on this my final cruise as their Captain, to command them, the best ship's company I have ever had.'

Captains are, perhaps, obliged to make this statement but with *Fearless* it was probably more often said with conviction than perhaps was normal.

Commander Shevlin[62] takes us back to the beginning of this commission:

Captain Hugh Corbett's arrival allowed me time to write the Ship's Standing Orders which I short titled as FEARSOs. By now the Executive Office had also been joined by the ship's first Master at Arms, L. D. Tuffnell BEM – not only the expected tower of strength but a tower of a man!

Then, on 10 July, **Fearless** *proceeded to sea for the first time, under the Red Ensign and the command of a Harland and Wolff appointed Master, to conduct a successful two weeks of Contractors' Sea Trials in the Irish Sea.*

One defect, however, was revealed. Going to sleep in my bunk for the first time, I learnt painfully that the new type, daytime settee/night time bunk was defective. As I slid between the sheets, the bunk decided that it preferred being the back of the settee, so it up-turned itself and squashed me against the ship's side! I was trapped, unable to force the settee back into its bunk configuration! Fortunately Mr Tuffnell had decided to undertake an exploratory night round. . . . I was amused to read some years later that the bunk had returned to its errant ways in Gibraltar.

In Belfast, on 19 October, General Moulton of the Royal Marines, visited and on 2 November the new Controller of the Navy, Admiral Sir Horace Law inspected the ship and then, on the 10th, the Commodore Contract Built Ships (CSCBS) conducted an eight-hour Terminal Date Inspection.

The final CSCBS inspection was carried out on 22 November after which the Commodore said he was not prepared to accept **Fearless** *into the fleet! However it was too late to change the commissioning arrangements. The main body of the ship's company moved onboard on the 23rd, followed 24 hours later by our first Embarked Military Force: a Troop of Queen's Dragoon Guards with two Saracen armoured cars and two Ferret scout cars.*

Although over 130 members of the ship's company had been standing by for eighteen months, the first Daily Orders were not issued from the Commander's ship-board office until Monday 22 November, just three days before Commissioning Day. Appropriately, thirty-seven years of Daily Orders began with the instruction that at 0730 that day Able Seaman Buckley and Able Seaman Davie were to report to the Motor Transport Section, Sydenham,[63] for transport to collect the rum ration from HMS *Sea Eagle*.[64] From the beginning, some will argue, the ship had her priorities in the correct order. Later that day the advance party moved into their mess decks and life on board HMS *Fearless* began.

While the press had been quiet during the building they were saving themselves for a field day once she had been commissioned which, the Ministry of Defence announced, would take place at Harland and Wolff on 25 November 1965. Local reporters and photographers were invited to tour the ship at 1400 the day before the ceremony and the London press to do the same at 1000 on the day itself.

By and large the press were impressed and although *Fearless* was due to be over budget by £1 million out of a second revised total of £12 million this still represented less than £1 million per thousand tons compared with a frigate which was, then, around £2 million per thousand tons.

At 1430 on 25 November, the Commissioning Order for the seventh[65] HMS *Fearless*, signed by Vice Admiral Sir Fitzroy Talbot,[66] C-in-C Plymouth, was read on the Tank Deck to the assembled ship's company in the presence of Lady Hull and her husband, now Field Marshal Sir Richard Hull, and Chief of the Defence Staff. The White Ensign was hoisted on a specially erected mast on the tank deck – the Irish weather was playing its part – as well as at the ensign staff, while the commissioning pennant was broken out at the masthead.[67] A dedication service, led by the Chaplain of the Fleet assisted by Catholic and Free Church padres, followed before Captain Corbett reported the latest addition to British defence capabilities to the CDS who addressed the assembly. Lady Hull and the Colonel Commandant of the Royal Corps of Signals[68] then made presentations to the ship.

Whether for an ulterior motive or not will never be revealed but the 1st Battalion Royal Irish Fusiliers's Piper, lent for the occasion, had earlier been entertained by the Amphibious Detachment SNCOs for far longer than was strictly necessary to get his drones in tune. At some stage in the ceremony a 'dreadful wailing' from the flight deck had heralded the sight of this lone piper making his unsteady way down the steep incline of the ramp towards the assembled ship's company, guards of honour and guests. He was met by the Detachment Sergeant Major and led away 'before any further disasters could occur'.

The ceremony was well covered on television in Northern Ireland but not on mainland Britain; air time being taken up by reports of a Unilateral Declaration of Independence in Rhodesia. None of that was of much interest to *Fearless*'s ship's company as celebratory parties began in the wardroom, the Chief Petty Officers' anteroom and the Junior Rates' dining hall. The fact that, according to the ship's log, it was 'snowing hard' by 1930 probably also went unnoticed to all but the duty hands.

The formality of commissioning could not have been delayed and so the Red Ensign was hoisted again the following day: a day spent storing ship for the first time with, no doubt, a good number of hangovers. Either the Naval Stores organization had sent too many stores or the ship's storing arrangements were faulty, but *Fearless* sailed with her dock full of boxes and containers that left no room for landing craft.

Then, at 1530 on 27 November 1965 following successful repeat trials, the CCBS accepted HMS *Fearless* for service in the Royal Navy: the White Ensign was re-hoisted plus the Commodore Amphibious Warfare's broad pennant and the commissioning pennant itself.

The First Commissioning Ceremony, 25 November 1965.

The ship's company were, in large part, delighted with their new home but not so that doyen of naval correspondents, the late Desmond Wettern of the *Daily Telegraph*. The week after the commissioning ceremony and having had time to reflect, he wrote, with some accuracy:

> *During a tour after her commissioning at Belfast last week one Senior Ratings' Mess I saw which was designed to accommodate 16 men had a clear deck space less than that to be found in an average bedroom. Even towel rails on locker doors were inadequate, measuring only about six inches in length. The Mess is certainly below the standards of accommodation to be found in many other warships today.*
>
> *Officer accommodation is also cramped. When only the ship's 30 officers were on board the wardroom was comfortable but the ship will carry a number of army officers as part of her crew [sic] and is designed to transport an entire infantry battalion or a Royal Marines Commando. These additional 40 or so officers will make the wardroom extremely crowded.*

Yet Wettern did have positive things to say:

> *The galley and cafeteria messes to some extent compensate for the crowded sleeping and recreation spaces. Senior army officers were greatly impressed by the galley. . . .*
>
> *As* Fearless *and* Intrepid *will be completed within less than a year of each other it will be impossible to fit improvements learnt from* Fearless *... in* Intrepid. *The two ships were built almost simultaneously because the entire amphibious warfare squadron which they will replace became obsolete some years ago and all six ships of the squadron had to be withdrawn within a few months of each other.*

Flight deck trials.

These themes were taken up by a number of other naval correspondents. The professional users, too, had their comments. The major complaint concerned the Flying Control (Flyco) position about which Commander Shevlin had been so critical. It has, though, to be remembered that, as Hugh Corbett has privately emphasized,[69] the LPDs were procured for Army use and that an Army brigade then, did not include helicopters. Nevertheless, Peter Shevlin's views had been listened to and his recommendations for a better Flyco were accepted in time, as were his views about the centre line barrier in the dock and the walkway for the line handlers.

Other comments rang true. On 31 October 1965 the *Sunday Telegraph*'s Naval Correspondent suggested that no ship, no matter how large and no matter how 'joint service', could effectively

Trials with docking an LCT Mk 8.

Tight fit. Note centre-line barrier in the forward half of the dock.

cover the area between Hong Kong and the Persian Gulf which had, previously, he argued, been the purlieu of the Amphibious Warfare Squadron: a Squadron that had, at any one time, consisted of at least seven ships – three 5,000-ton (fully laden) LST(A)s and four 800-ton LCTs with a Seaborne Tank Force embarked.

The same correspondent also regretted the demise of this fire-brigade force and rued the day that the government would have to rely on the RAF's Transport Command to move troops. In fact he missed – or purposefully ignored – the fact that six modern LSLs were also in commission and more than proving their worth. He also 'missed' the fact that HMSs *Bulwark* and *Albion* were at sea, both with nine helicopter spots (16 troop-lift helicopters per ship) and each capable of embarking and deploying a full Royal Marines Commando Battle Group of up to 900 men. The LSTs and LCTs had been elderly and slow; six knots in the case of some LSTs one year out of a bottom scrub.

Melding a crew with such a range of diverse capabilities and assets into one team was not going to be easy, despite the enthusiasm that stemmed from the Commanding Officer and that percolated down to the most junior seaman. Commander Charles Denman compiled an essay on how members should conduct themselves and, in

Corporal Tony Coppard and Major 'Tiny' Whitworth, at their assault stations.

its lighthearted way, helped to set the scene for the can-do atmosphere for which the ship quickly, and permanently, became renowned:

All those who serve in HMS Fearless *will be known as 'Fearless' Freds.*

Freds are made up mostly of Soldiers, or Milifreds, and sailors, or Nautifreds.

The Nautifreds are divided for disciplinary purposes into Officers (Offreds) and ratings (Manfreds) who, as is well known to one and all, are in every nice girl's top ten.

The older Offreds are also known as Brassfreds because of the sort of hats they wear. The Brassfreds are:

The Captain, Commanding Officer of the Ship, or Topfred.

*The Commander, Second-in-Command, Executive Officer or Xfred.

*The Engineer Officer or Chiefred.

The Amphibious Operations Officer or Tinifred.

*The Principal Medical Officer or Mofred.

*The Supply Officer or Payfred.

The Meteorological Officer cum Instructor Officer or Teachfred.

(* These are also known as Sergeants which, let's face it, could be confusing to the Milifreds.)[70]

There may also be on board two Bossfreds, conspicuous for their silverfreds amongst the gold, viz, the Commodore or Comfred and Brigadier or Brigfred. They will probably be accompanied by some Staff Officers. Staff Officers are picked for their intellectual ability and are known as Thinkfreds as opposed to the rest of us who are Dofreds or Serfreds.

The Manfreds are looked after by two Fiercefreds, the Master-at-Arms or Jauntifred, who is the senior Nautimanfred, and the Sergeant Major or Qfred, who is the senior Milimanfred.

For leave and so forth the Manfreds are divided into two, the Port Watch or Lefthandfreds, and the Starboard Watch or Righthandfreds.

For working purposes the Manfreds are divided in Departments, as follows:

The Seamen or Yoheavehofreds

The Mechanical Engineers or Plumfreds

The Electrical Engineers or Lfreds (nothing to do with the chaps who burn the cakes, that is done by the Cooks or Chipfreds cum Fried Fishfreds)

The Medical Department or Docfreds

The Supply Department or Pusserfreds

The Beach Unit and Landing Craft Crews or Phibfreds

We few, we happy few, we band of Freds

There are not many Freds to operate such a large ship so we must all be Flexifreds – The Offreds and Gentfreds must pull and haul with the Manfreds, to coin a phrase, and the Chipfreds must be one with the Phibfreds, so to speak. There can be no 'Not me, Chiefifred, I'm a Rad-fred' or 'Not my part of Fearless, *Fred' amongst us. In fact no room for the Fredbare.*

How to win Freds

As you go round the ship you will, of course, find all sorts and conditions of Fred – Fatfreds, Shortfreds, Loftifreds and so on. But whatever our personal preferences and prejudices we must always be prepared to put them into the background in the cause of Fredmanship. Or one Fred must at all times cooperate the hell out of other Freds.

Once more into the breach dear Fred

With all this keenness, kindness and cooperation we must also of course have candomanship. Nothing too difficult, nothing too much trouble for Fred, so that all the Admirals or the Fred and Fred Marshals we meet (you will find that all Senior Officers will tend to become Honorary Freds) will say when faced with an awkward situation 'A Fred, a Fred my pension for a Fred!'

Sub-Lieutenant (S) Peter Baseby[71] remembers his Commander (S) well:

Charles Denman[72] was a stalwart in those early days and one with some eccentric and endearing habits. One such involved his monocle. On occasion he would preside at the Commander's table when, if someone made a doubtful statement, his eye would open in silent amazement as he stared at the miscreant – and his monocle would fall neatly into his breast pocket. The effect on the nervous could be quite devastating! He was a much-loved character, relaxed and urbane as well as being an excellent 'wordsmith' as one might expect of a naval barrister who had served as Admiral Le Fanu's secretary in several appointments.

Peter Baseby remembers other snippets:

Early on, Captain Corbett decided that Fearless *merited her own Chaplain. After repeated badgering, the Revd. J.C. Venus was appointed to the ship – his first appointment in the Royal Navy. One of the Embarked Force Officers' cabins was taken over as the Vicarage. John Venus was an asset, fully justifying the Captain's insistence.*

Hugh Corbett quickly became much respected, though he never quite grew out of his destroyer handling habits as witnessed by one or two remarkably 'hairy' manoeuvres alongside! He was very experienced, a taskmaster and, of paramount importance, an enthusiast. He was to drive everyone, not least himself, hard and fairly but particularly the Commander, Peter Shevlin. Many times a day the ship's tannoy would bark out the order, Commander ring 213, *that being the telephone number of the Captain's cabin. He had two pet phrases,* Good God! *and* Don't you agree? *and so, very soon after his arrival a ditty circulated: 'Good God, Don't you agree? Commander ring 213!'*

Beachwork trials, Arish Mell.

LCVP troop trials.

HMS *Fearless* sailed from Belfast – under the White Ensign – for full power trials on 27 November and, with that milestone under her belt, anchored for the night in Bangor Bay. The next day she steamed through a gale towards Portland where, on 30 November, the first helicopter landed on at 1100: the Aviation Certification was issued on 2 December 1965.

On 1 December the first embarkation of two LCMs and all four LCAs[73] took place off Poole where the crews had been carrying out their own individual training. Colour Sergeant Howarth[74] had the privilege of bringing in his *Foxtrot Two* – the first LCM ever to dock in a Royal Navy Assault Ship – at 1508 precisely on 1 December followed, two minutes later, by Colour Sergeant Russell with his *Foxtrot One*. For this evolution, as for the thousands that would follow, the depths in the dock would be in the region of 5 feet at the 'beach' forward and 8 feet 6 inches over the stern gate's hinges. Nevertheless with a sea running the LCMs, lifted by a crest, could hit the underside of the flight deck with their open cockpits and then land heavily on the dock's wooden bottom in the trough. Few coxswains would be able to beach without touching the dock's sides or the central, longitudinal division, both of which were clad with massive wooden batter-boards to take the shock. Later, a newly joined Commanding Officer, after witnessing his first LCM-docking was to demand that the coxswain complete a Collision and Grounding Report after he had scraped along the dock's side – the acceptable method of keeping control while approaching the beach with just one clear foot either side of the craft. After trying it himself the Commanding Officer withdrew his request!

Docking trials. LCM Mk 9 with two Centurion main battle tanks safely embarked.

On 3 December the band of the King's Shropshire Light Infantry was embarked off Portland to play in the rain as *Fearless* sailed up the Hamoaze in Plymouth to make her first ceremonial entry. Shortly afterwards she entered a dry dock from which she emerged on 7 January 1966.

But it wasn't all work; the first Families Day was notable for one father. Chief Electrical Artificer Mike Walton brought on board his eight-month old son in a carry-cot and thirty-five years later that son, now the ship's Weapons Electrical Officer, returned the compliment when he invited Lieutenant Commander Mike Walton to visit. The Waltons were not the only father and son to serve in the ship.

This period also included a return to Belfast for the completion of some out-standing work including, while alongside Musgrave Wharf, a ship's company dance hosted by the city's corporation: from all accounts this magnificent party was not for-gotten by the guests for many years – if ever.

Apart from overload trials conducted by 43 Commando in March, many of the

Teething problems with an LCVP davit.

exercises were Army-orientated and an obvious Army regiment for training was 17 Port Regiment, Royal Corps of Transport, based at Marchwood; across the water from Southampton.

Another problem that faced this 'triphibious' ship – as Hugh Corbett called her – and which was particularly noticeable in the wardroom, was caused by naval officers' uniform giving no indication of the specialization of the wearer. Only the doctor and dentist, with red stripes between their gold braid, stood apart, but how were visiting Army officers (and, indeed, many Royal Marines officers) to know whether they were talking to a member of the Supply Branch, the Instructors Branch, an engineer and so on? A simple device, no doubt thought up by the imaginative Charles Denman, was employed. All officers, and not a few Chiefs and Petty Officers, were issued with the Army cap badge equivalent to their specialization: thus the Weapons Electrical members pinned the cap badge of the Royal Electrical and Mechanical Engineers on their uniform, the ship's communicators wore the badge of the Royal Signals and so on. It caused amusement and worked.

The first 'private' amphibious exercise took place across Saunton Sands in North Devon between 22 and 25 February 1966 and involved landing troops and vehicles from, for the first time, both the LCMs and Wessex helicopters. The weather was poor, which made it an even more useful preparation for the next landing which was in front of the international press corps at Browndown ranges in the Solent between 2 and 3 March. This time things did not go to plan although the embarrassing situation was saved by the very flexibility for which *Fearless* was already establishing her name.

Despite check soundings by the Amphibious Beach Unit *The Times* reported that the 'Navy forgot the tide' while the *Daily Express* commented, 'The day the Navy ran out of water and had to

Loading trials with a Wessex helicopter.

take to the air to gets its guests aboard its showpiece ship'. The *Daily Mirror*, declared simply, but in large letters, 'Slight snag for mighty *Fearless*'.

The problem was one as old as amphibious landings themselves – an unexpected and un-forecastable formation of a sand bank offshore due to heavy winds. The day was saved by a helicopter and a hovercraft – transport which, in practice, the press preferred! Nevertheless one officer on board remarked that:

> *Things do sometimes go wrong but it is better for them not to be exposed to the press. On board there were major senses of humour failures, raised voices, loggings even. The sort of situation when junior officers make themselves scarce!*

It was only the second time that a SRN-5 hovercraft had docked onto the ship's internal 'beach'.

Inevitably the staff of Flag Officer Sea Training (FOST) wanted to get their hands on this latest ship and that they did on 4 March with *Fearless*'s arrival at Portland Naval Base where she was to stay until 30th. Here the blind led the blind for the staff knew less about operating this new ship than did the crew – and they were still learning.

Engine room routines, fire fighting procedures and ship's administration were much in common with the rest of the fleet so these aspects were well covered with the expected work-up routines and tests. Ship-handling, ballasting, dock control, flight deck work and amphibious command, beach work, landing craft, control and communications were new to almost everyone, with each 'side' gaining experience from the other. Charles Denman was to write:

> The 'sea trainers' didn't really know what to do so we were 'let off' with only three weeks of leaping like gazelles from problem to problem – trying not to be caught out by the staff. Peter Baseby and I did get caught one Thursday afternoon: the day before pay-day (which was, then, paid individually, in cash). Working on the 'not us Chief, we're Pussers' principle we sneaked off to the Pay Office and started sorting out the money. We were having difficulties hearing ourselves saying 'Bloggs, shillings ten' so we took off our gas masks. Suddenly the door was flung open and the bright young Commander, Sea Training – Staveley was it? – said, 'Caught you!' Goodness knows what he thought he had caught us at but the general impression was that we should be hanging from the yardarm for a few days. Dear William![75]

The Amphibious Detachment was clearly an anomaly for the FOST staff who, according to Tom Potts:

> Required us to put out a fire which was burning on the jetty in oil drums, so the OCAD sent an LCM. These craft were equipped with powerful gas-turbine powered pumps for transferring ten tons of fresh water ashore to fill large rubber 'S' Tanks set up on the beach. This time the pump was used as a fire-hydrant. We put out the fire in five seconds flat and blew all the oil drums into the sea.

Another attempt by the FOST staff to test the ship's shore side, firefighting capability was foiled when the offending conflagration was simply bulldozed into the sea by the Amphibious Beach Unit's bucket-armed, Michigan tractor.

As with so many of these experimental evolutions, when it was HMS *Intrepid*'s turn to be put through the Portland mill the staff were ready for her.

Trials proved that the Army's RPLs[76] could fit in the after end of the dock in place of two LCMs and they could, as could any craft including the much larger LCTs, beach on the stern gate once the ship had disgorged its own craft and flooded up to leave the dry dock. Months later Captain (eventually Lieutenant Colonel, Royal Corps of Transport) David McLellan, was able to offer invaluable, operational advice on how to lift RPLs from Aden to Bahrain.

Mention has been made of overload trials. Towards the end of March 1966 and the culmination of the three-week Portland work-up period, 43 Commando, Royal Marines,[77] was embarked for Exercise MORNING GLORY between 23 and 25 March[78] which, apart from the basic military requirement of testing the assault procedures, was combined with an 'overload trial' to see just how many men, and with what inconvenience, could be carried beyond the ship's planned embarked force complement. The tank deck and all military cabins were crammed with campbeds and the decks of the LCMs were turned into open-air dormitories; while sufficient lying-down spaces could be found, the 'hotel services' were seriously stretched. The main galley coped in shifts, as did the wardroom, but all heads were overloaded and with every recreation space taken up there was nowhere to 'sit'. When, during the day, the upper decks were out of bounds due to weather or 'action stations' the ship was uncomfortable but otherwise the conditions were just about acceptable for very short periods.

The first amphibious exercise commanded by the Commodore Amphibious Forces,[79] part of Exercise LIFELINE, was conducted between 16 and 30 April 1966 and included parachute drops in eastern England and south Wales with the Royal Air Force providing offensive air support and air supply. The main exercise areas were the Castlemartin ranges near Milford Haven where, on

Entering the dock from the LCM coxswain's perspective.

24 April, with fixed wing aircraft screeching overhead, soldiers of the King's Shropshire Light Infantry and tanks of the 16th/5th Lancers, assaulted beaches defended by an enemy from 3rd Battalion the Parachute Regiment and a company from Italy's 8 Regiment of *Bersaglieri*. While this tested the ship's Amphibious Operations Room for the first time – and in particular the Supporting Arms Coordination Centre – another first was also being notched-up. *The Times* of 21 January had given prior notice that the Government was inviting military attachés from all Warsaw Pact countries to witness the Exercise's amphibious phase and the parachute drop by men of 16 Parachute Brigade. Previously all that the foreign attachés – and especially those from further east than Berlin – would have expected, would have been a static display held at a sanitized defence establishment.

In many respects the next exercise, STRIP PILLOW, off the Barry Budden training area on the north coast of the Firth of Tay at the beginning of May, was of more interest for it was not, quite, what had been envisaged in the days of *Fearless*'s conception. It was, though, a task for which she was highly suited. STRIP PILLOW was billed by the Army's Southern Command Public Relations office as 'the biggest ever airfield project attempted in Britain'.[80]

At Marchwood, over 27 and 28 April, the ship embarked 600 men from HQ 12 Engineer Group, 36 Engineer Regiment, Royal Engineers, 516 Specialist Team (Bulk Petroleum Royal Engineers),

51 Port Operating Squadron, Royal Corps of Transport and 35 Bulk Operating Platoon, Royal Army Ordnance Corps plus their plant equipment for the construction of a 5,000 feet long, emergency airstrip and associated ship-to-shore fuelling arrangements.

While the landing of the heavy equipment for the runway was reasonably straightforward for the LCMs,[81] the establishing of a pipeline direct from the ship to a tank farm was another matter. *Foxtrot Three* was detailed for 'tug' duties, requiring her to tow 325 foot lengths of pipeline towards the beach. Once 2,200 feet had been 'laid' *Fearless* returned to Portsmouth leaving the sappers to work on the airstrip itself while 350 tons of aviation fuel was pumped ashore from RFA *Brown Ranger* through *Foxtrot Three*'s pipeline. It was Captain Howard-Jones's task, with his 516 Petroleum Specialist Team, Royal Engineers, to pipe the fuel for another five miles, using equipment that he was trialling and which was in use during the Falklands campaign nearly twenty years later. On its completion, Argosy aircraft proved the runway and fuelling facilities before the whole construction was dismantled and removed by road.

The almost unending succession of trials and experiments were now halted for the first and much welcomed, foreign visit. Foreign visits, though, are not always rest and relaxation and this one to Brest with the Commander-in-Chief, Admiral Talbot, embarked, was four days of intensive sport, parties and ceremonials to celebrate VE Day. Also embarked were detachments from 43 Commando, Royal Marines and The King's Own Border Regiment whose soldiers provided ceremonial jetty sentries while the Royal Marines undertook the more naval duties of sunset and morning colours.

More work-up routines followed at Portland before *Fearless* sailed for Gibraltar and a mini amphibious exercise with B Company of the Royal Worcestershire Regiment. As Hugh Corbett has described, the ship spent some time off the north African coast where the water was deep

Canteen.

enough and clear enough for a session of 'propeller viewing'. What the submarine captain saw through his periscope required a docking in Gibraltar to rectify before a swift passage direct to the Loch Fyne Noise Range in west Scotland and the first official wardroom cocktail party from which, reportedly, the guests were determined not to leave. A ship's company party ashore was hosted by 'locals' who insisted that no modern or 'southern-style' dancing was allowed but 'Jack', never put off by these restrictions, entered into the spirit of the evening with gusto – and he too was reluctant to leave.

HMS *Fearless* sailed for the Middle and Far East on 13 September 1966. By her return in December 1967 she would have carried out her first two military operations, suffered her first casualty, steamed as far as Hiroshima, circumnavigated Africa and changed her Commanding Officer.

The passage to Malta was broken by the briefest of afternoon stops at Gibraltar in order that foreign service pay and allowances could be claimed as soon as possible.[82] Three days in Malta reminded the older hands of the delights of Valetta's 'Gut'[83] and Sliema's numerous tiny waterfront bars, while the younger element also had their eyes opened to the Island's other unique delights: delights that were left behind on 22 September as the ship made an average of 18 knots towards the Suez canal. The *Times of Malta* had given advance warning of the ship's visit under the banner headline 'HMS *Fearless* arrives today ... Navy's newest Assault Ship on Four Day Visit'. The Maltese were used to the Amphibious Warfare Squadron's LSTs and LCTs and were now fascinated by this capability compressed into one ship.

In his Report of Proceedings for the next formative weeks of the ship's life, Hugh Corbett wrote the following to Rear Admiral J.E.L. Martin, Flag Officer Middle East, under whose command the ship became as she approached Aden.[84] The report is presented almost in full (apart from some technical details) as it offers an insight into the joint service interest in this new concept as well as the social and operational pressures that came with it:

> I have the honour to submit the following Report of Proceedings.... The ship passed through the Canal on Sunday 25 September: as it was a busy day, Sunday was made for drill purposes into Monday, and Monday became Sunday. This allowed the ship's company a day of rest in which to become accustomed to the Red Sea heat: passing Tor Bank, the traditional site of Moses' parting the waters, at 1015 supplied the Padre with a ready made sermon. Fortunately the weather remained fair.
>
> A full power work-up trial was satisfactorily carried out in the Red Sea, and the air conditioning was proved to have benefited by the trials done off Gibraltar and the subsequent modifications carried out in Portsmouth. It had been hoped to do an economical steaming trial, but six hours delay in the Canal convoy necessitated too high a speed for one boiler.
>
> The ship anchored off Aden at 0800 on Thursday 29 September, a salute being fired to your flag. We exchanged calls in the forenoon and throughout the day the ship unloaded our 170 soldier passengers, destined for fifteen units in the Middle East Command, 25-pounder guns and 260 tons of ammunition brought out for the Federal Regular Army, and some special loads for other units. Friendships formed between our passengers and the ship's company stood us in good stead in the next month, and the Federal Regular Army showed their appreciation by presenting the ship with a plaque of an FRA soldier. The unloading took just under 10 hours overall from ship to land, which we were led to understand was a record.
>
> On Friday 30 September, Brigadier Bremner and members of his 24 Brigade Staff came onboard to give officers and senior rates a most interesting brief on the situation in Aden. His evident enthusiasm at the prospect of working with the ship was most encouraging, and we appreciated the trouble being taken to find troops to train with us, despite the heavy demands of Internal Security Duties upon them. We were also very pleased to celebrate the promotion of Sub-Lieutenants Dempsey and Fish to

Lieutenant: two stalwarts of the Communication's team, who had worked particularly hard on the passage out in an elaborate series of Communication exercises with Gibraltar, Malta, Germany, Cyprus and Aden which had steadily improved our performance.

On Monday, 3 October, I called on Admiral Sir Michael Le Fanu,[85] Major General Willoughby[86] and Air Vice Marshal Humphrey[87] and visited the offices of the Middle East Headquarters. On Monday, Tuesday and Wednesday, I entertained senior officers on board for lunch and the customary walk around the ship. Thus within a week of our arrival, the senior commanders were fully aware of what Fearless *had to offer, which was much to our advantage. In addition, over 300 officers and other ranks were shown round the ship officially, and many more informally, during the month.*

On Monday 3 October, six Centurion and two Chieftain tanks and other armoured vehicles of 1 Royal Tank Regiment were embarked. The next two days were spent carrying out driver training in the vehicle decks and practising landings ashore with their crews. On Thursday 5 the ship sailed with this force embarked to land them at Beverly Beach. No special problems were met; it was the first time that the ship had landed an initial wave of six tanks. Two Centurions were transported and landed by LCM without difficulty in an 18 knot wind (the authorized maximum for 2 tanks is 20 knots), and it is hoped that trials at home will not be long delayed, which will clear the LCM 9 to carry two Chieftain tanks in similar conditions.[88] This was the final exercise in the Middle East with tanks as they were due to be embarked for the United Kingdom the following day.

His Excellency the High Commissioner, Sir Richard Turnbull, flew on board to witness the exercise, going ashore immediately by LCM to see the final stages of the landing and returning on board for lunch.

The next few days were taken up with ship visits, formal and informal – staff officers, all ranks, school children, families and friends. Throughout the week, at every spare moment, over 100 deck landings were practised by Sioux, Scout and Wessex helicopters, giving valuable training to our Flight Deck personnel, and a number of pilots including Air Vice Marshal Humphrey being cleared for deck landing. Monday 10 October was complicated by the need to go alongside the BP Jetty in Little Aden to embark a paltry 40 tons of MOGAS: far too little by BP standards, yet too much for embarkation by bowser. There were frustrating delays waiting for pilots, also due to difficulty embarking so small a quantity and pipelines designed for 700 tons/hour or more. Initially, BP doubted our safety arrangements, though eventually impressed by our Damage Control organization.

At 1900 on Monday 10 October the ship sailed with 1 RTR's Recce Squadron embarked to land them up the coast for an operational patrol. Shortly before sailing, Admiral Le Fanu embarked to watch the operation. The ship arrived off Ras al Ara at 0500 the next day, anchoring about two miles from the beach. It had not been possible to recce the beach in advance and the first task for the Amphibious Beach Unit was to establish a suitable landing point. This had been done by 0530 and the first wave left shortly afterwards. The landing was completed by 0700 and the ship sailed for Aden at 0815. Although a small scale landing, this was the ship's first proper operation; it was rewarding to be in business after so many months of training, trials and exercises, and we were delighted that Admiral Le Fanu himself took part.

Security precautions were necessary in the Inner Harbour, with a number of sentries to keep small craft away, and a bottom search was carried out daily by our divers, who brought their time for the complete search down from 45 minutes to 25 minutes in the fortnight.

A number of officers and ratings visited the Radfan area during this period, and the majority of the soldiers in the ship's company spent time attached to shore units. I was flown by courtesy of 1 Royal Horse Artillery up to Habilayn, Musemir, Dhala and over the Radfan area and stayed the night with Lieutenant Colonel Bye, 45 Commando RM, at Habilayn; a most instructive and enjoyable visit. On one patrol, seven ranks and ratings were involved in a mine incident in which a RM from 45 Commando was injured; and Marine Harvey from the Amphibious Detachment suffered splinter wounds in the leg in a grenade incident near Aden police station.

24 Brigade carried out a two day familiarization period including two CPX[89] in the Assault Operations Room during this period. Though it was the same exercise setting as that used by 19 Brigade in April, the ideas on laying out the Operations Room were entirely different. I am beginning to suspect that the best Joint Operations Room would be one which could be adjusted like a meccano *set, to suit a particular operation: no two exercises we have done have required the same combination of personnel or facilities. The important thing is perhaps that the Operations Room has proved sufficiently adaptable to meet each occasion.*

On 21 October we held a Trafalgar Night Dinner in the wardroom which Sir Richard Turnbull, Admiral Le Fanu, Brigadier Jefferies, Air Commodore Sowrey and Captain George did us the honour of attending – a truly joint affair. It was Commander Shevlin's last occasion as President of the Wardroom Mess, and Admiral Le Fanu proposed the Immortal Memory: a happy occasion. On Sunday 23 October we had a crowded, informal party to say thank you to the very large number of kind people who had entertained us during our stay; Lady Le Fanu was this time the guest of honour, hoisted aboard in style in an LCVP.[90] Aden itself may be a silent, sombre city now the grenadiers and assassins lurk in shady corners; but there are many people who make light of it, and it has been a great pleasure to receive and offer hospitality to some of them in more relaxed surroundings. The ship's company also enjoyed much kindness and we had three families days onboard, as well as visits by schools and other organizations, in order to offer some return.

On Tuesday 25 October the ship embarked elements of 24 Brigade for Exercise FALAISE FRED ONE[91] before anchoring off Little Aden at 1900. Originally this exercise had been planned as a combined night landing exercise and tactical control of troops by HQ 24 Inf Bde but because of the introduction of Exercise FALAISE FRED TWO the tactical aspect was cancelled and only the night landing remained; for which the ABU set up its first beach in the dark. On completion of this exercise, the ship embarked the forces for Exercise FALAISE FRED TWO from Power House Jetty, Little Aden, while helicopters were flown in from Khormaksar and Falaise. Brigadier Bremner flew his pennant as Force Commander, consisting of 1 Irish Guards Battalion Group commanded by Lieutenant-Colonel Aylmer,[92] a troop of SAS under Major Hardy, some interpreters of the Federal National Guard under Major Yafai, plus one Scout and five Wessex II helicopters with Squadron Leader Braybrook as Air Commander. Mr Michael Crouch and later Mr Jim Ellis, arrived to give political advice. Just before the ship sailed, the well-kept secret was revealed that this was to be an operation and not an exercise.

The ship sailed at 1800 on Wednesday 26 October and at 0300 on Friday 28 stopped about four miles west of the operating area: from this position she launched both landing craft and helicopters. An almost simultaneous landing was made by helicopters and Geminis,[93] at the earliest acceptable light for helicopters landing on unprepared and unknown ground, closely followed by four LCVPs and two LCMs. The ship then closed to within three quarters of a mile of the village, but was forced to evacuate this position by a dense shoal of jelly fish which quickly blocked all four Turbo-Alternator intakes. Power was restored with commendable speed by the electrical and engineering departments. By this time the operation ashore was completed, and the ship was able to sail for Aden, having re-embarked the force by helicopter. This was the first time we had embarked an overload East of Suez – 566, of whom 138 slept in the Tank Deck – the first time we had ever re-embarked so large a force, and the first time we had operated with five Wessex on the flight deck. In an internal security situation, the ship had shown that she could give a long arm to the law while ensuring, through our operations rooms and extensive communications system, the close political and military control essential to such an operation at all stages. It had also been proved possible to react to good intelligence at short notice. But in Fearless *minds, the important thing was that this was 'Deeds, not Words'. For a year, we had talked about what we believed the ship could do: now, we had done it.*

The ship anchored at Little Aden at 0730, 30 October and landed the embarked force. At 1100 a presentation on the Operation was made to the Commander-in-Chief, his Service Commanders and a number of staff officers in the Assault Operations Room. We also embarked seventy-eight Army and RAF passengers and some stores and at 1400 sailed for Mombasa.

In lighter vein, in the six weeks since we left England I have felt that the ship's company of HMS Fearless has come of age. Our sports teams have begun to show fitness and achieve some good results. Sailing, encouraged by the expert eye of Captain George,[94] has made a start. Our first fishing competition showed promise for the future, though the big fish got away. The first two editions of a Ship's Magazine have appeared for the second of which Brigadier Bremner kindly provided a forward [sic] [and for the third of which Commander Shevlin has left us a backward (sic)]. Arts group and Musical groups are under-way. The Fearless Radio programme matured, and several performers were also heard on Aden Forces Radio. All in all, Fearless Fred is finding his sea legs and can look after himself as he will have to do in this ship which operates so much of her time on her own.

We cannot yet claim to be fully efficient: we need the sharpening influence of work with the fleet, and the peculiar layout of the ship and balance of our complement put some evolutions beyond us. The highest standards of appearance and maintenance will always be difficult for us to achieve.

Hugh Corbett mentioned his visit to Habilayn and the Radfan area over which 45 Commando and units of the British Army were operating. '45' was based at Little Aden with, initially, two troops permanently stationed at Dhala, in the mountains to the north and close to the border with Yemen. When the Radfan operations began, a mounting base was established at Habilayn (known to older hands as Fort Thumier) on the track that leads to Dhala, just above the escarpment and to the west of the Radfan proper.

Tony Coppard remembers, with some clarity, the incident to which his Commanding Officer refers:

45 Commando invited the ship to send up some sailors to see how life was ashore.

On that first evening we were invited to watch the nightly film (in the open) and of course when the sailors saw the seats in front of the screen were empty, they made a bee-line for them but as soon as the film started, shots rang out and bullet holes appeared on the screen. You have never seen matelots move so fast in your life. We rounded up the party and explained that this happened each night a film was shown, and that nobody actually sat in front of the screen, always to the side.

On our third day our patrol set off to visit one of the outlying picket positions on a hill some three miles away. The patrol commander, a Royal Marines sergeant, led the party of 'my' sailors plus two marines who had just joined: I, as the Corporal, brought up the rear.

Crossing a wadi the marine in front of me stepped on a mine. His foot had taken the full blast of the explosion so the Sergeant rendered what First Aid he could while I organized the rest of the party to move back to the wadi. On the main track I flagged down a passing Scout Car, to radio Habilayn.

The marine was airlifted to Aden where his foot was amputated. At the Regimental Inquiry the next day, it was discovered that a number of the sailors were Junior Seamen under the age of 18 and that the ship should never have allowed them into a theatre of war.

A number of unofficial accounts of the raid on Hauf have been published – including those in a history of the Irish Guards[95] – and one by the ship's navigating officer at the time, Lieutenant Commander Richard Perceval Maxwell, was published in *The Naval Review*. The official report on the ship's first operational task is paraphrased here:[96]

For two years intelligence reports had indicated that members of the Dhofar Liberation Front (DLF) had been using the small village of Hauf, a few miles inside the state of Mahra (EAP) from the Muscat border, as a safe refuge and a base for gun running and other dissident activities. Despite the fact that for many months these activities had been confirmed it had not been possible for the Authorities in Aden to take the necessary steps to eradicate this trouble. Nor for obvious political reasons had it been possible for the Sultans Armed Forces to cross the few miles into the EAP and take this action against the rebels to his regime. With HMS Fearless *newly arrived on station ... the C-in-C planned to mount a surprise operation at Hauf to demonstrate that the area was no longer a safe refuge for the DLF.*

Immediately it became clear that there would be a number of limiting factors on the naval side which would affect the planning. . . . The most important of these was that the information on the beaches was old[97] and unreliable. This in turn meant that no night landings were possible, that it might not be possible to land any vehicles and, in the worst case, no sea landings might be possible if there was too much wind and swell, in which case reliance would have to be made on embarked helicopters. The success of the operation depended on surprise and this ruled out any prior reconnaissance of the area. In the event the coastal minesweeper HMS Kemerton *was due to pay off for disposal. As she was scheduled to pass the area she was tasked to provide some photographic coverage which though necessarily distant was found to be invaluable.*

Because this was the first time that a Landing Ship Dock (LPD) was to be used in her primary role there were other unknown factors which had to be included in the planning and would be key factors in achieving surprise and in determining the timing of the operation. Primarily, these were, how far off shore could Fearless *be seen and heard and how much warning would be given by the noise of the helicopters, LCMs and LCAs.*

The C-in-C laid down that the aim of the operation was: To cordon and search the Hauf/Jadhib built-up area with a view to seizing Dhofari rebels and their equipment.

The plan, codenamed FATE, provided for the establishment of an outer cordon in six piquet positions flown in by Wessex helicopters to prevent escape and entry to the area. A special close cordon was to be established around selected houses believed to contain rebels while an inner cordon around the village would prevent escape – the troops for these two cordons being landed over the beach. Finally, screening and searching would be carried out by more troops which were to be landed over the beach.

To achieve this, HMS Fearless *embarked the Tactical HQ 24 Infantry Brigade, 1st Battalion Irish Guards, a number of miscellaneous small units. . . . Three* Hunters *from 8 Squadron were deployed to Salalah to provide air support if required.*

Hauf Beach.

The operation might well have been named FATED rather than FATE since once London had been informed that an operation was to take place both the Foreign Office and the Political Resident in the Persian Gulf at Bahrain began to have doubts about the wisdom of it, although both the High Commissioner in Aden and the Consul General in Muscat were convinced that the military operation should go ahead as planned. It was suggested that a postponement might be wise so that the operation could take place at a time when our actions in both Aden and Muscat were not under such close scrutiny at the UN. However, eventually as it was not wished to let the Sultan of Muscat doubt our willingness to fulfil our treaty obligations and as the presence of HMS Fearless gave an almost unique opportunity coinciding with dawn and high tide at the same time permission was finally given but this was not received until late on the 25th, little over 48 hours before the initial landing and less than 24 hours before the force sailed from Aden.

On 27 October gun functioning trials were carried out during the First Dog Watch – always an exciting sign that action is imminent. Reveille the next morning was at 0130 and Assault Stations piped at 0300. An hour later the first LCM retracted followed by the 'flying programme' just under an hour after that. The first Gemini inflatable boat 'hit the beach' at 0510. The airborne cordon was rapidly placed in position, the landing craft, having loaded in half the time originally planned reached the right beaches on time. Surprise was complete, there was no opposition and no casualties, 22 members of the DLF were taken into custody and later flown to Salalah where they were handed over to the Sultan of Muscat's Armed Forces. All troops were re-embarked by 1530 local.

The fact that the operation was concluded successfully does not mean that it was without incident or that no lessons were learned.

Hauf village.

The operation, timed for both dawn and high tide provided problems in operating a relatively large number of helicopters from a small flight deck, initially in the dark. Indeed none of the pilots had operated in the dark from an LPD deck. Coupled with these factors there was the need to launch five helicopters speedily yet not so fast as to increase the noise level and alert the inhabitants ashore and since only two helicopters could be launched simultaneously the first ones would have to loiter waiting for the others with corresponding fuel and weight problems.

The Chief of Defence Staff, who no doubt took a kindly interest in the ship that his wife had launched, wrote to the Secretary of State for Defence on 31 October 1966:[98]

As you were informed by telephone on Friday night Operation FATE was carried out successfully on 28th October.... surprise was complete.

22 members of the Dhofari Liberation Front, including three leaders, were apprehended and handed over to the Sultan of Muscat's Armed Forces. A small quantity of arms and documents was found. The local population was cooperative and the opportunity was taken to give medical treatment to about 40 of them.

In agreement with the Foreign Office, the Commander-in-Chief was informed that no press release on the operation should be made unless there was a leak, of which there has been no sign yet.

You may wish to inform the Foreign Secretary of the excellent effect this operation has had on the morale of our forces in South Arabia.

Hauf. The haul.

On 11 November the Naval Lessons from this operation were covered in Annex D to the Joint Force Commander's Report[99] which was forwarded on to the Second Permanent Under Secretary of State (Royal Navy) by Admiral Martin on 6 December. Factors relevant to future operations were:

Embarked force ... the total consisted of 52 officers, 88 SNCOs and 400 other ranks ... representing an overload of 22 officers, 52 SNCOs and 140 other ranks who had to be accommodated on camp beds....

Habitability ... on the Troop Decks under tropical conditions were as good as in United Kingdom waters.... The temperature on the Tank Deck was 10 degrees higher – averaging 80 degrees but the air circulation was good.[100] It is considered that an Embarked Force of this size could live under these conditions for up to 5 days without undue hardship or loss of efficiency.

Beach Reconnaissance ... the importance was re-emphasized. A calculated risk was taken in using an un-surveyed beach, and it was fortunate that dawn was within 2 hours of high-water as, near low water, the surf and swell over rocks made the beaches unusable by craft.

LCM Troops Lift.... 175 Guardsmen being landed, albeit with a 4 foot wade, but it put a lot of men ashore quickly. It is considered 300 could have been landed by one craft as follow up troops onto a secure beach....

Engineering Difficulties in Inshore Waters.... It is recommended that one turbo-alternator in each machinery space be fitted with a duplex seawater strainer so that (they) can be kept running whilst cleaning strainers should they suddenly choke due to jelly-fish, sand or other foreign matter[101]....

Aviation ... The on passage flying training followed by the heavy flying programme required by the operation involved the ship's Aviation Officer in very long hours closed up. The need for a second Aviation Officer in an Assault Ship was re-emphasized....

These were the official views: inevitably there were other opinions with the most important in Dick Perceval Maxwell's report which he forwarded, with the added comment that:

Apparently we were the first white men the village had ever seen except for a deranged Royal Marine – nothing personal – who had once appeared out of the desert and who died shortly after his arrival!

Dick Perceval Maxwell's comments are valuable for their nautical view of this operation which has often only been recounted from the landing force's standpoint, although it must be made clear that the Army were more than content with the Royal Navy's cooperation and efficiency, a view that was certainly reciprocated:

As Navigating and Operations Officer of HMS Fearless *my first task was to get the ship to the right place at the right time ... but there were one or two complications ... was the place shown as Hauf on the chart ... in fact the Hauf we were meant to attack.... [Secondly] to coordinate the arrival of the helicopters and landing craft it was necessary to position the ship accurately in relation to the village. This launch position had to be reached in the dark which in the circumstances meant fixing the ship's position by radar. Unfortunately the largest scale chart was only 10 nautical miles to the inch[102] ... was the chart accurate in detail and would the radar picture resemble it sufficiently to position the ship with the necessary accuracy?*

An RAF aircraft took vertical pictures of the coastline [and from these] it was possible to construct large scale maps of the area. To make absolutely certain a passing minesweeper photographed Hauf on its radar screen ... the chart was accurate and the features could [now] be recognized on radar.

Of the twenty four terrorists wanted twenty were captured[103] ... of the four who escaped two were later picked up in the screening process and the remaining two only got away after an exciting helicopter chase up the escarpment that lay behind the village.

Once it had been known that the landing had taken place Fearless *moved closer to the village and anchored about a mile offshore ... where [almost immediately] she suffered a complete electrical failure ... it was jelly fish ... and the ship was now immovable while we waited for this coelenterate menace to drift slowly by ... Hand grenades were dropped over the side but achieved nothing except to relieve the feelings of the command and shatter the eardrums of the suffering engineers below ... struggling to clear the intakes of their repulsive contents. ...*

The prisoners were flown to Salalah ... and the medieval mercies of the Sultan of Muscat and Oman.

The operation did not alter the course of history in the Arabian Peninsula ... the following year Aden was handed over to the National Liberation Front and the Dhofar Liberation Front [remained] active.[104] *However despite its failure in the long term the operation did have its lessons for the future.*

At higher command level it showed the remarkable effectiveness of the Joint Headquarters at Aden which in its short life achieved a measure of efficiency never matched by its opposite number in Singapore. This may have been partly a matter of size but I believe a more important factor was that all the key members of the staff worked together in the same building and were in daily personal contact.

At unit level the operation exposed some of the pretensions of the specialist. Here in miniature was a classic Commando Ship operation ... yet it was carried out by an Assault Ship, an RAF Squadron and an army unit who were still arriving in Aden while the operation was being planned.[105]

Fearless's *Middle East peregrinations did not end at Hauf or with the Radfan for she sailed from her jelly-fish-infected anchorage on 28 October, called at Aden on the 30th and left the same day having disembarked her Irish Guards and prisoners.* Fearless *sailed for a planned visit to Mombasa and a well-earned break from both exercises and operations.*

During the afternoon of Wednesday 2 November HMS *Fearless* crossed the Equator for the first time. The traditional ceremony was held on the Flight Deck where a large number of the ship's company, including the Commanding Officer, 'suffered the usual punishment'. Anyone who had crossed before and who, therefore, thought that he might have been safe from these indignities was treated as a 'repeat offender' and no mercy shown.

Mombasa and Nairobi, as they had done down the years, offered the sailors a choice of nightlife or wildlife with many taking advantage of both and, especially, visits to Nairobi for the former and the Tsavo Game Park for the latter. Some have mentioned that the roles of each location could have been reversed! Two members of the sick-bay staff visited the Kalindi Mission Hospital where the ship's out-of-date medical stores were gratefully accepted and the ship's company contributed fifty-three pints of blood.

A fact of rather more military interest – and a point not missed by the recipients of Hugh Corbett's ROP – concerned the heavy repair ship HMS *Triumph*[106] which was also visiting Mombasa.

Captain La Neice and I had an interesting discussion on the extent to which the roles of Triumph *and* Fearless *were interchangeable. We felt that* Triumph *with her ability to carry about 600 troops could, in certain conditions, fulfil some of the transport tasks of this ship. While* Fearless *might, to a limited extent, be able to carry out the escort support role of* Triumph. *We also believed that the two ships operating together could make a complementary team; they could carry a substantial force of soldiers, and the repair facilities and parking space in* Triumph *might allow a larger number of helicopters to be embarked for a longer period than is practicable in* Fearless.

On her return from East Africa on 13 November the intention had been for *Fearless* to give the troops in Bahrain the benefit of her presence but a signal was received shortly before her arrival in Aden stating that this visit was postponed.

While the ship refuelled at 0630 on 14 November decisions were mulled over whether or not to embark the vehicles earmarked for Bahrain as an outward sign that nothing untoward was afoot. At 1900 on the 16th orders were received to sail for Kharg Island at the head of the Persian Gulf and then Iran's principal deep water oil terminal. Yet with no vehicles, nor even the stores for the Gulf troops embarked, it did not take much guessing to realize that plans had been changed – but to where; that was the question.

Tom Potts was able to make an early assessment. Prior to sailing he had been warned that 'Skipper's Rounds' would include his map store in which he kept maps and charts covering, it seemed to him, the entire world. In preparation for the inspection he had painted the worn deck red and thought no more of it. The following morning, and with the empty ship now heading south, he discovered footprints leading directly to the cupboard which housed the maps of Mozambique. Only one other person on board held the key and sure enough it was Major Whitworth's shoes that had paint on them. On the first anniversary of her commissioning, the ship was again heading for an operational task.[107]

Safely at sea the Captain was able to inform his ship's company that the now-obvious change of plan had them bound for Durban to embark the 1st Battalion Royal Irish Fusiliers – the Regiment that had kindly supplied the lone piper for Commissioning Day – which was to be lifted out, at no notice, from its duties of helping to protect Swaziland from tensions in Rhodesia. The Regiment had been the first into South Africa in 1899 and was now the last to leave; a sudden move that

Royal Irish Fusilier Band beating retreat en route to Aden.

could have caused even deeper rifts with the United Kingdom. However, the embarkation went well thanks to good inter-service cooperation, helped in great part by the South Africans themselves.

The Battalion's move from Swaziland took six days by road and an RAF airlift of twenty Argosy[108] loads which continued on from Louis Botha Airport to the ship in South African Army lorries, with the Officer Commanding Natal Command, Brigadier Ferguson, personally smoothing difficulties with the Immigration Authorities.

In all 379 officers and men were embarked with fifty-one vehicles, twenty-nine trailers, fifty tons of ammunition and fifty-nine tons of loose stores. Apart from this tidy evacuation of the last British military force in South Africa, the operation was marked by the friendliness of the 'locals' who, it was anticipated by the Foreign Office, would make things tiresome. The opposite was true and the ship, at all levels, offered copious entertainment and informal visits: indeed the only complaint from the South Africans was that they had had no time to prepare any return parties.

Some of the visitors had flown 800 miles solely to visit the ship, including the founder Commandant of the UK's Joint Warfare Establishment, Air Vice Marshal Sir Leslie Brown. Commodore Johnson SAN who had served in the Second World War destroyer *Fearless* was unable to make the journey so commiserating signals of goodwill were exchanged instead. Hugh Corbett's Report of Proceedings summed up the operation.

> We had arrived in Durban prepared for coolness, if not a frigid reception:[109] we had no grounds to expect the South Africans to be particularly cooperative in the circumstances. None of the servicemen disguised for a minute that they associated the move directly with the Rhodesian crisis, and the Defence Review story cut no ice here. Several commented on the lines that they thought our politics were incomprehensible, but that it was nice to see a sizeable HM Ship again. We justified the short notice by the fact that **Fearless** happened to be available, and our timetable [required us] to get to Singapore by Christmas. Both had the merit of truth. I formed the strong impression that they would welcome more visits by HM ships, if these could be arranged [while] several expressed disappointment that the short notice prevented them laying on entertainment for us. We were given courteous and friendly treatment by the press, with little attempt to needle us on the political issues.... Natal and Durban are well known to be pro-British, and from what we experienced, they lived up to it to the full; an officer who had been in HMS Vanguard for the Royal Tour, said that this send off was more enthusiastic than on that occasion.... but it was also significant that there were no hostile demonstrations of any kind at any time.

A large number of locals saw the ship off before driving to the harbour entrance to flash their headlights as she sailed past while the band on board played *Auld Lang Syne*. Mrs Perle Siedle Gibson, 'The Lady in White' who had performed for passing ships during the Second World War appeared on the jetty to sing *Fearless* away with an aria – a gesture much appreciated. The Commanding Officer ended his report with high praise for his passengers:

> We entered Aden at 1000 on Wednesday 7 December with the Band, Drums and Pipes filling the Flight Deck with proud music and colour.... .
> Disembarkation of the Battalion proceeded to plan, [they had had] seven months unaccompanied service in Swaziland and were a well-knit and orderly unit, the best we have yet embarked ... on board for nine days, the longest period for which we have had so large an embarked force.
> Much good value was obtained in training, sport and recreation. Assault procedures were exercised, vehicles maintained, kits brought up to date (the Chinese laundry and 'Sew-Sew' were fully extended) as were a number of medical and dental treatments. The soldiers participated well in ship's activities [including] part-of-ship work. It was particularly fortunate that the Flight Deck was sufficiently clear

of vehicles for drill, and for the band to play, including Beating Retreat on the final night, a splendid floodlit occasion, and for recreation: by the end we were running short of deck hockey sticks and of old rope for grommets. . . .

Fearless could now be released to make her way direct to Singapore in time for Christmas. Surprisingly, as Hugh Corbett said, when the time came to bid farewell to Aden there was a marked sadness in the ship for they had made many friends professionally, socially and at every level. It was a pity, on both sides, that there was now no time to visit Bahrain – but the ship would be back.

On her departure for the Far East on 11 December 1966, at the end of two and half months under his command, Rear Admiral Martin forwarded his views of the ships' capabilities to the Second Permanent Under Secretary of State (Royal Navy) with a copy to the Commander-in-Chief Middle East, Admiral Le Fanu. He ended by stating that:[110]

> *There is no doubt that the Army and Royal Air Force in the Middle East have been quick to learn the lessons ably taught and demonstrated by* Fearless; *so much so in fact that her availability is among the first questions asked when a new operation or exercise is considered.*

To offer an encouraging 'taster' of the asset that the Commander-in-Chief, Far East Fleet was about to receive, this report was also copied to him, and a number of others who had vested interests in her capabilities. *Fearless* arrived in Singapore Naval Base on 21 December 1966 where her last months under her first Commanding Officer were to be another long round of flag-showing and 'acquainting'.

On 23 January 1967 the ship sailed for Penang, to collect the 2nd Greenjackets for an exercise at Terendak, remembered, rather surprisingly as it was their first such evolution, by a company commander, Antony Karslake,[111] solely because the whole Battalion took part in an assault landing on the west coast of Malaysia, 'otherwise there was nothing particular about the rest of it'!

The Malaysian sojourn complete, the ship returned to Penang for a four-day rest where she was to suffer her first death. One of the cooks, who had been on duty in the Senior Rates' servery at dinner, was not seen again until a week later when his body was found floating in the sea. It was believed that after his duties, he had gone to the forecastle and lain down on one of the huge mooring bollards from where, asleep, he had rolled over the side. John Nichol, flown ashore with one of the deceased's friends, could only identify the body by his tattoos and the servery key still attached to his belt. The Green Jackets helped with the shore-side arrangements and supplied a bugler for the funeral.

In Singapore, *Fearless* prepared for the first amphibious group exercise, planned to take place at Hong Kong, for which she sailed on 7 February in company with HMS *Bulwark,* the new LSL *Sir Lancelot* and several escorts: 3 Commando Brigade was embarked across the shipping with a number of the staff, led by the Brigade Major, John Mottram[112] joining by parachuting into the sea alongside.

After a rehearsal in Jason's Bay, the Task Group arrived in Hong Kong on 13 February where the original plan was replaced by a series of ship/unit exercises after which, as recorded in the Commission Book, the ship's company enjoyed a 'gay[113] week of rest in Hong Kong' before returning to Singapore on 4 March.

By now the nautical and military importance of the LCMs was established as explained by Colour Sergeant 'Styx' Westacott:

> *During August 1967 I had a 'pier head jump' to relieve one of the LCM Mk 9 coxswains. We were about to sail on exercise to pick up a tank squadron from a beach on the East Coast of Malaya. This would be the first time that I had undocked/docked an LCM. A nerve-wracking task in front of my*

trained crew. Nor had I ever seen a bridge-laying Centurion before: guess who had the job of picking up the bridge-layer, they only just fit, but on return to the ship the only position in the dock for the craft carrying such a load was the last man in. Not a great deal of room with limited vision over the top of the tank.

What did an LCM Coxswain do at sea? First and foremost he had his LCM to look after and the well being of his crew to consider, whether they were working on the LCM or any other job around the ship (stores parties being one of the most required). As coxswain you had signed for it and it was your responsibility, so there was the continuing maintenance to be carried out and the of checking of various systems, the Stoker RN having most responsibility because if the engines didn't work then the other systems couldn't work. As RM SNCOs we were also involved in normal Sergeants Mess duties (President, Treasurer, Secretary etc.) and although not a lot of scope for mess life such as at Poole, inter-mess life on board helped to pass the time on the long periods at sea and no matter what else was happening the Colour Sergeants and Sergeants were involved in some thing or other.

Our busiest time at sea was prior to any major exercises, briefings, making sure our charts were up-to-date, beach details, call signs, water, fuel and rations required. For that reason it was a good idea to be well in with the Chief Chef and Jack Dusty.[114]

Looking back on the experience I can say that serving in Fearless *as an LCM coxswain was the second best period of my career (best period is another story) bearing in mind we were the first. It was because of what we experienced and then passed on to those that came afterwards, that the Landing Craft Branch was able to achieve the high standards that it enjoys today within the Corps.*

Victorous Far East football team captained by Corporal Andy Dungay.

Fearless's initiation into fleet exercises had to wait until 10 March when she joined *Bulwark* north of Penang for a combined amphibious exercise and then, to celebrate, the following week was spent at the Naval Base for the Far East Fleet's Fleet Sports Week during which the ship acquitted herself reasonably well.

Sport played a major part in *Fearless*'s life with her football and rugby teams enjoying great successes over the years. The football team in particular got off to a good start thanks to Ken Trace – the Ballast Control Officer – who acted as Secretary. Fitness was achieved and maintained by Corporal 'Red' Skelton, Royal Marines. The Manager was CH (Joiner) R.B. 'Jock' Warrender. Ken Trace remembers:

> *I decided to make Corporal Andy Dungay of the Royal Engineers, Team Captain. With a soldier as Captain I felt it would integrate them more fully into the ship. However, despite all my endeavours, I could not get him to 'gee up' the team with the cry of 'Come on* Fearless' *– it was always 'Come on chaps!'*
>
> *The team, which nearly always included at least three soldiers (Lance Corporal Jupp and Sapper Fitzpatrick were other regulars) was extremely successful and rarely lost a match. The Big Ships' Cup was held in Singapore with the team fantastically supported by the ship's company who had banners, a Supporters' Club of over 200 and a number of rousing chants.*
>
> *On one occasion the team were having an off day and were losing to a very fit and industrious Royal Artillery eleven when, to my amazement, the Captain, Corporal Dungay, suddenly shouted, 'Come on* Fearless, *they're only a crowd of pongoes!' After we had sneaked a narrow victory, I said to him, 'Shouting* Fearless *was not too difficult, was it?' He agreed and the 'us and them' problem was resolved.*

There was some resentment from the military in Singapore that the Army members of *Fearless*'s company did not play for their parent regiments or corps such as, for instance, the Royal Engineers – Corporal Dungay and Sapper Fitzpatrick's Corps – or even for the Army team in the inter-services fixtures. The two major Far East football competitions were the China Cup and the Big Ships Cup with *Fearless* favourites to win the former but on a monsoon-affected pitch they were fairly beaten by a tough 42 Commando team. In the latter, the ship played eleven Cup games, winning eight of them only to lose to *Bulwark* (with twice the complement) at that ship's third attempt. Nevertheless, revenge was to be exacted on *Fearless*'s last night in the Far East.

On 27 March the ship sailed for Okinawa on the first leg of a Japanese and Korean cruise which also took in Hiroshima, while at Inchon[115] everyone – at every rank – received tremendous hospitality from the US and Korean services.

During the passages out and back the first long range communications exercise was conducted between the SBS and the Foreign Office although the ship's aerials were not, then, fitted for such work. Terry Radley (the Brigade Command Post's Signals Sergeant) was instructed to operate as close to 'field' conditions as possible. A Morse link of about 2,000 miles could, he found by experiment, be established from the radio compartment in the aftermost LCM and for many years it was from this position that such 'special forces' links continued to be established.

All 'runs ashore' and especially 'foreign runs ashore' have their highlights. Terry Radley remembers one from Okinawa:

> *I was on duty one evening and noticed a local taxi approach the Jetty to off load some sailors after which it drew away to the end of the jetty and instead of turning right it drove straight into the water. The Duty PO and I rushed to the upturned taxi which was gradually sinking. We managed to pull the*

driver out by his arm despite him having a broken collar bone. The ship was presented with a doll in a glass case by the taxi company but all the PO and I received was a rollicking for leaving the ship while on duty – funny people, sailors.

On her return from Korea *Fearless* spent six weeks in dockyard hands while her ship's company moved ashore to HMS *Terror* and the Army detachments – for once – joined units of their own. Many took the opportunity to bring their wives out for a holiday while local leave was available for those who wanted to get a little further away.

Fearless sailed on 10 June for a short work up in the Singapore exercise areas which included embarking 42 Commando, but after this the programme became uncertain because of riots in Hong Kong. To pre-empt further escalation *Fearless* was ordered to sail, on the 23rd, with a squadron of the RAF Regiment but was recalled within twenty-four hours. The routine then dissolved into 'order and counter order' until she finally sailed for Hong Kong on 30 June and an unexpected spree that lasted from 4 to 10 July. She returned to Singapore on the 13th.

On 6 June 1967 Captain Hugh Corbett – the great 'triphibious' enthusiast – handed over command to Captain Kerr who was not only as enthusiastic but whose time in command was to be equally as influential for the ship's embryo reputation. Nevertheless, it is worthy of comment that neither of these two protagonists of the amphibious art were to be promoted to Flag Rank, although in Mark Kerr's case some believed that later, non-military events in Gibraltar, may have had a bearing on this.

Chapter Four

Captain M.W.B. Kerr, DSC, Royal Navy

Second Commanding Officer
1967–1969
Later, Commodore

Far East, Persian Gulf, South Africa, Home Waters, Mediterranean, West Africa

Mark Kerr came to *Fearless* with an impeccable amphibious record having commanded HMS *Armada* and then HMS *Meon* as Captain Amphibious Warfare in the Persian Gulf. Earlier he had won the DSC while serving in HMS *Exeter* when she was sunk in the Battle of the Java Sea in 1942 after which he was a prisoner of war until 1945. He retired in 1972 as Deputy President of the Admiralty Interview Board and died in 1986.

The First Commission Book took the ship up to 1968 and in his *Tailpiece* Captain Kerr was to comment:

> *Before I ever reached* Fearless *her name was well known and even some of her exploits had become famous – all of this in so short a time since her completion.*
>
> *On arriving on board in June 1967 I realized why. Here was a ship that was not only new in construction but one that was new in conception and methods – and problems. For the most part the problems had been overcome; and, as her*

Captain Mark Kerr with a gin and tonic. Harold Wilson with a half of beer.

> *potential developed and was proved, she showed herself to be effective and versatile to an astonishing degree. Her first ship's company were imbued with a spirit that matched her capability welding* Fearless *into an operational unit which is second to none.*

On his departure he was to write in the Second Commission Book for 1968 to 1970:

> *My predecessor said that the first commission of the first of a new class of ship was a unique experience. My experience in* Fearless *has proved that this is equally true of the second commission; if anything the experience is enhanced because as the ship came better known – both inside the Navy and outside it – she more than fulfilled her reputation of being a 'can-do' ship. These things snowball and we have proved to the hilt the old adage that the more you do, the more you are asked to do; but what is more important we proved to ourselves that where* Fearless *is concerned the sky's the limit.*

Furthermore it is clear from the reactions of the many visitors that they agree with us – particularly those belonging to the other services and including the ones who may initially have been doubtful. And this attitude has extended even outside our own country, as we were invited to put on a demonstration for another NATO country which had shown interest in acquiring a similar ship.

Another Fearless *First was in the Spring of 1969 when we had a full complement of Embarked Force on board for over two months in the Mediterranean. This was the first instalment of the force to strengthen the southern flank of NATO.*

In between times, opportunities have been found for producing Calypsos, Concert Parties, and enough deck hockey to wear the flight deck thin, besides a lot of serious, and successful sport ashore.

For myself, my two years in Fearless *have been a wonderful experience. To have had the honour to command officers and men from all three Services has been rewarding and fascinating. And if some of the soldiers ended up by being very good sailors, and vice versa, this is all to the good. With a thoroughly integrated ship's company always ready, willing and able, there is nothing we weren't prepared to turn our hand to, and we can take modest pride in the fact that our commission must have made* Fearless *the most widely known, by both name and appearance, of all Her Majesty's ships.*

In bidding farewell to the finest ship I have ever served in, let me couple this with the hope that many of us may meet again in the future – at sea, ashore, or in the air.

Life under her new Commanding Officer continued much as before with exercises and inspections dovetailing with the less military attractions of that, now gone, way of life 'East of Suez'. Rear Admiral Peter Marsden, then the Deputy Supply Officer, recalls:

In mid August, shortly after Mark Kerr had assumed command, we were scheduled for our inspection by Flag Officer Second in Command, Rear Admiral (as he then was) Edward Ashmore. At a Deputy HODS meeting early that month we decided to do our darndest to outwit the Admiral and his staff. Our local intelligence sources were well developed by this stage of our deployment and we managed 'to come by' the location chosen for our Inspection Day landing beach. Armed with this vital information we hired a car and set off across the causeway into Malaysia with First Lieutenant, Navigator, Deputy Supply Officer and Beachmaster aboard. This recce enabled us to pre-select landing areas, and positions for field kitchens, casualty receiving/evacuation stations etc, so it was with some relief that when the signalled 'tasks' were received from FO2 they exactly matched our 'intelligence'.

Perhaps, therefore, it was hardly surprising that the Admiral's inspection report ended with the words:

The ship is well run and in very good heart. Fearless *can be relied upon to produce a sound solution to any problem posed and I am confident she would acquit herself creditably in any emergency.*

As Peter Marsden added:

The Admiral might have continued, ' … given the necessary notice!'.

Three weeks later and the day after her Army-captained football team had roundly thrashed *Bulwark* 5–0, *Fearless's* first sojourn in the Far East came to an end. On 9 September 1967, she headed north-west up the Strait of Malacca, but, being *Fearless*, there were still operations to be undertaken before she could make the final turn to port into Plymouth Sound. It was to be a busy journey home.

She called in at Gan to collect mail and allow an afternoon of 'swimming leave' – not that there was anything else to do there – and on 20 September secured between two buoys in Aden's Inner Harbour. She had brought with her a detachment of 10 Port Squadron RCT with two Michigan 75 tractors and one Mexeflote to assist with the back-loading of British troops as independence loomed.

To help further, two of the ship's LCMs, two LCVPs[116] and one of her own Michigan 75s were also sent ashore under the command of David Minords, to enhance 51 Port Squadron, RCT.

Meanwhile *Fearless* loaded a pot pourri of, mostly 'dead', vehicles and craft[117] destined for Bahrain, towards which she sailed on 21 September. At her second attempt, as it were, she entered that tortuous channel, Khor Kaliya, leading to the Mina Sulman jetty – the home-from-home of ships of the Amphibious Warfare Squadron. Among many, Commodore T.E. Fanshawe, Commander Naval Forces Gulf, called on Captain Kerr – not knowing that his nephew would take command of *Fearless* twenty-one years later.

Seven days later, with a pre-refit team from Devonport embarked, *Fearless* returned to Aden from where, after a visit from the High Commissioner, and the embarkation of as many vehicles as she could fit,[118] she returned to the Persian Gulf.

The highlight of this second visit was the visit of His Highness Sheikh Isa bin Sulman el Khalifa, the Ruler of Bahrain, who was not only impressed by what he saw but who considered *Fearless*'s arrival in his domain to be of 'considerable prestige value'.

Then it was back to Aden, via a short landing exercise on the well-worn beaches of Sir Abu Nu'Air, to embark a new load, this time of eight Wessex II helicopters, one Scout and one Sioux. Heading north she called at Muscat for an exchange of visits, including a day spent 'showing off' to officers and men of the Sultan's Armed Forces.[119]

Before turning south for the last time *Fearless* carried Support Company of the King's Own Border Regiment to Dubai, plus eighty-five vehicles – many of which she had earlier carried north to Bahrain.

British withdrawal from Aden, codenamed Operation MAGISTER, was covered by Royal Navy Task Force 318[120] and lasted, effectively, throughout the whole of November 1967 culminating on the 29th when the last British troops – 200 Royal Marines from 42 Commando – flew by helicopter to HMS *Albion*. *Fearless*, having 'done her bit' by helping to reposition a considerable number of men and tons of stores to other theatres had sailed for home via Durban on the 21st. Four days earlier, the two sisters had met for the first time when *Intrepid*, on her way to the Far East,[121] anchored off Aden.

Mark Kerr was quick to invite his opposite number, Captain Tony Troup, for dinner with the offer of passing on many snippets of advice garnered from empirical experience, but Captain Troup did little to endear himself for, as soon as his boat had left for *Intrepid* Captain Kerr 'exhaled a huge breath' and said to his assembled officers, 'Some people manage to make one feel very inadequate!'[122]

It had been a trying evening with the submariner holding forth about how amphibious operations should be conducted with the hint, perhaps, that all would change with his own ship's arrival on station. This was almost too much for the experienced, placid captain of *Fearless* who had, in addition to his previous amphibious command, also been the First Lieutenant of an LST(C), HMS *Narvik*.

The Suez Canal was closed as an after effect of the Arab-Israeli war a few months earlier and so ships were forced to take the 9,000 mile Cape route – a journey not entirely without incident, as problems with a shaft bearing required Herculean efforts by the engineers to ensure that they would be home for Christmas. She was, despite a 'mammoth' run ashore in Durban. This time the visit had been planned well in advance so the South Africans were waiting for her, socially and sportingly.

If the *Fearless* crew thought they were unlucky with their mechanical breakdown on the homeward leg then they were in for a surprise when two or so days after refuelling at Freetown,

Sierra Leone, they came up with the survey ship HMS *Dampier* with one of her two shafts fractured. She was under full sail, giving her at least an extra knot in the steady trade winds, and showing the correct day mark for a sailing vessel under auxiliary power.[123]

Fearless landed eighteen northern and southern Irish 'natives' at Cork on 19 December so that they would be spared passing through Britain as the country was in the throes of a foot and mouth epidemic. Without this detour they would have missed Christmas. Then at precisely 0745 GMT on 20 December the ship entered Plymouth Sound and her first commission was about to end. Since Bahrain, a trickle of 'second commission' crew members had begun to arrive on board.

One 'new boy' was the Reverend John Tyrell, the ship's second padre who, early one morning, was celebrating Holy Communion in the ship's chapel – which doubled as the Naval Staff Office. True to his training at the Navy's School of Catering, the diminutive figure of Steward Kwong Lee (just 4 feet 8 inches high) searched all the obvious places, knowing only that 'early morning tea' had to be delivered on time. It was – in mid communion, directly onto the altar, alongside the wine.

The commission was summed up in the Commission Book under the heading of *Those Magnificent Men and Their Landing Machines*:

'Picture', one of those writing chaps once said, 'if you can, a winkle'.

This exercise is fairly straightforward for those who happen to know what a winkle looks like. But it is A level stuff for those who have never seen one.

It is much the same with an Assault Ship. If you haven't actually seen one, it is, to put it mildly, very difficult to describe. Since Fearless *first burst upon, or should it be 'sailed majestically into', an astonished military world, our reception has been mixed. There has been the 'I don't believe it' or Doubting Thomas reaction, the 'Let's face it, Fred, from any angle you're ugly' or Surrealist school, and the most usual, or pop view, 'Isn't she big?'*

The 'Isn't she big?' view can be a serious trap for young players or Staff Officers in that the Assault Ship, like those favourite sweetmeats, has a hole in the middle, or non-fattening centre. Furthermore, quite a large slice of the ship, though not, thank heavens, all of her, is designed to sink. The ship is, therefore, not as big as she looks.

The effect of the hole in the middle is to turn the ship into what the aviators might call a twin boom job and the yachtsmen a catamaran. And in the twin booms are most of the living quarters.

Living in the twin booms or side pieces is not unlike living in a railway train, for they are long and narrow. Of course, living in a railway train can be quite comfortable if you've remembered to book your sleeper. But it is not so cosy if other customers have to bed down between the seats and in the luggage racks. This happens at what British Railways calls 'peak travelling periods' and we call 'overload'.

The lesson to be drawn from this is that, with the aforesaid hole in the middle, though excellent for tks and tpt, she is not quite so good for tps.

So 'big' is a relative word and we have some limitations. We are half as big as a Commando Ship – pour not a quart into a pint pot. But within these limitations we are nothing if not flexible. Even if we have not yet carried a double-decker bus we have, to crib from that air lift advertisement, carried: Generals Generously, Brigadiers Bravely, Admirals Admirably, Commodores Comfortably, Captains Capably, Colonels Correctly, Sergeants Safely, Corporals Cunningly, Privates Primarily, Staff Officers Sagaciously, Regiments Regally, Battalions Beautifully, Commandos Commendably, Dogs Disgustingly, Lorries Lavishly, Guns Graciously, Tanks Tactfully, Ammunition Amorously, Helicopters Handsomely, Aviators Amiably, Transport Tremendously, Sappers Serenely, Gunners Gratefully, Pioneers Powerfully.

This list is not exhaustive, it's just that about here one is inclined to run out of puff. And, to date, they have all been set safely ashore thanks to T.M.M.A.T.L.M., not forgetting D.V. and W.P.

In due course the author might have added that *Fearless* had:

Hosted Harold Hopefully and Ian Impartially.

Of interest to statisticians, her first commission had seen over 8,500 troops on board, over 1,850 vehicles carried and 2,700 official visitors entertained; nearly 3,000 deck landings had been made by just about every type of in-service helicopter and she had taken part in three active-service operations. She had steamed 77,158 nautical miles while the main galley had produced over one and half million meals. Mark Kerr had joined his men for lunch on the day the one millionth meal was cooked and sat next to REM Gerald Hunt from Barrow in Furness. They ate, for the record, soup, roast beef, Yorkshire pudding and vegetables followed by bananas and custard.

The ship's first major refit was also an occasion for many alterations and additions as well as a large repair list and lasted from January to July 1968. A factor pointed out by her 'new' Commander (E) was that after the experience of the first year – including lengthy periods on operations – much of the machinery needed modifying and in some places replacing with newer equipment. As the main machinery spaces were below the deck this required careful monitoring and a strict order of work. Flyco needed modernizing although it would not, yet, be brought up to the required standard for the unplanned amount of air activity. Two welcome additions were the fitting of the Fleet's first satellite communications and a radical re-design of the wardroom. Up to now the ante-room and the dining room were divided by a wide 'public' passage – the only fore and aft thoroughfare along 01 deck.

On completion on what was generally regarded as a 'good refit' – in large part due to the Devonport team that had flown out to Aden for discussions with the ship's staff – Captain Mark Kerr was directed by Admiral Sir John Bush, Commander-in-Chief Western Fleet, to re-commission HMS *Fearless* at Devonport on 19 July 1968 ' ... and to proceed forthwith ... for Home Sea Service and Foreign Service (East of Suez) ... '.

In fact the ship was not planned to sail for the first of her sea-acceptance trials until 12 August: a date that was met despite a small fire in the Ballast Control Room and adjoining fan room on the 7th, quickly doused by the Dockyard Fire Service.

The following phase of *Fearless*'s life was unusual and thrust upon her by a British Prime Ministerial attempt to reverse the Unilateral Declaration of Independence announced by Rhodesia's Prime Minster on 11 November 1965. Britain had declared this action illegal and, with the support of the United Nations (except South Africa and Portugal), was applying economic sanctions. Earlier attempts at a political settlement had failed partly because Mr Ian Smith would not agree to majority rule and partly because of rifts between the Zimbabwe African People's Union and the Zimbabwe African National Union. Mr Harold Wilson, believing that 'one last push' might produce a settlement between the two governments, had demanded a meeting with Mr Ian Smith on board the cruiser HMS *Tiger*, at sea in December 1966, off the north African coast.

Prior to that occasion Mr Michael Palliser, Mr Wilson's Private Secretary (PS), was telephoned by the Prime Minister (PM). The conversations, on a Thursday, went something like this:[124]

PM to PS: 'Michael, I know, we'll have the talks in a warship – find out which ship they can give us, we'll need it by the week-end.'

PS to MOD (Navy): 'The PM needs a warship for a conference and accommodation.'

MOD (Navy) to PS: 'I'll call you back in half an hour.'

MOD (Navy) to PS: 'I'll give you *Tiger* on Saturday.'

The talks ended in deadlock: minority white rule continued in Rhodesia. On his return to dry land the Prime Minister decided that, should there be a next time, and as politicians are prone to sea-sickness, he would have two ships – in harbour. Support for this was offered by the Attorney General,[125] reported to be a bad sailor, who was quoted as saying, 'I cannot give legal advice while cruising!'

And there was 'a next time', just under two years hence in Gibraltar, after which minority rule would continue while the country became ravaged by civil war until 1980 and full elections; elections that were to throw up Robert Mugabe as the Prime Minister of Zimbabwe followed by the granting of independence as a republican member of the Commonwealth. It is beyond the scope of this book to comment further except to say that Ian Smith had never seemed optimistic, for he must have known that, in the long run, the British – indeed the UN – would not accept a compromise on majority rule and that majority rule was against his own, deeply held, convictions and would 'never occur in his lifetime'. Before he left for Gibraltar he was quoted as saying:

> *I do not wish to raise any false hopes ... much wishful thinking is taking place. I must honestly tell you that as yet I can see no justification for this.*

He was right and the *Guardian* headlined a leader with the words, 'A 'No' from Mr Smith even before talks begin.'

Probably unhelpful was a cartoon by 'Jon' showing Mr Wilson greeting Mr Smith at the entrance to the conference while behind the Rhodesian stands a familiar figure. The caption reads, 'Mr (Enoch) Powell has come along to put over my (the Rhodesian Prime Minister's) point of view.'

For Mr Wilson's part, before leaving London he stated that to reach an agreement on Rhodesia:

> *I am prepared to go to the limit, but when I say 'to the limit' that means within the six principles we have laid down and two of those principles are the unimpeded progress towards majority rule and the ending of racial discrimination ... Mr Smith has got to move a very, very long way in order to ensure that we can get an agreement.*

Fearless's ship's company did everything in its power to ensure that the domestic and security arrangements were as near perfect as possible so that the politicians could concentrate solely on the task at hand. In many respects the subject of the talks and their outcome was of no military business of *Fearless* and her crew, yet if things had been so badly organized that the delegates were distracted then maybe some opprobrium and blame for failure would have been in order.

Thankfully that was not to be the case and so there we can leave the politicians to their work and concentrate on *Fearless* and her duties during Operation DIOGENES, an operation that was to test the patience and humour of her ship's company every bit as much as the stiffest amphibious landing. It was also to test the ship's communications and 'hotel services' to their limits.

Fearless's part began during the evening of Wednesday, 2 October, at 2200 to be precise, with the arrival on board of a signal[126] postponing Exercise LOVAT, due to start the next morning with a passage to the east coast of Scotland.[127] A Royal Marines Commando with its men, vehicles and equipment had loaded – all they lacked was the ammunition due to arrive that night. No further details were forthcoming until 1100 the next morning when a visit by the Chief Staff Officer to Flag Officer Carriers and Amphibious Ships outlined, in strictest secrecy only to the Commanding Officer, the 'possibility' of the operation taking place. A further visit by the Officer in Charge of Defence Communications at 1800 confirmed that the operation was 'on' but that all outward signs of a change in plan were to be kept to a minimum. An hour and half later a conflicting order was received from the Ministry of Defence stating the outline requirement 'if it should take place'.

The embarked force remained on board but at 0400 on Friday another signal from the MOD confirming that DIOGENES would take place coincided with an order from the Commander-in-Chief Western Fleet to sail. At 1100 *Fearless*, having offloaded her embarked troops, slipped from No. 7 berth, anchored in the deeper water of Plymouth Sound, docked down, and sent the Commando's vehicles ashore by LCM. As planned for Exercise LOVAT, four Wessex Mk V helicopters from RNAS Culdrose now landed on and were lashed for sea.

At 1500 on Friday, 4 October *Fearless* sailed for Gibraltar and as soon as Special Sea Duty Men had been stood down Mark Kerr was able to tell his crew of the destination but no more. Speculation, as always, was rife with the most popular guess being Mexico to act as guard ship for the Olympic Games! When the truth was revealed, one Chief Petty Officer was quoted in the *Daily Telegraph* as saying 'the groans could be heard throughout the ship'. The truth came via the media's inability to honour an embargo, obliging Mark Kerr to report:[128]

> The press statement announcing the conference was to have been made at 081200Z in London. In view of the great secrecy that was being maintained, the clear implication was that Ships' Companies were not to be informed of DIOGENES until this time. In these circumstances, it was unfortunate that Reuters put out this information nearly an hour before this deadline. This information was received quite openly in the ship and the secrecy maintained by the Command was made to look a bit foolish.

From here onwards many stories emerge, almost all of which coincide with the official report, written by the Commanding Officer, but for the main thread we rely on the unofficial journal of the Commander (S), John Carlill.[129] Snippets from other members of the ship's company – and from Captain Kerr's official report – are added in rough chronological sequence.

> On our way south we were joined by a Wessex helicopter bearing the temporary Captain of HMS Kent.[130] It was a fortuitous choice as he had been involved in arranging the previous talks in HMS Tiger. Conflicting signals began to arrive from different Government agencies in Whitehall that merely added to the confusion; accommodation on board was being allocated arbitrarily and seemingly without knowledge of the internal re-arrangements carried-out during the recent refit.
>
> The final insult came when the Captain's quarters were requisitioned and he was relegated to a cot in the Sick Bay. He took it all in tremendously good part but the ship's company was less than best pleased. Amid all the confusion it became very clear to me that one person was needed to take charge. Clearly it could not be the Captain, the Commander had to run the ship's routine and the Engineer Officer would need to be able to go below if we were to be at sea.
>
> Heads of Department were summoned for Mark Kerr to bring us up to date with the developing situation which was being conducted at Top Secret level and to appoint me as the coordinator.
>
> My shopping list of requirements was endless. Hand written chits flew off the end of my pen and were rushed to addressees. All were received in the spirit intended and things began to happen immediately. Fortuitously, we had the only reservist in Parliament on board.

Lieutenant Commander Keith Speed, RNR,[131] had joined *Fearless* for his annual reserve training. He had been elected the Conservative Member of Parliament for Meriden in March 1968 – seven months earlier – and was now able to offer, in his words:[132]

> Political advice to Captain Kerr and his team on the various changes the ship might require in order to act as headquarters for the Wilson/Smith talks. I also spent some time with everyone else giving her a fresh coat of paint.
>
> I was told that my presence on board as a newly elected Conservative Member of Parliament would not be welcome whilst the talks were going on. As a result I was transferred for several days to HMS Troubridge.

Gibraltar with HMS *Kent* outboard.

John Carlill continues his story:

> Keith Speed was the greatest help to me prior to our arrival at Gibraltar and before any announcement was made. I breached my confidence and told him what by then was pretty obvious but still under wraps. I had to do this as he was to be landed on arrival in Gibraltar as his presence on board could have been an embarrassment to the Prime Minister. From (him) I got useful background information as well as accurate guesses regarding the likely composition of the UK delegation and personalities.
>
> Both ships entered Gibraltar naval base and secured alongside the South Arm with Kent outside Fearless and angled-in so that the fo'c'sles of both were close together with a short brow joining them. A Conference Room was created in the dining part of the wardroom with a UK delegates Mess/Bar/ Meeting Room in the other half. A sound-proof temporary bulkhead was created to separate them. Cabins were allocated and re-allocated, sketch location plans prepared and fire and other emergency procedures outlined in non-naval language. Special arrangements had to be made for the unknown number of female members in the Whitehall party. Accommodation ashore had to be arranged for displaced officers.

There were conflicting requirements as the MOD (Navy), oblivious to the fact that *Fearless*'s wardroom had been altered during the recent refit, was advising from the original builder's drawings which, naturally, the ship no longer possessed. The ship was being asked to reinstate the fore-and-aft passage way that had divided the dining room – now the Conference Room – and the ante room, which would remain as such for delegates within the Conference Citadel. These 'new' bulkheads had to be constructed then lined with noise-proof tiles.

Amusingly, the on-board Job Card (Naval Form S2018 (1967)) had to be filled in by the ship's technical office and countersigned by the Shipwright Lieutenant as being an official task to be undertaken by his team. Under the main heading of 'Description' appears the following instruction: 'Major and minor alterations to be carried out. Items manufactured, signs painted etc for summit conference to be held on board whilst ship is in Gibraltar.'

Under this, on the day he departed, the Prime Minister was to write;

With very warm thanks for a job superbly done. Harold Wilson.

What he must have seen were the boxes which had had to be filled in by the authorizing officer. These read:

System/Structure:	Conference Requirements
Location:	Shipwide
Ship:	Fearless
Requisitioned by:	Rt. Hon H. Wilson
Rank:	Prime Minister
Department:	Labour
Date:	8.10.68
Serial No:	H.339
Man-hours:	735 – 15 Shipwrights
	126 – 3 MEs.
	14 – 2 Seamen

Accommodation caused one of the bigger headaches for Captain Kerr and Commander Carlill as the Commanding Officer was to outline – among many factors – in his list of comments to FOCAS, Rear Admiral Fell, when it was all over:[133]

Relations between delegates and Ship's Officers ... were at all times cordial and relaxed ... the officers who had duties in connection with the Conference were comparatively few, nevertheless the Delegates appeared to welcome such mixing as came naturally, and there was the minimum of the 'we' and 'they' attitude which could so easily have arisen if there had been less contact. Furthermore the perhaps over-demanding attitude which is sometimes in evidence with the denizens of Whitehall and Westminster was conspicuous by its absence. Any tendency there may have been in this direction was quickly and satisfactorily nipped in the bud by a small incident when the (Commanding Officer) had to put his foot down firmly. The initial surprise that this caused was followed by a greater respect for the ship and a more sensitive attitude on the part of the Delegates, which in turn had the effect of enhancing the already very good relations that existed. . . . .

In this connection, it is considered bad policy for the Commanding Officer to be required to give up his quarters for anyone other than a member of the Royal Family or a Senior Officer of his own Service.[134] It cannot be denied that the Navy is held in less regard than formerly by civilians, and any willing self-denigration on the Navy's part can only encourage this unfortunate tendency. The Commanding Officer of one of Her Majesty's Ships holds a unique position, and any action which erodes this position is resented inside the Navy and is misunderstood outside the Navy. This point was brought home to me very clearly by the attitude of my own ship's company. . . . .

More cabins than had actually been asked for were made available ... in the event this proved to have been a wise precaution ... The Delegates repeatedly expressed themselves surprised and gratified at what they found and the Prime Minister himself claimed that words failed him, from a politician, strong language indeed. . . . .

If the complete disruption of officer accommodation is accepted there is no doubt that the ship can be turned into a very satisfactory location for such a Conference. However, this disruption is very complete, and it is suggested that the success of the arrangements on this occasion should not be allowed

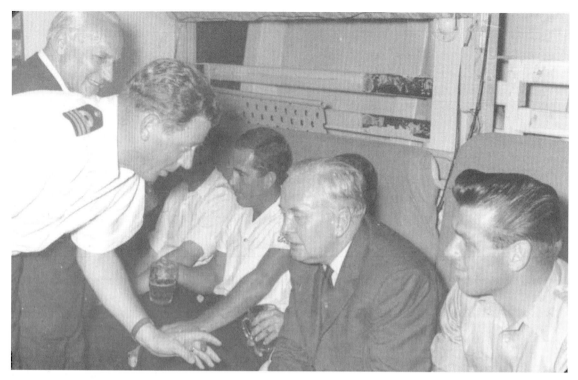

Caption from the Wardroom Line Book, 'That's it. One more beer, then you leave!'

to encourage politicians to ask for such facilities for any occasion of less importance than the conference which has just been held. . . . As opposed to the officers, ratings accommodation was hardly encroached upon at all. The only space they lost was the Senior Rates Dining Hall which was turned into a dining room for officers without bar facilities. An ad hoc bar was arranged on the upper deck where an awning proved sufficient protection in the prevailing good weather.

John Carlill:

A car pool had to be organized. Facilities for the Media (TV, Radio and Press) had to be set-up with all the problems of power, lighting and internal communications. Tight security onboard was easy enough but restricting access to the Conference Citadel presented difficulties. Chinese Stewards had to go about their routine domestic business, the electrical staff had to maintain and check lighting and air-conditioning, refuse had to be disposed of and so on. Armed sentries were to be positioned discreetly and checked and relieved. Security passes had to be prepared. 'Rubber-neckers' and the inquisitiveness of all ranks would get in the way and would need to be dissuaded.

The ship arrived in Gibraltar on 8 October and at 1415 secured at 48 berth, South Mole. HMS *Kent* secured alongside *Fearless* half an hour later and the two Commanding Officers, together, called on the Flag Officer Gibraltar, Rear Admiral Ian Jamieson, DSC.[135] There had been very little time to rearrange *Fearless* domestically and physically and what was ordained had to be built with the few raw materials she carried. There were precious few hours between berthing and 'action stations', for Mr Wilson's party arrived on board at 0015 on the 9th. John Carlill:

When the time came for the British delegation to arrive it was later in the evening than previously planned. This tested our flexibility from the outset as an informal reception and buffet supper had to be put on hold for a couple of hours. In a way it worked even better as they were all tired and just pleased to be our guests and to enjoy being made to feel welcome.

The Rhodesian Delegation had arrived at a leisurely 1645 that day by boat from Flag Staff Steps direct to *Kent* in order, such were the sensitivities, not to cross *Fearless*. The first of four full days began the next morning – 10 October. Other visitors came and went amid frenetic, preparatory activity: General Sir Gerald Lathbury, the Governor of Gibraltar, called on the Prime Minister at lunchtime to be followed at tea time by Sir Humphrey Gibbs, the Governor of Rhodesia but, as Mr Wilson had taken over the Commodore's suite of cabins, these visits – including full ceremonial arrivals and departures – were perhaps less of a hindrance than to those at lower levels.

Ian Smith welcomed on board.

A Conference Citadel with single access embracing all the spaces used by the delegates was achieved by cutting off from the rest of the ship all the senior officers' accommodation and wardroom with the adjoining flats and passageways and the forward two thirds of the junior officers' cabins. The Citadel also took in the Assault Operations Room and the Main Signal Office on 03 Deck.

This not only eased security but ensured that people unused to a ship's layout were confined to a simple section without too much danger of becoming lost.

Much of this partitioning was undertaken at sea – once the confusions over the new-look wardroom had been ironed out – but the noise-proof tiles could only be fitted after the ship arrived at Gibraltar along with the supply of other items not normally, then, carried aboard a British Man of War. These included, as a token list, typists' desks and stools, soft lavatory paper, shower caps, sanitary bins, flower vases and flowers, deck chairs with arms and, perhaps not unexpectedly, extra spirit measures!

In addition to sentries, a Royal Marines Orderly Corporal was permanently posted outside the Prime Minster's – the Commodore's – cabin. John Carlill again:

> *During the course of the next few days I was to have many opportunities to talk informally with both Mr. Wilson and Mr. Smith. Both were charming to me as indeed were both of their delegations.*
>
> *Although the least pompous of men and one with a very quick sense of humour and repartee Mr Wilson nevertheless liked to make an 'entrance'. On more than one occasion he told the Royal Marine sentry not to open the door onto the for'ard Sea Cat deck until he had great clouds of smoke pouring from his large pipe.*
>
> *Somehow he never got used to the certainty that for once there would be no one waiting to be impressed on the other side. Another thing that surprised and intrigued him was the fact that the* Kents *had become Rhodesian supporters for the duration of the talks. The Prime Minister was to discover this for himself when he tried to engage them in light-hearted banter across the guard-rails. They were polite but no more. It just didn't work.*

Captain Kerr was to raise this point in paragraph 15 of his report:[136]

> *The lower deck, as ever loyal, respectively 'supported' their own Delegation in each ship.... There were certain aspects in common with the supporters of a football match – my team, right or wrong.*

Harold Wilson meets the LCM coxswains. L. to R. Bluey Smith (now deceased), Styx Westacott, Bill Cordy. Major Douglas Mayhew (now deceased) with his back to the camera.

By Sunday 13 October – the fourth full day of talks – and after a short church service on *Fearless's* flight deck attended by both delegations, there was growing excitement throughout the two ships that matters might be drawing to a close; which they did at 2200 that evening. Mr Smith left an hour later clutching an ultimatum for his cabinet from Mr Wilson who, among other concerns, was determined not to see the Commonwealth destroyed by the actions of this breakaway state. The next day Mr Wilson gave a press conference in the Naval Base and another for lobby correspondents on board then, just before lunch, he thanked both ships' companies on *Fearless's* flight deck and at 1240, after a final instruction to 'splice the main brace', *Fearless* sailed for the United Kingdom. Two and half hours out of Gibraltar Harold Wilson's order was 'executed'.

Yet even the seemingly innocent, neutral ground of a church service had generated problems. Well in advance it had been accepted that both Prime Ministers would read a lesson each; accordingly, *Kent's* padre, the Reverend Peter Hudson,[137] had allocated Mr Smith a passage which included the words, 'Thou shalt love thy neighbour as thyself', while that chosen by the Reverend John Tyrell, *Fearless's* padre, for Mr Wilson, thundered, 'If the world hate you, you know that it hated me before it hated you.... . Remember the word that I said unto you, the servant is not greater than the Lord. If they have persecuted me they will also persecute you'.

Both Prime Ministers refused to read lessons that day, leaving Mark Kerr with just one: he chose the marginally less evocative passage selected by *Kent*.

John Carlill:

> *The Prime Minister told me that, in part, he blamed himself. Mistakenly, he had treated Mr. Ian Smith as the small-time politician he had met previously in HMS* Tiger, *whereas in the meantime he had grown into a man of considerable political stature.... .*

In anticipation of success we had made discreet arrangements onboard for a celebration party. Unhappily, it was not to be. A handshake had to do. I was surprised to be called to the gangway where the Prime Minister and the Captain were chatting together. It seemed that Mr. Wilson had delayed his own departure in order to thank me and say goodbye. It was a thoughtful gesture and one that I appreciated greatly.

On arrival back in Devonport we promptly embarked the Commando Group again and sailed for a major tri-service exercise in Northern Ireland.[138] No rest for the wicked!

But there were less official stories and they slowly filtered out. One in particular – involving Marcia Williams's bunk – has drifted down the years with modifications and embellishments. As it is not apocryphal (although many believe that it is) here is the definitive version from John Carlill in a tale he calls 'Bunkum':[139]

The Captain and I had an unspoken understanding that neither of us would turn-in until the last member of the British delegation was safely back onboard. About 11 p.m. one evening the telephone on the bulkhead of my borrowed cabin rang. The call was from one of the Prime Minister's press advisers.[140] *I had not met him as he did not mix with his colleagues:*

'The naval car that brought Mrs Williams[141] *and me to the Rock Hotel earlier this evening is no longer here. I told the driver to wait.'*

'Good evening. What time did he drop you off?'

'About 7.15 p.m.'

'Well he may have misunderstood you because he certainly could not have been spared from the ship for over four hours just waiting at the hotel.'

'Well, Commander, what should I do as we wish to return to the ship?'

'If you were a sailor you would take a taxi or if you were an officer you would probably walk.'

'I do not intend to take either of those courses. Send a naval car immediately.'

'We only have one driver at night and he may be out on a duty call. In the circumstances, it would be quicker and more appropriate, if you were to take a taxi.'

'Send a car as soon as you can.'

I went out on deck to calm my anger and, in passing, told the Captain what had transpired. I was pretty fed-up but, nevertheless, arranged to send a car – but in no great hurry. In due course the returning car came to a halt abreast the bow. Its passengers got out and hurried on board. They swept past the Officer-of-the-Watch and Gangway Staff without a word and ignored both the Captain and me. They were the last of our delegation to return and so the Captain and I felt free to turn-in ourselves. It had been a long day with a disagreeable ending.

Next morning, and just as I was going in search of an early breakfast, the Prime Minister's Principal Private Secretary[142] *knocked on the cabin door. There wasn't any room for him to sit down so we stood while he told me his problem.*

Apparently, Mrs Williams had been so angry about being kept waiting for a car the previous evening that she had forced her way past the Royal Marines sentry on the door to Mr. Wilson's quarters, woken him and complained at the way that she had been treated. The Prime Minister, not best pleased at having his sleep so rudely disturbed, had instructed his PPS to find out what had happened. I was then told by the PPS that I was to give him my 'reasons in writing' forthwith. This I declined to do.

I went on to explain that I was responsible to the Captain and not to the Prime Minister. He needed to ask the Captain to obtain any such report from me. Of course, although perfectly correct, this did not go down too well, and I was told not to be difficult, and just get on with it. Once again I declined to do so.

In an effort to get me to change my mind the PPS, himself an ex-wartime Brigadier, decided to tell me what had happened after Mrs Williams had left the Prime Minister's cabin. Apparently she had gone to her cabin, the one vacated for her by our Engineer Officer, got into her night attire and, as she settled herself into the bunk, it had promptly folded into its daytime position of settee, trapping her inside.

Her cries for help were muffled by the bedclothes and it was some time before she was able to extricate herself.

It was rumoured that the Royal Marines sentry, outside the Prime Minister's quarters, just a few feet along the cabin flat, delayed before coming to the rescue. He had been the butt of Mrs Williams's anger a few minutes earlier and did not want to risk a second dose – as it was, her behaviour had already got him into some trouble.

At this point I excused myself and reached past the PPS for my cap.
'Where are you going?' he demanded.
'I am off to tell the ship's company at breakfast what you have just told me. If you listen carefully you may hear their roar of laughter.'
I thought no more of it but, when I was one of the Prime Minister's guests at lunch later that day, he did remark with a twinkle, 'I hear there was some trouble with the naval transport last night, Commander.'
'A load of bunk, Sir.'

In the covering letter with this story John Carlill wrote:[143]

I never discussed the incident with either Mrs Williams (as was) or Gerald Kaufman. First, because there was no need and second because both were self-important 'fish out of water' and there was a lot of amour propre flying around.

Incidentally, the poor Royal Marines sentry on the Prime Minister's cabin door was on a charge the following morning for allowing Mrs Williams to get past him!

He then added, rather enigmatically:

I could tell you more but will not.

In early 2003 both Lady Falkender and Gerald Kaufman were approached for their memories but Mr Kaufman declined to offer any story[144] which is a pity for his dinner partner that night in The Rock Hotel wrote tantalizingly:[145]

I can only remember now a little of what it was like, but they are very wonderful memories for me. . . .
I am sorry that Gerald Kaufman has declined to participate, but I do remember that he did have a story that was very funny. . . .

Others have slightly differing views on those days; Colin Robinson, the Commander (E), wrote,

There were a number of very nice people on board, including the Cabinet Secretary, Sir Burke Trend and several of the Garden Room girls. Most people liked those who were lodging in their cabins. Not I though. Mine had been occupied by Marcia Williams and another by Gerald Kaufman, both of whom managed to make themselves heartily disliked in the ship. . . .

The PM tackled Mark Kerr about (the staff car incident) who, no doubt unwisely for his future career, was absolutely furious and refused, point blank, to take any action against the driver, telling the PM that his ship's company had better things to do than drive Marcia Williams and Gerald Kaufman around in the small hours . . . Marcia also got laughed at because of (my cabin's) bunk incident. . . . For all the press presence on board the only place these episodes were (accurately) reported was Private Eye.

All on board both ships liked (Ian Smith) enormously. A lean, stringy, laconic Rhodesian who had been a successful fighter pilot in the war, he seemed in marked contrast to our podgy Prime Minster whose war had been in the Board of Trade.... It was impossible to hide the fact that when the day was done the PM would be steadily working his way through our best brandy and cigars but that in public he made much of drinking beer and puffing at his pipe....

Certainly the conference did not do Mark Kerr any good (which it should have done) but John Carlill who as Commander (S) had really managed the thing from start to finish in his capacity as 'hotel manager' got an OBE for his pains and finished up a Rear Admiral. The rest of us just rather enjoyed it as something out of the ordinary.

Captain Kerr was to conclude his report with these words:

This Summit Conference has been an uplifting and stimulating experience. The inconvenience and disruption to the ship was counterbalanced many times over by the knowledge that the moment was an historic one and that we were privileged and fortunate to have been able to contribute to it. Such comments as are offered ... should be seen against this greater background and in the context of aiming at the unattainable – perfection.

Perfection may be unobtainable but the ship came close, and especially so when one remembers the tight schedule coupled with the significant fact that all preparation was carried out at sea – apart from the tiles, soft paper and flowers of course.

The Commanding Officer's report was straightforward and aimed at easing the way for any future ship tasked similarly and yet, probably because it pulled few punches, it was not given wide publicity. Indeed the report and the covering letters by both FOCAS and C-in-C Western Fleet were regarded by a senior civil servant within MOD (Navy) as: 'Not suitable for wide distribution but will be extremely useful if a similar operation arises again.'[146]

The Prime Minster had been happy with the arrangements on board *Fearless*, if not with his discussions with Mr Ian Smith (nor, possibly, with the behaviour of some members of his own team), for he was swift with the following signal sent from RAF Comet 1001 'en route Gibraltar to London':

To Captain Mark Kerr ... As my colleagues and I and members of the British Delegation leave Gibraltar I send to you, your officers and entire Ships Company of HMS Fearless *our warmest congratulations on the magnificent way you all responded to the demands we put upon you. It was a pleasure to be with you. Our heartfelt thanks and good wishes go with you all as you sail from Gibraltar. Harold Wilson.*

In a later private letter to Mark Kerr[147] he wrote:

I am confident that you all share my hope ... that despite Mr Smith's inability to accept on board Fearless *the honourable settlement open to him he may still on reflection decide to do so.... If eventually a settlement emerges HMS* Fearless *can claim a distinguished part in it....*

The use of Her Majesty's ships as political conference centres with all the military and personal disruption caused was to be the subject of many internal discussions, concluding with the general naval view that such exercises should be avoided at all costs. Although it should be acknowledged that the Royal Navy had a close interest in the conclusion of the talks for, if successful from the British point of view, the Beira patrols in the Mozambique channel – that attempted to prevent embargoed oil from reaching its destination – could be withdrawn and at least three warships and one Royal Fleet Auxiliary released back into general service just as the Russians were overtly building up their presence in the Mediterranean.

Nevertheless, many considered it an inappropriate use of two major and busy warships whose time could have been better spent.

Before this conference, *Fearless* had, in many respects as far as the general public were concerned, been just another large warship – unique perhaps – but one not worthy of much detailed interest beyond the military. Now she was headline news and the country knew more about her than any other ship in the fleet: they even knew the dimensions of Harold Wilson's cabin, the colour of the carpet, the subject of the pictures on the bulkheads and even the size of his (and his alleged mistress's) bunk. From Gibraltar onwards, whatever *Fearless* did, she would be 'news'. Before the talks started the *Daily Express* had headlined:

> *The all-purpose* Fearless: *carries tanks, troops, hovercraft – and the hope of two nations.*

... while the *Daily Mirror* suggested much the same:

> *The Summit Aboard The Ship They Call The Trouble-Shooter.*

On completion of the talks Harold Wilson presented two signed photographs of himself, one for the wardroom and one for the ship's trophy cabinet. While on passage home the wardroom photograph attracted much graffiti so the PO Steward, PO Wong Ngau, 'believing this to be the image of someone of at least mandarin status', decided that the officers were not to be trusted and removed the picture with the intention of displaying it only on special occasions.

Almost as many versions of the truth surrounding the fate of the two photographs began to circulate as there were concerning Marcia Williams's nocturnal adventures. The truth has never been fully established despite official inquiries and MOD press statements, yet a number of facts were never in doubt to those 'in the know'. One of the originals was indeed 'hidden' by PO Wong as described above; one copy was disfigured with a moustache and beard and one was definitely 'lost at sea' – and that makes three pictures, although the second and third are probably the same. Some months later and after 'Questions in the House' two signed photographs miraculously reappeared for the press to photograph just in time for Mr Wilson's next visit, off Lagos in March 1969. They could not both have been the originals for one had certainly been given a 'float test'!

Nevertheless, snippets that still bear credence should be shared. The first occurred on the ship's arrival in Plymouth on 17 October where she enjoyed considerable attention, including an invasion of the wardroom by all manner of visitors, one of whom asked where the picture of the Prime Minister was displayed. As Mr Wilson was not on board and as the only two photographs on permanent display in the wardroom were of the Queen and Prince Philip an officer laughed off its absence by saying, 'It was put overboard to see if he could walk on water'. Unfortunately the questioner was a *Daily Express* reporter and so, inevitably, the next day's papers caused embarrassment or amusement depending, slightly, on the reader's position in the naval hierarchy.

It was not, though, to be the end of the matter but, for the moment, more important things beckoned in the form of Exercise SWOP for which the cancelled Exercise LOVAT was to have been the work-up period. The Army's Strategic Command Public Relations Press Release set the scene:

> *The largest exercise ever to be held in Northern Ireland in peace-time,*[148] *involving over 6,000 servicemen, will take place in October. Code-named SWOP, it will be a Joint Services exercise, and as well as Northern Ireland will involve the Isle of Man. The aim is to practise Joint Service techniques in a limited war setting, including amphibious operations.*
>
> *The main tactical phase of the exercise will take place in County Down and the Magilligan area of County Londonderry between 17 and 27 October 1968 when a land force in Northern Ireland*

represented by 39 Infantry Brigade[149] supported by the North Irish Militia will counter an invading force of 24 Infantry Brigade supported by the Royal Navy, 45 Royal Marine Commando and the Royal Air Force.

A Joint Force Headquarters ... will be established at RAF Colerne, near Bath, to control the invading force and a concurrent command post exercise in the Isle of Man.... .

On 16th October, Headquarter 24 Infantry Brigade (Plymouth) and 45 Royal Marine Commando will board the Royal Navy Assault Ship HMS Fearless and two of the Army's Logistic Landing Ships, Sir Percivale and Sir Tristram. They will be joined at sea by Tank Landing Craft of the Royal Corps of Transport. Other forces, including the 2nd Battalion Royal Regiment of Fusiliers ... will board the Logistic Landing Ships ... to join the battle.... .

At the wash-up and acknowledging the Irish Guards' experience during Operation FATE, the Commander 24 Infantry Brigade[150] summed up his formation's part[151] with the now familiar theme: 'Exercise SWOP' was the culmination of a year's training by an Infantry Brigade Group. Though no doubt numerous mistakes occurred, the general feeling of all concerned was that there is no black magic involved and that the techniques can be learnt quickly. '

The Army Brigadier's report went on: 'The present doctrine is that assault landings are the prerogative of Royal Marines Commandos and the Army role is intervention when opposition is likely to be minimal.'

It is not certain where he would have read this 'doctrine' for it never has been a claim of either the Royal Marines or the Navy but it does make sense that, as the Navy's Sea Soldiers are used to living aboard and operating from ships, when such landings have to be conducted, the Royal Marines should be the first – but not the only – choice.

The same Army commander made a further telling comment when he rued the absence of an Amphibious Beach Unit, which is strange as *Fearless*'s was deployed but the passage of time now hides the reasons behind this comment. Included in his notes on the discharging of cargo he made the observation that: 'Had it been possible to beach the LSLs or the LCT, the discharge rate would have been extremely high and the LCM crews would not have been overworked.'

This view underlines a long-standing complaint about the misuse of LSLs over the years by preventing them from beaching and thus speeding the logistic build-up ashore. The simple, but rather limp, excuse was that, as civilian ships, each beaching had to be treated as a grounding and thus the ship needed to be docked to check for damage each time. When one considers the use to which the LCTs and LSTs were put (and they had been designed and built quickly during the war years) when two or three beachings a day were the norm in the Gulf of the 1960s it will be seen as an incongruous ruling.

Mark Kerr commented[152] that, in future, better use could be made of the LSLs by having one earmarked as a hospital ship: an LPD, he argued, was not the right ship for dealing with casualties.

As far as loading his ship was concerned he felt that Mountbatten Hard in Plymouth (then owned by the RAF) was subject to too many restrictions and 'cannot be counted on as always been available'. Alongside this comment someone, presumably on the staff of FOCAS to whom the report was addressed, had written in pen, *Bloody Crabs*. The unreliability of the Mountbatten slip – although perfect at most states of the tide, with the right gradient, the right forming up spaces at the inland end and with good exits to the main roads – was to be noted over the years, but the RAF continued to try and prevent its use by any, other than its own air sea rescue launches. Mark Kerr moved on to another 'tricky' area – paraphrased here for brevity: 'The SBS had not considered a landing possible under the sea conditions prevailing and so did not mark the beach. The SBS Commander should be under the effective control of the Naval Commander and not, emphatically, under Joint Force Headquarters.'

Again, a hand-written comment was added in the margin, *Who decides?* It was, Mark Kerr believed, not up to the SBS to deliberate on such fundamentals; it was for the SBS to report and allow the commanders to weigh up the risks. In this case the decision had been made to land without the initial beach markings (which would have been useful) with the result that one craft broached on the beach, but this, foreseen, risk had been acceptable to the commanders. Captain Kerr's last comments involved the LCM crews:

> *The LCMs had finally landed 88 chalks although the weather throughout had been against them ... and for much of the time poor visibility made the transit to the beach anything but easy and vectoring from the ship was needed; for example one crew were in their craft working for 63 hours out of the 76 hours of the unloading.*

The, now familiar, written comment appeared in the margin: *Enough crews?* The answer then, as always, was 'No' and was to become a running sore when compared with the concern over an aircraft's pilot's carefully-regulated hours. It is agreed that a coxswain falling asleep at the wheel may not have the same consequences as a pilot being similarly affected with his controls but....

The press, having 'noticed' *Fearless* in Gibraltar, could not let her go and headlines such as 'Now *Fearless* Takes Lead Role In "Invasion"', '*Fearless* In Northern Ireland "Invasion"' and '*Fearless* Starts Ireland Attack' and even 'Invasion of Ireland' had been blasted across the news pages of broadsheet and tabloid at the start of SWOP.

Over the next weeks she was to embark the 1st Battalion Royal Welch Fusiliers and C-in-C Plymouth for visits to Bristol and Cardiff before moving on to Bristol and back to Devonport. From there she paid a visit to Bremerhaven (and a ship's company trip to Berlin) but the Commanding Officer was disappointed by the few visitors: a fact he commented on in his Report of Proceedings:[153] 'Interest in navies, indeed in all the services, is at a very low ebb among the Germans at present.'

During the return leg the Welch Fusiliers were replaced in Portland by a battalion of the Royal Regiment of Fusiliers; required on board as part of a damage control exercise with an Embarked Force. C-in-C Western Fleet landed on by helicopter for the overnight passage to Plymouth and so, as *Fearless* entered Plymouth Sound on 12 December, her 1968 perambulations came to an end.

It had been quite a year but the next was to be equally as busy and would take her back to the Far East and include another Harold Wilson extravaganza.

Fearless sailed on 15 January 1969 for the Mediterranean and her first extended, operational deployment, Exercise SUNTRAP. The ship, with her Embarked Force of Royal Marines, Life Guards and Royal Artillery personnel, formed the first instalment of an enlarged British Naval presence on NATO's southern flank. The reason for this deployment's importance was that it was the first, fully-integrated, embarked force the ship had carried that was also balanced and ready for battle: indeed, as mentioned above, it was declared to NATO.

45 Commando Royal Marines, commanded by Lieutenant Colonel John Richards,[154] who, with his headquarters and Zulu Company (commanded, unusually, by Captain 'Buckey' Sykes, USMC) represented SUNTRAP's infantry element. A flight of three Wessex helicopters from 845 Naval Air Squadron commanded by a Royal Marines pilot, Lieutenant John Holdaway, and a flight of two Sioux from the Brigade Air Squadron, commanded by Lieutenant Richard Hawkins, RM,[155] supplied the air lift. Offering armoured support was a troop of Life Guards with four Saladins and four Ferrets commanded by Captain Seymour Gilbart-Denham[156] while 8 (Alma) Battery of three 105-mm pack howitzers, commanded by Captain John Perry, RA, provided artillery support. An SBS team under Lieutenant Vic Courtice, RM, was also embarked.

The night of 7–8 January was spent ammunitioning ship before *Fearless* was ready to sail for Gibraltar, which she did on 15 January. She hoped for a fast passage for the use of the Sardinian

Training Area, inland from Capo Teulada in the far south, had been unexpectedly brought forward by the Italians. However, the ship's log records[157] that when she slipped at 0918 the barometer was already at 978 – and 'falling' and with the wind logged at SW Force 5 clearly a full gale was on its way. By teatime speed had been reduced to five knots. The log further records that: 'During the afternoon two injuries sustained in the tank deck. Speed further reduced to one and a half knots while loose palletized stores re-secured.'

This first twenty-four hours sorted out the sailors from the landlubbers although it is fair to say that most places at dinner throughout the ship that night were dressed in military – as opposed to naval – uniforms! Mark Kerr was to report[158] that the Force 8 and associated sea conditions had forced *Fearless* to heave-to but that with gradually improving weather conditions the next morning he was able to work, in steps, up to 20 knots in order to try and make the planned arrival time at Gibraltar. In fact, the lost day could not be recovered. Colonel John Richards's view was similar:[159] 'For the first two and half days the ship experienced the worst weather of her present commission and it was not only the embarked force that suffered. At least, most of our stores, vehicles and aircraft were secure and seaworthy even if we weren't. '

The run ashore in Gibraltar on 18 January was just that! Few sailors touched land but the majority of the Embarked Force ran to the top of the Rock, celebrated their safe return with a beer and were back on board well before the ship sailed at 2100 – but everyone had qualified for Living Overseas Allowance. On sailing, the ship had acquired a civilian film crew and eleven ranks from the 2nd Battalion Royal Anglian Regiment; one of two battalions from Gibraltar's resident military force.

The Cape Teulada training area is well known to 'southern flank warriors' and allows for amphibious landings, air assaults and tracked manoeuvre inland: it is usually blessed with dry and calm weather. However this did not prevent the Sardinian recce party suggesting that it would be wise of the embarked force to waterproof its vehicles – a tedious and dirty business in those days – which in the end was proved to be unnecessary as few vehicles had a wade in more than two feet: the drivers reckoned that the Recce Team – and the Colonel who gave the order – owed them a drink, which they never enjoyed.

The SBS were inserted by Gemini inflatable raiding craft after dark on D-1 to check the beaches and then act as part of the enemy; a night helicopter landing of a rifle troop followed – before night vision goggles – to secure the beach perimeter in order for a first light, beach assault by the remainder of Zulu Company who arrived simultaneously with the guns, under-slung from the Wessex. Support troops and vehicles landed by LCM and then, with the beach secure and an arms-length established against counter-attack, the armoured cars secured a line of observation 5,000 yards inland. Two swift Zulu Company attacks followed using helicopters and supported by the armour. It was typical of an amphibious raid to achieve a limited purpose and this time even the Royal Marine with his rifle considered it as successful as did the headquarters staff.

The exercise highlighted – not for the last time – the lack of what in the Helicopter Carriers was known as the Assault Supply Organization which did precisely what its title implied: it was the onboard team – a permanent part of the ship's company – that brought forward from magazines and stores, all the combat supplies as and when needed, then arranged for their timely passage ashore. In the assault ships this team had to be supplied by the embarked force who, naturally had no spare men for the task and who, anyway, were not familiar with the internal layout, 'assault routes' and, of more importance, the ship's personalities involved. It was a problem that was never solved and Colonel Richards highlighted it thus:[160]

As you know there is no Assault Supply Organization as such in the LPD and with all the ship to shore administrative traffic anticipated we wondered just what sort of problems would arise without one. In the event it worked remarkably well, mainly I think because of the (Quartermaster's) LPH experience. I think we were right to try and solve the problem without setting up a pre-determined organization. Had we provided, say, an officer and 10, I'm sure they would have all earned their pay. In the event one of our NCOs and two Marines proved to be almost, but not quite, sufficient.

As this was the first Royal Marines Battle Group to be embarked in an assault configuration in an assault ship, John Richards' views were awaited back in Plymouth. He concluded his first report with facts that will still sound familiar to embarked forces, throughout the fleet and down the years:

We have all settled in well on board and accept the inevitable business of having to provide working parties when we want to train. Having ammunition stowed on the tank deck is a nuisance as it adds to the already large watch-keeping bill. The wardroom is a happy one and this of course makes a big difference in overcoming any differences of opinion. I do my best not to become involved in day to day administrative problems but with no Second in Command to deal with the Commander and with an Adjutant very much junior to all Heads of Department the normal LPH way of dealing with things is not possible. I am, of course, very fortunate in having a very experienced, charming and joint-minded Captain to deal with.

Then it was back to Gibraltar where the older and more adventurous naval and marine hands would have agreed with the Colonel's words:

I'm afraid Gibraltar has not much to recommend it these days, particularly in winter when there is no swimming. There is a tense political situation and travel across the border is not ... allowed.... It has little to offer as far as the marine is concerned beyond the main street shops and bars.... On Friday we sail for Taranto. John Perry, the Battery Commander, is busy planning to fire his guns from the flight deck and Seymour Gilbert-Denham is going to attempt another first by replacing a Saladin's main gear box whilst we are at sea....

During this brief stay much of the embarked force officers' time was spent planning for an amphibious assault against Gibraltar's defence, Exercise ROCK APE, to take place and, purposefully, to fail, during the ship's passage home towards the end of March. Colonel Richards was not keen on the idea:

Briefly ... the Embarked Force will attempt to capture the Rock! Everyone from the Governor down apologized profusely for involving us in a totally unrealistic venture but the aim is to test some of the defences and naturally we are happy to provide this service, even if it does stretch our imagination somewhat. The only point I made was that, as a Royal Marine he couldn't really expect me to enjoy failing to take the Rock, of all places. Still, if it convinces the Spaniards that an amphibious attack is not on, then we will have done our duty I suppose.

On passage between Mediterranean ports Colonel Richards was obliged to highlight additional problems that would need facing in the future, although they were never to be satisfactorily resolved as most future commanding officers would discover.

Training on board ... was difficult in spite of excellent weather. The Flight Deck was in almost continuous use by the helicopters and the ship went to action stations and held damage control exercises which mean the troops being confined to their mess decks. The Flight Deck, originally intended as a space for embarked force vehicles and training, and the occasional visiting helicopter, is now regarded as being almost for the exclusive use of the air department. It's only available to us if they don't want it. This is inevitable, I suppose, if the LPD is being used as a mini LPH under existing LPH rules. I do

Deck hockey or 'This is no time to be praying'. (Wardroom Line Book caption.)

wish, however, that our helicopters, like our other vehicles, were under command in these circumstances so I could then allocate priorities! . . . Our periods afloat are not going to be very long in fact so I am not too concerned; however if we were to remain embarked for protracted periods then the problem could be more acute than in the LPH.

45 Commando re-embarked for what many regarded as the highlight of the deployment – a two and a half week self maintenance period in Malta: an island that, thankfully, had yet to be taken over by the package holiday business and which was still welcoming to ships of Her Majesty's Navy. The bars and brothels of the 'Gut' beckoned before a *carozzi* ride back to the jetty (providing there were not too many dead *carozzi* horses in the way – a fabled excuse for being late back on board) and a final *dhyisah* journey across Grand Harbour. On this visit neither the ship's Captain nor the Commando's Colonel recorded any serious problems which either meant that 'Jack' and 'Royal' were becoming less adventurous or that the 'Gut' was becoming tame.

Exercise SUNTRAP, Wessex and Sioux.

On 3 March *Fearless* berthed in Grand Harbour, shortly after which the Commando and its supporting arms disembarked to live with, among others, the 3rd Battalion Parachute Regiment while a large number of Exercise SUNTRAP's families took advantage of RAF indulgence flights to take up

temporary residence. Tropical routine was established with the afternoons and evenings free for anyone not on duty. Football, Malta's national pastime, was popular but the Parachute Regiment was able to call on the services of Sir Stanley Matthews which some might have considered cheating, yet in practice, all sporting events confirmed and sealed already good relations between the ship, resident units and Maltese.

This gentle maintenance period was brought to a sudden halt thanks, once more, to Mr Harold Wilson's love of naval life when a signal was received from C-in-C Western Fleet[161] during the evening of 13 March indicating the 'possible operational requirement' for HMS *Fearless* to sail on the 15th, but 'no action is yet to be taken'. This was followed the next evening by a signal from MOD(Navy)[162] giving the broad outline of the operation – for the Commanding Officer's eyes only – and ordering the ship to sail. Throughout the evening of 14 March and the very early morning of the 15th, the recall system, so often practised at home, swung into action with many a rap on front doors followed by a brief, sleepily-received and thoroughly unwelcome, statement.

By 1500 on 15 March all men and vehicles had been re-embarked, machinery quickly re-assembled, stream raised and mooring lines slipped. Although Mark Kerr had, during the forenoon, briefed his ship's company that they would be sailing early – that day in fact – he made no hint at their ultimate destination although the Maltese papers and the BBC left few in doubt that it was to be West Africa. Even so, it was not until late on 17 March – the day before he brought *Fearless* into Gibraltar – that he could confirm that the ship's destination was Lagos and that her role was 'to be flag waving in support of the Prime Minster'.

The Maltese supply organization had worked magnificently by providing, at no notice on a Saturday morning, three months of frozen stores as the ship had been running down prior to her return home. A signal was sent ahead to Gibraltar demanding, from experience, the necessary 'conference stores' plus additional tropical clothing.

For the second time in this commission, politically-generated groans could be heard through the mess-decks but, as always with a good ship's company Mark Kerr could write with conviction in his Report of Proceedings: 'Despite the disappointment and the domestic implications of the changes to leave dates, (everyone) rose to this new demand and morale remained high.'

Morale might well have remained high but that did not prevent a *Daily Express* headline which ran, 'Navy Rescues Bridegrooms' followed by the news that fifty-seven prospective grooms[163] had to be flown home from Gibraltar thanks to 'Mr Wilson's mission to Nigeria'. The newspaper ended with the comment: 'One can foresee questions in the Commons on the cost to the British taxpayer.'

It was hoped that those questions would be asked of the Wilson government and not the Royal Navy. Media speculation roared again over *Fearless*'s employment: the *Sunday Times* declared a 'Mystery Mission for *Fearless*' while the *Observer* had her sailing to 'The rebel Island of Anguilla' in the West Indies, although the paper failed to comment why, then, was it necessary to unload the embarked military force.

Fearless arrived in Gibraltar at 0700 on 18 March, unloaded the majority of the Battle Group, stored ship and sailed for Operation ESTIMATE at 1519 taking with her, rather inconveniently, all the embarked force vehicles, armoured cars and guns.[164] The cynical might, with reason, make two comments: firstly, NATO commitments took a lower priority than Harold Wilson's whims and secondly, until the ship's return, three front-line units – 45 Commando, the Life Guards and the Royal Artillery – would be curtailed in their operational capabilities. In its leading editorial of 18 March the *Daily Telegraph* summed up the feeling of people of most political persuasions when it declared:

> Fearless, *with a great song and dance, was sent to the Mediterranean as a contribution to NATO's strength there in view of Russia's recent activities, and as evidence of Britain's new 'Europe-*

mindedness'. Two days before she was to start operating she is taken away post-haste and sent to provide bogus drama for yet another of Britain's apparently never-ending post-colonial involvements.

Nigeria was in the throes of a civil war and had been since 1967 after the Federal Government under General Gowon refused to grant the Ibo leaders the autonomy they demanded. The direct result of this act led to the Ibos declaring the independent state of Biafra whose forces then seized the Mid West and even threatened the capital, Lagos, itself using arms from France, Portugal and South Africa. Russia and Britain were, similarly and controversially, supplying the federal troops. Adding to the tensions was the diplomatic recognition of Biafra by Gabon, Ivory Coast, Tanzania and Zambia. The Organization of African Unity (OAU) had tried to end the war while famine of an almost unprecedented scale swept across Biafra. Mr Wilson who believed that his intervention could bring peace to this potentially oil-rich member of the Commonwealth was quoted as saying:

> *That his (the British Prime Minister's) purpose in coming (to Nigeria) was not to seek to interfere in matters which can only be settled by Nigerians but that it was rather by discussion, examination and analysis of the facts to do what was possible within the limitations of being a non-Nigerian to mitigate the sufferings of Nigeria.*

During the passage down the west African coast there was plenty of time for the ship's various musical groups to indulge in some fun-poking at their current predicament. A popular shanty went like this:[165]

> *Our Father is a British Captain.*
> *Served for thirty years or so*
> *So I asked him if he'd tell us*
> *Were the Hell we're going to go.*
>
> *Oh, No Jack, No Jack, No!*
>
> *It's been hinted in the papers*
> *Harold Wilson wants to stay*
> *Is it this, or is it capers*
> *Up and Down Anguilla Bay*
>
> *CHORUS*
>
> *Have you got the slightest notion?*
> *Hasn't anybody guessed?*
> *Shallow Bay or Deepest Ocean?*
> *North? Or South? Or East? Or West?*
>
> *CHORUS*
>
> *Captain, Sir, the future's cheerless*
> *It's to Hell we'll all be bound!*
> *One last thing Sir – Will the Fearless*
> *Evermore see Plymouth Sound?*
>
> *CHORUS*

The *Fearless* Calypso offered a different slant and suggested that she had had to be the obvious choice as *Number Ten* was already painted on her side.

> *Well I'm sad to say*
> *Fearless is sailing away*

Won't be back for many a day.
Instead of Northward bound
We are turning around
Gotta meet Harold Wilson
In Lagos town.

Oggie, Oggie, Oggie.
We'll never get home
Oggie, Oggie, Oggie.
On the sea's we will roam.
The Government says we should never drip
But please Haslemere get me offa this ship.
Oh, Harold Wilson
It has been heard to say
Is putting in
For separation pay
Three times in two years
On ships of the Line
So now he's shouting
Roll on my time.

CHORUS

Oh, Splicers for 'G! members'
Limers for 'UAs'
That's all we get from Wilson's stays
They're using this ship like Wilson's Den,
Even on the side is painted Number Ten.

CHORUS

From a Dhyisah man
We got the buzz
That we weren't sailing
Back to Guzz
Confirmed by the BBC Radio Man
We're being used for Conference talks again.

CHORUS

This time the Prime Minister elected to stay with the British High Commissioner but was allocated the Commodore's suite should he feel the need. About eighteen members of the delegation were, though, accommodated on board, causing far less disruption than previously – and that only to the wardroom officers. There was considerable relief, openly expressed, that neither Kaufman (who remained ashore – apart from attending the Prime Minister's private dinner in the Commodore's Dining Cabin on 30 March) nor Williams (who was not in the delegation) were included in this figure: more entertaining and fun visitors were four secretaries[166] – Garden Room girls – plus Cabinet members, FCO officials and various communicators, among whom were three more ladies. One notable visitor of standing was:

> Leonard Cheshire.[167] *There entirely unofficially in theory, but in fact he came clean and told us that he was asked to exploit the situation from both sides ... what was true and what were lies....*[168]

One of the main excuses for using *Fearless* was her secure communications fit but this very nearly backfired as Captain Michael Walker,[169] the Officer Commanding 621 Signal Troop remembers:

> *As we approached Lagos we lost all HF communications with the UK and tried to call via Malta and Cyprus, eventually raising a CW (Morse) path through Mauritius to the UK but this did not meet the expectations of the Cabinet Office whose only precedence for a message was FLASH. We established an HF path over the Sahara Desert into Gibraltar and then into a landline circuit back to the UK. We were not involved in the meetings but there was a real urgency to send a vehicle to the airport to pick up daily newspapers from the UK for the delegates so they could see the impact of the visit in the media back home.*

Before arrival at Lagos every member of the ship's company was required to have a fresh TAB inoculation, including the eldest who might, after a lifetime of boosters, have been excused. As the Commanding Officer, the Commander and the Commander (E) were the only members of the ship's company to suffer splitting headaches and violent shivering, the Surgeon Commander considered the success rate to have been pretty good. However, when Mark Kerr challenged this medical view the doctor, pleased with the results, replied, 'After all, there were only three such cases'. Mark Kerr's reasonable retort was, 'Then they were the wrong three'.

There were one or two seamanship problems that needed to be addressed in advance for it was not absolutely certain that *Fearless* would fit in Lagos harbour which had, officially, been dredged to 28 feet whereas, in the ballasted condition to float out the LCMs, she drew 32 feet aft. In the event she did squeeze in by mooring between two buoys – in order to stop her swinging into even shallower water – during the late afternoon of 26 March.

Although the talks were held on land Mr Wilson returned to the ship each evening at any time between 1900 and 2200, on board the Captain's 'barge', a Fairy Huntress speed boat, to return ashore at about midnight.

The Prime Minister's hands-on intervention did not reach its planned conclusion and the ship was released from her duties on 31 March. Biafra capitulated in 1970 although that was not to be the end of the famine and suffering of the Ibos: the United Kingdom continued to supply arms to the Federal troops.

To return to the saga of 'The Photographs' which Desmond Wettern again raised in the *Daily Telegraph* by reporting that the loss – 'which was bound to be discovered by the Prime Minister himself when he came aboard at Lagos' – was now the subject of an internal Ministry of Defence enquiry 'but the findings were not likely to be made public'. The matter was even discussed, briefly, in the House of Commons, when a Conservative member[170] expressed his disgust that, 'If the Royal Navy are going about throwing the Prime Minister's picture into the ocean the public ought to know about this affront to the Queen's First Minister'. Michael Walker was involved:

> *On a quiet Saturday afternoon at sea a message came in from MOD Navy demanding a response to yet another story about the 'missing photographs'. As Duty Signal Officer I took the signal up to the Captain who was a perfect gentleman and much respected as our Commanding Officer for his attention to detail and sense of correctness but with a sense of humour. He took a message pad and in answer to the question on the disappearance of the Prime Minister wrote that we had merely opened the frame to clean the photograph and it had 'flown to heaven'. I realized that I had been present at a moment when one of those famous naval signals had been drafted. He overcame my mild protestation with the words 'Make that'.*

The Captain sent a second signal which said, simply, but enigmatically:

> *All pictures presented are still secure.*

Signal from the MOD.

The delayed journey home was uneventful but enlivened by the ship's first Arts and Crafts Exhibition run by the Commander (E), Colin Robinson:

> *Easter Sunday. I got stuck into running (the Exhibition) for four hours in the Dining Hall assisted by volunteers including the Chief ERA, Chief Shipwright, Chief Bosun's Mate and the Sergeant Major. It was a terrific success (as) we had over 50 entries, largely paintings and drawings but a good sprinkling of models and craftwork. We estimated that over 4/5ths of the ship's company attended. We displayed the pictures on hardboard sheets hung from pipes and fan trunkings ... and for almost the whole time there were never less than fifty people looking.... . Five prizes were awarded by a heavily-primed Mark Kerr: one of my watchkeepers, for a very good seascape in oils, the Sergeant Major for oils and charcoal drawings, a Corporal for matchstick work-boxes and a Stoker for a model of* Fearless, *2'6" long made from 11,000 matchsticks!*

The passage north was notable for another reason: it was to end in the farewell to the Commanding Officer as recorded by Colin Robinson:

> *As we neared home the wardroom dined out Mark Kerr and presented him with a set of four, silver, dolphin candlesticks that we had bought in Malta and which were now in a lovely, baize-lined, fitted case made by the 'Chippies'. He was quite overcome and made a speech from the heart stressing the importance of amphibious expertise, drawing on the Royal Navy's great history in that respect; pointing out how easily such skills could be lost and imploring those of us who had learnt so much from* Fearless *to do our utmost to keep it alive.*

For reasons which seem to have drifted into history Captain Mark Kerr took his departure from *Fearless* standing in the bucket of one of the Michigan bulldozers. Although a cliché, it was, indeed, the end of an era. The ship had been built, accepted into Naval service, bloodied in action – a small action admittedly – boosted NATO's southern flank and twice deployed as a diplomatic tool on the international stage.

What neither Hugh Corbett nor Mark Kerr had said was that this period in *Fearless*'s life, commanded in turn by them was by far the most important. *Fearless* was not only 'first of class' but, to coin a phrase was, to the Royal Navy, 'first of concept' and if these two commanding officers and their ship's companies were to have 'got it wrong' then the repercussions might have reverberated down the years. They got it right and laid the benchmarks for the subsequent (nearly) four decades. Nevertheless, the next years were not to be plain sailing for such a flexible ship with a 'can-do' attitude.

In short, *Fearless* had quickly come of age through hard-won experience: she would be put to task again and again in the growing knowledge that there really was not much that she could not do.

Chapter Five

Captain J.R.S. Gerard-Pearse, Royal Navy

Third Commanding Officer
1969–1970
Later, Rear Admiral, CB

Home Waters, South Africa, Far East, Persian Gulf

Fearless's third Commanding Officer, Captain Roger Gerard-Pearse, had already commanded three ships before – HMSs *Tumult*, *Grafton* and *Defender* – and would then command HMS *Ark Royal* and finish his naval career in 1979 as Assistant Chief of Naval Staff (Operations). Roger Gerard-Pearse writes:

A few memories of Fearless. *I took command on 17 April 1969 when she returned to Devonport on completion of the talks that Mr Harold Wilson had had in Lagos.*

The Commodore's dining room carpet was badly stained with red wine and my Chinese Leading Steward was horrified that Harold Wilson had toasted the Queen's health in red wine and not port and had spilt most of that on the carpet!

Our commission was the last of the old general service commissions when we all remained for 2–2½ years. By the time we returned to Devonport after about 17 months in the Far East we certainly had one lad who had joined as a boy and had passed his exams for Leading Seaman before we paid off. We had no trickle drafting.

She was the first air-conditioned ship for most of us and in spite of cleaning the filters very

Captain Roger Gerard-Pearse.

thoroughly a 'flu virus went round the whole ship's company on our passage from Devonport via Cape Town to Singapore and we were unable to take part in the inter-service sports meeting the day after we arrived in Singapore.

We had a rendezvous with Intrepid *in the Indian Ocean when we gave her our Home Fleet Orders and she gave us her Far East Orders. She also sent over a soaking photograph of Harold Wilson which they said they had picked up out of the sea!*

We took the Mayor of Cape Town – a delightful man who had been a Dockyard Matey in Chatham Dockyard – from Cape Town to Simonstown where we showed off our amphibious capabilities to the South African Navy.

We had embarked for trials an amphibious, 3 ton lorry and a hovercraft and, after a visit to Port Dixon in Malaysia, we embarked the Tunku Abdul Rahman from Kuala Lumpur by helicopter. He wanted to ride in the 3 tonner in the Straits of Malacca and there was a degree of consternation on board when the lorry broke down with the Tunku in it.

In Tokyo I went ashore in our hovercraft to a golf match and we broke down in the middle of the harbour, a little later the Gurkha regiment that we exercised with in Brunei were most impressed when we landed by hovercraft for a party at their mess just off the beach!

One of our best visits was with FOF2 FEF embarked[171] to Bangkok and he arranged for me to accompany him on a memorable visit to the two war graves, one on each bank of the River Kwai. They were immaculate with the head stones representing soldiers and sailors from very many Commonwealth and other countries.

We were the only Royal Navy ship in Tokyo for 'British Week' which was opened by Princess Margaret and we provided the Guard of Honour for the opening ceremony. We took four bands to Tokyo, the Queen's Own Highlanders (Seaforths) from the Middle East, an RM and RAF band from Singapore and the Duke of Wellington's band from Hong Kong. (They all embarked in Hong Kong.) So we had music in every corner of the ship! They worked hard and were very popular during British Week. I found out, on our way from Hong Kong to Japan, that all the bands and my ship's company were on different rates of Living Overseas Allowance. Despite vigorous protests to C-in-C Far East Fleet that this was unfair – as we were the lowest rate of LOA – and that we should all be on the same, highest, rate; after nine months of haggling we got nowhere.

In those days LOA was stopped after sailing from the last port before reaching the United Kingdom. Consequently, when Durban was to be our last port on our way home I managed to get a 36 hour stop in Madeira for mail!

As we were having an extended Far East leg, we were allowed to give leave to half the ship's company in the UK and other places over Christmas. This worked splendidly and no one overstayed their leave. For the other half we had two periods of a week in the Cameron Highlands in Malaysia and I flew up with John Neville-Rolfe, my (F), for a couple of nights to see the sailors catching huge butterflies and playing soccer in a cool climate. We had members of the ship's company spread across the United Kingdom, Hong Kong, Japan, New Zealand, Australia and South Africa.

On one occasion we took a Gurkha band to Fremantle for a week to make money for the Gurkha Benevolent Fund. It was a marvellous visit and we were the only ship there.

It was a wonderful commission with an excellent ship's company and we did a large variety of interesting things.

Rather more formally he was to write the following in the Commission Book before he left:

It is never easy for the ship, or indeed the new Commanding Officer, when the Captain joins in the middle of a commission. However for my part I knew that I was fortunate in taking over a happy and efficient ship and it was clearly my main concern to maintain this. Just over twelve months away from home, with some good visits in the Far East, was the planned programme. During the East of Suez leg we have visited or, at the time of writing hope to visit, Cape Town, Singapore, Hong Kong, Borneo, Tokyo, Australia, Bangkok, Penang, Bahrain and Durban. We have of course done some work between visits and sometimes a great deal during visits!

Together with the west of Suez leg this surely satisfies our main reason for joining the Navy? To see the world.

I am sure that you will all remember this commission for a variety of reasons but I suggest that the lasting impressions of baths in Japan, or girls in Fremantle will enable you to spin a very good yarn.

I hope that I will have the chance to meet many of you again and I would like to take this opportunity of wishing you all the best of luck and a good draft chit.

Fearless arrived in Devonport from her Nigerian jaunt on 10 April and there she was to stay for seven weeks before beginning a seventeen month Far East deployment on 4 June 1969. Eight days later she 'crossed the line' without having put into Gibraltar to qualify for the elusive Living Overseas Allowance and berthed at Cape Town on 19 June. Despite warnings of local opposition to visits that both previous Commanding Officers had received from a nervous Foreign Office, the receptions, both socially and in the media, were almost overwhelming while, yet again, it was made clear, ashore, that any adverse comments were directed towards Her Majesty's Government and not Her Majesty's Ships.

Unfortunately, as far as LOA was concerned, Cape Town was not a British port and so it was to the Farquhar Islands, south of the Seychelles, that the ship now headed, and off which she anchored – at Mirs Point – on 30 June. Few on board knew anything of these islands – the *Station Guide Book* suggesting only that they were coral atolls inhabited by about 250 people and produced coconuts – other than that they were part of the British Indian Ocean Territories and that was good enough for the allowance to begin; if a run ashore could be achieved.

To meet the 'rules', a landing had to be effected and so a flotilla of one dory and two Gemini inflatable raiding craft set off across the ocean swell to search for a break in the reef. This tiny amphibious reconnaissance party consisted of one Royal Marines Colour Sergeant (coxswain of the dory) and two Corporals (coxswains of the two Geminii) with the Commander (E), the dentist and a sick bay 'Tiffy' as passengers. While beaching, the dory, with the Commander, was swamped but both Geminii remained dry – much to the amusement of the junior hands. This motley crew was immediately met with a request for dental checks – quickly rescinded – and beer, which they had, fortuitously, brought with them. In return, coconuts were offered as well as a pair of cowrie shells for the Commanding Officer. The shore party then re-embarked – the Commander in a Gemini this time – and thus the regulations for LOA had been met, although swimming and coconut collecting parties were landed later, just to make sure.

Far East beach work. Laying Class 30 trackway.

Gan was the next port of call for fuel before *Fearless* could begin the last leg to Singapore which she reached on 10 July only to be told by the port health authorities that as so many of her ship's company were suffering from a form of 'lurgi' picked up in the Mozambique Channel she would not be able to take part in any sporting or military programmes. The most significant of these restrictions was a ban on entering the Inter-Services Sports Meeting the day after her arrival; thus denying her the opportunity to stamp her mark until rather later.

It was also a militarily awkward start to her second Far East tour as a waiting Army force was prevented from embarking. However, once out of quarantine, she carried out exercises in the South China Sea, Malaysia and Brunei over the next six weeks or so, interspersed with welcome two- or three-day respites at Singapore Naval Base where, no doubt, the Tanglin Club, Pebble Bar, Gino's a Go Go and every 'establishment' in Bugis Street were well frequented, depending, possibly, but not exclusively, on rank.

One exercise, JULEX 69, (with 42 Commando, Royal Marines embarked), included more than twenty ships from Australia, Malaysia and New Zealand but this was to be one of the last 'imperial gasps' before the United Kingdom's withdrawal from 'east of Suez'. The *Sun* newspaper of 5 September 1969, commented with the headline 'Why sailors don't see the world . . . ' adding that *Fearless* was the only major British warship 'now overseas'. The paper went on to explain that only about fifty of the Navy's 200 ships and submarines were away from home and that fewer than 10,000 personnel were serving at sea outside home waters.[172]

Despite this impending withdrawal of British forces from the Far East – with the implication that we did not want to stay, nor were wanted – *Fearless* was invited to move to Man o' War Anchorage off Singapore town itself for the 150th anniversary of the founding of Singapore by Sir Stamford Raffles. Here she was in full view, and floodlit at night, from 8 to 12 August while visitors, from the most senior invited officials to the thousands of curious sightseers, were ferried

Floodlit.

SRN 6 docking.

'to and fro' by landing craft. The embarked SRN 6 hovercraft docked and undocked across the stern gate for seemingly, non-stop demonstrations of dry landings.

Exercise HAPPY HUNTING was conducted off Seria, Brunei, between 16 and 22 August with the 2 Battalion Gurkha Rifles. Michael Walker remembers it well for one specific reason:

> *In Singapore we were about to embark up to 1,000 Gurkhas in overload, austere accommodation to take part in an exercise when Commander (S) asked about their diet and the question of curry. 'A good idea,' says I having served with the Gurkhas. So a 4-ton truckload of curry and rice was loaded and off we sailed to Brunei to pick up the 2nd Battalion Gurkha Rifles.*
>
> *The first words the Commanding Officer said on embarking were 'I have ordered the men to eat the British rations on board'. The Commander (S) looked daggers at me but the ship's company enjoyed real curry prepared under the guidance of the Gurkha cooks while the Gurkhas ate the British rations with equal relish. A classic example of how life on board worked well and made for a happy and purposeful ship's company.*

On 1 September the ship was in Singapore for a short period of Assisted Maintenance in preparation for Hong Kong and the Tokyo British Week. 42 Commando's unarmed combat team was embarked – a brave move, perhaps, when intending to give displays in the heartland of judo – as were sporting teams and single-decker buses (a number of London double-deckers having been shipped in by more conventional methods earlier) and two military bands to join those already 'in theatre'.

There can be no doubt that this week in Tokyo and, crucially, HMS *Fearless*'s part in it, was a huge, almost unparalleled, success best summed up by Commodore T.W. Stocker, Commodore Amphibious Forces, in his Report of Proceedings[173] to the Commander Far East Fleet. The following brief extracts are relevant to HMS *Fearless*.

Her Royal Highness, Princess Margaret, formally opened British Week on Friday 26 September at a ceremony in the National Theatre attended by many prominent Japanese, including Her Imperial Highness Princess Chichibu, as well as British personalities. . . . The dress circle was a mass of white uniforms provided by officers and ratings from Fearless and Stromness. The Royal Marines Orchestra played superbly for half an hour before the Royal Party's arrival and set the tone for performances by all the British Bands.

In fact, Princess Margaret admitted to being rather nervous until, 'She looked up and saw a sea of familiar British naval uniforms'.

The Commanding Officer, HMS Fearless, and I attended the first day (of the Highland Games) as the Royal Marines Bands and Queen's Own Highlanders (pipers) were performing. Prince William, a Second Secretary at the Embassy, formally opened the Games. The venue, in an obscure suburb of Tokyo, was difficult to find so, having reached the general area, I persuaded Captain Gerard-Pearse to demonstrate the highland fling to a local. This he did with such success that the Japanese face, after a moment's astonishment, lit up with understanding and we were successfully directed to the right place. . . . The 'Games' consisted of half a dozen Scottish dancers demonstrating their skills and a similar number of tough Highlanders who tossed cabers, put shot and threw hammers with gay abandon around the small dusty arena – in fact with such abandon that the caber landed in the midst of the marching Queen's Own Highlanders Band. Quick reaction by the two rear ranks saved what could have been a serious accident.

The five bands – Fleet Commander's, 3rd Commando Brigade, Queen's Own Highlanders, Duke of Wellington's and Far East Air Force – were given a very full programme . . . One major snag arose over victualling as the Japanese idea of a meal – consisting of raw fish, bean curd and a small cup of tea – is not enough to stoke a fully operational British bandsman. Frequent protests to the British Week Office achieved little improvement so Fearless did her best by producing bag lunches and by serving numerous meals at odd hours.

Inevitably in the middle of such events there are tiny moments of political or diplomatic concern which are more often in the eye of the functionary than the people who matter. The ship's company had seen this during their visits to South Africa and now, even more surprisingly, during British Week in Tokyo.

Publicity for our visit was initially very poor. Only 1,200 visitors boarded Fearless on the first day she was open to the public as no announcement had been made of this. The British Embassy was clearly playing down publicity for two reasons: they did not want to take any limelight from British Week before it was formally opened and the Ambassador was evidently concerned about a warship's presence stirring up student pacifism to the detriment of British Week. At the opening ceremony, the Duke of Wellington's Band was told by a junior Embassy official to 'lose itself out of sight'. Rightly the Bandmaster disregarded him.

My view was that they could not have it both ways bearing in mind our contribution to the Week, and I considered protesting to the Ambassador. However, in the event, I authorized Captain Heathcote RM (the Public Relations Officer) to deal direct with the local press if the Embassy still proved adamant. Fortunately they did not and things improved.

Over 5,000 visited Fearless the second day she was open and, in any case, by this time the buzz had got round that the Navy was not only here but that they had brought all these magnificent bands. . . . Princess Margaret's gesture in inviting Captain Gerard-Pearse, my wife and myself to lunch at the Embassy was specifically to thank us for the part the Services were playing.

Thank goodness a naval officer has a more mature, if not detailed, understanding of international relationships than does a Foreign Office Third Secretary, thus proving, not for the first and almost certainly not for the last, time that Lord Palmerston's words, uttered in the nineteenth century, were still apposite, 'If I want a thing done well in a distant part of the world I always send a Captain of the Royal Navy' – and he had been Foreign Secretary himself for a total of sixteen years.

It wasn't just the diplomats trying to spoil the British armed forces' involvement, mother nature also considered intervening but, clearly not wishing to meddle with such a defiant ship, thought better of it:

> *Typhoon* Elsie *caused some concern: had it curved towards Tokyo we would probably have had to shift berth into Tokyo Bay with considerable disruption to the programme. Fortunately it went elsewhere ... but tropical storm* Flossie *caused some dirty weather and an exciting solids RAS with* Stromness *on 7 October.*
>
> *British Week was officially declared closed by the Lord Mayor of London, Sir Charles Trinder ... on Sunday 5 October when, during the preliminary speeches, praise for the bands was particularly enthusiastic. Which was just as well for the massed bands of COMFEF and FEAF presented an impressive closing fanfare which then broke into* Auld Lang Syne. *This was, apparently, the signal for everybody to descend on the Lord Nelson[174] where there was open house and a delightfully informal party, and when supplies were exhausted there, many went on to a reception for participants in British Week at the Akasaka Prince Hotel. At both these parties bandsmen and other servicemen of all ranks mingled freely with the Ambassador, Lord Mayor, and both Japanese and British businessmen so that the week ended in an atmosphere of much bonhomie.*
>
> *Everyone had been struck by the interest, friendliness and goodwill shown by the Japanese at all levels for they had seemed genuinely to regard the British as their longest-standing and closest friends in the Western world or, for that matter, anywhere else and constantly reminded their British visitors of past ties and, in doing so, regretted the United Kingdom's departure from the Far East as much as anybody.*

Hong Kong was revisited so the crew could wind-down – ? – in the China Fleet Club and the less regulated bars of Wanchai before Exercise SEA HORSE off the New Territories preceded preparation for yet another social extravaganza: Fremantle in Australia.

Fremantle had long been anticipated as a deployment highlight and the Australians did not disappoint. Neither did *Fearless* disappoint her hosts for she also had the Pipes and Drums of the 10th Princess Mary's Own Gurkha Rifles and the Gurkha Engineers embarked. Sailing on 10 November 1969 from Singapore, the Navigating Officer had allowed a week for the journey to Fremantle's Victoria Quay during which time the Gurkha pipers tuned their drones and 'grace' notes and the 'Pommies' practised their 'Strine'.

Hospitality was in the finest Australian tradition including private excursions into the outback while, in return, the band played on. Major Jimmy Nobbs,[175] second in command of the Gurkha Engineers based at Kluang in Johore wrote:[176]

> *We had four major engagements for the ten day visit and a number of minor ones, including a performance for the local television station. Beating Retreat on the evening we arrived at Fremantle was the most spectacular. The wardroom had a cocktail party on the fore-deck and we assembled the band, unknown to the guests, in a warehouse adjacent to her berth. At the appropriate time everyone was asked to move to the flight deck and when all were there the ship was suddenly darkened and the band struck up.* Fearless *used her searchlights to light the area.*

The ship, though, was due its own entertainment on the return journey as Jimmy Nobbs explained:

We had brought with us seven junior soldiers who had trained as dancers – or Marunis in Gurkhali. With the Commander (S)'s help we cleared the wardroom's dining room and assembled the Marunis there unknown to the ship's officers. Marunis are dressed as young women in typical Nepalese finery. Then, at the right moment, I opened the curtains that divide the dining room from the ante-room, the lights came on and there, sitting on the deck was this young 'woman' who rose to her feet and performed one of the Nepalese ceremonial dances. The overall performance, including other dancers, lasted about 35 minutes. The Commander – Arthur Checksfield[177] – had asked the Captain down to watch it.

The following day I was asked by the Captain if we could put on a repeat performance for the ship's company. I was about to offer anyway – providing the ship did not 'blow soot' which would have ruined the dancers clothes and that we reduced speed and sailed a course that would damp any rolling. Some of the movements are intricate and need a very careful balance.

Gurkha dancers.

The ship's company appreciated our efforts whole-heartedly and after it was all over I was asked to the CPOs' Mess for a drink – and did not feel too bright the following day.

1970 brought much of the same as far as exercises and 'showing off' were concerned but with the added attractions of Bangkok, the Persian Gulf and Devonport. A Combined Services Sports Meeting was held in Singapore between 5 and 15 January with the ship fielding her Army and Royal Marine members without adverse comment from those ashore.

The five-day visit to Thailand's capital between the 18 and 23 February was in company with HMSs *Andromeda* and *Whitby* and the RFA *Tarbatness* carrying a Naval Sales Mobile Exhibition. *Fearless,* with FOF 2 FEF embarked, was moored some miles from Bangkok at New Port but, according to a number of 'non-attributable accounts', this made little difference to the amusements experienced by the majority of the Ships' Companies. Bangkok has, of course, considerably more to offer than stunningly attractive girls so it is pleasant to hear that the Royal Barges and temples were also given the full tourist treatment. Then it was back to Singapore before the end of the month to load 42 Commando for a rendezvous with the newly arrived HMS *Bulwark*.

Exercise FLYING FISH, held off the coast of Malaysia, was conducted in appalling weather at the end of which, Captain Ian Lamb,[178] the new OCAD, Beachmaster and experienced Landing Craft Officer, was ordered to conduct a night, tactical withdrawal on a falling tide with un-waterproofed vehicles. The Beachmaster had attended the Brigade briefing in the BARV – which had caused some excitement as it crashed through the jungle towards the 'O' Group where, against his advice, this re-embarkation was ordered.

Result – lines of Gurkhas up to their necks in water wading out to the sand bar in the middle of the night and chasing LCAs being bounced further and further down the coast in the pounding surf. Also the Brigade Commander appeared when all was falling about my ears – which was all I wanted – and at some stage threatened me with Court Martial. . . . Fortunately Roger Gerard-Pearse got me out of that. . . .

For the second time *Fearless* bade a sad farewell to Singapore Naval Base and headed west, on Monday 13 April 1970, nearly nine months after her arrival.

There was a particular reason for visiting Bahrain as this was now the headquarters of British Forces Middle East, and an organization anxious to test its own ability at managing amphibious operations. After an uneventful ten day passage, via Dubai for fuel, *Fearless* entered the waters she knew well from Operation MAGISTER, with her crew determined to show that they could operate as successfully off a desert as they could off a jungle. Exercise ENTROLD's aim was to: 'Exercise units of British Forces Gulf[179] and HMS *Fearless* in joint warfare techniques, in a Counter Insurgency setting such as might be expected in the Gulf.'[180]

The 3rd Special Boat Detachment (permanently deployed in the Gulf) was tasked as both enemy and friendly forces depending on the phase of the exercise. The Exercise Director was the Commander Naval Forces Gulf on board *Fearless* while the Joint Task Force Commanders were the ship's Commanding Officer and the CO 4th Battalion Royal Anglian Regiment. Embarked, too, were Wessex helicopters of 78 Squadron RAF who fitted in well with naval flying procedures; mutual praise passing in both directions and highlighted in the exercise 'wash-up' reports. The well-known *Fearless* 'jointery' was more than able to ignore the long-held (but sometimes understandable) animosity that can exist between the two services and, anyway, the Squadron was no stranger to the ship for it was 78 Squadron's aircraft that had been embarked for the raid on Hauf in 1966.[181]

Considering that no detailed planning could take place before *Fearless*'s arrival and that there was no time for rehearsals, then the official view that, as a 'joint exercise, it was an undoubted success' was probably fair but ... if the object of an exercise is to highlight areas of concern then ENTROLD proved useful for the local forces. The list of points that needed attending to was lengthy. *Fearless*'s own part was noteworthy for the lack of lessons that she, herself, needed to learn.

At this remove in time it is presumptuous to comment but such fundamentals as no recent beach surveys – and then only of one beach with no alternative – and no darkening of ships, especially minesweepers landing special forces and sweeping lanes prior to the approach of the landing force, should not have needed re-learning. There was criticism of the medical command structure; casualty reporting procedures; casualty categorization and disposal. One serious 'safeguard' casualty took eleven and a half hours to reach *Fearless* for, rather surprisingly, no medical officer had been appointed to give direction and to coordinate. Over the years these particular aspects were to be streamlined to almost flawless perfection.

One recommendation suggested that 'careful thought should be given to the feasibility of LPDs carrying some Mexeflote sections to enhance the amphibious capability when no LSL is present'.[182]

Fearless played her part by landing and recovering a battalion of troops and so with grateful thanks from HQ BFME for helping to point the way towards the required standards, she was released to continue her journey home via Durban where, once again the British Government was working its gloomy predictions as Roger Gerard-Pearse's Report shows,[183]

The ship's Liaison Officer warned me on arrival that the British Consulate were playing down the visit for fear of political repercussions, arising from the Cricket tour controversy. However, the Press showed an active and friendly interest in the ship from the start, and very favourable newspaper articles appeared each day throughout the visit. In addition, news of the visit was broadcast three times on the SABC and five times on the Natal Regional Service.

There is no doubt from the friendly and hospitable treatment that we received, that the political fears of the British Consulate were unjustified and the excellent first leader in the Daily News, *shows clearly why this was so.*

On Saturday 23 May all Chief Petty Officers onboard were hosts to 180 local people ranging from Airways Office Managers to Hospital staff.[184] *The Reception was undoubtedly a great success from every point of view, and the opportunity to do this was greatly appreciated by my Chief Petty Officers.*

A brief call was made at Cape Town to embark a rating from HMS *Tartar* who needed to be invalided back to the United Kingdom and as always the chance to land and collect mail was welcome, thanks to the Fleet Mail Service's renowned efficiency.

Of importance at this stage in many overseas deployments were the onboard sporting activities and, inevitably, a Ship's Operatic and Dramatic Company production; this latter event even deserving a mention in the Commanding Officer's Report of Proceedings:

An extremely slick SOD's Opera ran for two nights in a very professional looking improvised theatre in the Tank Deck and the show received 'Rave' notices from the Art Critic in the Ship's Newspaper, The Amphibian.

There was, though, one final run ashore. Funchal in Madeira had been chosen as the last chance to buy rabbits and where *Fearless* was fortunate to be given an alongside berth for forty-eight hours thanks to the efforts of the British Consul, Mr P. G. Blandy who, along with a number of Anglophiles on the island, was particularly hospitable. Also alongside was the educational cruise liner SS *Uganda* so visits were swapped and a soccer match arranged between the civilian crew and members of the Amphibious Detachment.

So successful was this visit that Roger Gerard-Pearse recommended that *Fearless* return to Funchal on her next journey south. But she was to pass this way only twice more and then on her way to and from the Falkland Islands; occasions that allowed no time for such pleasures. On the way south she was anxious to get to war and on the way back anxious to get away from it.

The only incident to mar the occasion was an accident to Able Seaman Corlass who, while hoisting the ship's whaler inboard after a fishing trip, fell and suffered a range of breaks and damages. He and a medical escort were immediately flown direct to England thanks, again, to the efficient Mr Blandy.

A rendezvous with a long range Shackleton for a mail-drop was the sign that 'Blighty' was getting near and thus the signal to prepare for the mandatory 'up-channel parties';[185] although for those Special Sea Duty Men who had to anchor the ship in Plymouth Sound at 0545 on Friday, 12 June this might have been a bit early! It was a foggy morning with a Dutch coaster close to *Fearless's* allotted spot but so overawed was she by a 12,000-ton apparition looming out of the fog that she quickly weighed and disappeared into the murk.[186]

Fearless's luck held for even HM Customs Service cleared the ship before the start of working hours – by no means a normal routine for that organization – and by 0830 she was also de-ammunitioned and ballasted down, allowing the LCMs to collect families for the passage up the Hamoaze. The penultimate entry in the Commanding Officer's Report states that:

By 1130 visibility had improved and the families – 700 in total – had a grandstand view of HMS Ark Royal *on her way to sea (before we) berthed alongside Number Six wharf at 1200.*

After lunch the families disembarked and a proportion of the ship's company proceeded on long leave in the knowledge that those returning could look forward to their ship being in dockyard hands – but for how long – for the fitting of Skynet and for a new Commanding Officer. The timings for a planned, brief Docking and Essential Defects remained undecided as Roger Gerard-Pearse's final sentence states: 'Since (the exchange of signals) there have been conflicting statements from the dockyard and it now appears that we are going to have a six months DED.'

Fearless would be in dockyard hands for the last rum issue on Black Friday – 31 July 1970 – a loss that would be mourned by everyone; while nearly everyone also understood the reason for its passing. Warrant Officer Moss Pearson, the next commission's Detachment Sergeant Major, was to comment:

> *The stopping of the tot was a Godsend really as we could then have a gin and tonic or a beer which was far more civilized. Four measures in harbour or two at sea was the ration and it did mean that we could offer a guest something other than rum or beer.*

While *Fearless* struggled with her refit, concerns were already being raised in Whitehall over the future of both LPDs and thus of amphibious warfare itself. Just five years after the introduction of the first LPD – and only three after the commissioning of the second – a Labour Government was expressing doubts about the existence of the Royal Marines and their associated ships. On 8 April 1970 the Commandant General, Royal Marines, General Sir Peter Hellings,[187] had a private meeting with Dr David Owen,[188] the Under Secretary of State (Navy). While many contentious issues were raised by the CG, such as the Government's proposed closure of both Deal and Eastney Barracks, so were future tasks for the Corps allied to the expected loss of the LPDs. In a confidential résumé of the meeting[189] to his Chief of Staff, General Hellings was moved to state, when referring to the closure of the barracks, that: 'I doubt that he (Dr Owen) took much notice and the impression I was left with was that he was firmly determined on his own course irrespective of argument, although perhaps I am wrong.'

The sentiment of the General applied throughout the meeting and especially to the manning of amphibious ships and, thus, the future employment of the Royal Marines:[190]

> *Dr Owen ... is aware ... of the Navy's inability to man the future fleet[191] and that when the manpower economies begin to bite it will affect ... the LPDs and finally the LPHs.... I pressed him for a new construction ship with a crew of perhaps 200 built on RFA lines, civilian designed and built and he seemed to think this was a better approach. He criticized Bath and their very expensive new design LPH of £25m ... he was interested in the LSL design and felt that perhaps we should explore a 'blown up' copy or something on these lines.*
>
> *Finally we came round again to his fear that the Navy ... would not be able to man the amphibious ships ... and it was well worth the Corps bearing this in mind and diversifying their role.*

While Dr Owen was keen to sow the seeds of diversification he showed little understanding that the Royal Marines without ships would be so emasculated as to be pointless and yet, earlier in the meeting, he had discussed the Northern Flank, NATO and snow and mountain warfare training and thus, by implication therefore, the need for specialist shipping. He was also aware of the hostility towards the Royal Marines shown by the Army's GOC Southern Command, Sir Michael Carver, from whom much of this overt 'constructive dismissal' of the Corps was emanating:[192]

> *He (Dr Owen) was keen to know if there was any pressure from the army and expressed the view that as far as politicians were concerned they were very much behind supporting any diversification of the*

Corps' roles. I told him that we usually got good warning of any impending attacks ... and that the stage was reasonably quiet. He asked about Carver and I expressed the view that he seemed less antagonistic at the moment.

Not all enemies of amphibious warfare came from within the ranks of politicians and the Army, as extracts from the Chiefs of Staff Committee Meeting[193] of 10 February 1970 reveal. The need for amphibious forces and ships was subject to intense Parliamentary review. Under the heading *Amphibious Forces in the 1970s* the COS Committee replied to an invitation to comment on a Reinforcement Study that had suggested the reduction of the United Kingdom's NATO commitment:

Para 6. The contrary view is ... that a NATO commitment (should not) be used for justifying such a decision and that a military case for continuing the amphibious forces throughout the 1970s in view of our new-style European policy, has still to be made.... .

Para 16. The Navy naturally support the paper, The Army will agree.... .

Doubts continued and were not alleviated by, apparently benign, comments in Parliament:[194]

PQ 8431A

Mr Patrick Wall (Conservative. Heltemprice):[195] *To ask the Minister of State for Defence if he will make a statement about the future of the amphibious forces.*

Answer

Lord Balniel: The UK amphibious forces, including the Royal Marines Commandos, will continue to form an important part of our contribution to NATO and they will be available for service wherever required.

Which was, between the lines, not very encouraging.

Although few in the Fleet knew it, the future of amphibious warfare was in the balance and it would be only a few years before the Government of the day, encouraged by antagonism from the Army and Royal Air Force, could finally admit in the 1974 Defence Review, that it did not support amphibious warfare.

In the meantime it was to be the introduction of the Dartmouth Training Ship role that, paradoxically, prolonged the final demise just long enough for the two LPDs to be involved in the greatest watershed of their lives. The country would not have considered victory in the South Atlantic an option worth pursuing had neither ship been in commission.

In Devonport Captain Roger Gerard-Pearse handed over his command of *Fearless* on 20 October 1970.

Chapter Six

Captain B.J. Straker, OBE, Royal Navy

Fourth Commanding Officer
1970–1972
Later, Rear Admiral, CB

European Waters, West Indies, Mediterranean, Norwegian Arctic

Captain Bryan Straker had commanded HMSs *Malcolm* and *Defender* before *Fearless*. He retired in 1981 as Senior Naval Member on the Directing Staff of the Royal College of Defence Studies and summed up his time in command through a series of notes:

> *Post-refit, Devonport Dockyard:*
> *Commissioning service*
> *Before this on Pre Commissioning Trials; went off to Scilly Isles and delivered via LCM, JCB to Tresco home of Dorrien-Smith family: consequence – two 15 cwt trucks of daffodils and camellia's for Commissioning Service.*

> *Mini work up at Portland:*
> *Wore flag of new Flag Officer Sea Training – Rear Admiral Gerard Mansfield – in my personal view – most brilliant Flag Officer I had ever met.*

Captain Bryan Straker with Lady Hull cutting the commissioning cake.

> *New engineer officer (Commander Willie Erskine) put on 15% list (via ballast tanks) in 10 minutes. Chieftain tanks did not like it, nor did troop accommodations!*

> *Chinese cooks and stewards (Hong Kong and Beijing) sat under wardroom tables in gas masks and tin hats throughout work-up.*

> *Only Chinese defaulter (gambling) – I asked Chief Steward (perfect English) a point of order. After about ten minutes of Cantonese – 'He say No!'*

> *Did round Britain schools liaison tour to eight ports.*
> *With boys on board overnight to next port. In words of Chinese Chief Cook – 'Never cook so many chips in my rife!'*

> *Rough weather*
> *On way to land commandos in North Norway,* Fearless *rolled 35° thus putting wedging of LCMs and vehicles to interesting test.*

Delayed leaving Devonport for West Indies for 36 hours until wind dropped to Force 9 – only then Wessex V helicopters at Culdrose could unfold blades to fly on board. This didn't stop a helo from Teeny Weeny Airways (RM Air Squadron) dropping in (on) to deliver to me a farewell gift of Regimental ice bucket from 3 Commando Brigade. To make up time we then crossed Atlantic at 22 knots! Bit short on fuel on arrival San Juan, Puerto Rico.[196] At the same time a LSL was losing a Mexeflote in Biscay

Firsts!

Did amphibious exercise with Italian LPD named Impavido *– translated means either* Fearless *or* Intrepid!

As far as I know – first Seacat ground firing trials at tank models on US firing range at Vieques, Puerto Rico. 50% success rate.

As far as I know – Fearless *did trials to introduce dark blue 'woolley pulley' (spell as you like) into naval service.*

Bryan Straker took command on 20 October 1970 after which his time was confined, unlike previous Commanding Officers, to the Atlantic fringes and the Mediterranean – including the Limassol wine festival – but was no less exotic, hardworking, taxing, instructive and fun for that.

There was a problem yet to be sorted out that had been simmering for some time and it took a new and wise Detachment Sergeant Major to nail it once and for all. On joining the ship Warrant Officer Moss Pearson,[197] Royal Marines, was disturbed to find, as he had been warned he would, that the Army members of the Amphibious Detachment no longer felt part of the Detachment nor, even, as members of the ship's company:

The army were reluctant shipmates as my predecessors had made them mess separately from the Royal Marines: they wore khaki all the time and were made to look inferior. I was at Hamoaze House[198] when I was promoted and sent to Fearless *with instructions to sort out the problems. It wasn't difficult to solve as I drew up a Watch and Quarter Bill that incorporated the army fully, then I mixed them into the Marines barracks forward and made an army JNCO 2IC of each mess-deck. I had a bit of resistance but it worked well in the end.*

A short time afterwards I asked permission to put the army into the RM/RN No. 8 dress for working but retaining their regimental/corps identities by wearing their belts and berets. This went down very well as in the evenings when they discarded belt and beret they felt part of the ship's company. This was particularly helpful when we had army personnel embarked as 'our' army felt superior – believe it or not!

The ship's company moved on board in November 1970 then, with Christmas and the New Year behind them it was possible to fix a date for *Fearless's* third Commissioning Day. Friday, 12 February 1971 was chosen with Field Marshal Sir Richard and Lady Hull the premier VIPs along with the Commandant of the Joint Warfare Establishment, Rear Admiral Gueritz[199] who had wartime experience in amphibious warfare.

The ceremony – held in the tank deck for the third time – followed the set naval format beginning with the Captain reading the Commissioning Warrant in which Admiral Sir William O'Brian, Commander-in-Chief Western Fleet, directed that *Fearless* proceed forthwith on a General Service Commission. The next day it was back to 'defect rectification' until 25 February and a month at Portland.

Sufficient experience had now been built up by FOST's staff to give the ship a fair and relevant test which she passed well; so well in fact that the staff lined the wall as she sailed with each member bearing a huge placard and a single letter that, together, spelt FOST TAKES GOOD CARE OF YOU. Indeed it had.

Effectively, the commission began with NELSON'S TOUCH and MOON LADY, described as 'consecutive national amphibious exercises mounted and carried out between 30 April and 13 May 1971'. Originally these were to have been three months apart and, for once, those at the lower end of the command chain were to consider it a success while the commanders and planners, although professing to have learned a great deal, found many areas that were unsatisfactory or which needed serious re-thinking. These ranged from poor beach reconnaissance by the SBS to the matter of alcohol for Embarked Force SNCOs now that the tot had been abolished.

NELSON'S TOUCH required the ship to load, transport during an opposed transit and land, elements of 24 Airportable (Army) Brigade in Carradale Bay, Mull of Kintyre. As far as *Fearless* was concerned all went well apart, that is, from the battalion she took up – the 1st Battalion the Duke of Wellington's Regiment – having a different manifest to that which she then took to Denmark – the 2nd Battalion Royal Irish Rangers. This caused understandable irritation to the Amphibious Operations Officer who was expecting, in accordance with the exercise instructions, the same number of men, split in the same proportions between the ranks.

This was easily resolved but not so some of the confusions that occured during the second exercise, MOON LADY, south of Copenhagen, which was unfortunate for FOCAS, Rear Admiral Treacher,[200] had decided that this would form the basis of *Fearless*'s Operational Readiness Inspection. An added excitement was close surveillance by a number of Soviet bloc ships.

In the various wash-up reports[201] by the senior commanders a number of problems were raised – some of which should not have happened while others were the fault of nature for which, maybe, quicker solutions might have been sought. Nevertheless, such is amphibious warfare and its close dependence on the elements but, even so, the ship's ORI Report was perhaps better than it might have been. Indeed, Bryan Straker opened his own résumé with the words: 'Many lessons were learned but regrettably some need not have been apparent had more thought been given to pre-planning by HMS *Fearless*.'

Even before the first exercise had begun two LCMs were damaged at Marchwood as a result of which the ship suggested that the slip should be modified to take her landing craft. Admiral Treacher's response was: 'No modification approved – LCMs used wrong part of the hard.'

Exercise MOON LADY. LCVP, LCM and a mexeflote with track-laying Michigan tractor embarked.

But a more serious problem was generated during the MOON LADY landings. A grandstand had been erected at the back of the beach from which many senior Warsaw Pact and NATO officers had been invited to witness the landings. The beach, according to Captain Ian Lamb,[202] was flat, featureless and, apart from two houses that were not on the chart, devoid of any fixing marks even in broad daylight:

> In the beach recce book, plus a SBS confirmatory recce, the horizontal photograph gave a view of a beach backed by a continuous band of thick pine trees broken in one place, almost behind the beaching point, by a white building. Simple we thought. No! Over the intervening period the tree line had covered that building but exposed another some 400 yards to the north. Hence on the run in, both Lieutenant Vaughan Turland, my 2IC, and I, identified our target and 'broke vector'. We managed to impress – or otherwise – the assembled NATO and Warsaw Pact hierarchy by appearing from an unexpected direction.
>
> The SBS had also confirmed there was a bar off the beach over which we were unlikely to get the LCMs: no problem, as the vehicles were all waterproofed – except that neither the SBS nor the book mentioned soft clay between the bar and the beach. Fortunately we got the BARV and the Michigan through but my four-tonner was not so lucky. . . . Incidentally, you can get 276 fully equipped Irishmen into an LCM by raising the ramp and squashing them up a bit. The first part of this exercise was most certainly a cock-up.

Ian Lamb admits this mistake while Bryan Straker's report was obliged to confirm it:

> H Hour was in daylight at 0630. Due to a combination of loose vectoring, incorrect vectoring, incorrect recognition of beaching points, an ineffectively positioned SBS radar reflector and failure to accept The Brigade Commander's advice when he was airborne in a Sioux, the first LCVP wave beached 400 yards to the North of the correct beach. The laying of a danbuoy at the seaward end of the boat lane would also have alleviated the situation.
>
> LCMs grounded on a sand bar 120 feet offshore. Beach reports and SBS recce indicated this possibility. What was not expected was that the sub-soil under water was clay. The water depth at the ramp of the LCM was 3–3½ feet followed by a 130 foot wade. The ABU Michigan and the 4 tonner bogged badly.[203] No vehicles could be landed in these conditions. A 112 foot roll on-roll off Mexeflote pontoon was brought in by two LCVPs but it was 20 feet too short. 'Captive ferrying' was tried but was too slow. It had to be beached hard every time. So the remaining Mexeflote was called in to form a diagonal causeway. At this moment thick sea mist came down and the Mexeflote lost its way. It is recommended Mexeflotes have UHF communications and a radar reflector when working with LPDs in the future. Eventually at H Hour + 4 hours 25 minutes the causeway was built and the first vehicles landed over it, 3 hours late. Alternative methods of overcoming the beaching problems might have been considered if the available beach information had been studied more closely beforehand. It is recommended that sub-surface samples should be taken when the SBS carry out checks in the future.
>
> The fog partially lifted shortly after the diagonal causeway was built. 17 LCM loads were landed from the LPD and 14 from the LSL. LCVPs landed six Land Rovers as a training evolution. . . . The LCM programme was finally completed at 1900 – 4 hours later than was planned but still within the Brigade's deadline of 2000.

One problem that was encountered and which would re-occur over the years, was the relative rank and status of the OCAD/Beachmaster when compared to the local Military Commander ashore. This was highlighted by 24 Brigade's Commander, Brigadier Perkins,[204] who wrote:

> Command on the Beach. If any events begin to go wrong on the beach it is to be assumed that the senior army officer present, probably a Lieutenant Colonel or the Brigade Commander will endeavour to

Exercise MOON LADY. BARV salvaging a Bedford 3-tonner.

put things right. It is unrealistic to expect that they refrain from exercising their authority because, technically, it is a naval problem. The crunch has come and we are now involved in joint command rather than, as hitherto, joint planning! It is therefore essential that the relative junior officer who commands the Amphibious Beach Unit can work jointly through periods of stress with someone considerably his senior.

Two factors are raised here: one is that a Royal Marines Captain is – or rather was – the equivalent rank of an Army major and thus at the same level as the Brigade Major[205] and secondly, but of more importance, the approach, the water-gap, the beach itself and its exits are dangerous places even in peacetime with breaking waves, unexpected runnels and soft sand all crossed by heavy vehicles. Nature tends to be in charge and it is here that an expert team which has been trained to confront and overcome all types of amphibious eventualities has to be in control. Beachmasters down the years have fought off well-intentioned but misguided advice from 'more senior' but inexperienced meddlers whose involvement so often tends to make things worse.

An encouraging word in the ear or warning of unknown outside factors is, obviously and sensibly, welcomed, well-received and weighed up along with other considerations, but the Beachmaster has to remain in command and any attempt by an Army officer – or even a naval officer – of whatever rank, to 'take charge' is wrong. Thankfully, Admiral Treacher was wise to the realities of the problem and snuffed out any damaging changes with the words:

Events on the beach did not go well to begin with but I consider that the problem was local. I would not recommend any change in the respective duties of the Officer Commanding ABU and the Military Commander ashore, which are laid down in Joint Services Publication No. 4.

Initially, Ian Lamb's coxswains, and then he himself, were presented with a series of problems, and not all of them of their own making. In solving them satisfactorily and within the Brigade Commander's time limit, if not within the time sought by the planners, he and his ABU were able to regain the situation; but he still remembers that that might not necessarily have been the case had the Army's unwarranted interference been allowed to gain momentum.

On arrival in Plymouth on 21 May Her Majesty's Customs refused to board before 0800 – as had been planned – and thus, with no prior warning, disembarkation could not begin until 1030 with all the knock-on effects that mindless contempt can throw up.

Following the Operational Readiness Inspection and a brief spell in Devonport, *Fearless* was offered up for three periods of *Meet the Navy* which took place between Greenock, Leith and Sunderland. The ship that was now so well known to the public was again swamped with inquisitive visitors anxious to see where Harold Wilson had so publicly failed to make foreign policy history. If they had known of Marcia Williams's nocturnal adventures they might have wanted to take a peep into the Commander (E)'s cabin as well.

To placate the Pompey natives a Dockyard Assisted Maintenance Period (DAMP) was held alongside in Portsmouth Naval Base between 4 and 16 June before *Fearless* loaded her most unusual Embarked Force so far: thirty-six members of the British Olympic Yachting Team, their seventeen yachts and a number of motor cars, all destined for Kiel Week or *Kieler Woche 71*. Bryan Straker reported to FOCAS:[206]

> *Fearless* sailed from Portsmouth on 16 June having embarked several members of (the Team). The embarkation was carried out via one of the LCM 9s, a swift and easy method. Kiel Week was everything the Western Fleet Guide Book promised to be – and more. It is an amalgam of Yachting Regatta, Navy

Olympic yachts load for Kiel Week.

Week, Kiel City Week and high level diplomatic activity.... Fearless arrived two days before the official start ... providing an excellent opportunity to ... give the kidneys an excellent 'warm through' before requiring them to work at maximum capacity ... There was no doubt that the hospitality received and extended at all levels, but particularly by the Federal German Navy, was on a scale rarely enjoyed these days.

Fearless arrived off Kiel Light at 1020 (18 June).... A German Band oompahpahad on the jetty and the C-in-C Western Fleet's Royal Marines band counter-pointed on the Flight Deck.

With ships from Germany, the Netherlands, France, the United States, Denmark, Portugal, Belgium and Sweden, the calls and return calls – not to mention those between the Commanding Officer HMS *Fearless* and the Flag Officer Germany, the Territorial Commander, the *Minister Präsident* of Schleswig Holstein and the *Oberbürgermeister* of Kiel – were taxing on time and liver but once completed Captain Straker could relax with his ship's company into a serious marathon of sport, parties and sightseeing. The success of *Fearless*'s part in all this, plus the smooth running of her own programme, was due, in very large and gratefully-acknowledged measure, to two outsiders: *Kapitänleutnant* Walther Gühmann, the ship's liaison officer and the British Naval Attaché, Bonn, Captain J.M.H. Cox.

Snippets emerge from the official report to offer glimpses into the life of a British Warship at *Kieler Woche 71*:

A LCVP took part in an 'obstacle course' overnight motor boat rally ... the race instructions were in German ... obliging the LCVP to follow the leaders, but they claim to have won the drinking and dancing (at the end) ... the only non-German boat to enter....

On Sunday 20 June Kiel Week got into top gear. An International Naval Protestant Church Service was held in HMS Fearless's tank deck led by Chaplains from the German, Netherlands and Royal Navies....

At noon the British Forces Broadcasting Service, Germany, allocated all its Family Favourites broadcasting time to Fearless....

At 1400 a NATO Press Conference was held on board ... the German Navy showed considerable interest in the 'through deck cruiser' (while) the USN Press Liaison Officer distributed ships badges and yellow rubber goods which raised some eyebrows until they proved to be balloons bearing the name USS Patterson....

Naval cutter races throughout the week ... Cocktail parties throughout the week – sometimes two on the same evening (and) the junior rates fraternized very considerably ashore.... 20 officers whose ages and heights had to be reported two months in advance were well paired off at a magnificent ball ... and 150 ratings were entertained at other dances to all of which English speaking partners had been invited.... The Ship's Fleet Chiefs and Chiefs gave a cocktail party....

One Naval Officer with a scar on his face was held in very high regard in the Student Halls where duelling is illegal but still practised ... and the Doctor won a serious beer-drinking contest....

Soccer, sailing, basketball, volleyball, rifle shooting and ten-pin bowling tournaments ran throughout the week....

A children's party was held on board ... as was a dinner by HBM's Ambassador Sir Roger Jackling ... a unique event as it is the only occasion on which high powered Civil Service dignitaries dine formally on board any warship during the week....

Sir Roger also invested Dr Hessenhauer, Chairman of the Anglo-German Society, with the OBE on board....

Our paying guests (the British Yachtsmen) held a party on board for a great number of International Yachtsmen including, in an unofficial capacity, Their Majesties King Constantine and Queen Anne-Marie of Greece....

Of the many recommendations for the future the last read: 'A vast quantity of milk should be carried as pre-reception stomach lining.'

Even Kiel Week had to come to an end. With the yachts re-embarked, *Fearless* slipped and proceeded to Portsmouth on Saturday, 26 June during which, just to remind everyone that she was also a warship, she exercised a nuclear fall-out transit, which must have confused the yachtsmen, then, to confuse the Navy, the ship anchored off Dover to clear customs, land the band plus a number of yachtsmen and to: ' Embark a party of 80 Ministry of Defence civilians for passage to Portsmouth ... many (of whom) were better looking than the departing passengers with (their) hotpants and mini-skirts a cheering sight.'

Three more sessions of *Meet the Navy* – in addition to those she had hosted before Kiel – were conducted between Southampton, Cherbourg and Avonmouth at the end of which Bryan Straker wrote:

> *The ship's company have had to put up with a great amount of inconvenience (and) while few complaints have been heard the general feeling is that (we) have now contributed our fair share to* Meet the Navy.... *. After leave my company will be keen to get abroad, including reasonably long sea passages when (we) can settle down to a steady routine. Most of all, the ship needs more exercises to improve amphibious skills.*

The ship was not yet free from her social and publicity obligations for a party of foreign Naval Attachés, including the Pakistan Naval Staff Course, were entertained to a wardroom mess dinner and she gave a comprehensive amphibious display for Navy Days between the 28 and 30 August while also hosting 26,883 visitors. Then it really was back to military work – although whether or not the Limassol Wine Festival comes under that category will be a matter of individual 'taste' – with Exercise DEEP FURROW in the Mediterranean.

During this period Captain Straker had become increasingly aware that many of his 'Army' embarked force wore lightweight, khaki woollen jerseys when 'in the field' as a middle way between combat dress and khaki service dress. The SBS had been wearing a heavy version for some time with a draw string around the neck and this design had slowly and unofficially crept across to 'mainstream' Royal Marines, but had yet to find favour within the Royal Navy. Now the Commanding Officer decided that as an informal but smart alternative a thick, blue jersey, reinforced, as were the military ones, at the elbows and shoulders, would reduce wear, tear and expense. His original view was that they should be worn only by watch-keepers so a number were procured, issued and much approved. There was some opposition but eventually, thanks (it is generally agreed) to the trials conducted on board HMS *Fearless*, the 'woolly-pully' became accepted into the naval service.

Prior to DEEP FURROW, *Fearless* was berthed alongside No. 10 Wharf which was not ideal for embarking a military force as it had no cranes and was too shallow to allow docking by LCMs. However, by 1 September, Headquarters 3 Commando Brigade and its vehicles had been hoisted aboard by the ship's own 15 ton crane and despite a short delay, when it broke down, all was secured on time.

South of the Sound, ammunition and general stores were brought on board by Vertrep[207] and jackstay and once all was stowed, *Fearless* was able to 'benefit from the welcome opportunity to sail in company with three frigates and carry out an anti-submarine exercise with HMS *Dreadnought*, who was returning home'.

During the three day visit to Gibraltar, qualifying for LOA, four Wessex V helicopters were embarked from *Bulwark*, after which this 'Med Deployment' followed the near-standard procedure of landing and recovering Royal Marines, interspersed by social and military visits to Italian ports and accompanied, as usual, by unseasonably bad weather and trouble with the boilers.

Mention must be made of one or two out-of-the-ordinary experiences which Bryan Straker was to recount in his Report of Proceedings.[208] While at anchor off Limassol the ship had been obliged to assume a modified form of Awkward State 3 as the military authorities warned of possible saboteur activity because General Grivas[209] was in the area. On 19 September a sentry reported a suspicious sighting. A full bottom search was activated, beginning within twenty minutes of the 'pipe' and which was completed in twenty-five minutes; both timings reflecting creditably on the diving team.

A less dramatic and more pleasurable episode was British Night at the Limassol Wine Festival when members – and one in particular – of the ship's company took part on the open air stage in the Municipal Gardens. 'This was well received . . . by the strong section of local teenage girls who gazed in admiration at the impressive agility of my floodlit muscleman,[210] flexing his biceps in time to appropriately dreamy music – he received a rapturous ovation . . . '

Exercise DEEP FURROW itself took place in the Souda and Saros Bay areas of Crete and off the Turkish coast. Amphibious assaults by Royal Marines and the USMC were conducted from both *Fearless* and *Bulwark* and when all were recovered the ship sailed for Istanbul where she anchored for the major post exercise discussions headed by her two embarked Commanders, Commodore R.W. Halliday DSC as COMAW and Brigadier P. Ovens OBE MC of 3 Commando Brigade.

Brigadier Ovens was able to show that a wise, amphibiously-experienced Brigade Commander does not need to resort to threats of courts martial to get things moving on a beach. During DEEP FURROW for instance, not only was his car written off due to an enthusiastic driver moving it out of one perceived danger into the path of the Michigan but his Land Rover driver then:[211]

> Took his feet off everything in four and half feet of water. . . . The Brigadier must have thought we had it in for him but he was very good about it and instead of sending a 'senior' officer to take charge, simply realized that on a beach the ABU is dealing, constantly, with real enemies – the weather, topography and, more than often, unrealistic timings imposed by those who have no idea what beach-work involves.

Her Majesty the Queen was visiting the area in the Royal Yacht *Britannia* and as it was deemed awkward to 'meet' in foreign territorial waters *Fearless* weighed anchor at 0330 (local) from Istanbul to make a fast passage through the Sea of Marmara in order to clear the Dardanelles by 1230 that day – just one hour before *Britannia* was due to enter. In fact, her Majesty did see *Fearless* from a hill top and was reported to have been considerably cheered by the welcome sight of: 'One of my own ships passing through the Dardanelles.'

Fearless continued straight to Malta for a brief but pleasant maintenance period – pleasant that was for almost everyone but the engineers who, troubled with continuing boiler and evaporator problems, spent much of their time cleaning both and conducting a thorough investigation of the ship's complete hydraulic system, helped by a representative from McTaggart Scott. Their caution was well-founded for soon after this gentleman's arrival the whaler, while being lowered, 'ran away' and impaled itself on the guard-rail stanchions. No one was hurt but it was a vindication of the earlier worries.

The whaler was replaced at sea during a RAS with RFA *Regent* following which *Fearless* entered Cagliari where, in celebration of Italy's Armed Forces Day, two 21-gun salutes were fired as soon as she had moored. Ceremonial is important in a 'capital' ship employed on such duties but such were the manning restraints that even the simplest of things had to be borrowed, as Moss Pearson recalls:

> The Captain was bemoaning that we would be on a Med deployment without a bugler but after a word with the Band Sergeant ashore he was over the moon. That little favour served me well as a few

Rugby team. Back row (left to right): P.O.N. Pearce, A.B. Nye, Mne. Williams, Mne. McKenna, M.E.A.(H) Earl, L.S. Carney, M.E.A.(H.) Charlton (Capt.), A.B. Foat. Front row (left to right): Mne. Mitchell, M.E.A.(H) Brown, P.O. Read, Captain Straker, A.B. Jones, Mne. Spray, E.M. Lloyd.

years later I was late for a meeting in the West Indies when I took the 1st Raiding Squadron there for an exercise. The chairman was my ex-Captain:[212] *he immediately jumped up from his chair and shook me by the hand. As I was the only non-commissioned officer there it was quite a relief.*

Fearless returned home via bad weather, Exercise SARDINIA 71 and a Remembrance Day Parade in Gibraltar, held on the jetty and considered a suitable occasion to christen the ship's new 'organ, portable, not-so-small, electric'. Moss Pearson again:

> *Our Army Catering Corps Sergeant Mick Cowley, said that all he ever did was cook so ... I eventually said that if he wanted to be a Guard Commander of a Royal Marines Quarter Guard it could be arranged. I would ask Mick Jones*[213] *to drill him for a week in the tank deck and he could do the job. He blanched at first but another couple of drinks later he said he'd do it! Mick gave Mick a week of private lessons*[214] *and then, when he was ready, with the Guard itself. The great day dawned as we entered Gibraltar and the ABU's Cook Sergeant sailed through his ordeal with flying colours. In the Mess afterwards we had the happiest Sergeant of the Guard I have ever seen.*

Bryan Straker's ego was also boosted in Gibraltar for, after jogging back from playing tennis, he ran effortlessly up the brow in his tracksuit to be accosted on the flight deck by a junior seaman shouting, 'Are you the new club swinger, mate?'

A few days later, on 17 November, the customs were more accommodating and *Fearless* was able to enter the Hamoaze as planned, allowing Bryan Straker to end his Report of Proceedings with news of his ship's company's health: 'Very good. The Ship's VD record ... never more than one case in each port and none in Istanbul.'

Rolling through 70 degrees in the North Sea.

Tank on pedestal to prevent rolling on its springs and then breaking away from the securing chains.

With two, five-bladed propellers fitted, the hull scraped and anti-fouled and the topsides re-painted it was back to work in early January 1972 – delayed for three days by Plymouth Dockyard's lack of progress – and *Fearless*'s first foray into the Arctic after noise ranging at Portland and the embarkation at Rosyth of elements of 45 Commando, plus their supporting light helicopters.

Unlike other passages across the North Sea to Vest Fjord this was anything but uneventful with at least one 35 degree roll, each way, recorded. Understandably this swing through 70 degrees was too much for the BARV which decided to move with the ship as did the two aftermost LCMs. On the flight deck a four-ton lorry made a similar bid for freedom, all requiring courageous efforts to secure. On taking over from Douglas Mayhew, Ian Lamb had asked what kept these two LCMs apart at sea. 'Mass and friction', was the reply and, until this passage, neither had been put to the test.

An additional aim of supporting the Royal Marines' annual cold weather training – Exercise CLOCKWORK – was to test the ship's own systems in the extreme cold but, as luck would have it, 1972 was a 'warm' Norwegian winter with much colder weather, including a foot of snow on the upper deck, as soon as *Fearless* returned to Newcastle on 21 January.[215] In the meantime though, support of the Embarked Force continued while the ship acted as target for Norwegian submarines and fast attack craft.

In the middle of all this a beach recce was interrupted by the first, recorded, unofficial beaching of a *Fearless* landing craft when *Foxtrot Six* struck a rock:[216]

> *On 16 January attempts to carry out Arctic beach trials were frustrated when the LCVP carrying the recce party ran aground on a rock two miles from the ship. Apart from the two LCMs which had sailed to recce Salangen and its approaches all the efforts of the Amphibious Detachment were concentrated on the salvage of the LCVP. Two LCVPs were secured either side of the grounded craft on the rising tide with strong-backs to prevent them listing. In addition a life raft was positioned in the engine room and*

Foxtrot Six comes home.

inflated. At about 2230 the combined efforts of the LCVPs, the life raft and the rising tide succeeded and all three landing craft floated clear of danger. Once safe inside the ship's dock the LCVP was drained and craned on to the flight deck.

Ian Lamb[217] commented that it could have been much worse but that, luckily, the LCVP had remained impaled on the rock and could sink no further: he was, though, professionally saddened that the ship decided to turn this event 'Into an evolution and took the recovery – for which (he and his men) were fully trained – out of (his) hands. Thus a superb training exercise was lost.'

With no harm done other than to the coxswain's pride, his engines and hull – all reparable, including the Corporal's morale – this near disaster would have been of almost incomparable value in high-latitude, winter, seamanship training. For small craft in a busy waterway it might seem inexcusable to run aground on a well-tabulated reef but, in support of the coxswain, the only charts available to him then were monochrome photocopies run off from the ships microfilm system onto flimsy, water-absorbent paper. In winter, many of the buoys – lit and unlit – are prone to removal by ice floes anyway. In this case the rock was not marked at all, the position and depths of the surrounding reef itself were uncertain and the navigation marks were missing.

A second, foul-weather crossing of the North Sea back to Rosyth had to be endured, thence a much heralded visit to Newcastle – it snowed – where the many 'locals' among the crew took a last look at home for six weeks. A ship's company dance was held, although it began in a near-disastrous fashion as the booked Palm Court Violins knew only Victorian tunes. A hasty '999' call to a local disco: 'Restored equilibrium – at least in the eyes and ears of (my) youngsters.'[218]

Both boilers needed cleaning but the incentive was strong, for the immediate future included a brief return to Plymouth and, more exciting for many, a West Indies deployment with elements of 24 (Army) Brigade embarked.

Colour Sergeant Bernie Todd explaining the intricacies of LCM handling to the First Sea Lord.

The weather was no better in Plymouth Sound with storm force winds forcing the laying of a second anchor, the cancelling of all flying and small boat operations and, although unconnected, the work to rule of PAS personnel. HMS *Intrepid*, under command of Captain William Staveley, was able to help load the ship by lending her LCMs during a brief lull, yet even so *Fearless* was to sail for a major deployment without the correct issue of charts and other victualling and armament stores – such can the defence of the country be held to ransom by Government employees. Her own LCMs could not be used to do the PAS work as they had, by then, been pre-loaded with Wessex V helicopters, safer in a landing craft for a transatlantic passage than on the flight deck.

Heavy seas and strong winds continued to dog *Fearless*. At 1700 on 2 February, she sailed into worsening weather which continued unabated until a few days out of her destination, Roosevelt Roads, where she arrived with her forecastle breakwater bent back a foot, one of the forward Sea Cat launchers damaged, a hole in the *Fairy Huntress* – the Captain's barge – and several upper deck lockers crushed or carried away. The accompanying three LSLs with their Mexeflotes, one of which was lost, and a frigate had had an even worse time. After a cursory licking of wounds, the first phase of Exercise SUN PIRATE, a Brigade-scale landing, could begin in the US Navy's Virgin Islands training areas, including the island of Vieques: but not before the older hands had re-acquainted themselves with the notorious Black Angus night club in San Juan, Puerto Rico.

Interestingly, another strange decision by one of Her Majesty's Representatives abroad occurred – perhaps *Fearless* was jinxed in this matter – as the Consul General in San Juan: 'Did not consider it appropriate to invite guests from San Juan to attend (the official reception to show the ship's appreciation) nor to attend himself.'

Eyes were raised at this serious omission, which was not of *Fearless*'s making, by those who might reasonably have expected an invitation.

SUN PIRATE's second phase of individual company-group training took part in the altogether less overtly-military area of the British Virgin Islands and was centred around Tortola where, during a lull on 21 February, a large proportion of the ship's company took advantage

Bryan and Emile Straker.

of an 'official' banyan on Beef Island and where the wardroom held the obligatory reception for local dignitaries.

Four days in Bridgetown, Barbados, was the price to be paid for eleven days on exercise and where, again no doubt, the better-off hands were this time able to re-acquaint themselves with the Breadfruit Tree Inn – an altogether more sophisticated evening than those to be found in Puerto Rico – or, for those less well-off and probably most of the officers, the Coconut Creek Country Club. Further down the financial pecking order, the Nelson Street bars found favour.

Men gave blood, under-privileged children were amused, the ship's cricket team won their match, official receptions were exchanged, visits to the local rum distillery were endured, the dock (with the stern gate permanently lowered) acted as a non-stop marina for the dinghy sailors, and the embarked soldiers constructed a pathway, a bridge and a playground for St Gabriel's School. The Commanding Officer met his namesake, Emile Straker, who was leader of the 'number one band' in the West Indies – The Merrymen – and discovered a common ancestor. After this unlikely revelation the ship's company patronized Emile's large, alfresco night club, The Caribbean Pepperpot, where they were greeted each evening with cut-price rum.

Despite there being 975 officers and men on board there were no charges of drunkenness or misbehaviour of any type.

So, all in all, a reasonably typical, West Indies, end-of-exercise, wind-down period. The Commanding Officer was, though, obliged to add a corollary to his report,[219]

> *A number of younger ratings experienced their first sexual encounter with a coloured girl which on the whole proved expensive – one MEM 2 paid $25 BWI for his pleasure and had $40 BWI stolen at the same time.... Full instruction was carried out on passage by the Medical Officer but despite this five sailors and seventeen soldiers 'caught colds' ... I might add that the majority of these soldiers had arrived from another ship.*

Whether the MEM, to add to his woes, was one of this latter number is not revealed.

Now the Liverpool girls had hold of the head rope[220] and after a ten day and rather calmer passage than the outward one, *Fearless* arrived off the Bar Light at 0800 on 9 March to face disembarkation of her Army embarked force, a heightened security alert thanks to the IRA, and a very full sporting and social programme beginning with a ship's company dance in a converted LCT in Salthouse Dock.

During the Atlantic crossing an Amphibious Detachment 'first' had been celebrated on 3 March when a Regimental Dinner was held by the Sergeants' Mess in the Senior Rates' Dining Room. It was suggested and organized by the indefatigable Warrant Officer Moss Pearson who readily obtained permission from an enthusiastic Commanding Officer. Sergeant Mick Cowley, the Army Catering Corps cook of Guard Commander fame, devised the menu, Marine Ranson trained two volunteers, Marine Wilson and one other, as stewards in the Commodore's quarters and invitations were sent to the Captain, First Lieutenant, Commander (E), the Master at Arms, Mr Davies, and the ship's military officers. Spirits and wine were served as appropriate, the port was passed and toasts drunk – including one to Bryan Straker for whom this was also a farewell thank-you present from his Detachment Senior NCOs. It was, as Moss Pearson points out: 'A very special and unique occasion for us.'[221] It was pretty special and unique for Captain Bryan Straker as well and equally appreciated.

This sad occasion for the ship's fourth Commanding Officer was not allowed to pass unmarked at Liverpool either for someone tipped-off the other moored ships, ferries and tugs and so, as *Fearless* slipped for the last time under Bryan Straker's command on 13 March 1972, every ship on the Mersey sounded its siren as she sailed towards the Irish Sea, Portsmouth, an assisted maintenance period and a new captain.

SNCOs' dinner. Commander (S) Jefferson, Colour Sergeant Jimmy Green, CO, WO Moss Pearson, Captain Lamb.

Always when entering a dockyard for a maintenance period there is speculation on whether or not the ship will leave as planned. As *Fearless* slipped slowly past HMS *Victory* in a gentle drizzle, a West Country member of the ship's company, finding himself in Portsmouth for an uncertain length of time, was heard to mutter: 'They took her in for a refit over 100 years ago and she is still here, so what hope have we got?'

In his foreword to the Commission Book that was to be published nine months later, Captain Bryan Straker wrote:

> *There is an awful lot to recommend serving in an LPD and of course* Fearless *in particular. The main thing to recommend this commission is her splendid ship's company – and if you want a diverse life, where else do you find Royal Marines diving and driving aeroplanes and sailors doing all these things and forming a 'Blue Beret' Platoon which lands in support of the Embarked Force – and not only in the Internal Security role.*
>
> *With only two such ships in the Royal Navy* Fearless *is bound to be in great demand, as the succeeding pages in this book will show. In a word – work hard and play hard.*
>
> *I personally am very sorry to leave you and wish you every success for the rest of the commission.*

Captain Bryan Straker handed over command on 20 March 1972 and, heading for an office, was towed away on a huge desk fitted with quills and other such antiquated bureaucratic equipment.

Chapter Seven

Captain S.A.C. Cassels, Royal Navy

Fifth Commanding Officer
1972–1973
Later, Admiral Sir Simon, KCB, CBE

European Waters, West Indies, Mediterranean, the Norwegian Arctic

HMS *Fearless* was Captain Simon Cassels' fifth command after HMSs *Vigilent, Roebuck, Tenby* and *Eskimo*; later he was to command HMS *Tiger* and retired in 1986 as Second Sea Lord, Chief of Naval Personnel and Admiral President of the Royal Naval College Greenwich. He writes:

My time in command consisted almost exactly of nine very active months, followed by six months in refit.

It began unexpectedly. Bristol's Lord Mayor was about to pay a formal visit to Bordeaux to mark the 25th anniversary of the twinning of the two cities, supported by HMS Bristol. *But* Bristol *had engine trouble and could not sail. So* Fearless *took her place, accompanied – appropriately – by HMS* Bacchante. *After much ceremonial on arrival, enlivened with certain French variations, this was an enjoyable visit for everyone onboard.*

Then to the ship's main business. A long steam through the Mediterranean to Dhekelia,

Captain Simon Cassels escorting the Grand Duke of Luxembourg.

Cyprus, to rehearse RM Commando landings and recoveries before a major NATO southern flank Exercise DAWN PATROL, first near Kavalla, in Greek Thrace, followed by the west coast of the Peloponnese. What better introduction to the complexities of 'amphibiousity'.

The long haul back to Devonport – via Malta – followed, then to Rosyth, inspection and further exercises in the Orkneys, this time with the Royal Netherlands Marine Corps. While at Rosyth, the Grand Duke of Luxembourg included Fearless *as an unscheduled extra on his State Visit. Back to Devonport and thence to Lisbon for a most important foreign visit – as Flagship for C-in-C Fleet (Admiral Sir Edward Ashmore) – the first since 1966. After Bordeaux thoughts dwelt on what ceremonial quirks might be in store. Thankfully none. The whole programme was faultless.*

After a Meet the Navy visit to Swansea, Fearless *was exercising near Cape Wrath when I was summoned to the then novel Skynet Portacabin. A familiar voice (my immediate predecessor – Captain Bryan Straker) told me on the scrambler to break off and proceed at once to the Clyde for further instructions. On arrival a FOCAS staff officer came onboard and told me what the ship had to do. Thereafter Operation MOTORMAN was on: first taking the Scots Guards to Belfast, then back to the Clyde to embark AVREs[222] for 'inserting' into Londonderry. No signal was ever sent: everything was done by word of mouth.*

After embarking the AVREs, the ship had to hide until dark, then make for the entrance to Lough Foyle. Memories of a remote spot from my navigation course sprang to mind: hard to detect onshore or from seaward. Thence to the Foyle. A filthy night: pitch dark, pouring with rain.

After Summer leave, the main event was the major NATO northern flank (and an unidentified object on the bottom of a fjord . . .).

Fearless *returned to the Mediterranean – to Dhekelia, Volos in Greece, Malta and finally to exercise with the French off Corsica. The worst moment was trying to refuel ships in company in viciously heavy seas while heading ever closer to the coast.*

After a few days in Toulon, it was back to Devonport to prepare for refit. Lady Hull, who had launched the ship in 1963, visited with her husband, Field Marshal Lord Hull. The lunch party for the Hulls seemed a fitting finale to the busy life onboard.

Among the main events, my lasting impressions of those nine months are:

While steaming quietly towards Gibraltar, a Royal Marine playing a classical guitar in evening concert to a spellbound audience on the fo'c's'le.

At Lisbon, the impeccable precision of the RM guard.

At Swansea, the crane hoisting a severely disabled boy in a car onto the flight deck so that his father could drive him down the ramp to the tank deck and LCMs. The boy had spent many hours making an 'Airfix' model of the ship.

Off the Isle of Man, a 'fun' day with Intrepid.

At Volos, berthed stern to the jetty. The civic and military guests arriving together. Only one inspected the Royal Marine guard on the stern gate: the Archbishop.

The number of VIP visits, including Lord Carrington (Secretary of State for Defence) twice.

The extraordinary response to the challenges of MOTORMAN.

The skilful LCM handling by the Colour Sergeant Coxswains.

The many hours steaming to and from the Eastern Mediterranean and the Arctic Circle.

Above all, the well-knit, lively and happy ship's company of 'Friendly' Fearless.

Lord Carrington's visits were looked forward to for he had taken the amphibious cause to heart – and *Fearless's* role in it – although his enthusiasm was not always to fall on receptive ears. He had, too, been the First Lord of the Admiralty who had overseen the procurement negotiations for the LPDs and then signed the build contract.

Captain Simon Cassels took over command on 20 March 1972 while *Fearless* was in Portsmouth dockyard preparing for a two month Mediterranean deployment with elements of 3 Commando Brigade, Royal Marines. Because of the change of plan involving Bordeaux she sailed on 11 April with only the advanced party embarked.

The fifty or so nautical mile passage up the Gironde and Garonne rivers at night – never straightforward in any ship at any tide – was a test even for *Fearless's* Commanding Officer, a navigation specialist. HMS *Bacchante* led the way – each ship having embarked a pilot off the river's entrance – reporting back alterations to charted depths and navigational marks. For much of its length the river's minimum charted depths are in the region of just twenty-three feet and, in some places, rather less. Simon Cassels subsequently reported,[223]

It became evident that this (passage) does require more careful planning than usual and even then timing is dependent on the amount of water in the river. . . . The passage down river was more critical in that it started at low water at Bordeaux and ended on a fast falling tide. . . .

Chinese laundry team, early 1970s.

Petty Officer Wong.

Leading Seaman Collins receiving the Fleet Seacat Aimers Trophy from FOCAS.

In between these two transits the ships enjoyed:

A heavy programme of social and sporting events – if anything too heavy, although it was appreciated that this was on account of the special nature of the visit.[224]

The fiercely independent inhabitants of the region enjoyed the sight of a frigate named after the Greek god Bacchus,[225] lit up each evening alongside their town jetty and bearing the pennant number F69. One Frenchman assumed that she had been given this number temporarily, just for the visit!

From *Fearless*'s new Commanding Officer's point of view, having FOCAS embarked was an added concern, especially as Simon Cassels was living ashore with his wife. Each morning he would return on board for ceremonial Colours to be greeted by: 'A catalogue of horrors noted by JDT[226] during my absence. Hardly an encouraging start to my time in command.'[227]

The social programme was, indeed, heavy with few finding it heavier than the embarked Royal Marines Band who were required to perform many times a day as FOCAS himself commented to Commander-in-Chief Fleet:[228]

Bandmaster Williams and his musicians from your band made a number of appearances and, as I would expect, created a very good impression. The musical highlight of the visit was a band concert … by the Royal Marines bands and bands of the French Army and Air Force. The finale was a rousing performance of Colonel Bogey *in the modern theatre of St Medard-en-Jalles, received with immense enthusiasm by a very full house. The performance was followed by a generous* vin-d'honneur *which very nearly proved disastrous for the Royal Marines who still had to Beat Retreat at the Ship's Reception before their working day was over.*

The problem was three-fold: the band was counter-marching among tram lines along the jetty, the *vin d'honneur* had, as officially reported, been generous and the senior bugler/drummer,[229] whose duty it was to mark the various evolutions with a tap on the drum – unnoticeable to non-musicians – had benefited greatly from that generosity. The sunken metal tracks and the wine combined into a two-pronged assault that not only forced the drummer to weave an uncertain course through the counter-marching but led him to tap out his signals at the wrong moments. The newly arrived OCAD and Beachmaster, Captain Ewen Southby-Tailyour,[230] who had relieved Ian Lamb in Liverpool, was not so impressed as the ship's French guests who, rightly, praised the band for continuing with near perfection while ignoring the 'mis-directions'. As a result of their pleas, no disciplinary action was taken: the French considered it amusing, their own fault and a fine tribute to their hospitality.

Despite all the vineyard and distillery visits, and those to the bars and clubs plus the overwhelming bonhomie and private invitations offered by the people of Bordeaux, there were no cases of ill-discipline. One sailor broke his leg while ice-skating and was returned to the ship by the rink's manager himself.

At the 'other end' the senior officers were honoured by an invitation to lunch with the Prime Minister of France, Monsieur Chaban-Delmas, who was also the Mayor of Bordeaux, while Major Ken Robson,[231] *Fearless*'s AOO, laid a wreath at the memorial in the Anglican Church commemorating those members of Lieutenant Colonel Blondie Hasler's Operation FRANKLIN and who were drowned or murdered by the Nazis in December 1942. A more recent act of courage was also honoured with the announcement and presentation of the C-in-C's Commendation to AB Stephen

AB Stephen Crossdale being presented with the Commander-in-Chief's Commendation.

Crossdale for rescuing his companion when their Rigid Raiding Craft had been overturned by a large wave the previous November.

Seven thousand people visited HMS *Fearless* and as she sailed in company with *Bacchante*, those who had crowded the jetty – many with handkerchiefs to their eyes – then jumped into their motor cars to drop flowers onto the flotilla as it passed beneath the Pont d'Aquitaine, two miles down stream. It had been a truly memorable visit, even to those well versed in such matters.

Fearless arrived in Gibraltar on 20 April, landed the Commander-in-Chief Fleet's Band, loaded the balance of the Commando Brigade's Headquarters and sailed that same day for Exercises DOUBLE BASS, the preliminary 'in-house' rehearsals for the major NATO, 100-ship Exercise, DAWN PATROL. Of interest, the Brigade Major[232] of Brigadier Oven's[233] 3rd Commando Brigade was now Major Julian Thompson,[234] Royal Marines, who, just ten years later almost to the day, would, himself be the embarked Brigade Commander for the Falklands campaign.

Off Cyprus *Fearless* met *Albion*, with 42 Commando and 848 Naval Air Squadron on board, to conduct an administrative landing at Dhekelia before re-embarking their respective units and sailing for the first of DAWN PATROL's full-scale amphibious landings: deterrent operations close to Kavalla village in Greek Thrace.

These landings were the new Beachmaster's first since joining *Fearless* and, having listened to Ian Lamb's tales of problems on the beach, he was anxious to get off to a good start; not only in the eyes of the Landing Force and its Commander but also in the eyes of his own Amphibious Beach Unit. Beginner's luck prevailed for the pre-dawn weather was excellent, the gradients as expected, the water gap and the beach exits un-mined. The Brigade was transferred ashore without one drowned vehicle or wet foot. Things were to get even better for, as the sun brought clarity to the surroundings, two large camper-van vehicles were spotted parked among neighbouring sand dunes, each with *Adventuretrek* painted in large letters down their sides.

A jovial, fit-looking gentleman eventually appeared rubbing his eyes and asking how many men were there in the ABU and for how long would they be staying. The curt reply from the Beach Unit's Colour Sergeant Bill Evans – a man of immense beach experience – was '20, two nights and this is a NATO exercise for which we have clearance'. We needn't have been so on our guard for part of the subsequent conversation went something like this:

127

You are not going to believe this but I am an ex-Royal Marines Colour Sergeant who now runs an adventure company which usually caters for middle-aged London couples who want to get away from it all on organized camping holidays. If you look towards Kavalla you will see all my permanent tents. This week is different. Eighteen of the twenty places have been bulk-booked by a group of single Australian girls from Earls Court hell-bent on a massive hen party! They fly in this evening but there has been a delay and will arrive too late for dinner in the local taverna.

This was too good to be true – indeed, a Greek version of the fictitious Coach Load of Nurses from Larnaca[235] that never turns up – and so bets were soon laid on who would achieve a first strike and how quickly. Yet, and yet … an air of disbelief enveloped the ABU, for such things do not, in reality, happen; but this one was about to, and it did, with the Army Catering Corps Cook Sergeant, Mick Cowley, preparing pusser's-issue chicken supreme on his 'hydro-cooker' in the sand after the girls had arrived – lit, un-tactically, by the BARV's searchlights. Pudding was, inevitably, tinned peaches in syrup with sweetened condensed milk. It might not have been very military but even the most curmudgeonly of critics would understand the ABU's predicament!

It was not the first meal in Greece that the 'sheilas' had been expecting – nor for which they had paid – but it was more memorable for that. A veil must still be drawn over the rest of the night except to say that with all Embarked Force vehicles and personnel up in the hills and not expected to return for forty-eight hours, a run ashore was organized using the BARV as transport once a simple re-call system had been agreed, should exercise plans change. In the morning the Beachmaster held his first and last parade on a beach: everyone was present (there was one black eye), bets (quite a few – and even the most optimistic expectations seemed to have been achieved) were honoured and the marines and soldiers dismissed to their duties. Luckily a film crew from Telstar Productions, which had joined in Gibraltar to make a documentary about an Assault Ship's activities, were shooting elsewhere.

The major, international, DAWN PATROL landings were held along the beaches of Kyparissia, on the west coast of the Peloponnese, between the 11 and 14 May and where the British beach was alongside that of the Americans. This exercise, similar to so many from the ship's perspective, was notable for three events: the unexpected and active railway line which required a wooden 'fording' system for both tracked and wheeled vehicles and a careful eye on the timetable, supplied by a local farmer; the very high percentage of American drowned vehicles, even in the shallowest of water gaps and the BARV being armed with a large-calibre gun.

Prior to the landings the ABU had decided that it could not be seen to be less well-equipped than its American counterparts and so a suitable length of drain pipe was fixed to the BARV with cooling jackets, flash hiders and other authentic-looking add-ons. Unfortunately, the first to be taken in by this simple subterfuge was the ship's own Gunnery Officer who demanded to know where the ammunition was

Wardroom Line Book view of Athens.

WELL, HERE GOES MY GOOD CONDUCT BADGE !

The armed BARV.

being kept for, as it was not in his magazine, it must be illegally stowed. A couple of gins and some sweet talk unwound him but not so the USMC Major the following day who, on seeing the BARV, hull-down in a sand dune, enquired by what authority 'you Brits are operating a weapon not declared to NATO'.

The Beachmaster, rather than admitting a childish piece of amusement, for he sensed good sport, declined to tell the truth. At the post exercise discussion or 'wash-up', held in Athens, the matter of 'illegal weapons' was raised. American patience was tested further when their Brigadier General was told by a senior Royal Navy officer that they had been the butt of a simple – but obviously effective – example of British humour.

As PXDs go this was probably one of the largest and most comprehensive with which *Fearless* was ever involved. Luckily, the cruiser HMS *Blake* bore the brunt of the social events while those not involved in the official functions were able to sample the delights of La Placa and plate throwing. The Commanding Officer, though, was under pressure that had begun with the arrival of the 'new' FOCAS, Rear Admiral Lygo.[236]

After an enjoyable, leisurely lunch with the Ambassador, I returned to the quayside mid-afternoon to find no boat as arranged. Eventually one came and on stepping on board I was told that the Admiral was there already. The fur flew. He had sent a signal advancing his time of arrival. Frantic search through signal logs. No sign of receipt. Not accepted by the Admiral. Black mark No. 2. Weeks later a check of FOCAS's out logs revealed that the signal had never been sent.[237]

With prescience (and following a request from the Naval and Air Attaché, Captain John Lawson, RN) Simon Cassels had, well before Exercise DOUBLE BASE, landed a team led by the Deputy Supply Officer, Lieutenant Commander Mudge. Among many of his tribulations Brian Mudge was actively hindered by the US Air Base responsible for the secure movement forward of, for example, mail and stores, claiming that they – the Americans – had no knowledge of the NATO exercises, despite accommodating several members of the USN's 6th Fleet. While this example of obfuscatory behaviour continued throughout the whole PXD period it was due much to Brian Mudge's extreme patience that – at every level from Ambassador to Junior Seaman and from logistic re-supply of Land Rover axles to arranging football matches – the visit to Athens of the British ships went so smoothly and was so popular. So popular, indeed, that *Fearless* requested to return during her next Mediterranean Deployment in September.

Saturated with work and play *Fearless* sailed for Malta and home on 20 May, a passage remembered by more than just Simon Cassels for one particular reason:

> An 'Entertainment' held on the fo'c's'le one evening. The sea was flat calm, no wind, speed reduced. There were several amusing sketches. But my most vivid recollection is of a Royal Marine (name, alas, forgotten) playing a classical guitar. Those assembled were spell bound. There is no other word for it. You could have heard a pin drop and there were demands for encore after encore.

Devonport, Rosyth for Exercise STRENGTH TRIAL with FOCAS and the Royal Netherlands Marine Corps embarked, Kirkwell and Lisbon were next; of which Lisbon was special. In the meantime STRENGTH TRIAL was of interest as it was the first 'outing' for the newly formed Commando Logistic Regiment and although not embarked in *Fearless* – the LSLs would become the Regiment's more usual mode of transport – they would become closely linked.

Relations between the United Kingdom and her oldest ally, Portugal, had been strained since 1966 because of the Beira patrol and blockade: it was now time to put affairs back together with *Fearless* chosen as the Commander-in-Chief Fleet's Flagship for this important diplomatic visit, but the irony was not lost on the press that this was also the ship that had hosted the Smith – Wilson talks. The *Sunday Telegraph* ran a piece on 25 July 1972 supporting the visit and praising the Portuguese:

> Portugal, increasingly pilloried by the United Nations for the firm hand she keeps on her African possessions, is to receive an official gesture of goodwill.... (The Admiral's) arrival may help to cool the resentment which the Portuguese naturally feel at the Royal Navy's blockade of Beira in Portuguese East Africa, part of our sanctions against Rhodesia.... It will also give the Admiral an opportunity of thanking the Portuguese for the humane and forbearing way in which they have never hesitated to admit sick or injured British sailors from the blockading ships to Beira hospitals....

With a Royal Marines Captain's Guard and Band fallen in on the flight deck, *Fearless* berthed port-side to *Doca da Rocha* at 0900 on 30 June 1972. Admiral Sir Edward Ashmore[238] arrived ten minutes later to receive the first General Salute and from then onwards timings were critical to the morning's success as no less than seven more visitors, each warranting a General Salute and inspection, were to follow at very close intervals. There were plenty of chances for Sod's law to intervene and shades of Bordeaux came to the Commanding Officer's mind – as it did to the Guard Commander's. At Bordeaux the VIPs had arrived in the wrong order and thus in indecipherable uniforms but the Bandmaster – Mr Williams – had saved the day by playing the same musical salute for each caller, but Bordeaux had been a social visit whereas this, in Lisbon, would have had a diplomatic 'fall-out' if things went wrong. They did not, and:

> Despite some cars being spotted hiding behind warehouses to await their turn all went smoothly with the Portuguese highly amused to learn of our concern when told about the French shambles.[239]

Eight guards in Lisbon commanded by the author.

As always on these occasions so much depends on the British Naval Attaché and the rapport he will have forged with the ship's liaison officer flown ahead well in advance – sometimes weeks in advance. It was by general agreement a 'magic' visit with immense and genuine friendships formed and hospitality given and received and if there had ever been any concern over British foreign policy – as in South Africa – it was voiced towards Her Majesty's Government and not to Her Majesty's Royal Navy. In fact, as the *Daily Telegraph* reported on 29 July 1972, the day before the ship's arrival:

> *The guest list for a party Admiral Ashmore is giving aboard* (Fearless) *tomorrow night reflects the way in which emotions over the Rhodesian question have changed in Lisbon. It includes many of the most important figures in Portuguese civilian and military life.*

Once again, the success of a sensitive diplomatic occasion rested fairly on the heads of the young stewards and cooks under the command – and direction – of the Commander (S). Of course others were – are – involved, but these members of the ship's company were very much in the front line. If VIPs don't remember much about the Guard of Honour or the reception at the head of the brow they do remember the food, how it was served and whether or not the Band was up to scratch.

With Anglo-Portuguese relations back on an even keel and the C-in-C flying home, *Fearless* made a fast passage towards Devonport and the altogether different delights of Swansea. As she crossed the Channel a Mayday call was intercepted just before dawn on 6 July from the *Robin John*, somewhere dead ahead. Speed was increased. *Fearless* assumed the duties of scene-of-search command and lowered her LCVPs to quarter the Plymouth fishing vessel's last known position. Tragically, apart from a few books from the casualty's wheelhouse, nothing was found and the crew were 'missing presumed drowned'.

Quote from Douglas Barlow the Bosun 'Wait till he sees my parrot!' (Wardroom Line Book caption competition winner.)

Swansea was socially important for the ship and had been requested by the town itself. Following a families' day in Plymouth Sound, 200 schoolboys remained on board for the journey across the Bristol Channel and a tight squeeze through the ninety-foot-wide lock into Swansea Harbour – made even 'thinner' as the flight deck catwalks all but overhung a swing bridge. All the usual entertainment was laid on including the required party for handicapped and under-privileged children but the one event that gave most pleasure is described by Simon Cassels:[240]

> *A father told me that his severely handicapped son, aged about 12, had painstakingly made an 'Airfix' model of* Fearless. *Was there any chance of his seeing over the ship? The only way to get the boy onboard was to hoist him in father's car by crane onto the flight deck. (Breaking all health and safety requirements – Dad accepted liability.) While still in the car he was driven down to the tank deck and into an LCM, much to the boy's delight. Local press took up the story.*

Getting out of Swansea for a rare meeting of siblings was more difficult than getting in as the Commanding Officer explained in his Report of Proceedings:[241]

> *After several delays due to other ship movements the ship sailed from Swansea at 1215A on 17 July. A cross wind in the lock made passage through it difficult and the berthing incident which subsequently occurred has been reported separately.... . The opportunity to engineer a meeting of sister ships was noticed almost by accident so it was a happy occasion when HMS* Fearless *and HMS* Intrepid *met for five hours in the North Channel on 18 July. A* Beira Bucket[242] *competition was held in* Intrepid.

Ship's hockey team early 1970s. Back row (left to right): C./Sgt. Carlise, Lieut. Scott, P.O.(P.T.I.) Ballard (Capt.), P.O.EL. Slight, Surg. Lieut. (D) Harkness, Lieut.-Cdr. Mudge. Front row (left to right): C.P.O.M.A. Cherry, Lieut. Cooper, P.O.M.E.M. Burk, A./L.C.E.M. Dean, App. Hopper.

Teams were transferred by light jackstay together with various key officers who were keen to study the changes required by the Dartmouth Training Squadron role. On completion of the transfer, Fearless *maintained close station at 'chucking up' range in a vain attempt to redress the advantage one expects the home team to gain. Finally at 1700 my teams conceded defeat by a narrow margin and returned by LCVP. . . .*

Despite Government assurances, amphibious warfare was now on the descendent in the United Kingdom and it would get worse – and include a war – before any reversal would take place. By coincidence, on the day that the two amphibious flag ships met, the *Daily Telegraph* offered a brief comment on the future:

The Navy's amphibious forces will be halved next year when the assault ship Fearless *. . . becomes the Dartmouth Training Ship and her sister ship* Intrepid *starts a long refit. This will leave only the Commando ships* Bulwark *and* Hermes *. . . neither of which can carry anything heavier than the standard three-ton lorry. The rundown of the amphibious forces starts next month when the* Intrepid *takes over from the frigates* Eastbourne, Scarborough *and* Tenby *. . . The withdrawal of the* Intrepid *next year and her replacement by the* Fearless *are particularly serious moves at a time when NATO is emphasising the policy of 'flexible response' to the Warsaw Pact's overwhelming superiority in troops and armour. . . .*

By cutting off its nose to spite its financial face, Whitehall was making fools of Britain's armed forces in the eyes of the country's allies . . . while, unknowingly, *Fearless* was on her way to an amphibious operation – and nearly without her LCMs. These had not been required in Swansea nor for the forthcoming Exercise WRATHEX – a Supporting Arms Coordination Centre Desk[243] and Naval Gunfire Support exercise off the live firing range at Cape Wrath. Major Ken Robson, despite being offered the opportunity to leave them in Plymouth for a period of self maintenance, wisely advised the Commanding Officer that to sail without the ship's main armament, no matter for how short a time, was not a good idea. He was more right than he could have guessed.

A brief background to the situation in Northern Ireland is necessary to put *Fearless*'s part into perspective. By 1972 security in Northern Ireland had deteriorated to the point where large swathes of suburbs were 'no-go' areas for the Royal Ulster Constabulary and the military. Republicans, in Belfast's Andersonstown , in Londonderry's Bogside and Creggan districts had effectively sealed themselves off from the outside world behind massive barricades of solid materials; some of these obstructions were mined. Passage past was only by courtesy of the IRA which planned its murderous deeds from the sanctity offered by these cantonments and from which they would sally forth to shoot, bomb and maim before returning to comparative 'safety'. By the summer of 1972 the Government had decided that it was time to re-establish law with force.

Meanwhile, in company with HMS *Zulu*[244] who would supply the Naval Gunfire Support from her two 4.5-inch mountings, and with elements of Headquarters, 3 Commando Brigade, 848 Naval Air Squadron, 95 Commando Forward Observation Unit and 29 Commando Light Regiment Royal Artillery with its 15-mm pack howitzers embarked, *Fearless* was placed – to add realism to the enterprise – on a conventional war footing once she arrived off Cape Wrath on 26 July. The guns were landed, as were the Royal Artillery's Forward Observation Officers while the Royal Artillery's Liaison Officer Naval Gunfire Support (RALONGS) was embedded in *Zulu*'s operations room. All augured well as *Fearless*'s SACC Desk began dovetailing the Royal Artillery's firing serials with those of the frigate. Simon Cassels takes up the story:[245]

At about 1530 a signal from Commander-in-Chief Fleet was received indicating that Fearless *would probably be required to sail at short notice to lift an infantry battalion to Northern Ireland. I advised the Fleet Gunnery Officer of this and had him flown ashore to confer with Lieutenant Colonel W. Morris the CO of 95 Commando Forward Observation Unit and Lieutenant I. MacKenzie of D Flight, 848 Squadron, on how best to continue in* Fearless's *absence. He returned . . . and informed me that . . . with the essential elements of the SACC ashore it could go on with a modified tempo. . . .*

I was then summoned to the Skynet Portacabin. A familiar voice (Bryan Straker, now DN Plans) told me on the scrambler to, 'break off, go to the Clyde and await further instructions'. On arrival there, one of FOCAS's staff officers came onboard and told me what the ship had to do. Thereafter MOTORMAN[246] *was 'On': first taking the Scots Guards to Belfast, then back to the Clyde to embark AVREs for 'inserting' into Londonderry. No signal by W/T was ever received or sent: everything was done by word of mouth.*

Fearless sailed at best speed for the Gareloch in western Scotland where she was met at the Royal Corps of Transport's slipway at Rhu on 27 July by Major Neil Carlier, Royal Engineers,[247] the Army GSO2 on FOCAS's staff. Simon Cassels, in his report, would write:[248]

For the rest of the day Neil Carlier was on board or ashore briefing those concerned and resolving problems as they arose. The smooth execution of Fearless's *part in Operation GLASSCUTTER was largely due to his well-directed efforts at this early stage.*

Fearless's role was two-fold: first, she was to lift an infantry battalion to Belfast and, secondly, she was to deploy four armoured bulldozers directly into Londonderry after dark, if a landing place on the banks of the River Foyle could be found. These Armoured Vehicles Royal Engineers or AVREs were never to be referred to as tanks lest the politicians be accused of deploying such

AVRE demolishing a Bogside barricade.

vehicles in an internal security situation: shades of Hungary and Poland haunted their minds. Nevertheless they were built on Centurion chassis and, in addition to their dozer blades, they mounted a fearsome demolition gun that would smash through the barricades.

With no aircraft of her own, the first of *Fearless*'s two recce teams, consisting of Major Ken Robson, the Ship's Communications Officer, Lieutenant Commander Bruce Lemonde, and two LCM Coxswains, Colour Sergeants Johnny Keogh and Johnny Mumford, was lifted off by Army helicopter during the evening of 27 July with the aim of establishing what was practical and how to communicate directly with the ship from ashore. Meanwhile the Second Battalion the Scots Guards embarked that evening.[249] The next morning the second recce team, consisting solely of the Beachmaster, flew by civil airline to HQ Northern Ireland to establish where best to disembark the AVREs into Londonderry.

The banks of the Foyle do not lend themselves to clandestine landings by anything larger than a canoe and certainly not for, effectively, main battle tanks from LCMs. With the help of the detachment of Royal Engineers at Fort George on the west bank of the River Foyle, about two miles above the Foyle Bridge, a beaching position was chosen just outside the perimeter security fence, which had to be breached and then guarded. With considerable, after-dark scooping and three rolls of Class 30 trackway rolled down it by hand and then pegged, this makeshift beach would, it was hoped, accept wheeled scout cars and tracked bulldozers.

The risks were deemed acceptable and the chances of executing a clean landing considered fair, bearing in mind one or two unusual factors: it was a steeper incline than would be considered 'normal'; the trackway would, because of the way it is rolled and, in this case unrolled manually, be laid upside down with the smooth surface upwards and it was only Class 30 and not designed for heavy tracks.

With three rolls laid on top of each other and all held in place by massive pickets into the earth, the Beachmaster reckoned that it might just hold. In due course Simon Cassels was to describe the beach thus in his Report of Proceedings:[250]

> *Londonderry. Chart 2486. Position 252 degrees from Pennyburn Light 450 yards. A hastily constructed beach of mud, gravel and rocks which required five hours of Royal Engineers work before being suitable. Due to the manoeuvres on the beach use of the ship's Class 30 track-layer would be impracticable. If notice is given trackway could be re-laid and the perimeter fence re-breached. Suitable for LCMs only 3 hours before high water springs for re-embarkation and 3 hours either side of high water springs for disembarkation. The beach is exactly the width of a LCM and should be approached with extreme accuracy. Distance, LPD anchorage to Beach: over 26 miles. A 'one off' beach in a secure area.*

Fearless sailed at 0900 on 28 July – earlier than ordered – just in case the arrival time in Belfast was brought forward and that evening the Guards Battalion was disembarked allowing Simon Cassels to write that they: 'Had been an exemplary embarked force which I am sorry to see leave.'

They, or their successors, would again be taken to war in an LPD – twenty years hence.

Fearless left Belfast at 0100 on 29 July, to steam back to Rhu and the waiting AVREs of 26 Armoured Engineer Squadron, brought through Europe on low-loaders from the British Army of the Rhine and then via an Army LCT, HMAV *Audemer*,[251] to the south coast of England. They were accompanied by Ferret Scout Cars, all under the command of Captain Steve Taylor, Royal Engineers, and embarked into *Fearless* via LCMs by 1300. Detailed planning could now begin for the night passage up the River Foyle with the Beachmaster studying charts, tides, timings and arranging simple reporting lines. Captain Cassels takes up the story in another amalgamation from his correspondence:[252]

After embarking the AVREs, the loads were covered by tarpaulins and sections of the ship's condemned, Flight Deck ceremonial awning. The operation however did not appear to evoke much interest among onlookers ashore or afloat. I was told to hide the ship until dark, then make for the entrance to Lough Foyle. Memories of the west coast of Scotland from my navigation course sprang to mind. There was an ideal spot, not overlooked by land, hard to pick out from seaward and remote enough for the LCMs to swing their compasses, test their radars and rehearse the navigation and communications plans. I therefore sailed at 1200 shaping initially for Girvan and Stranraer before anchoring in Proaig Bay on the east coast of Islay at 2359. The seclusion of this spot was better than I expected. There was only one crofter's cottage to be seen, apart from Jura House four miles away.

While on passage to Proaig Bay HMS Gavington[253] was made available and so the forenoon of the 30 July was devoted to rehearsals in Carskey Bay, Mull of Kintyre. Plans were revised for her employment which was to conduct an accepted patrol pattern in the Rathlin-Foyle area for as long as possible then follow the LCMs up river, keeping some 8–12 miles astern of them, acting as a communications link as far as Redcastle Light.... .

Thence to the Foyle. Fearless *closed to within 3.5 miles of the Tuns buoy at 2045 at which time the Beachmaster and OC RE Detachment were collected by two army helicopters and the LCMs retracted.*

It had long been decided that the Beachmaster, once he had given his 'O' Group to the ship's Communications Officers and Navigator plus his own coxswains and communicators, would be of more value at the beaching point to ensure that it was not only secure but that transit lights were correctly placed as they had to be at a precise angle to the shore line to ensure the deepest water in the final approach. Simon Cassels also believed that the ship's navigator, Lieutenant Commander John Ainger, should be responsible for the navigation:[254]

In the event the cold, dark night with rain and poor visibility while ideal to deter others from looking too closely made conditions far from pleasant for negotiating a narrow channel for the first time by blind pilotage.

They were scarcely any better for the recovery when thick fog persisted for much of the way. The LCM radar, Type 975, was reassuringly good in all craft throughout.

The LCMs set off, put the AVREs ashore and withdrew. It was a relief when they were seen returning. Yet, in the same instant, came the order for them to return and recover the AVREs. Now the thickest of fogs had set in. Altogether a most testing feat of navigation: the Foyle is no picnic at the best of times.

The LCMs had sailed from a position 3.5 miles from the Tuns buoy at the entrance to the River Foyle and from there were 'shadowed' by HMS *Gavington* as far as Redcastle Light in the Republic – indeed much of the deep water channel runs within a few hundred yards of the Republic's shore and well within rifle-shot range: not that it made much difference which side of the border shots were fired from as both were equally as likely. In the event there were none, as it was dark, raining and with visibility down to about half a mile.

On the banks of the Foyle the Beachmaster heard the darkened craft and switched on two dim, beach transit lights: the first craft lowered its ramp at 2351 and immediately a Ferret roared up the steep bank followed by the Centurion bulldozer which, surprisingly, did no damage to the trackway. The other LCMs followed onto the single-point beach: it took just twenty-six minutes for all the AVREs to form-up, ready to advance. Even without a torch it was easy to see that each armoured vehicle now had ROYAL ENGINEERS painted in large white letters along their sides so that the world's press would be in no doubt that these were not 'the cavalry'. Between the two words someone had stuck a *Fearless* transfer: the Mighty Lion was in action again.

The nautical plan required the LCMs to return, for not only would they be targets at dawn with nowhere to hide, but the tide would shortly preclude any further movement: the Beachmaster travelled with them and they entered *Fearless*'s dock at 0300. The warning order to repeat the round journey – the operation ashore having been more swift and more successful than expected – came at 0800 but the first LCM was already on its way by the time the confirmatory signal was received a few minutes later. This second double transit of the River Foyle, with the OCAD now back in command but with John Ainger still navigating, was conducted in daylight in thickish fog and without incident, despite the IRA's nest having had a stick poked into it. All LCMs were recovered by 1500 when *Fearless* closed her stern gate, de-ballasted and weighed anchor. Summer leave had been delayed but now she was free to re-join her original programme and head for Plymouth Sound after dropping off her Scottish liberty men at the Gareloch.

On the flight deck a party had been arranged at which all LCM, AVRE and Ferret crews were welcomed back. As with almost everything *Fearless* did it had been a joint effort from the ship's command and communications teams, to the Engineering Department and, especially in many respects, through to the Supply Department who, once more had successfully embarked, bedded and fed a complete Army battalion for two days with no warning. The Medical Department, too, had been on full alert throughout this time – just in case. Simon Cassels commented:

Captain Stephen Taylor, RE, welcomed back from Operation MOTORMAN with a cake baked by PO Ck Yeung Cheong Sing.

The AVRE and LCM crews returned tired but happy. Everyone in Fearless *was thrilled and very relieved that the operation had been successfully carried out without a casualty. The operation was very much a 'whole team' affair so I am reluctant to single out officers, ratings and other ranks for particular mention. I wish, however to commend the following. . . .*

Simon Cassels ended this ROP with glowing praise for not only – and quite rightly – John Ainger[255] upon whom the timely and safe landing of the AVREs had relied, but also for the four LCM coxswains:

C/Sgt J. Keogh[256] (Foxtrot Three) C/Sgt J. Mumford[257] (F4), C/Sgt B. Todd (F2)[258] and C/Sgt B. Phillips (F1) for their high professional skill as Coxswains of their respective LCMs during the long passages of the Foyle, when they alone of their crews were exposed to potential sniper fire, and in their expeditious off- and back-loading on the beach at Fort George.

Problems with beaches were not quite over. While unloading the AVREs at RAF Mountbatten's slipway at dawn on 2 August the Beachmaster was placed under close arrest by the Station's Duty Officer. Somehow this administrative Squadron Leader had been left out of the 'orders-loop' from the highest echelons of the MOD and, seeing LCMs and 'tanks' on his slipway in the half light, had rushed down in his best uniform to tell them that they could not do what they were doing without his permission 'which I will not give!' While the ABU was conducting this tricky offload of very heavy vehicles on a slimy slipway, the Squadron Leader was told to 'shut his eyes, and pretend he had never seen anything!' As two Flight Lieutenants were marched down to the beach to effect the arrest, the OCAD sped past in the Commander (E)'s open sports car which, too, had been unloaded. The RAF, not being slow to report a 'slight' to its dignity, had already signalled Captain Cassels.

The old problem of comparative ranks of Royal Marines Captains and RAF Squadron Leaders was the catalyst.[259] But HMS *Fearless*'s wiley Commanding Officer was equal to the task and immediately dispatched the ship's AOO – a Royal Marines Major – to:[260]

Put the Squadron Leader straight: not least of all for trying to prevent an operational offload that had been sanctioned from Number 10.

No more was heard and everyone was able to proceed on their delayed summer leave to return ready for a major NATO exercise, STRONG EXPRESS – this time on the northern flank.

Numerous signals of thanks were received on board, only one of which survives and that from the Commander 8th Infantry Brigade:

Many thanks for your assistance during Operation CARCAN. The delivery of the AVREs so successfully contributed greatly to achieving the aims of the operation. Please pass to all concerned my appreciation for the excellent work and example of cooperation and teamwork.

As with so many ships in dockyard hands in those days, sailing was often delayed by industrial action and then, when everything appeared 'ready in all respects for sea', shoddy workmanship would cause further delays. As Simon Cassels recounts, *Fearless* was no exception:

Industrial action in Devonport Dockyard affected the undocking programme and preparation for sea. Both stern glands leaked unacceptably on first flooding up and the dock had to be pumped out again. The glands were refilled by the Dockyard but similar unacceptable leakages occurred on the second occasion. . . . Various trades being 'out' on selected days precluded full repair before the ship's sailing date so a temporary repair to last until the refit was effected by caulking. . . . Further enforced delays hampered ammunitioning, storage and cranage. . . .

Such was the way Britain's Navy went to war in the latter half of the twentieth century, and it was usually the long-suffering, hard-working and flexible serviceman who was left to 'make things happen'. Against the odds, *Fearless* with Headquarters, 3 Commando Brigade and elements of the Commando Logistic Regiment embarked, sailed on time on 7 October. She collected a United States Navy SEAL team from USS *Mount Whitney*,[261] the 1st Raiding Squadron of Rigid Raiding Craft from the Amphibious Training Unit, Royal Marines at Poole[262] and then proceeded to Europort to pick up a rifle company of the Royal Netherlands Marine Corps.

From *Fearless*'s point of view, Exercise STRONG EXPRESS, held in the waters of north Norway around Harstad and the Lofoton Islands, was memorable for two events: the detaching of the LCUs under independent command of a 'third party' and for the ship herself running aground – although many on board may not have known of this last event at the time. Otherwise, in company with other NATO ships, the exercise was a reasonably standard series of large-scale landings of UK, Dutch and US Marines along the coasts and fjords, dovetailed with nautical manoeuvres at sea.[263]

Two of these landings involved LCMs being detached, for the first time, from the ship's control to that of the landing forces. Up to this date no LPD Commanding Officer had been keen to lose control of what was, in effect, his main armament and apart from the odd night laying up at an anchorage or on passage between ports as navigational exercises, the LCMs had remained under the command and control of the Ship's Operations Room. Ewen Southby-Tailyour, in his book *Reasons in Writing*,[264] takes up the story:

> Before 1972 landing craft had been tied very much to their parent ships, which meant that if the shipping left the AOA, landing craft support was lost to the Commando Brigade. In the Mediterranean, Persian Gulf and Far East this loss of mobility had been acceptable as the troops moved inland but in North Norway the problem was more acute. Fjords bisect many lines of advance and offer the only guaranteed methods of movement in winter when enemy action or avalanches can close valleys and roads and blizzards prevent flying. Without use of the sea lanes this loss of flexibility can seriously hamper the Commando Brigade.

There was another and perhaps more realistic reason why the LCMs were not allowed to 'play away': it was taking a long time for successive LPD Commanding Officers to accept that the Colour Sergeant coxswains were capable of independent command, including both ocean navigation and inshore pilotage. Understandable perhaps, but to use the LCMs only in ship to shore, controlled passages was a waste of experience and, of operational importance, was denying Brigade Commanders a vital asset. Simon Cassels and the Commanding Officer of 45 Commando during Exercise STRONG EXPRESS, Lieutenant Colonel Sir Steuart Pringle,[265] were to change all that and set a precedent for the future.

The Italian San Marco Battalion was acting as enemy in a blocking position at the head of Reisenfjorden some fifty miles from *Fearless*'s position. It was Colonel Pringle's aim to rout them but, a frontal landing would be obvious and, with the Norwegians as 'enemy', bound to fail as *Fearless* herself would, under normal circumstances, be required to approach the Amphibious Operating Area (AOA) before launching her craft. The Italians knew that too and considered their position reasonably invulnerable. Ewen Southby-Tailyour again:

> In 1972 the Commanding Officer of 45 Commando ... asked if Fearless's craft ... could be detached for a night raid while the ship went to sea. Surprisingly ... Simon Cassels, took no persuading to detach two of the LCMs, allowing me to establish a Forward Operating Base on the edge of the fjord, with my Headquarters in one of the holds of the lead craft. As the ... Commando could not fit in my two craft I asked HMS Albion[266] if she would lend me her four LCAs.

Her OCRM, Lieutenant Roger Dillon[267] … was a superb ally in this experiment. That night we loaded 45 Commando into the boats, secured the LCAs alongside the larger LCMs to produce only two radar echoes and showed (when necessary) the lights of fishing craft. The Commando was then landed fifty miles away just short of the head of Reisenfjorden, across unrecce'd beaches (another radical departure), from where they attacked the defending Italian San Marco battalion in the rear, while we returned, again undetected by Norwegian Coastal Forces as we steamed close to the cliffs (sometimes as close as half the width of an LCM and therefore in the radar echo of the cliff – or so we had hoped).

The Italians were not amused, nor were the rather stuffy NATO umpires who Colonel Pringle had 'forgotten' to brief. Two nights later we carried out a similar raid with two companies against a Norwegian Coastal Artillery Fort on the island of Grytoy.

The second and smaller exercise was conducted under the command of the OCAD and the Dutch Company Commander when the LCMs carried out an un-recced, covert landing of RNLMC personnel by night onto the cliffs and rocks of Koreneset Fort on the island of Grytőy. On passage from a lying up position to the east of Harstad, the flotilla of LCMs was challenged by Morse light from the 'enemy' base at Kråkenset but as the craft were showing the lights of fishing boats and had a Norwegian 'spy' on board who knew the identification signal for civilian craft during times of tension, they were allowed to proceed un-harassed by Norwegian fast attack craft. The men were landed by rubber craft, launched over the lowered ramps, to take the equally un-amused Norwegian defenders by surprise.

Thus was re-born the well-established concept of independent landing craft operations which was to be used with effect in the Falkland Islands before being officially recognized with the formation in 1984 of 539 Assault Squadron, Royal Marines.

Further ship-controlled landings took place at the head of Droysendet fjord on completion of which it was necessary for *Fearless* to weigh anchor and take a short cut through a deep, narrow but well defined pass named the Finnlandsneset Gap and into the larger Solbergenfjorden.

At 05095Z in the morning of the 23 September one or two of the sleeping ship's company were woken by a shudder and a slight heeling of the ship that lasted a few seconds. The confident – and remarkably calm – bridge team knew that they had not hit the bottom: they also knew that a Russian submarine had been reported in the area. Simon Cassels was later to write:

Having anchored one night tucked away off the main fjord to avoid detection, the ship bounced over some obstruction on returning at first light with a ghastly bang, shake and quiver. My heart sank. Visions that this marked the end of my career. Later that morning divers inspected the hull and explored the area where the incident had occurred. One pitometer log had been bent from vertical to nearly horizontal; mercifully the screws and rudders were undamaged. At the crucial 'step' between the two fjords there was nothing to be seen on the sea bed. Reams of paper supporting the notorious Form S.232, required for collision and grounding incidents, followed – just deserts for a former navigational adviser to the Admiralty Board. In dry dock on return to Devonport, there was unmistakable metal-to-metal scoring on the hull running intermittently for some feet aft from the log opening. The inference was that a Russian midget submarine monitoring the Exercise had bottomed on the 'step' overnight. By chance the pitometer log had struck a mast or the conning tower. Having been so rudely woken, the Russians made a hasty exit to avoid further detection.[268]

The ship returned to Rosyth, via Europort to disembark the Royal Netherlands Marine Corps, where the LCMs were ordered to act as gash barges for the returning amphibious fleet: a task which was cancelled at the last moment but not before a disturbed OCAD had made as many representations as he thought he could get away with. Once again, it seems worthy of comment that the country's defence capabilities were being affected by the industrial action of Government employees. Simon Cassels:

> *The ship anchored west of the Forth Road Bridge. . . . Throughout this period due to the industrial situation in Rosyth shore support available was minimal. . . . Gash disposal facilities were not available to the ships assembled in the Forth so the LCMs were initially requisitioned by the Port Admiral Rosyth for use as gash barges. Fortunately this drastic measure was not required. It does however highlight the limited knowledge of the way in which a LPD operates in the Fleet as a whole. The LCMs and their crews had been working hard during the exercise ... great deal of extra craft running was already required to make good the lack of PAS effort. Moreover as the ship was due to deploy to the Mediterranean in two weeks time due to a programme change[269] I had planned for as many of the ship's company as possible to take weekend leave. In the circumstances using the LCMs as gash boats would have stung the Amphibious Detachment hard.*

Although due for a refit there was, unexpectedly, *Bulwark*'s Mediterranean deployment to be 'endured' to show solidarity with NATO's southern flank. Thanks to another case of industrial action, the LPH was still in dockyard hands, unable to meet her long-standing commitment to the Southern Flank.

Before this news was received, *Fearless* had begun planning for a lengthy period in dockyard hands, due to start in October and, as part of the lead-up to one of the most major refits of her life – with a considerable list of substantial Amendments and Additions – her stores holdings had been run down. Now these stores, including food and other consumables, needed building up again but with industrial action in Rosyth and Portsmouth preventing RFA *Resource* herself from stocking up, this process would not be easily reversed as Simon Cassels stated in his ROP:[270]

> *The support given by PSTO(N) Portsmouth and his staff in arranging this large stowing at short notice was excellent and almost everything required was made available. . . . The evolution did, however, once more prove convincingly how much more economic in time and manpower RAS is compared with a stowing in harbour. On this occasion it took two days and consequently delayed the ship's original sailing date by two days.*

Yet more dockyard-induced, mechanical failures dogged the ship – she had had to enter Portsmouth on one engine[271] due to a luboil pump failure – and now, after repairs, the same pump failed again. A strike in a different section of the dockyard affected the operational readiness of the ship so, at no notice, the repair was taken on by the Fleet Maintenance Group who worked all night in order that she could sail for Gibraltar during the afternoon of 12 October.

Bad weather forced the cancellation of the rare opportunity to fire the Seacat missiles but at least *Fearless* was able to complete her storing during a RAS (Solids) with RFA *Olna*, only to have this curtailed due to a failure of the refrigeration plant: the transfer of frozen food was instantly stopped after just fourteen days of frozen provisions had been received. A representative from the makers, York Shipley, flew to Gibraltar so by the time the ship reached Malta all was back to normal.

On arrival in Grand Harbour the four Wessex V helicopters of B Flight, 848 Squadron, were craned from the LCMs onto the flight deck and 41 Commando Group under the command of Lieutenant Colonel R.A. Campbell, Royal Marines, was embarked: *Fearless* may not have had the capacity of *Bulwark* but her presence was still welcome. In practice she was employed as little more than a troop ship and, once the Embarked Military Force had been landed into their Cypriot training areas, there was no more for her to do until the Commando needed lifting back to Malta. During her brief stay at anchor off Dhekelia she flew the flag of Flag Officer Malta, Rear Admiral

J.A. Tempelton-Cothill and entertained various military, diplomatic and civilian dignitaries from the local Sovereign Base Area. With those social tasks completed and, at more junior levels, runs ashore satisfactorily achieved, *Fearless* was free to revert to the role of 'private ship' and head for Greece.

By popular acclaim from the ship's company – after a form of informal ballot had been held across the Divisions – the main run ashore was to be Volos, on the east coast, north of Athens.

> *With a view to investigating possible navigational training areas for the future when Dartmouth Midshipmen will be embarked the passage was planned via the island of Stampalia and the Santorini passage. . . . In addition arrangements had been made for an expedition by two LCMs (with a number of hiking parties embarked) via the Khakis Channel. . . .*[272]

On arrival *Fearless* moored with her stern gate lowered onto the waterfront making access easy, which was just as well for on the Open Day she was nearly overwhelmed with visitors interested in seeing the largest British warship to visit since 1964. Although this visit had had to be arranged at very short notice it was an undoubted success with over 100 ship's company taking part in 'expeds' and extended banyans among the local islands: a success due in no small part to the enthusiasm of the British Naval Attaché in Athens, Captain John Lawson.

On the formal and social sides full programmes were set in motion – memorable, for some, by the arrival of girl friends first met during the earlier visit to Athens; John Lawson being particularly diligent in this regard!

> *One expedition inside the Gulf of Volos . . . was made by a party of 20 in an LCM and LCVP to a spot named on Admiralty Chart 1196 as Fearless Cove. . . . How it got its name is not known . . . a small diving team pinpointed a wreck marked Position Approximate on the chart. . . .*
>
> *In his speech the Mayor mentioned how much the town enjoyed the return of the Royal Navy. . . . He hoped* Fearless *presaged more visits in the future . . . The sentiments were clearly genuine and for our part we were struck by how well the ship's company was received ashore, especially in the countryside. . . .*[273]

Almost as one might have expected, mechanical defects nearly spoiled everything:

> *On leaving Volos . . . at 0930B on 31 October the main circulator for the starboard engine tripped on overspeed due to a blocked suction. The weed clearing ejector was (activated) . . . (but) the main engine was therefore unusable during a critical period in the harbour entrance . . . by dropping the port anchor the tugs were able to control the ship in the freshening wind.*

41 Commando needed lifting back home, a task for which *Fearless* was joined by *Intrepid*, who then, at dawn on 6 November, led the way into Grand Harbour. For their part the *Fearless*'s crew were looking forward to a fourteen-day Assisted Maintenance Period which, as Simon Cassels noted in his final Report of Proceedings only staved off the increasing list of major defects that would need attention during the course of his ship's forthcoming extended refit in Devonport.

With her defects stabilized there were one or two tasks yet to be completed: depth charge trials at Malta's Marsaxlokk; Exercise CORSICA 72 and visits to Calvi and Toulon. For this last visit *Fearless* and *Intrepid* lay alongside each other; an occasion that spawned numerous mess-deck exchanges.

Then, at long last, it really was time for the much needed refit and, in some areas, rebuild. The Army also took the opportunity to remove its ranks from the Amphibious Detachment, including the whole of the Royal Signals Troop. Their duties, plus those of the BARV crew, Vehicle Decks Party and Michigan tractor drivers would now be undertaken by Royal Marines.

Fearless entered Plymouth Sound on 10 November 1972 and the next day steamed into Devonport Dockyard. Simon Cassels remained in command to oversee the start of this programme before handing over on 18 June 1973 after what he described, in part, as:

> *An occasionally frustrating but full and varied time, much of it at sea either exercising or under way at high passage speeds ... The ship's company has taken the extra running time in good heart and, indeed, it has been possible in many ways to turn it to their advantage....*

When it was produced a little later Simon Cassels wrote the following in the Commission Book as a form of Epilogue:

> *Captain Straker mentioned in his Foreword that* Fearless *was bound to be in demand – working hard and playing hard. The last nine months have been no exception: two major NATO exercises, four national exercises, five foreign visits, schoolboys galore, not to mention the ship's part in Operation MOTORMAN.*
>
> *All this you have done cheerfully and well, and it is with good reason we have come to be known throughout the Fleet as Friendly* Fearless.
>
> *It has been a great privilege for me to command such a well-knit, responsive and happy ship's company.*
>
> *My best wishes to you and your families for the future, and may this book help you share and cherish your memories of this fine ship with them. God bless you all.*

Chapter Eight

Captain J.B. Rumble, Royal Navy

Sixth Commanding Officer
1973–1975

European Waters, West Indies, Mediterranean

HMS *Fearless* was Captain John Rumble's second command after HMS *Torquay*. He retired from a MOD communications appointment in 1979 and died in 1996, before this book was conceived. Commander John Lock, his Executive Officer, has written on his behalf: 'My account covers the period April 1973 to December 1974 when I was relieved by Commander Jeremy Dreyer.'

John Rumble took command of HMS *Fearless* on 18 June 1973 to find his ship as deep in a major refit as possible. The ship's company was living ashore in less than ideal conditions while the duty watch were appalled during rounds each night to find that the dockyard hands were sleeping off their daytime excesses in the mess decks, for which they had demanded beds and bedding. When challenged by a ship's officer, a dockyard manager admitted that the average working week involved just nine and a half hours' labour.

But all bad things do come to an end and after three major delays a Refit Completion Date Inspection was fixed for 6 November 1973 to be followed by a month of trials, repairs, more trials, the first of a three-phase Portland work-up, more trials and the acceptance of the Dartmouth Training Ship role from *Intrepid*. Christmas leave was welcome but, after so long 'at home' so was the coming West Indies deployment. John Lock:

Captain John Rumble with HRH Princess Margaret.

In addition to the usual repair, overhauls and A's and A's the ship was also prepared for the role of Dartmouth Training Ship involving the fitting of Portakabins for use as classrooms. The aviation facilities were greatly improved with the repositioning of the Flyco one deck higher than before; a new Air Maintenance Control Room; white floodlighting for the Flight Deck and an Aircrew Briefing Room. Facilities for a permanent ship's flight were still unsatisfactory with no covered space for major component changes or protection of parked aircraft from the ravages of salt and condensation. Nevertheless it was intended to embark a flight of two Wessex for the training cruises for familiarization of trainees and general usefulness. The Aviation Department complement was increased.

Please Admiral, can we stay and watch the bomb go off?

There were a number of spurious threats during the refit to worry the new Commander.

In addition to the raising of Flyco by a deck the other significant change was the filling in of the after Sea Cat Deck – 02 Deck – to produce not only the Aircrew Briefing Room and stores but a Warrant Officers' Mess on the starboard side, aft. John Lock:

Refits are seldom easy and this had been no exception. Officers and ship's company lived ashore in HMS Drake *with the junior rates quartered in below-standard Nissen huts that did little for morale. The Dockyard were having difficulty keeping to programme and the completion date was postponed three times to the point where any further delays would have jeopardized the planned operational programme and assumption of the Dartmouth Training role. Dockyard delays bore on ship's staff work to clean, paint and set to work in readiness for the move back on board and for sea. Consequently it was necessary to extend daily working hours to 1800 for the last seven weeks in refit. The dockyard also increased their effort but it was dispiriting to see the night-shifts going to the empty mess-decks to sleep or play cards and the Lagger's Union constantly demanding more concessions and safety clothing which were then not used.*

At last, however, the work was done, the people embarked, the Port Admiral's inspection took place and the ship cleared to start a four week Post Refit Trials (PRT) programme. These were not without incident and twice had to be aborted. Firstly the lubricating oil to the Main Circulator failed and the port engine had to be shut down, then, two weeks later it was the starboard engine's turn when overheating in the superheater tubes occurred. On both occasions the ship had to return to the Dockyard for repairs. Nevertheless progress was made and the first deck landing by a Wessex from Yeovilton was achieved with the aircraft greeted in Fleet Air Arm style with champagne on the flight deck. Back in Devonport work was further interrupted by the mass of autumn leaves carried downstream in the Tamar that blocked the intakes to the generators. Another minor but messy frustration was caused by the vast numbers of starlings choosing to roost on the dockyard cranes close alongside. For some reason the cranes could not be moved. Ships are better off at sea.

On one occasion, while in the basin, a tragedy was narrowly averted. Late one night the Duty Lieutenant Commander and Duty PO were doing upper deck rounds when they heard faint cries for help coming from over the side. The Officer of the Watch, Lieutenant Rick Banfield, was seen wet and bedraggled on the gash barge alongside. He had fallen through a hole in a catwalk into the basin luckily without injuring himself and was recovered by ladder.[274]

Post Refit Trials were followed by a short, intense work-up in the Portland areas. FOST produced the usual thorough Staff Sea Check highlighting those areas of organization that needed attention. Many of these were already known but it is always daunting to see ones shortcomings so starkly laid before one. In this period the LCMs were embarked from Poole and on return to Devonport the ship berthed on Intrepid *to transfer the Dartmouth Training task, officers and equipment. It was about this time that the Captain brought his two most attractive daughters on board causing quite a stir in the wardroom.*

The shortened trials and work-up programme put a heavy burden on all, but particularly on the Technical and Supply Departments. All were eager to move ahead but were constantly having to step

The refit dragged on. 'Paf' Grant's Wardroom Line Book's view.

back and put to rights equipment that should have emerged from refit in good working order. In particular all the main ballast pumps were unserviceable and the machinery control system gave constant trouble. Such set-backs and frustrations are common to all ships after refit and part of the naval life. Fearless *was in no way worse served than other ships but the pressures of delayed completion, squeezed trials programmes, bad weather, the twin roles of Assault Ship and Dartmouth Training Ship, autumn leaves and incontinent starlings certainly made for an interesting time. Christmas leave brought a welcome respite for everyone.*

Fearless was designed and built as an amphibious warfare ship with no provision, nor intention, to train large numbers of young officers or Officers Under Training (OUTs). A clash between the two tasks was inevitable even if this was confined to the operational programme. There had to be a good understanding between the FOCAS and MGRM staffs and it was very much up to the wardroom and Ships Company to see that the clash did not develop into a Royal Navy/Royal Marines tug of war. Intrepid *had taken on the role when she was a worked up and dedicated amphibious warfare ship whereas the new commission in* Fearless *had to learn both roles from scratch. Luckily the full staff of two Seamen Officers, three Instructor Officers, a Fleet Chief Petty Officer and four Petty Officers transferred from* Intrepid. *The penalties were a further reduction in some Communications and amphibious warfare billets and some infringement on amphibious warfare spaces. OUTs occupied the Embarked Force mess-decks in the starboard dock wall while the starboard side of the Upper Vehicle Deck became a training area filled with Portakabins. The Royal Marines retained full use of the Lower*

Vehicle Deck and the dock remained fully operational. Ship's boats were used for training while the landing craft were often used for 'officer of the watch manoeuvres' by the Midshipmen. When OUTs were on board at the same time as an Embarked Force the Supply Department was stretched to the limit in feeding everyone. All meal times had to be staggered, including those in the wardroom.

The primary training objectives were coastal navigation and practical seamanship including seaboats, boat running, anchorages, OOW manoeuvres and Replenishment at Sea. The operational programme had to cater for these needs and on long ocean passages the staff had to devise useful alternatives. The Portakabins in the tank deck were fitted out as classrooms with furniture, chart tables, radar displays and some 'navaids' that could be used without interference to the ship systems.

Should a real operational need have arisen there were contingency plans to disembark the trainees and staff and bring the amphibious warfare complement to full strength. The Granada incident in January 1974 and the Turkish invasion of Cyprus that summer were possible instances but in the end came to nothing as far as the ship's internal organization was concerned.

It is undeniable that the training task did impinge on the amphibious warfare role as indeed the training requirement itself was inhibited to a degree by the amphibious warfare programme. Nevertheless it can be fairly said that the combination worked as well as could be expected.

Tank deck fitted for DTS duties with Portakabin classrooms.

Nor, of course, was it a bad thing, from the amphibious warfare point of view, for the officers under training to have such an intimate introduction so early in their careers.

In early January 1974 the first batch of OUTs was embarked, numbering 32 Sub-Lieutenants and 110 Midshipmen. Three days later the ship sailed for Portland and a short amphibious warfare work-up. This was to be the first time that the two roles were undertaken together and COMAW, Commodore David Smith, embarked for the exercise. The plan was to carry out a short exercise landing troops and tanks over the beach at Arish Mell using both landing craft and helicopters. Ten Chieftain Tanks, an ARV and other equipment from C Squadron 4/7 Royal Dragoon Guards were embarked by LCM while the ship was moored to a buoy in Portland. Eighty-six troops from the RCT Junior Leaders Regiment were flown on by helicopters from 848 Squadron. The troops' introduction to life at sea included a night on camp beds on the half deck. The Supply Department managed well in feeding an embarked force, OUTs and a full Ships Company.

The weather once again intervened and due to the lack of an RFA oiler, fuel had to be taken on at the Outer Coaling Pier. As the wind increased to full gale and gusting more, the berth became untenable and had to be left. Conditions in the harbour made manoeuvring hazardous to the extent that an anchor was needed to assist the turn to line up with the harbour entrance. The order to 'stand by' was misheard and both anchors were slipped while the ship was moving downwind. They did their work with memorable effect and held fast without dragging but the swing into the wind produced the inevitable elbow in the cables and the likelihood that the ship would then drag. In the conditions the only solution was to slip one anchor without delay and seek the safety of the outer harbour. The slipped anchor was not buoyed and despite the efforts of divers has never been recovered. Next day it was replaced with one from Intrepid, *refitting in Portsmouth. All in all an eventful week that also included a flood in the provision rooms and canteen stores necessitating the writing off of a considerable quantity which had to be replaced by vertrep from RFA* Regent *at short notice.*

John Lock mentions the loss of the port anchor in Portland harbour. The forecastle officer, Lieutenant Colin Day,[275] misheard in the gale, the order to 'Stand by both anchors' as 'Let go both anchors', nevertheless his prompt action did, in the view of some – but not the Commanding Officer – save the ship which was stopped almost dead in her tracks, facing the sea wall, before she began to swing head-to-wind.

On 18 January the trials and work-up were complete, the ship fully stored, helicopters embarked and struck below, and at anchor in Plymouth Sound ready to sail for Trinidad and the first Training Cruise. Once clear of the Channel the weather improved and the ship settled into passage routine with the opportunity to continue internal training and to start to enjoy life. Ever since the previous summer, life had been one continuous battle to extract the ship from refit and create a cohesive and worked-up entity from the varied elements that made up the company. The transatlantic passage was the chance to further the process. . . .

. . . and to prepare for the possibility of a small military operation.

In 1973 Edward Heath had agreed with the Prime Minister of Grenada, Sir Eric Gairy, that the island should receive independence and that power would, therefore, be transferred on 7 February 1974. Local opposition parties were against independence on the grounds that the already failing economy and high unemployment could only worsen. In January police had fired into demonstrations, killing one man who happened to be the father of one of the opposition party leaders, Maurice Bishop. The situation was volatile. While on passage to Trinidad, Fearless *was ordered by MOD (Navy) to prepare contingency plans to evacuate British nationals and give whatever humanitarian assistance that might be needed. Plans were drawn up but in the event not executed so the ship was to play only a minor role,*

John Lock the new Commander took over a lively wardroom.

although on arrival in Port of Spain that was in the future and an official from the Foreign Office duly arrived on board for a series of two-way briefings. His task was to fly to Grenada by civil airline, contact Government House to assess the situation, gather information and report back by radio. Our task was to instruct him in the use of radios, cryptography and firearms, all of which were new to him and made

Clive Lloyd's cricket coaching session.

him naturally a little nervous. Off he went and a few days later reappeared on board justly pleased with himself and a good three inches taller for a successful James Bond style mission. The situation in Grenada remained uneasy with public service workers on strike but the airport was open and the threat to British residents slowly passed. Independence celebrations on 7 February were carried out by candlelight as power supplies were down.

In the meantime, the West Indies cricket team led by Clive Lloyd was host to an MCC side for the first of a Test Series and, as so often, *Fearless* was considered suitable neutral territory for a joint reception. Two cricket bats were autographed by both teams to be auctioned in aid of the ship's favourite charity, the Children's Burns Unit at the Royal Naval Hospital, Stonehouse. Clive Lloyd also offered some impromptu coaching to the ship and although the result of the first Test Match is well-recorded – England lost[276] – that of the match between the ship's cricket team and the West Indies is, fortunately, not recorded at all!

Rumours of unrest in Grenada had been circulating before the ship sailed from the United Kingdom – indeed there had been a tiny piece in the *Daily Telegraph*, just enough to suggest the procurement of relevant charts and maps. With little intelligence, other than that the 'enemy' was the quaintly named Mongoose Gang, the Amphibious Detachment was ordered to prepare for the evacuation of British nationals from Grenada. Throughout the Atlantic crossing, Command Post and communications exercises were conducted as well as advanced weapon training but without the full briefing that awaited the ship from the Foreign Office on arrival in Port of Spain, only an outline plan could be considered. This was based on the understanding that all evacuees would assemble in the capital, St George's, where they would be met by a Royal Marine protection team and led, by night, to waiting landing craft beached at the head of either Clarkes Court Bay or Prickly Bay; two and three miles, respectively, south of the capital.

On arrival in Trinidad, representatives from the British High Commission briefed the ship's command team on the situation and their preferred method of safeguarding the British inhabitants of Grenada. It was up to the AOO to produce formal orders and a communications plan that would be taken to the island by the young Foreign Office gentleman mentioned by John Lock.

A wardroom cocktail party was held, during which the orders were to be handed over to the Foreign Office, so it was unfortunate that the AOO was 'taken ill' that evening. The OCAD was summoned and, although not aware of the detail of the verbally-agreed plan, an extemporized one was swiftly drawn up with the aid of the ship's Communications Officer then typed by the Detachment Clerk, Marine Lemonde. The British High Commission official – prevented from leaving early through various acts of social subterfuge – then left and the Foreign Office gentleman was dispatched to Grenada.

From the top floor bedroom of a St George's hotel another Foreign Office employee, this time from Grenada's High Commission, was, if all else failed, to flash a torch to seaward where, during the period stipulated in the 'new' orders, *Fearless* would be hovering, hull-down, over the horizon. A Royal Marines signaller would be perched up the main mast with a pair of binoculars.

The whole affair fizzled out while the ship was 'hiding' off Bequia and the West Indies Dartmouth Training Ship deployment could continue – without further interruptions – to Antigua, Virgin Gorda, Long Island Bahamas, Miami and Nassau which, for once in *Fearless*'s illustrious life, was probably just as well.

All ships visiting Antigua try and do something for Nelson's Dockyard at English Harbour and for this visit Fearless *had brought out three reproduction careening capstans made by the shipwrights in HMS* Vernon. *These were erected and installed by a party of Midshipmen who were visited at their work by Pierre Trudeau,[277] on holiday at the time.*

At Virgin Gorda Fearless *joined a Fleet Assembly where, between 12 and 15 February a total of fourteen RN and RFA ships were at anchor in the sound – nor was there a shortage of admirals. C-in-C Fleet, Admiral Sir Terence Lewin, flew his flag in* Kent *while the outgoing First Sea Lord, Admiral Sir Michael Pollock, made his farewells. There was much visiting between ships, competitive sport and banyans. A constant swell runs through the sound making for interesting boat handling for the Midshipmen and RM Landing Craft crews alike. An LCVP fell victim to the scend on a beach and broached, needing twenty four hours of effort by the Beach Unit to recover.*

Which they were allowed to do under their own arrangements.

Finally the fleet weighed and with all ships manned, made a farewell steam-past for the First Sea Lord in Bulwark. *On completion* Fearless *detached for Long Island Bahamas. This is a long low-lying island across the Tropic of Cancer with a small population and little then in the way of facilities but ideal for exercising the ship's disaster relief organization and yet more boat running. The Midshipmen were given the job of surveying the Diamond Roads anchorage under the guidance of the Navigating Officer perhaps repeating an earlier one done by Columbus when he visited in 1492. At Long Island as at other ports the helicopters were used for familiarization flights for OUTs in either the front seat or the rear cabin.*

The arrival in Miami was perhaps not as smooth as it might have been for as the brow was being hoisted out the crane lost power leaving the Captain, Commander, ceremonial gangway staff and Royal Marines Guard frustrated on the Flight Deck while an amused CBNS Washington paced the jetty. After half an hour power was restored and the Admiral came up the brow to be piped aboard by Midshipman Bell-Davies, his son. The usual visit activities ensued with a reception for local notables including Douglas Fairbanks, Junior[278] when several guests sent their own photographers ahead to record their arrival at the top of the brow. One charming guest announced on arrival, 'Gee I've just gotta take a bath'. All things are possible and she was shown to the Commander's cabin with a Maltese Steward as sentry: the Commander meanwhile, gallantly, remained on the gangway. The Royal Marines Band, which had cross-decked from Bulwark *at Virgin Gorda, Beat Retreat to much acclaim from the visitors. A Children's Party organized by the highly competent and practised team had the pirates making impromptu changes to their routine when the disadvantaged children turned out to be in their late teens.*

The last visit was the first to Nassau by a large Royal Navy ship since independence less than a year before. A twenty-one gun salute to the Governor General on arrival aroused considerable local interest. He lunched on board but the ship had not been briefed that he was a strict vegetarian. He was charmingly insistent that no alternative be found and so the hosts hurried through their fillet steaks while His Excellency satisfied himself with one small potato and a few peas. Despite the embarrassment it was a happy occasion.

On sailing from Nassau, two social events took priority during the initial stages of the eleven-day passage to Cawsand Bay, Plymouth. They are worthy of mention as examples of many such events that dotted the ship's life: a SODS Opera and a money-raising 'country fayre'.

Most SODS operas follow a reasonably predictable pattern and are not as unstructured nor as coarse as non-naval people might suppose. There is a tendency towards variations on old favourites such as recitations of *The Death of Lord Nelson*, *The Green Eye of the Yellow God* or Kipling's *Gunga Din* but these will be interspersed with remarkable and hitherto unknown talent on some musical instrument as Simon Cassels, rather movingly, had discovered in the Mediterranean. This time a highly plausible take-off of the accident-prone Frank Spencer, Michael Crawford's character in the TV series *Some Mothers Do 'Ave 'Em* was offered by a Leading Hand.

The mix and standard of 'reviews', 'skits' or musical offerings will depend on the skill and taste of the elected organizing committee and whether or not there is a professional band embarked to help move the evening along. Inevitably, and for many, the purpose is to poke harmless fun at 'the command' and other ship's characters (who will probably be taking part anyway) through relatively benign satire.

On this occasion a Royal Marines band was embarked and a group of middle-ranking officers decided to write a 'new' vignette based on the plight of the Uckers[279] phenomenon, the Yellow Blob. Roughly speaking – depending on whether or not 'jungle' rules apply – a blob is formed by one counter landing on another of the same colour thereby preventing any overtaking by other pieces of a different colour until a six is thrown. The plan was simple: to the tune of *If I Were a Rich Man* a 'counter' dressed in ten inflated lifejackets and covered in yards of yellow bunting would bunny-hop around the flight deck in front of the audience, bemoaning – in song – the fact that any other coloured piece could knock him off the board. This was the cue for a second similarly-attired 'counter' to jump on the first one's back. Together they could now sing *Now I am a blob job* ... at which the third member of the cast would come pirouetting into sight wearing a square 'tutu' around his waist with the number six on each side and carrying a bucket of water which, so went the plan, would be thrown over the double 'yellow' blob to, as it were, knock it off the board.

With the ship's gentle motion in the slight tropical swell and the fact that the two 'counters' and one 'dice' had felt that this performance could not be conducted entirely sober, coupled with induced giddiness as the bucket was swung round and round, the 'dice' – as should have been expected – misjudged his footing. Having swept through the band, scattering violins and drum sticks, he gently and sedately toppled over the edge of the flight deck and disappeared from view; apparently into the dark, mid-Atlantic ocean. The first on the scene from the front row was the Commanding Officer who, looking down into the netting a few feet below deck level, saw his Senior Instructor Officer lying in a mild, smiling stupor with the now empty, galvanized iron bucket clutched across his chest.

All 'yellow blob' participants were required to report to the Commanding Officer's cabin later although none could work out quite what was out of keeping with the occasion: indeed it had been unanimously voted the best laugh of the evening. However, Instructor Lieutenant Commander Sam Poole never made Commander and left the Royal Navy shortly afterwards.

The 'country fayre' was altogether – but not entirely – a more serious if not sober affair as it was the last money-raiser for Stonehouse Hospital's Burnt Children's Ward before the ship's return. The usual stalls were set up on the flight deck and among many other delights and entertainments the ship's company were invited to bowl for 'pigs', knock down coconuts or hurl wet sponges at the Bosun whose head jutted through a suitably decorated and annotated board. Inevitably 'village tarts' touted for trade – and charity.

Again, there were variations on a theme with the most popular an animated fruit machine. Four straight-faced, Chief Petty Officers stood in line, the first with a clenched first raised from the elbow at forty-five degrees while the three to his left stood to attention each with a large paper sack at his feet. On paying the set fee for three 'goes' the punter would pull sharply down on the clenched fist at which the other three would rummage in their bags before, together, pulling out a 'goodie'. The bags, of course, contained one each of ten items, not all of which would have been found at a village fête nor on a the wheels of a genuine fruit machine: among the standard requirement of apples and oranges there were beer cans and – not often – on a secret signal between them, each would hold up a condom for the once-in-a-while jackpot winner. It was the most popular stand and, alone, accounted for the largest proportion of the total raised. John Lock:

The spring cruise to the Caribbean had been primarily devoted to the training task but had also allowed all departments to recover from the effects of the refit and the curtailed trials programme and work-up. The ship now felt more confident and ready for the dual role of amphibious operations and Dartmouth training. Although training would continue, the first four weeks of the summer cruise to the Mediterranean would mainly concentrate on amphibious warfare.

Before sailing on 16 April 1974, Commodore David Smith and his staff embarked with an advance party of 3 Commando Brigade HQ and Signals Squadron. A four hour stop, off Gibraltar, was all that the programme allowed but was enough for a 'Top of the Rock Race' before the ship continued to Cyprus. En route a RM Scout helicopter was launched to investigate a group of Russian warships comprising one Don Submarine Support Ship and three Riga class frigates. The Commander 3 Commando Brigade, Brigadier Roger Ephraums, and the balance of the Embarked Force joined at anchor off Malta.

Two amphibious exercises were scheduled. The first, DOUBLE BASS, from Dhekelia Roads on the south coast of Cyprus would be a necessary rehearsal for the major NATO exercise DAWN PATROL. The latter started with the seaborne forces gathering in Kalamata, Greece, before sailing through the straits of Messina and on to a landing in Sardinia.

Once again the Mediterranean in summer – Taranto, Venice, Soudha Bay and Izmir for instance – provided excellent training grounds as well as some good runs ashore for everyone. There is no doubt that the DTS role allowed for an enviable cruise programme and a collection of memories:

Secured between buoys off St Mark's Square in Venice and floodlit after dark the ship was an impressive sight for the throngs of tourists. Sir Ashley Clarke, a former Ambassador to Italy, author and founder of the Venice in Peril Appeal, gave a lecture and tour for some forty Ships Company and Trainees. Culture of a different sort came on board in the person of Ernie Wise.

Circling and photographing more Russian naval ships in the Kithera Channel on passage to Malta. The Moskva *Helicopter Carrier, a Kara Missile Cruiser and two auxiliaries gave everyone a close up view of our potential enemy.*

Two weeks in Malta for a Self Maintenance Period and the annual admin inspection by FOCAS made for a busy time. Full tropical routine was worked to get the best return from working hours as well as good shore leave. The Maltese Cooks and Stewards were given maximum leave to be at home with their families.

A peaceful anchorage at La Maddalena at the northern extremity of Sardinia. A dinner ashore for the Captain and Padre was rather spoilt when returning on board at high speed in the Huntress. *The Coxswain, engaged in conversation with the Captain, passed on the wrong side of the end of the breakwater. In the quiet after the impact some late night strollers were heard to say 'Oh that must be the American Navy'. The Captain indignantly and perhaps unwisely corrected them. This was one occasion when the Commander decided not to meet the Captain on his return on board.*

The Sea Inspection by FOCAS took place at Portland on 18 July. An unusual item was a Royal Visit by HRH Princess Margaret and her two children then aged thirteen and ten years. During a Bofors demonstration HRH remarked that her daughter did not like loud noises, unaware that Lady Sarah Armstrong-Jones was an enthusiastic onlooker at the mounting. As much of the visit as possible had been rehearsed beforehand but HRH managed to inject the unexpected when she asked to see the dock gate opened. Perhaps she had been prompted by a member of the inspecting staff.

It was at this time that a Greek-supported military coup had overthrown President Makarios in Cyprus and the Turkish army had invaded the island on the north coast. On returning to Devonport for summer leave and Navy Days Fearless *and a number of other ships were ordered to be at seventy-two hours notice to sail for Cyprus with an Armoured Car Regiment with the possibility that they might have to evacuate British nationals from the island. Despite this, leave and AMP were unaffected although arrangements were made to recall all men on leave if necessary. In the event the ship stayed in Devonport.*

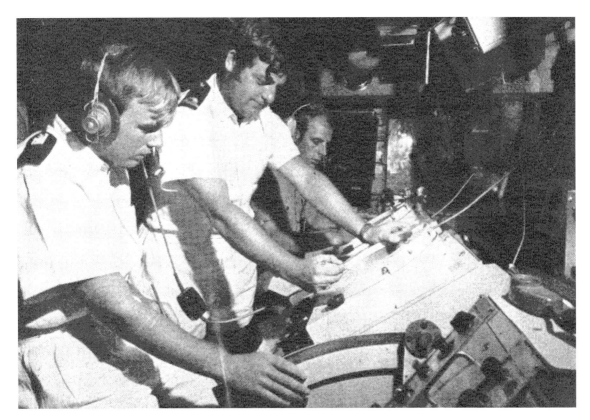

Officers under training.

The autumn of 1974 saw a third Training Cruise combined with amphibious warfare exercises. Following summer leave Fearless made short visits to Antwerp and Le Havre. Both cities were celebrating the thirtieth anniversary of their liberation from German occupation thus making much ceremonial work for the Royal Marines Guard and Band. In Le Havre the liner France, pride of the French Merchant Navy, was about to be paid off causing much anger and a threat by unions to close the port. It seemed sensible to leave the berth to avoid being locked in. Steam was raised in record time using just the Duty Watch of the ME Department and a successful move made to an anchorage. A UK tabloid was pleased to use the headline 'French Strikers Rumbled'.

The NATO Exercise NORTHERN MERGER started in Barry Budden followed by a passage phase to Obskol in Denmark where sea conditions prevented the use of LCMs, thus forcing a change to a helicopter landing. There was some concern that the command arrangements for the exercise with the Brigadier in Fearless and the Amphibious Group Commander in Hermes would lead to delayed decision making exacerbated further by poor communications. On completion a detachment of Royal Netherlands Marines were disembarked in Den Helder. Attention then turned to the training task with visits to Rotterdam, Kiel, and Eckenforde before returning briefly to Devonport.

A chance meeting with the Federal German Navy Training Barque Gorch Foch occurred one cold clear night in mid Channel. Under full sail and floodlit for our benefit she made a fine and rare sight. Two more different Training Ships it is difficult to imagine.

The next eight months of Captain Rumble's command repeated much the same pattern as in 1974 with West Indies[280] and Mediterranean cruises for young officers interspersed and often coinciding with, amphibious warfare exercises; one of which was held in the Baltic and the other in Norway.

John Rumble's last months in command included a deck landing by a Harrier flown by John Farley, a Hawker Siddeley test pilot. This event, for which the national press were invited to watch from the Isle of Dogs, took place at 1500 on 24 June 1975 while the ship was anchored off the Royal Naval College at Greenwich and came shortly after the Government had announced its decision to develop the Maritime Harrier for service with the Royal Navy.[281] *Fearless*'s visit had been arranged to coincide with the Atlantic Treaty Association Seminar sponsored by the British Atlantic Treaty Committee. This seminar, held in the College, was addressed by Mr Frank Judd, the Under Secretary of State for the Royal Navy and was devoted to naval problems associated with the North Atlantic, North Sea and the Channel. The Harrier was part of an on board equipment exhibition for the international delegates[282] who also attended a reception hosted by the Commander-in-Chief Fleet, Admiral Sir Terence Lewin.

On completion of the seminar the seventy-three embarked Midshipmen from nine nations (including Tonga's Prince Tukuaho whose parents, the King and Queen, were also guests of the ship) were landed to continue their studies back in the West Country.

As a wind-down period for the ship's company and flag-showing exercise, *Fearless* sailed for Casablanca and Madeira before embarking on a long refit in Devonport just nineteen months after her previous, mammoth session in dockyard hands. Under John Rumble's command she had steamed over 44,000 miles and visited thirty-nine ports on both sides of the Atlantic.

While both LPDs were enjoying their refits, operations and exercises, their future remained under intense debate. The latest scare was briefly summarized by the Government thus:[283]

> *The Government agrees ... that a long term Defence Review was necessary due to the worsening economic situation since the 1974 long term costing, but did not accept that the Defence Review was based on unrealistic projections of economic growth. The committee expressed reservations about the effects of the cuts on the British contribution to NATO, and the Government notes their concern but points out the need for some reduction in this area. Some changes have been made to the original proposals in response to representations from NATO allies. ... The Government is confident that the savings made by the Defence Review will be sufficient to keep defence expenditure within the agreed limits.*

This resulted, in April 1975, with the Director of Naval Plans, now Captain William Stavely (lately of HMS *Albion*) being obliged to circulate a paper[284] on behalf of the Assistant Chief of Naval Staff which he headed, *Concept of Operations for the Amphibious Force 1976–1985*. The relevant passages include:

> *The implementation of the Defence Review will, as far as the UK Amphibious Force is concerned result in ... the disbandment of 41 Commando Group, the loss of one Wessex V helicopter squadron, the premature disposal of HMS* Bulwark *by 31 March 1976, the transfer of HMS* Hermes *to a primary CVS role in April 1976 and the retention of only one LPD in an operational role while the other will be at more than 30 days notice. ... These decisions, coupled with the proposals to end a reinforcement commitment to the Southern Flank of ACE will have considerable implications on the concept of amphibious operations from April 1976.*

The paper made one or two major assumptions that would also affect amphibious operations over the subsequent years, paraphrased here: 'An amphibious capability will continue to be declared to SACLANT and one that will be capable of landing a tactically grouped force ready to deploy rapidly to combat positions without initial reliance on port facilities.'

It is difficult to understand how this was to be achieved with one LPD (assuming full-time serviceability) and no dedicated LPH and especially so as the paper went on to expand on the ground forces that would need to be transported, landed, supported and, perhaps, withdrawn tactically to be re-deployed:

> *The Commando Forces declared to SACLANT will consist of a Brigade Headquarters, two Commando Groups with 1 Amphibious Combat Group of the Royal Netherlands Marine Corps together with combat logistic elements will be available for reinforcement of the Northern Flank or the Island Commanders plan.... One Commando Group with one RNLMC company under command, mountain and arctic trained and equipped, will be available for the reinforcement of Northern Norway all the year round....*

Yet the amphibious shipping, from the mid 1970s, was planned to be one CVS – with only a secondary role as LPH – one LPD and the LSLs, whose availability 'will depend on operational priorities at the time to be decided by the Chiefs of Staff'. The one remaining Wessex V helicopter squadron would deploy 'shipping them by sea or flying them independently to the area of operations'; both fraught options and a fear highlighted in a later paragraph:

> *Once Soviet forces are in action the Norwegian Sea will provide a very hostile environment and NATO surface forces will operate North East of the Greenland, Iceland, United Kingdom gap at considerable risk.*
>
> *Consequently these factors dictate that NATO strategy must be based on reinforcement of the Northern Flank during a period of tension....*

The next Conservative administration was four years away and if anyone hoped that that Government would – if elected – usher in amphibious sanity then they were in for a surprise.

Chapter Nine

Captain L.A. Bird, LVO, Royal Navy

Seventh Commanding Officer
1975–1977

Home Waters, Norway, Mediterranean, West Indies

Captain Lionel Bird assumed command of HMS *Fearless* from being the British Naval Attaché, Paris. His previous commands had been the Motor Gunboats HMSs *Gay Centurion* and *Gay Charioteer* followed by the Frigates HMSs *Exmouth* and *Brighton*: he had also served as the Commander of HMY *Britannia*. He retired in 1981 as Chief Staff Officer (Plans) to Commander in Chief Naval Home Command.

Dickie Bird's opening remarks below could have been made by every Commanding Officer involved with a major refit in a British dockyard which, for the LPDs, seemed to come round rather quickly. He writes:

Captain 'Dicky' Bird and Chief Petty Officer Mick Ahern.

I took over Fearless *from John Rumble on 13 August 75, just as she was going into refit at Devonport. This was again a period when dockyard officers were constantly looking over their shoulders, being only too well aware that a government, totally* in hoc *to the unions, was paying far more attention to the demands of shop stewards than the advice of management! During dockyard visits by Ministers – and particularly those by Frank Judd[285] – the presence of a militant steward, Bill Coffin, throughout a dockyard tour was insisted upon during which he was effectively given equal time and status as the Admiral Superintendent and the General Manager! It was some years before Margaret Thatcher brought such nonsense to an end. The resulting low morale and disillusionment – not to mention a total overtime ban throughout the yard! – required ship's officers to perform a constant balancing act to complete the refit package and get their ship operational again; we got out on time but with difficulty and at a cost of undergoing some sea trials and work up serials simultaneously – not ideal! We could not have achieved this without the considerable experience, as a dockyard officer himself, of the Marine Engineer Officer, Commander John Bowen.*

While we refitted, Intrepid *undertook the dual role of LPD and Midshipmen's Training Ship in the leap-frogging mode of the two ships.* Fearless *duly emerged during summer '76 to sea trials and then work up at Portland; this was followed by a liaison visit to our 'twin' town Worcester – no attempt being made to take* Fearless *herself up the Severn to the city – but an LCM was sent instead! Participation in Navy Days at Plymouth at the same time as giving summer leave followed; stretch was a word frequently heard and written in Ministry of Defence and staff circles at this time, Ship's Companies were not convinced that 'they' in London understood the real meaning and implications![286]*

So to September and sailing with Commodore, Amphibious Warfare (COMAW), Richard Franklin and the Brigade Commander, Brigadier John Richards,[287] embarked to participate in the major biennial NATO autumn exercise in defence of the Northern flank, TEAMWORK. The huge fleet that assembled reflected the effort that NATO used to put into exercising defence of the Northern Flank at the height of the Cold War – now so easily forgotten. During this exercise, the writing of this history might have been very different but for the quick-witted nous of the officer of a middle watch – a Lieutenant – who ordered 'Hard a starboard. Full astern both engines' before pressing the Captain's call. I was on the bridge in seconds and in time to watch a large, black silhouette passing close across our bows and down the port side! It was a US destroyer apparently oblivious to our presence.

Full LPD role over for a while, and back in Devonport to embark Portakabins and 67 Midshipmen bound for ten weeks sea training in the Mediterranean; but our operational amphibious role was at least partially maintained with exercises with the Royal Marines; elements of 41 Commando were embarked at Civitavecchia before operations with them at Malta and later working with the Royal Green Jackets at Gibraltar; and then, following the Mediterranean deployment, a few days exercising with the RNLMC off Den Helder – all these latter activities, much to the relief of Amphibious Operations Officer, that engaging personality, Major Tim Downs,[288] who clearly viewed Midshipmen's training as a threatened complete take over of their – the Royal Marines – ship by the blue water part of the Navy!

At Venice, one saw the extent and gravity of the problem of saving the beautiful buildings of that historic city as bells and hooters announced that another high tide was about to flood St Mark's Square and nearby streets – yes, there is tide in the Adriatic though not in the Mediterranean. At Toulon we briefly flew the Flag of Flag Officer Carriers and Amphibious Ships (FOCAS), Rear Admiral Eberle,[289] for a liaison visit to his French equivalent.

The importance and gravitas attached to Remembrance Sunday by the French came as a surprise to some; our hosts were delightedly impressed by the performance of our guard and band – the Junior Band of the Prince of Wales Division – at ceremonies on the day.

Between the visits to Venice and Toulon and while acting as a participant in the filming of the next James Bond film, The Spy Who Loved Me,[290] *off Malta, the ship went to the aid of a burning Greek freighter,* Nostros Vasso Athene; *a long, weary and sometimes fraught day was spent alongside her suppressing the fire while towing her slowly to an anchorage off Grand Harbour – fortunately it was flat calm. Foam was flown on board in quantity by helicopter from Hal Far. The freighter's crew leapt on board* Fearless, *suitcases in hand, clearly thinking that any attempt to save their ship was hopeless and set about with dangers.[291] Years later a small salvage award was made[292] – much diluted by the additional claims of tug crews and others from Malta who only came in on the act after the day had been won!*

To 1977, and the spring Caribbean cruise with RFAs Tidespring *and* Stromness *in company was largely devoted to training Midshipmen, though there was brief participation in a major United States national exercise while operations with units of the RNLMC were carried out at and off Curacao. Were the Dutch Marines sparsely fed by their own? – perhaps a policy of battle hardening? They certainly took a voracious liking to RN cooking whenever embarked – we called them the Dutch Devourers!*

Visits were also made to Port of Spain, Cartagena, Kingston in Jamaica, Port au Prince, Charleston and Bermuda; on departure from Port of Spain, we rescued a capsized catamaran and crew. Port au Prince was remarkable for a seemingly always smiling people living at or near the bread line, but at the same time totally honest; there was no need to lock one's car or worry about pick-pockets! Here,

Commander Tim Hale's judgement and sense of humour, in which he was not lacking, was stretched when, just minutes before slipping, the Master at Arms reported a junior Cook absent until he was seen 'streaking' down the jetty – 'Sir, she just would not let me go! And eventually threw all my clothes out of the window!'.

At Bermuda, I had the honour of hosting a farewell dinner on behalf of the Royal Navy for the imminently retiring Governor, that engaging personality, Sir Edwin Leather – an hilarious evening but also noteworthy for richly and most interestingly recounted views on recent political events and history!

As always in the Dartmouth Training Ship/Squadron, the summer was spent in Europe with visits to Copenhagen, coinciding with Denmark's Liberation Day to mark the end of Nazi occupation, Bordeaux for the Annual International Trade Fair, Dartmouth for College liaison, Kristiansand and Kiel for Kiel Week. All on board found that European prices tested bank balances – the just appraisal of service personnel's worth to nation and NATO that followed Margaret Thatcher's election was still nearly two years away. There was amusing confusion at Bordeaux where the local French dignitaries, press et al had constantly to be reminded that Bird was no longer Naval Attaché in Paris, his immediately preceding appointment in which he had cause to be frequently in the region, but was now Captain of Fearless; *and that Michael Howard was now the Attaché and not commanding* Fearless! *The Trade Fair is a major event in the* Bordelais *calendar to which our band and Royal Marine Guard again added that something extra, particularly on British Day.*

At Kiel Week, our Ambassador in Bonn, Sir Oliver Wright, graciously asked to co-host the Captain's lunch for which he offered his own quite excellent selection of Isle of Wight wine; the Germans were unanimous in acknowledging Sir Oliver as just as great a connoisseur of the white grape as their best. His more important fame as one of our outstanding post-war diplomats needs no elaborating. This lunch was the last major occasion for which culinary preparations were made by Chief Petty Officer Cook Yeomans, a real master of his craft; eloquent testimony to this was frequently expressed, perhaps most pertinently at my dinner party for the great and good in Bordeaux; French friends were so impressed that they jocularly accused me of hiring a noted local traiteur[293] *to provide the meal; when CPO Yeomans was invited to join us for a glass of port, he received what can only be termed as a rapturous ovation.*

Summer in the Baltic where, in an apparent thawing of the Cold War, the ship was saluted instead of ignored by a passing Soviet cruiser – better informed about my seniority than we about his?

The Silver Jubilee Fleet Review at Spithead was a welcome ray of sunshine in a period of bleak economic austerity for all of us; not only in the Service, but in the whole country; in Whitehall, there had been serious consideration given to not holding it at all as a cost saving measure; in Fearless *one noted the marked impression that it made on everyone, but particularly the Midshipmen. I invited Admiral Mountbatten to speak to them on the eve of the great day; this he did, presenting prizes and having tea with the winners and others. At seventy-seven years old, he retained all his famed presence and ability to hold the attention and admiration of his audience. FOCAS, now Rear Admiral Staveley also elected to attend, even though he did not approve of the event and its concept; but then he wouldn't would he? – unless, of course, he had issued the invitation himself?*

The Review culminated in a steam past the soon retiring First Sea Lord, Admiral Sir Edward Ashmore, after which we sailed for Devonport to disembark one hundred and forty Midshipmen and embark Headquarters elements of 3 Commando Brigade for participation in Exercise FOREST VENTURE.

No account of this period would be complete without mention of our sports prowess; in both codes of football we had considerable success although winning a final always alluded [sic] us; Lieutenant Commander Allan Johnson coached a fine rugby side which was led on the field by one of his senior rates, 'Taff' Connely; a fine number eight who played for Combined Services and got a trial for Wales.

The only officer who commanded a regular place – others played at times – was the Captain's Secretary, Roger Jackson at scrum half: an interesting commentary on the game's success in broadening its appeal across the whole social spectrum, for a generation earlier all HM Ships' rugby teams would have been officer dominated. The ship's football team had something of an icon in an exciting and most effective striker; 'Mac' McDonald could hit the ball like a rocket and he was well served with chances by the more constructive Keith Whitely.

Navigator Rodney Preece led a cricket team that was able to challenge shore establishments on equal terms, though the Jamaica Defence Forces at Kingston proved a hand full! Regular practice under the right conditions was, of course, a problem – partly eased by the rigging of a net in the dock while crossing the Atlantic.

I handed over my last seagoing ship – the first being Frobisher *in April 1946 – alongside in Devonport on 24 August 1977 to Captain Richard Thomas, sadly, now the late Richard Thomas.*

Moist eyed from the cheers of the ship's company, as I stepped ashore, a dockyard rigger further touched me with, 'That must have warmed the cockles, Sir, we haven't seen that here for quite a while.'

After thirty-eight weeks in refit and 'under new management' a planned completion date had been set for 28 May 1976 but this was postponed due to a failure by the Dockyard to complete the necessary evaporator and auto control trials. It was not until 4 June that Dickie Bird was able, for the first time, to order 'Obey telegraphs' and proceed seawards. Dockyard problems continued to plague *Fearless* as the Commanding Officer noted in his Report of Proceedings for the period:[294]

Labour troubles also bedevilled Sea Trials which had to be totally re-cast ... (allowing for) very little training to be completed. The ship had to return each evening at about 1800 to disembark trials teams who would not work overtime ... in this context opportunity was taken to spend a short weekend in Guernsey ... much appreciated by all on board.

Nevertheless he was also keen to point out:

Given the labour ... problems of the Royal Dockyards of today, the refit had been a good one and the ship achieved the distinction of coming out on time although the sailing date had to be slipped three days. I believe it to be of the utmost significance that this was achieved ... by not allowing any slippage of completion date until the last possible moment. ...

Even so, all checks, trials, rectifications and FOST inspections were not completed until 1 September by when the ship was at last ready in all respects to resume her duties as an LPD. This settling in period had also seen a re-dedication service and the brief visit to Guernsey where she was delayed leaving due to a major defect in the port main engine. However with independent landing craft operations now accepted by the Commanding Officers of LPDs, two LCMs, *Foxtrot One* and *Foxtrot Two*, each with a LCVP embarked, sailed for Cardiff and thence on to Worcester, a city with whom the ship had established a 'liaison'.

The re-dedication service had been held alongside in Devonport Dockyard when, once again, Field Marshal and Lady Hull honoured the ship with their presence; the cake being cut, traditionally, by Mrs Barbara Bird and JMEM Mellor, the youngest rating in the ship, while the band of the 3rd Battalion the Royal Regiment of Fusiliers played.

So, by the beginning of September 1976 and with Navy Days and 22,000 visitors behind her, *Fearless* was ready for work and quickly back in the business of pre-sail conferences, opposed transits of the North Sea and Norwegian fjords, deterrent landings, amphibious assaults and offshore manoeuvres. Exercise TEAMWORK '76 was no different with Brigade Headquarters embarked plus 42 Commando and elements of the RNLMC and Army units within the

Commando Brigade spread across *Fearless* and various LSLs. The land phases of this NATO autumn exercise were held in Denmark and subsequently the Namsos area of Norway while, in toto, TEAMWORK covered almost the entire 12 million square miles of the Atlantic Command and involved over 80,000 personnel, more than 200 ships and 900 aircraft. It was also noted for its generally bad weather which added to the training value and lessons learned:

> *The main operational lesson ... was that as we no longer have an LPH available it is inevitable that the ship will be used as an LPD/H.*[295] *It had not come fully prepared. However with the cooperation of 845 Squadron the work up in this sphere was done 'on the job' and this, though obviously not the right way in the event, achieved the aim.*[296]

Fearless was back on 'Charlie' buoy, Plymouth Sound, by 27 September, landing her embarked force via LCMs, before proceeding up the Hamoaze the next day; but there was to be no respite for over the 29th and 30th she embarked Portakabins, changed her role to that of the Dartmouth Training Ship and prepared for a Mediterranean cruise; towards which she sailed on 4 October 1976.

At this time[297] the *Daily Telegraph*'s naval correspondent, Desmond Wettern, had one of his articles headlined *Navy Cut to One Cruiser* before tabulating the state of the fleet's major warships. This abbreviated version gives the gist of his concerns during the autumn of 1976:

> Ark Royal: *late into refit – because of delays to* Hermes's *refit*
> Hermes: *operational date delayed again, this time by a further three months*
> Eagle: *awaiting scrap*
> Bulwark: *being mothballed*
> Tiger *and* Blake: *one in commission, the operational date of the second 'vague'*
> Fearless: *designed purely for landing tanks ... armament limited to close-range missiles and small guns – training Midshipmen*
> Intrepid: *being mothballed as part of the defence cuts announced last year*
> Destroyers ... *half of the eight missile destroyers are in dockyard hands.*

One night in Gibraltar brought forward the qualifying period for LOA and that having been achieved, *Fearless* sailed for Civitavecchia and the recovery of 41 Commando[298] from Exercise DISPLAY DETERMINATION. A training period with the Royal Marines ended in an invaluable two-day Exercise, WILD THYME. This was, as it were, a 'private exercise' which not only practised amphibious procedures but introduced the ship to the problems of conducting a civilian evacuation. At the culmination of a landing – by helicopter due to bad weather – ninety women and children (all volunteers from the Commando plus a handful of Midshipmen) were evacuated from Kalafrana and returned to Valetta by sea. The experiment was considered excellent value with HMS *Fearless* now better able to face a day of evolutions under FOCAS's[299] critical eye as part of the ship's annual sea inspection.

But if Malta had satisfied the amphibiously-minded then Venice would do the same for the culturally aware, although the ship arrived at the height of bad flooding as Captain Bird mentions. The ship, impressively flood-lit each evening, berthed at the *Rive dei Setta Martini*: ten minutes walk from St Mark's Square.

The next stage of this Mediterranean deployment had been planned as 'the quietest and slowest for the benefit of Midshipmen training'. However, in Dickie Bird's words: 'It quickly became the fastest and most exciting phase with poor weather, two replenishments at sea and an intensive flying programme that saw the 1,000th deck landing since re-dedication.'

After dawn on 6 November the ship embarked, by helicopter from Malta, a film crew for the closing scenes of the Bond film *The Spy Who Loved Me* in which a space capsule, crewed by Roger

Moore and Barbara Bach (making love at the time), is saved when it floats into the dock. It had been hoped that the stars would have taken passage but this was not the case as Gareth Owen explains:[300]

> *Sir Roger never shot a foot of film on board … the end sequence in the film consisted of a second-unit location shot of the probe approaching the dock of the ship. It was then a quick cut to a Pinewood water-set with actors Bernard Lee, Desmond Llewelyn and Walter Gotell looking down into the probe. … As is often the way with film-making; much is deception!*

The filming did not go uninterrupted for not only were conditions for camera work far from ideal but, paradoxically, when the weather was perfect outside events took charge. As the first scene was about to be shot the ship was called to the aid of a 6,500 ton Greek freighter, the *Nostros Vasso Athene*, burning fiercely five miles off Malta's north-east coast and already being abandoned by her crew. The fire, out-of-control by the time *Fearless* arrived, had begun in the engine room and

Salvage off Malta.

spread swiftly to the accommodation. Fire-fighting was made even more hazardous by the ship's deck cargo which included eighty 5-gallon drums of oxidizing acid, three drums of benzine, two tons of paint and no fewer than twenty-three tons of lighter fuel.

Nevertheless by manoeuvring *Fearless* alongside and sending across fire-fighting teams led by Lieutenant Commander Peter Luce and CMEM Brian (Mick) Ahern the blaze was eventually brought under control and safe enough for the casualty to be towed, alongside, towards Grand Harbour. Both Peter Luce and Mick Ahern were to be awarded the Queen's Commendation for Brave Conduct.[301]

This was a most professional operation carried out under trying circumstances yet one which, in her Commanding Officer's words: 'Markedly enhanced the crew's confidence in their equipment and ability.'

With her duty of care passed to the Maltese dockyard authorities, *Fearless* was free to return to her role as film star: a more amusing task, that was completed the next day and which subsequently attracted the signal:

> From James Bond film unit to HMS *Fearless*. Many thanks for a good shoot. A highly eventful week when many were stirred but none were shaken. Signed 007.

Fearless returned home for exercises with the Dutch off Den Helder and Christmas in Devonport. The new year, 1977, began with a Dartmouth Training Ship cruise of the West Indies for which she replaced an LCU with an Army Ramped Powered Lighter[302] for delivery to Belize.

During the Atlantic crossing and not only for the benefit of the young Officers Under Training, the 'usual' exercises were conducted. Daily man overboard drills, a rendezvous with a Maritime Patrol Aircraft, steering gear breakdowns and replenishments at sea with her accompanying RFAs, *Tidespring* and *Stromness* were practiced. On passing Ponta Delgardo in the Azores a LCVP was dispatched inshore to collect mail as 'the conditions were unsuitable for the Wasp'.[303]

Otherwise the cruise followed the ordained pattern: exercising with the Dutch Marines at Curacao (when the 'Dutch Devourers' enhanced their gluttonous reputation) and assisting the US Marines at Roosevelt Roads in their Exercise CARIBEX. Much of this time was spent in company with HMS *Tartar* whose presence added greatly to Midshipmen training. A social highlight was the embarkation of the British High Commissioner to Jamaica, Mr John Drinkall CMG, for passage to Haiti where he was also the British Ambassador and where the ship arrived – not by coincidence – in time for the first day of Mardi Gras. By invitation, HMS *Fearless* entered a float; a model of the ship mounted on a 4-ton lorry was preceded through the streets by the Corps of Drums[304] who then played non-stop for six hours to 'not inconsiderable acclaim'.

This was probably the highlight of the deployment despite Charleston and Bermuda being next on the itinerary where, at the latter, the ship hosted the retiring Governor, Sir Edwin Leather, with all the attendant pomp of a farewell for which the Royal Navy is renowned.

In his Report of Proceedings[305] Dickie Bird felt it necessary to raise the perennial problem of machinery defects, emphasizing that the whole of Exercise CARIBEX had been, of necessity, conducted on one engine and that the engineering staff had had to work in shifts not only at sea but also throughout the visits to Port of Spain and Carthegena. It is interesting, too, to note that in his next – and last – Report of Proceedings five months later[306] Dickie Bird was to write: 'In many ways it is a pity that the ship is now due for a DED with all its attendant disruption and an inevitable increase in unreliability as the disturbed equipment is bedded again.'

Fearless arrived in Devonport on 16 March 1977 for a month's Assisted Maintenance Period.

A change was in order as the ship embarked detachments of the British Army's 8th Field Force for the briefest and simplest of landing exercises across the Browndown beaches of the Solent[307]

Night shoot.

on the 20 April. There was nothing unusual in this other than it helped the Army to continue in its belief that there is no mystique in such undertakings.

By the end of April it was back to training midshipmen, hosting official receptions, runs ashore and all the on board exercises that keep a modern warship – and its embarked trainees – on its toes. A visit to Copenhagen was followed by one to Bordeaux: the latter being conducted in much the same style as when *Fearless* had been under the command of Simon Cassels. On this occasion, though, blood was given by some fifty of the ship's company in exchange for wine! Over 5,000 people visited during two afternoons.[308]

If a variety of small exercises are glossed over plus a visit to Kristiansand – notable for offering little in the way of recreation or entertainment despite the gallant efforts of the British Consul – two more noteworthy events were to take place before Captain Bird handed over command: in chronological order these were a visit to Kiel and the Queen's Silver Jubilee Review at Spithead.

The visit to Kiel was as before (although without the yachts) but particularly memorable for it heralded the end of Chief Petty Officer Cook Yeoman's time on board. This last of his extravaganzas was a luncheon for the British Ambassador to Bonn, Sir Oliver Wright, held under an awning on the forward Seacat deck from where His Excellency and his senior German guests could watch the international array of warships gathered for *Kieler Woche*. As so often, the Royal Navy's reputation – and, as a spin off, that of the country – rested not on the guards, floodlighting, behaviour ashore or on the sports pitches or standard of boat-work, but upon the skill of an individual. Dickie Bird:[309] 'The setting could hardly have been better ... and was the last major occasion prepared by CPOCK Yeoman who has given sterling service to the ship for the last three years. I am indeed sorry to lose him.'

On 21 June *Fearless* sailed for Spithead where she anchored early on the 24th with her 150 Officers Under Training employed in painting: previous attempts at Kristiansand having been curtailed by bad weather.

> *The Silver Jubilee Review made a marked impression … on everyone on board at the time. None could fail to be favourably impressed with the organization and execution … not only by those who planned it but by those who presented their ships to mark the occasion … a moving experience only surpassed by the Review itself.*[310]

The full programme of visits, ceremonial, training, flag showing and intensive amphibious work in testing conditions continued with the visit by Lord Mountbatten, a steam past the retiring First Sea Lord, Admiral of the Fleet Sir Edward Ashmore, an amphibious exercise – FOREST VENTURE – off the west coast of Scotland with 3 Commando Brigade, Royal Marines which also included landings across Saunton Sands, before a final docking in Plymouth on 15 July.

Captain Lionel Bird's time in command was over on 24 August; marked by the emotional farewell from his ship's company of which he was so proud. His last words were:

> *On return from the Falklands, the Queen's Harbour Master at Portsmouth, Captain James Weatherall, invited me to join him in his barge when he went out to lead her into her berth; a brave sight, though without one LCM and all her gallant crew. One proudly shed a final tear.*

Chapter Ten

Captain W.R.S. Thomas, OBE, Royal Navy

Eighth Commanding Officer
1977–1978
Later, Admiral Sir Richard, KCB, KCVO, OBE

Mediterranean, European Waters, West Indies

Captain Richard Thomas's family.

Captain Richard Thomas commanded four ships before *Fearless*: HMSs *Buttress*, *Wolverton*, *Greetham* and *Troubridge*. After retiring from the Royal Navy in 1992 as the United Kingdom's Military Representative to NATO he was appointed Gentleman Usher of the Black Rod, Serjeant-at-Arms to the House of Lords and Secretary to the Lord Great Chamberlain until 1995.

As Captain Thomas died in 1998, before this anthology was begun, it has not been possible to include his views as Commanding Officer. However one of his Reports of Proceedings[311] exists and from that it is possible to gain a brief insight into his opinions. The following is an abridged version in which, straight away, he was obliged to comment adversely on a Dockyard refit:

I assumed command ... on 24 August 1977. At that time the ship was completing an eight week period for Docking and Rectification of Essential Defects. Devonport Dockyard was unable to undertake the full workload because of financial restraints and because of delays in the accepted package completion date. This did not delay the ship from sailing on 13 September for the Autumn deployment but it did throw considerable strain on the Officers and Senior Ratings of the technical departments who had to work long hours to get the ship ready on time. It also meant that the machinery spaces were well below standard. Dockyard work on the LCMs had been progressing very slowly and unsatisfactorily and as a result LCM Foxtrot Three remained unserviceable on board until 2 November.

As the duty Dartmouth Training Ship, *Fearless* sailed for the autumn deployment with 105 young Officers Under Training but this time she had also embarked a number of Marine Engineering Artificer Apprentices from HMS *Caledonia*.[312] Salerno Company from 41 Commando, Royal Marines, was embarked for transit to and collection from, Exercise DISPLAY DETERMINATION with the USMC in Turkey. Away for nine weeks, *Fearless* visited all the 'normal haunts' such as Gibraltar, Malta, Venice, Greece, Sardinia and those in southern France before returning on 24 November to land her trainees and embark the 1st Amphibious Combat Group of the Royal Netherlands Marine Corps.

One visit of diplomatic importance was that to Navarino in Greece between 19 and 20 October 1977 for the battle that had taken place there 150 years earlier is historically famous as the last sea fight of the sailing navies. A combined fleet of twelve British, seven French and nine Russian line-of-battle ships, led by Vice Admiral Sir Edward Codrington in HMS *Asia*, defeated a combined

The Chapel and Naval Staff Office. Note the 'ecclesiastical' chairs.

Turkish-Egyptian fleet after a four-hour fight. This time *Fearless*, with the British Ambassador to Greece, Sir Brooks Richards,[313] embarked, was accompanied by one French warship and eight from Greece.

As soon as she returned to Devonport another role change took place prior to a brief exercise with the Royal Netherlands Marine Corps off Den Helder before Christmas leave and the Caribbean with trainees.

Richard Thomas's thoughts on the training schedules are of interest as they are the most detailed to appear in a Report of Proceedings. It will be noticed that although the Report in question[314] related to a Mediterranean deployment, a small Embarked Military Force was briefly involved. Passage times between ports were arranged at slow speeds to allow the maximum time for pilotage, watch-keeping and other associated duties on the bridge and in the machinery spaces:

> *A good balance between sea and harbour time was achieved. This together with a long spell of excellent weather and slow passage speeds between ports provided the ideal background in which to plan and execute OUTs and MEA Apprentice Training.*
>
> *The general standard of OUT classes was encouraging: they were all well motivated and entered into all activities on board with gusto. The instructor officers, whom my training staff told me were unimpressive last deployment, were particularly enthusiastic. The main party of OUTs who were on board for the full deployment consisted of 24 Royal Navy and 40 International Midshipmen. Some concern was felt at the beginning that the Royal Navy contingent would not get a fair deal in these circumstances but this proved unfounded.*
>
> *The Royal Navy Midshipmen went from strength to strength and by the end I would readily have accepted all except one into my wardroom. They were sufficiently trained to undertake the duties of Second Officer of the Day in harbour, Second Officer of the Watch at sea and assistant Divisional Officer in a frigate.*
>
> *Three factors detract from their time on board: the first and the one that looms largest in their minds is the requirement to return to BRNC to undertake professional exams, the basic preparation for which had largely taken place months beforehand; the second is that there appears more in their syllabus than is required before they embark on the next stage of their sea training in the Fleet and this requires them to spend time in the classrooms on board to the detriment of their practical training; and the third is that having been trained for sea they have to return to academic training ashore at this juncture.*
>
> *Many of the above remarks apply to the International Midshipmen, the best part of whom are very much among the front runners. Indeed the standards obtained by most of those with a good understanding of English are satisfactory. However, some of the foreign students on board for this deployment have been poor. I believe we are asking too much of them and this is putting them under such pressure that we are in danger of demoralising them rather than building up their self confidence. The trouble is something more than a fundamental difficulty over language – they do not have the basic sophistication of a broad based education that others have. They therefore have great difficulty in keeping up and it requires very careful programming to stop them holding others back without making them feel very clearly second class citizens.*

The Commanding Officer was equally enthusiastic over his MEA Apprentices:

> *The addition of the MEA Apprentice Training Task has been on balance an advantage to the ship. It has enabled the ship's company to recognize more clearly the ship's training role and the competition generated between the MEA Apprentices and the OUTs is a useful benefit. As those ratings will be fully-fledged senior ratings by about the same time as the Midshipmen become fully-fledged officers it is obviously beneficial for them to gain this general training on the side.*

Ship's Amphibious Operations Room. SACC desk on the right.

Richard Thomas never forgot the prime purpose for his ship's existence and that it was important that the planners in Northwood did not forget either. Should the need arise 'out of the blue' HMS *Fearless* had to be able to meet the amphibious challenge with no notice:

> *The worry, often expressed by my ship's company, is that the standard of amphibious operations is falling and the depth of knowledge is becoming shallower at an ever increasing rate. I consider that the ship needs considerably more opportunity for operational training in company with other units before I can confidently provide an efficient LPD in support of NATO contingency plans or an efficient command platform for an embarked CATF.*

There were other worries:

> *The current problems concerning pay are undoubtedly colouring my ship's company view of life. While I believe that my officers' main concern is with comparability with their civilian friends and differentials within the service it seems that the ratings particularly resent the fact that others outside the services get overtime and productivity bonuses which cushion them against the worst effects of restrictive pay policies. The public support given to the services during the current fireman's strike[315] has boosted morale but I regret that I believe that this boost will be short lived and that morale will continue to decline on this score until light can be seen at the end of the tunnel.*

170

This Report of Proceedings ended:

> *Notwithstanding the above points I have, on returning to sea, been impressed by the high degree of motivation, skill, loyalty and pride displayed by my Officers and ship's company. They provide an excellent background against which to train young officers and ratings but they crave* operational opportunity.[316]

The next year, 1978, brought much of the same but still no operations: nevertheless by the time *Fearless* returned from her final foreign deployment she had, in the months under Richard Thomas's command, trained 586 young officers,[317] 203 MEAs and had visited nearly fifty ports.

The ship had, too, received an unwelcome piece of publicity that, although not of her making as it were, hit the headlines. In August, Junior Seaman Adrian Clark, was court-martialled at Plymouth, sentenced to three years' imprisonment and dismissed the service. Large headlines in newspapers of every hue carried the tale of a 'Sailor (17) jumped ship for the love of a barmaid, a Lovelorn tar gets the yo heave-ho',[318] and while this was nothing new as sailors are always being seduced by siren voices and hour-glass figures – let alone Maltese barmaids – the circumstances on this occasion were unusually dramatic. Other headlines gave more clues; 'Landing craft seized by lovesick hijack tar', 'Love sinks sailor who seized boat' and 'A hijack for the love of Anna'.[319] During the ship's last night in Malta the previous May, Adrian Clark had slipped ashore on a civilian, painting catamaran, despite having had his leave stopped. His mission was, in his own words to a colleague, 'To go on the trot' with his girlfriend, a Miss Anna Mangion who was – but apparently not all the time – blonde, about mid-thirties and working at The Silver Jubilee, a Valetta bar.

A patrol of three Royal Marines was dispatched to arrest him, which was not difficult as Miss Mangion's home address was well known. JS Clark was escorted to an LCVP but during the short journey across Grand Harbour he produced a 9-mm service pistol, two magazines and 274 rounds of ammunition. Ordering the craft to return with the words 'I have a ticket to take me back' the coxswain had little choice but to obey and once alongside Clark ran off. Later that day he was arrested by the Maltese Police, fined £135 for possession of a firearm and released back into Royal Naval custody. At his court martial it was revealed that the pistol had been cocked but unloaded and had been intended merely for shooting game against the possibility that Miss Mangion would not wish to entertain him for long, forcing him to live rough across the Maltese

On passage.

countryside. No doubt there was also an internal inquiry about how a weapon and ammunition could have been acquired by a Junior Seaman.

Fearless's last sojourn in the Mediterranean, between the end of September and the end of November 1978, saw her take part in that year's NATO Exercise DISPLAY DETERMINATION but otherwise she enjoyed a total commitment to training. Her Royal Marine Detachment celebrated the 314th birthday of their Corps on 28 October with a Regimental Dinner given by the SNCOs' Mess while on passage between Malta and Alexandria when the Commanding Officer, helped by his AOO, Major Anthony Langdon,[320] cut a cake and led a toast. A fanfare heralded the cake's arrival played, not by a Royal Marines musician, but by three buglers from the Green Jacket's Depot at Winchester: such was the happy 'jointness' of an LPD's life. Warrant Officer Sammy Carlisle – Navy hockey player and the senior Royal Marines signaller on board – remembers the evening well with the added rejoinder that 'The Drafting Officer did not make a blunder when he made this draft chit out for me![321] I had two great commissions in *Fearless* and it was a sad day when she was taken out of service':

> *Fred Chapman – the Detachment Sergeant Major – encouraged some of us to write words to the tune of the Eton Boating Song which included a verse about the Beachmaster:*
>
> > *… This is Captain De'Ath, sometimes known as Joe … He's got a little Mitchy, BARV and Bucket too, and sits around the beach all day with sod all else to do …*
>
> *Eventually the Mess President stood and said, 'Gentlemen, the Captain is leaving,' but the Captain replied, 'Am I?' then stood and removed his* Fearless *cummerbund to reveal that his Mess Dress trousers were held up by a Royal Marines stable belt. A great touch.*

One of the duties of a Royal Marines Colour Sergeant was that of Upper Deck SNCO, responsible for, among many varied duties, the hoisting and lowering of the LCVPs. Geoff Haywood[322] remembers:

> *Lowering and hoisting LCVP's with passengers – Embarked Force or libertymen – even in calm conditions needed a close understanding between Controlling Officer, Coxswain and Crew. In rough seas, at night or after a couple of bounces on the falls, split second timing and a confidence in each other was a must and would change the looks of apprehension and concern to ones of relief and a fuller understanding of the skills used in this operation.*
>
> *We took every chance possible to practise, including when the ship was moving slowly ahead and swapping boats from davit to davit. Did I hear, 'We can't do that Colours, the numbers will all be wrong.' 'If you say so, Sir. We'll swap them back again but meanwhile will paint the other side with a different number ready for the next port visit!'*
>
> *Maintaining the screens took up much of the time and after an exercise when the boats themselves showed signs of long hours at sea this was a real chore. On occasions the use of non-recommended ship's husbandry skills acquired over the years was the only way to keep the Commander happy. Thank God for rust killer acid because it removed the most stubborn of grime at a wipe – but the colour faded. 'Must be a different batch of paint, Sir', or 'It's the way the sun keeps shining on it!'*

Across the Mediterranean, northern Europe and the Caribbean *Fearless*'s sporting teams held their own but she also boasted sportsmen with a more nautical flavour. During this last period of 'active service' a crew skippered by Charles Abrahams sailed *Chaser*, one of the services' yachts from HMS *Hornet*, to meet the ship in Gibraltar. Because of the unusual mix of ranks among the crew[323] (for those less-enlightened days) bad weather (including a split mainsail) and the thoroughly

Cartoon presented to Captain Richard Thomas by his Warrant Officers.

professional manner of the voyage, the passage made news. When *Chaser* finally entered Gibraltar, after what was acknowledged to have been a 'difficult' voyage, her crew's efforts were nationally applauded.

On 29 November 1978 Richard Thomas brought *Fearless* into Plymouth Sound after his third Mediterranean deployment, disembarked the Officers Under Training, sailed for Portsmouth and on 1 December closed the ship down in preparation for a period in reserve and refit. As she entered harbour, flying her paying off pennant, she was followed in by her four LCMs in formation.

Chapter Eleven

Reserve, Refit and a Defence Review
1978–1981
Portsmouth, South Shields

Commander F.A. (Tony) Collins,[324] Captain Thomas's Executive Officer, took HMS *Fearless* into reserve but most believed that the chances of being called up were slim.

This three year period of *Fearless*'s refit would see the election of a Conservative Government in 1979 but instead of heralding a renewal of interest, Mrs Thatcher's Premiership would propose the destruction of naval amphibious capability.

For nearly two years *Fearless* lay unloved by all but a scratch crew until the 4 July 1980 when she was towed to South Shields for a refit by the newly reconstructed Tyne Shiprepair Group which had won £20m worth of business; largely on the back of a no-strikes agreement with the unions which also allowed for the mobility of the work force between all the yards within the group and thus the abandonment of demarcation lines.

Commander Collins was relieved by Commander F.D. Wilson who, in turn, was relieved by Commander John Kelly,[325] as *Fearless*'s Senior Officer. John Kelly would revert to Executive Officer on the arrival of her next Commanding Oficer, Jeremy Larken.

With the arrival of Mrs Thatcher as Prime Minister in 1979 came Mr John Nott,[326] first as Secretary of State for Trade and then, in 1981, as Secretary of State for Defence. Acting under his leader's orders he set about a Defence Review which was summarized, later, in the Eighth Report of the Parliamentary Select Committee on Defence:

> The review which took place under Sir John Nott's tenure at the MoD ran from January to June 1981. It was conducted in the international context of a Soviet military build-up and the domestic context of a severe economic downturn and the introduction of cash planning to control public spending. As our predecessors put it, in their Report on the 1981 Statement on the Defence Estimates:
>
> > The Secretary of State ... says that the right balance must be re-established 'between inevitable resource constraints and ... necessary defence requirements'. In other words, the Government's commitments to spend money on defence have outstripped the availability of funds. ...
>
> > The main cuts under the Nott review were to fall on the Navy ... one of the three carriers (Invincible) and the two amphibious ships Fearless and Intrepid were also to be cut. Out-of-area, or expeditionary warfare capacity was therefore to be further significantly reduced. ...

In his book *Amphibious Assault Falklands*,[327] Commodore Mike Clapp expanded on the saga slightly as the demise of the shipping was running parallel with the demise of his job:

> Already the position of Commodore in 1982 had become another pawn in the game of cuts. It had been disbanded about four years earlier, only to be resurrected about two years before the Falklands crisis. ... Perhaps the best example of why we in the Royal Navy felt frustrated is summed up by Mr John Nott's Parliamentary Statement made on 25 June, 1981, when he said, in part:
>
> > It is for this reason that while we shall complete the new aircraft carrier Ark Royal we intend to keep in service in the longer term, only two of the ships of this class with their heavy demand on supporting anti-submarine and air defence escort. The older Hermes will be phased out as soon as

the second of the new carriers is in operation.... . We shall maintain the three Royal Marines commandos ... as we place great value on their unique capability, but we shall dispose of the two specialist amphibious ships Fearless *and* Intrepid *rather earlier than planned.... .*

Yet, the 'unique capability' of the Royal Marines referred to by John Nott was, in large measure, due to the flexibility afforded by the doomed specialist amphibious ships. As Mike Clapp put it:

By the spring of 1982 the LPHs and all but one of the light fleet aircraft carriers had gone. All that remained to support amphibious operations (themselves under threat with the planned demise of the LPDs) was the Invincible class – not much more than small helicopter and Sea Harrier platforms and the ageing, and threatened HMS Hermes. *With no airborne early warning or tanker capability and the much reduced range and weapon load of the otherwise remarkable Sea Harrier, and with the running-down of the amphibious shipping we were close to impotency in our ability to project power ashore which has, arguably, been the primary role of Navies over the centuries.*

In fact the Defence Secretary was to spare the LPDs in February 1982 as a direct result of a visit made to *Fearless* and to Royal Marines, Poole, on 23 November 1981. Many naval officers believed, however, that to keep *Fearless* and *Intrepid* running they would have to sacrifice destroyers, and that was, in some quarters, even more unpopular: a view highlighted by Desmond Wettern in the *Daily Telegraph* of 26 February 1982:

The reprieves have caused dismay in the Navy. It is felt it would be far better to have retained the 19,500 tonne carrier Invincible, *now sold to Australia, and other anti-submarine ships in preference to costly (LPDs) designed in the early 1960s that land tanks and vehicles on to open beaches ... considered irrelevant in the NATO area.*

Sir John Nott was happy to state that he changed his mind as he had not been content with the 'totality' of what he was being 'forced to do by Mrs Thatcher' and that that, coupled with the self-evident view that the Royal Marines without their amphibious shipping would be emasculated and difficult to support in their long-term future, was a cut that, for him, would be 'too far'.[328]

Meanwhile, *Intrepid* returned to Portsmouth on 26 November 1981 to assume the less-than-glamorous position of being 'preserved by operation' – but only until the next year, 1982; after that she would be scrapped. *Fearless* was on her way towards operational readiness but only until 1983 or 1984 when she too would be placed on the disposal list.

Chapter Twelve

Captain E.S.J. Larken, Royal Navy

Ninth Commanding Officer
1981–1983
Later, Rear Admiral, DSO

West Indies, Norwegian Arctic, South Atlantic, Northern Europe, Mediterranean

Captain Jeremy Larken's previous commands had been the submarine HMS *Osiris* followed by the destroyer HMS *Glamorgan* and then the submarine *Valiant*. After commanding *Fearless* for which he was awarded the DSO following the Falklands campaign, he was Commodore Amphibious Warfare, flying his broad pennant in HMSs *Intrepid* and *Ark Royal* and retired in 1990 as Assistant Chief of the Defence Staff (Overseas).

Captain Jeremy Larken.

The Falklands Campaign broke as an almost complete surprise for those who were to fight. Fearless abruptly found herself a major cog in a large and intricate, yet flexible, military machine that quickly became a crucial instrument of UK national will and government policy.

The day was Thursday 1 April 82. Fearless was one week into a three-week maintenance period. Much equipment had been opened up, nothing reassembled.

Next morning I was awakened early by a call from the Commander, John Kelly. Fearless *had been placed on priority for war stores second only to the submarine strategic deterrent. On Tuesday we sailed from Portsmouth for the South Atlantic. The amphibious Commanders, Commodore Michael Clapp[329] and Brigadier Julian Thompson[330] joined by helicopter in the Channel. The Amphibious Force gathered around us and we set course for Ascension Island, some half way to the Falklands.*

I had taken command of Fearless *in May 1981 when she was a sorry sight, hugely high and dry in a floating dock in which she was undergoing a major overhaul. While doing our best to support the admirably pragmatic Geordies, a major aim was to form a close-knit team of fish-heads, marines and aviators. We set the principle, then unusual in the surface fleet, of everyone achieving an accredited standard of whole-ship (as opposed to simply departmental) knowledge. Competence and integration advanced even amidst the unpromising environment of South Shields with its fantastic density of pubs per square mile and other distractions.*

Fearless *worked up at Portland during the autumn of 1981. We were becoming an operational team. Hard-driven, even if there was much to entertain as well as to test and exasperate. Under the tireless eyes of FOST inquisitors, ancient Bofors anti-aircraft guns on the bridge wing platforms would respond to the early morning mock attacks by Hunters with sporadic blank fire before jamming. Bang, Bang … Bang, Bang … silence … Whoosh went the Hunter close overhead! Six months later in San Carlos they would fire on and on with relentless efficiency. Missiles hung-up on launchers. . . .*

New Year 1982 saw Fearless *deploy to the West Indies by the northern great circle route. This was my decision and a poor one, based on inadequate research. We encountered hurricane conditions mid-Atlantic, not unusual for the time of year, and damaged two helicopters lashed to the flight deck, one terminally and thus not available for the Falklands aircraft inventory.*

After some exhilarating tribulations, such as hi-jacking a British widow's yacht from Trinidad following the murder of her husband to forestall its indefinite impounding at Port of Spain, the deployment took Fearless *to the Netherlands island territory of Curacao. The port incorporated an army encampment, Camp Allegro, converted to a recreation centre which proved enormously popular with my sailors and marines, the true nature of which became clear to me subsequently. The padre conceded wanly that it had taken Camp Allegro to really put the ship's company into foremost fettle! I did not complain. We embarked the Commander-in-Chief Fleet, Admiral Sir John Fieldhouse, for a short visit during which he enjoyed a traditional ship's company concert held on the vehicle decks, where five hundred voices nearly lifted the Flight Deck heavenwards with* Hearts of Oak *and* Rule Britannia*. The Admiral turned to me and said, without conceivable premonition 'What if we were to go to war tomorrow?'.*

We re-crossed the Atlantic, embarked a major contingent of Royal Marines at Plymouth together with the amphibious maritime and land-force commanders, Michael Clapp and Julian Thompson and proceeded to north Norway around the Lofoten Islands for major exercises. With the Commodore's encouragement, again without premonition, I experimented in manoeuvring Fearless *to use huge fjordal land features as protection against line-of-sight attack by fast-jet aircraft. Driven simply by sound strategy, the succession of such decisions, both planned and opportune, advanced the ship's operational readiness and our ability to apply her capabilities in a war theatre.*

Fearless *sailed south from Portsmouth on Tuesday 6 April with an unprecedented operational load. My people and numerous helpers including normally rule-bound dockyard workers and the teenage sons of my Deputy Weapons Officer moved mountains to reassemble and store the ship. Four large helicopters, artillery ammunition, light tanks and many lesser vehicles packed into every conceivable corner. False decks were created from a cornucopia of stores. Topping up to some 1,400 people, we broke all previous records.*

The task of achieving the relatively modest metamorphosis from a worked-up state to a war footing was now mainly a matter of human relations and education in war imperatives and stratagems. We took the morale pulse from day to day. One evening during our three week pause at Ascension Island, the very same Royal Marine Band that had unleashed such carefree enthusiasm but two months previously boarded to give a concert. The event was well attended but subdued. Concerned at first, I concluded correctly, that sober stocks were being taken of our prospects. We accepted that our likely fate was to sail south to the Falklands to face hazards new to us all.

I was determined there be no jingoism. When the Argentine cruiser General Belgrano *– of comparable size to* Fearless *– was sunk by HMS* Conqueror*, I briefed hour by hour on the number of her ship's company reported saved. Soon HMS* Sheffield *was also lost.*

Immediately following the landings at San Carlos during the early hours of 21 May 1982, it fell largely to Fearless*, on the Commodore's behalf, to organize the stationing of ships in the anchorage. Here the recent Norwegian fjord experience proved invaluable. We anchored ships packed together*

Hiding in the Arctic alongside a fjord.

around the relatively slight major land features in a way that would inconvenience the Argentine fast-jet, weapon-launch flight paths. Flaws in our initial calculations led to hits on two logistic ships, the bombs happily failing to explode.

Thereafter no strikes on troop- or cargo-carrying ships in the anchorage were achieved. In case Argentine daylight intelligence of this unconventional arrangement might encourage high-level night attacks, we had all ships moved to dispersed positions at nightfall, resuming the compact formation before dawn.

I had also to decide from where to fight Fearless. *My small 1960 vintage Operations Room was filled entirely by the Commodore and his staff. Moreover, our ancient air-defence radars saw nothing beyond the surrounding hills, from amongst which attacking aircraft would emerge some ten seconds from target (e.g.* Fearless). *Having endured the first air attack as a frustrated supernumerary without even a radar monitor at my disposal I decided to migrate to the missile/gun-direction platform at the very top of the ship, a level above the navigational bridge. This was better. From here I could see incoming aircraft as soon as anyone else. I could direct the manoeuvring of the ship to present the least target and best weapon arcs to the Argentines' favourite flight paths. I had first-hand observation of each attack on the anchorage and its results, and could provide a deputy's eyes for my Commodore. I could, moreover, set a direct example to my people, some fifty of whom were on the upper deck manning weapons from missile launchers to infantry automatic weapons.*

This was a period of ceaseless activity. Almost every night, during some fourteen hours of total darkness, Fearless *deployed from the anchorage. The aim might be a special forces insertion, the meeting and escorting of the submarine HMS* Onyx *into the anchorage for a pit-stop and out again a few hours later, or the escorting of a convoy outbound, to rendezvous with another to be escorted back. The rule was to be within the relatively safe confines of the defended San Carlos anchorage by the first glimmerings of daylight – even if on two notable and nerve-racking occasions we did not achieve this.*

Two splendid Johns, Kelly the Commander and Prime the Navigating Officer, took turns at conducting the ship during part of these night-time forays once we were clear of Falkland Sound while I cat-napped in my sea-cabin, microphone in hand. John McGregor, the Marine Engineer Officer, led teams to succour bomb-damaged consorts. Stewart Thompson the Supply Officer and Phil Moore the Deputy Weapons Electrical Officer, both flew helicopters left-hand seat, as did John Kelly. The Chaplain, Peter Hudson,[331] buried Argentine dead at Goose Green, a harrowing task.

Following the loss of the Cunard container ship Atlantic Conveyor *with much of the force's military helicopter lift, the Commandos and Paratroopers moved forward some 50 miles to invest the northern approaches to Port Stanley, by yomping, heavily laden, across the Falklands in the rain. Formations of the reinforcement brigade who were to take the southern flank were not equally robust in pure fitness terms. It thus became necessary to take these newcomers forward by sea along the southern extremities of the islands by night.*

Intrepid *took the Scots Guards, launching them by landing craft some considerable distance short of their destination. They survived harrowing hours in very bad weather, amongst other nasty hazards, under Ewen Southby-Tailyour's redoubtable command.*

Next day I persuaded the Commodore to let Fearless *take the Welsh Guards that night, notwithstanding the serious disruption to command communications that this would cause for some hours. The plan was to take two of my landing craft (two had to be left behind in San Carlos), rendezvous with* Intrepid's *four off the entrance to Choiseul Sound, send four of the six forward with the Welsh Guards embarked to Bluff Cove and bring two back to San Carlos. I was determined to get nearer to their destination of Bluff Cove or Fitzroy this time, whilst avoiding the footprint of a land-based Exocet site the Argentines were believed to have established south of Port Stanley. I had to be back at San Carlos by first light. This all involved some nice navigational calculations.*

We sailed in nasty bumpy weather and proceeded south through the Falkland Sound and Eagle Passage, then north-east. We reached the rendezvous in good time, calm sea and comparatively docile weather. Unknown to me, due to weather, command and control dysfunction beyond either our knowledge or control, Intrepid's *landing craft had been unable to sail to meet us. I waited longer than we should have dared, finally launching our two landing craft with half the Welsh Guards and legging it back to San Carlos. Twilight, then full daylight found us still forcing our way back up the Falkland Sound. The Argentine Air Force did not call our bluff.*

It was decided that Fearless *could not again be released on such an extended and tenuous communications tether from the Land Force, and that she was anyway too crucial a command asset for such high-risk exposure. To underline the point, one of the two landing craft then launched,* Foxtrot Four, *never returned. She was destroyed two days later with six of her crew in a savage and pyrrhic air strike.*

Colour Sergeant Brian Johnston and his wife, Evelyn.

A week later it was all over and Fearless *was anchored in Stanley Harbour. Onboard as my 'guest' was the Argentine late Malvinas Commander, General Mario Menendez. We had some interesting discussions. The General had a final advantage however; he kept 'Spanish' hours with siesta to the local clock, whilst I was working a 20 hour day based on UK time (four hours ahead of the Falklands)! He poured the whisky, with which I had had his cabinet stocked.*

The Duke of Edinburgh did us the great honour of greeting us at Plymouth. On 14 July 1982 we arrived in Portsmouth to one of the fine welcomes accorded to ships returning from the South Atlantic. We took leave and then re-deployed, first to the Mediterranean and then again to the West Indies before I was relieved by Roger Trussell in March 1983.

On 6 June 2002 I paid one further farewell visit to Fountain Lake Jetty. On this last occasion I was asked to lay a wreath for the gallant crew of Foxtrot Four *on the ramp of a replacement,* Foxtrot Juliet, *berthed against the ship's lowered stern door: thus I bade farewell to the great ship.*

While some may have taken heart that, because she had been refitted and because there was now a Conservative Government, *Fearless* had a future. They would have been wrong. The following answers to Mr Trotter's[332] written question in the House of Commons on 1 July and to Sir Patrick Wall's written question[333] on 28 July 1981 show why:

> *Mr Trotter:*[334] *What will replace (*Fearless *and* Intrepid*) when they are withdrawn from service?*
> *Mr Goodhart:*[335] *As indicated in Cmnd. 8288 it had already been decided that these ships would not be replaced when paid off. On present plans they will be phased out when their next refits fall due.*
> *Sir Patrick Wall: What was the original cost of* Fearless *and what would be the estimated cost of a replacement at current prices?*
> *Mr Blaker:*[336] Fearless *originally cost £10.6 million. It is not possible to provide an estimate for the replacement cost of this ship since there are no plans to replace her and therefore no basis on which to formulate a cost estimate.*

On 15 June, 1981, Jeremy Larken had assumed command of a ship not only in deep refit but under threat of disposal within two years. *Fearless* was still in South Shields but she managed to sail on 16 October for the usual work-up exercises. It was during one of these 'in house' practices that, on 23 November, the Secretary of State for Defence, John Nott visited. He had stated a wish – some say it was suggested that he should state a wish – to be shown an LPD's capabilities and to be briefed by the Commanding Officer, the Commodore Amphibious Warfare and the Brigadier commanding 3 Commando Brigade Royal Marines. Later in the day the case for amphibious warfare was further driven home at Royal Marines, Poole and the announcement reversing the original decision eventually made in early 1982.

Jeremy Larken was not the only newcomer to amphibious warfare for Surgeon Commander Douglas Whyte[337] – among others – had also joined during the refit and was soon to be plunged into sea training routines with an unfamiliar ship and sickbay:

> *On my arrival there were many small Sick Bay matters, which needed completion and securing despite a ship's refit not being a topic covered in my medical education. . . .*
>
> *The Sick Bay staff quickly took up their allotted roles on board while getting to know everyone was an essential task, enhanced when the ship completed FOST's inspection during Oct/Nov 1981. Here everything and everyone was put through 'the mill' from dawn to midnight every day. Little did we realize then what a bonus BOST would turn out to be. The Sick Bay staff and the whole ship's company developed a team spirit that I have never experienced before or since.*
>
> *Although being an Aviation Medicine specialist was an added bonus for the ship's aviators, routine medicine and casualty treatment was the stock in trade. Indeed, on our first trip in January 1982 across the Atlantic mundane treatment of seasickness (including fluid balance) for first timers experiencing Force 12 gales became the common feature early on.*[338]
>
> *Later, in San Carlos,* Fearless *worked 20 hours a day but only because the Argentines did not fight at night. The first two to three days took some adjusting with everyone running on adrenaline.*

Fearless's first deployment, seven months after Jeremy Larken took command, was to the West Indies as the Dartmouth Training Ship, between January and March 1982, beginning with the bad weather that both the Commanding Officer and Medical Officer have mentioned.

There was, though, an unusual incident during this otherwise 'standard' training cruise and one that involved a murder. While *Fearless* was in Port-of-Spain the yacht *Nyn* arrived from England, but not long after an intruder broke in, strangled the skipper, Michael Crocker, and knifed his crew, David Drake. Details remain sketchy but the initial press reaction was one of thanks to a team of volunteers from *Fearless* who had cleaned up the vessel. The British High Commissioner, David Lane, wrote to Jeremy Larken on 1 February 1982 expressing his thanks and admiration to:

> *The members of your crew who so amply volunteered to clean up after the tragedy. . . . As you will have seen from the local press, their action has not gone unnoticed, and can do nothing but enhance even further the already high reputation which the Royal Navy enjoys in Trinidad.*

The local press was supportive, particularly as two young seaman from *Fearless* had been held up at knifepoint during a run ashore in Port-of-Spain. 'What makes the attack of the men of *Fearless* so horrible', quoted one local newspaper, 'is the goodwill, indeed the love, that they and their crewmates are showing to the people of our country.' The press even highlighted that over two days the ship had given at least ninety pints to the local blood bank.

The next headlines, and particularly those in the British press, began to take a different slant. 'The Navy Sails off with murder yacht' declared the *Daily Express* while *The Times*, with a smaller by-line said, 'Warship carries Crocker yacht' and, as *The Sun* had it, 'Navy sails into death boat row'. Behind this reporting was the simple fact that, following a request from Mr Crocker's widow, Tricia, *Fearless*'s shipwrights built a cradle in which to bring the ill-fated vessel home. Unfortunately the Trinidad police publicly, and perhaps stating the obvious, cried that the Royal Navy was removing 'the scene of crime'. The Trinidad and Tobago government became increasingly angry over the Navy's involvement especially as the police had yet to apprehend the killer. John Donaldson, the National Security Minister, said: 'I find it curious that crew members of the visiting battleship find themselves on the scene of a local murder, cleaning, mopping up and whatever.'

In due course the press reports fizzled out and an eighteen year-old local was brought to trial.

By 5 March 1982 *Fearless* was back in Plymouth undergoing a role change in order to participate in Exercise ALLOY EXPRESS in north Norway. Despite the 'moratorium on defence spending' which hit amphibious and landing craft training especially hard, the Royal Marines were determined to keep these arts alive right up to the last moment if necessary. It was during this deployment that *Fearless* left behind LCU *Foxtrot Four* and replaced her with one of Poole's landing craft, known colloquially as *The Black Pig*. This cuckoo in *Fearless*'s dock was crewed by *Foxtrot Four*'s team under the command of the greatly experienced Colour Sergeant Brian Johnston whose temporary command was a standard LCU converted for extended sojourns in the Arctic winter. Among many additions were a sectionalized, glass fibre canopy and extensive heating elements in the fuel and water tanks as well as under the exposed decks.

Fearless reached the northern Norwegian port of Harstad in a blizzard, through which the light grey of all the landing craft could easily be spotted: it was decided immediately, although not in the original trials directive, to paint *The Black Pig* in a disruptive, two-tone pattern using light colours. The only paint available in any bulk on board, apart from 'ship-side grey' with which she was already painted, were black and brown. This was considered better than nothing and was applied liberally. The results had not been anticipated but *The Black Pig* now disappeared into the background of the surrounding fjord especially when she was close inshore among the cliffs and rocks. A similar camouflage scheme was to become standard for all minor landing craft.

Otherwise the winter exercise was pretty much 'NATO-standard' but enlivened for some on the return journey by a 'black velvet'[339] party held in *The Black Pig*'s tank deck to thank everyone, at all levels, who had helped with the arctic trials. It was subsequently rumoured that following this lengthy extravaganza the Commanding Officer of HMS *Fearless* was not seen for twelve hours!

In Plymouth on 22 March to unload military personnel and stores, the ship began the familiar role change to training duties and even found time to embark a number of her crew's sons for the short passage back to Portsmouth. Also embarked for this brief coastal journey was a party of lads from the ship's affiliated Worcester Sea Cadet Unit plus a handful of Royal Marine cadets from the Bristol Filton Sea Cadet Corps. The Royal Marines' detachment put on a firepower demonstration

The Black Pig in North Norway.

of all infantry weapons used by the Corps although the most memorable event for young minds was the berthing of *Fearless* between HMS *Leeds Castle* and HMS *Intrepid* in Portsmouth: the latter in the process of being decommissioned.

Meanwhile in the South Atlantic, Argentinian scrap metal merchants were busy laying the seeds for the United Kingdom's first major amphibious operation since Suez which, in turn, would ensure that *The Black Pig*'s Norwegian trials would remain relevant for the future – as indeed would those of her parent ship.

On Wednesday, 31 March British intelligence confirmed that the Argentinian South Georgia operations were now being used by the junta as a cover for more dramatic events: an invasion of the Falklands themselves was actually underway with reports reaching Whitehall suggesting that the islands would be invaded on 2 April (bad weather had delayed Argentine plans by twenty-four hours).[340]

In London during the evening of that Wednesday, intense arguments raged within Mrs Thatcher's government on the sense – or otherwise – of facing-down this aggressive expedition; but how and with what, bearing in mind that Mr Nott, in concert with the Army and Air Force Chiefs of Staff, were of the opinion that the Falklands were now a lost cause. The United States Navy also considered the re-capture of the Falkland Islands to be a military impossibility. The only voice among 'the Chiefs' in support of such an expedition was that of the First Sea Lord, Admiral Sir Henry Leach.[341]

Mrs Thatcher, in her memoirs,[342] described Admiral Leach as 'quiet, calm and confident'. When she asked him precisely what he could offer he replied:

> *I can put together a task force of destroyers, frigates, landing craft and support vessels. It will be led by the aircraft carriers HMS* Hermes *and HMS* Invincible. *It can be ready to leave in 48 hours.*

This was the first positive opinion received by the Prime Minister. Events and decisions occurred in rapid succession after that and while many may consider, quite understandably, that the Argentinians had invaded as a result of signals sent by Mrs Thatcher's government, it was, paradoxically, her determination – once the invasion was a fact – that allowed the Royal Navy to prosecute what was always going to be a risky enterprise, with remarkable success.

Argentinian forces landed on the Falkland Islands during the night of the 1–2 April and yet it was not until 3 April that Jeremy Larken was ordered to bring his ship to four hours' notice and prepare for Operation CORPORATE: for which he was given just three days to store to a war readiness state and sail south.

One of *Fearless*'s boilers had been un-bricked: two days earlier, the re-bricking programme had been set for five weeks. Refuelling, arming and storing took place simultaneously while Health and Safety inspectors, had they been allowed anywhere near, would have prevented almost every activity in sight.

Fearless sailed on 6 April and that evening, in Lyme Bay, the remaining headquarters staff led by Commodore Mike Clapp (Commodore Amphibious Warfare) and Brigadier Julian Thompson (Commander 3 Commando Brigade Royal Marines) joined by helicopter in a rising gale. The landing was conducted outside safe flying limits: the first of dozens of occasions that peacetime regulations were to be disregarded.

Accommodation on board at every level was tight with the AOO, Major Mark Gosling, responsible for Embarked Forces' accommodation, faced with a near-insoluble problem. He coped imaginatively by turning the gunroom into a temporary dormitory and billeting comparatively senior officers in 4L1 mess-deck: years later to become Wrens' accommodation. Storage was equally tight with both fore and aft passages on 02 deck covered with a layer of compo boxes that, effectively, reduced the deck-head by about twelve inches.

Fearless arrived off Ascension Island on 17 April so low on fuel that she was unable to float out her LCUs. Slowly the amphibious fleet assembled and briefings were conducted while an intensive re-stow of hastily embarked stores continued day and night. Once *Fearless* had refuelled, her four larger landing craft were able to take part in this mammoth task as well as, with the LCVPs, ferrying men and vehicles ashore for training.

The day before her arrival at Ascension, the Carrier Battle Group Commander had, unannounced, landed on board for a first meeting with his two co-Task Group Commanders: Mike Clapp and Julian Thompson. In many respects this meeting tended to muddy rather than clear the waters of Amphibious Task Force planning as explained by Julian Thompson in his book *No Picnic*:[343]

> *Instead of listening to the outcome of some twelve days' work and analysis by Clapp's and my staffs, which resulted in us having a pretty clear idea of the various options, we were treated to a staccato procession of pedagogic questions which bore little relevance to the facts as we understood them. One of the ideas that was forced upon us for examination was to land at the extreme end of West Falkland in order that an air-strip could be constructed by my engineers to take Phantom air-defence fighters. That my engineers had neither the plant nor the numbers to carry out such an ambitious project, which would have taken a large force of contractors months, all within easy range of the Argentine Air Force, was dismissed. Landing on West Falkland would also necessitate another amphibious operation on East Falkland. This in itself was reason enough not to contemplate such a move. Fortunately the notion was killed at the Council of War[344] the following day. I could sense my staff's outrage at this cavalier treatment.*

Another of the 'ideas' forced upon the *Fearless* team is covered in a paraphrase from Mike Clapp's book, *Amphibious Assault Falklands* and from Sir Lawrence Freedman's *Official History of the Falklands Campaign*:

> *Finally, (we were) instructed to consider another and even more alarming (scheme) ... a 'feint' lasting two or three days using* Fearless, Fort Austin *and* Resource *as well as some LSLs. This required me to disembark some of my staff (and some of Julian's) to a destroyer, while* Fearless's *group, acting as decoys, would close the Argentine coast in order to draw the Argentinian Air Force so that we could initiate an air battle. At the same time the two staffs would be closer to the Falklands coast in the destroyer 'making amphibious noises over the radio' simulating an assault. This raised two obvious concerns: one was the safety of* Fearless *herself – we only had one ship capable of commanding a landing – and the other was that both my and Julian's Task Group would be left leaderless. . . . .*

As only the Commander Task Force at Northwood had the authority to issue such an order to the Amphibious Task Group ships the idea was dropped.

The stay at Ascension Island was frustrating for all because of the uncertainty over whether the Amphibious Task Group would sail south or return north. Nevertheless, the weeks allowed other ships to catch up, including the swiftly-recommissioned *Intrepid*, who arrived just in time to meet the rest of the Task Group before it sailed. *Fearless*, as did a number of other ships, embarked tons of sand with which to fill bags for the more exposed upper deck positions around, for instance, the Bofors on each of her bridge wings and the upper-deck machine gun nests.

Frustration was rife with the political situation disturbingly uncertain enough for Jeremy Larken to write in his Night Order Book:

> *20/21 April – at Ascension Island: Political situation has not improved – call me for any serious deterioration.*

Training of ground troops was intensive but more so for the two Army battalions who had never been to sea and who nicknamed the LCVPs and LCUs, into which they were crammed twixt ship and shore, as rubbish skips – perhaps forgetting, as some unkind nautical types were wont to point out, what rubbish skips are designed to carry! In fact 2 Para only managed one rehearsal loading into the LCUs from the *Norland* – forces of circumstances and timing that were to have a knock-on effect later.

With an air and sea blockade unenforceable and with international diplomacy equally unable to reach a solution acceptable to the British government, the Amphibious Task Group sailed south on 6 May certain, now, that it would be conducting operations in the Falklands before returning to the United Kingdom. *Intrepid* sailed two days afterwards, as a result of her late arrival. She caught up quickly.

When she did, a jackstay transfer was organized with *Intrepid* off *Fearless*'s port side during which it was noticed that her starboard funnel badge was back-to-front with the rifle of the Combined Operations insignia pointing astern: in the old days this would have incurred serious penalties for a Commanding Officer involving rounds of port. *Fearless*'s Chief Yeoman was invited to point out this sartorial error across eighty or so feet of water by semaphore to his opposite number – discreetly using his hands in front of his body. Captain Dingemans's instant reply to Jeremy Larken was: 'A wise man should keep his arse covered.'

As the amphibious flagship, *Fearless* had her own additional duties to keep her occupied. Not only was she home to twice the normal overload of personnel but she was the focus for considerable staff activity, putting further pressure on the Supply and Secretariat Department as well as the Aviation Department and its tiny flight deck. Throughout the days and many nights, as the Amphibious Task Group forged southwards, hundreds – possibly thousands – of men flew in and out in all weathers while, on board, they, too, needed to be fed, watered, briefed and, occasionally, bedded down.

Fearless was designed for this work but now, not only was the Brigadier commanding the equivalent of five Commandos and a Logistic Regiment, he also had considerably more minor units under command than had ever been practised. Additionally the Commodore was, or was about to be at any one time, commanding forty-seven merchant and naval ships, three naval air squadrons, two fleet clearance diving teams and numerous other smaller units. The Communications Departments of the ship and embarked staffs were as overworked as any, especially as almost every signal received and sent had a higher than normal classification and a faster than normal routing requirement. There is no doubt that of all the ships sent south HMS *Fearless* was by far the hardest worked.

The embarked aircrew from 846 Squadron, whose aircraft were split across at least ten other ships[345] but whose Commanding Officer, Simon Thornewill, was on board the amphibious flag ship were also hard pushed. David Lord, the Squadron's QHI[346] sums up with a personal view which says it all for the embarked aircrews over the years:

I cannot explain why Fearless *was always the first of the pair of LPDs to be mentioned, but she was always acknowledged as the leader, the tip of the amphibious shipping arrow. She was a durable and happy ship and Junglies[347] were made welcome. Even high-spirited aircrew antics in the wardroom were tolerated with remarkable restraint. The briefing room forward of Flyco and abeam the Photo shack was our working space. Successive Junglie detachments kept it well ordered and functional as a routines office, briefing room, safety equipment, flying kit and map store. Junglie pilots were typically confined to a 6 man cabin forward of the wardroom. What stories that cabin could tell; personal traits were laid bare and largely tolerated, friendships cemented, dislikes aired and enemies consigned to their fate. A stock of Johnny Walker Red Label was always to hand for medicinal purposes. It was not unusual for the cabin deck to become an impromptu sleep-over space for one or more itinerant Junglies, wandering the flight decks of the Fleet in that venerable workhorse, the Wessex HU Mk V. Finding themselves washed-up, with no prospect of a return to their own Mother until the dawn's early light, they gravitated to the 'Junglie Grot'. None complained.*

Our most illustrious neighbour was the Bish (Ship's padre), for whom the Junglie Grot must have been a vision of Dante's inferno.

Lieutenant Commander Featherstone was Fearless's *AVO. His San Carlos broadcasts of the status of Air Raids were eagerly monitored and closely adhered to by the Junglies plying their trade unloading shipping. When he said 'SCRAM' you cleared off, to find a convenient niche in the surrounding hills, and watched and waited for the 'All Clear'. He kept a cool head and his sense of humour. The Junglies liked him.*

Non-aviators sometimes remark on the lack of a hangar in Fearless *and* Intrepid. *The inability to conduct complex aircraft maintenance within the shelter of a well-lit hangar was a grave short-coming. Tactically, once the darkened ship began its advance into an Amphibious Objective Area, night-time maintenance of embarked aircraft prior to H-Hour was all but curtailed. We must have done alright in the Junglie squadrons because the new LPDs,* Albion *and* Bulwark, *are devoid of hangars as well. . . .*

The first of the two definitive briefings for the landings – Operation SUTTON – was held on 13 May when Brigadier Julian Thompson gave his Orders Group covering the initial assault and the immediate aftermath. This was held in *Fearless's* wardroom where the senior landing force Commanding Officers sat in comfortable armchairs in the front row, almost upon the lectern and screen. Behind them, on less comfortable seats, sat the Operations and Intelligence Officers, the Officers Commanding smaller units, the supporting arms coordinators, communicators, air and landing craft commanders and Beachmasters, staff officers and liaison officers from ships and other units. At the very rear of the briefing, the most junior commanders and staff perched or knelt on the wardroom table, pushed hard against the starboard bulkhead. Although no longer a surprise, San Carlos – chosen by the Commodore and Brigadier – could at last be confirmed as the point of entry: a decision agreed and endorsed by the Task Force Commander, Admiral Sir John Fieldhouse, in Fleet Headquarters at Northwood.

The second major briefing, the Pre-Landing Conference, was held by Commodore Mike Clapp on 15 May under similar cramped conditions but attended this time by the captains of all ships (war, auxiliary and merchant) plus their navigators, Principal Warfare Officers and, where appropriate, the Senior Naval Officers embarked in merchant ships.

Yet despite the intricacy of the military and naval plans so carefully prepared and dovetailed over the preceding weeks and with everyone knowing precisely what their duties were and with the whole landing sequence approved, a major change was ordered on 18 May by Admiral Fieldhouse. Mike Clapp describes the situation in *Amphibious Assault Falklands*:

Now all waited for the final word to 'Go!'. Instead that evening we received an invitation to move two of the units out of the luxury liner, Canberra. *I had always made it quite clear that the bulk of the men would have to land from the ships in which they sailed, the silence from Northwood allowing us to believe that this was acceptable. Now, the only way to cross deck was by landing craft, an unlikely event in the South Atlantic with the onset of winter and about 300 miles from the nearest land – and that hostile.*

The invitation to redistribute the men was unambiguous but as each marine or paratrooper carried between 70 and 100 pounds, the helicopter lift for well over 1,000 such laden men was unacceptable. My concern now was that we were taking troops from a ship they knew well and from which they had all practised their assault procedures and were putting them into unfamiliar ships already grossly overloaded – and that certainly was a risk. Canberra *had been designed to allow hordes of untrained, blue-rinsed Americans to escape with some safety from a fire. She also had enough life rafts for all her passengers but neither* Intrepid *nor* Fearless *could boast the same at 'overload plus'.*

Where to put the men was one thing, how to get them there was something else altogether. During the night the wind had dropped leaving a very long, six-foot, benign swell running and little sea. It was easily agreed that both *Fearless* and *Intrepid* could risk lowering their stern ramps and float out their LCUs – probably the furthest from land this evolution had ever taken place or, as Mike Clapp put it:

> *LPDs had launched LCUs in heavier seas but always close to outside 'engineering' support if, say, it had been impossible to raise the stern gate again or pump out the ballast tanks. The order was given and probably the most remarkable mid-ocean, cross-decking exercise in (amphibious) history took place.*

In *No Picnic*, Julian Thompson wrote:

> *The Captains and Ships' Companies of both LPDs responded in their usual swift and flexible way. In* Fearless *Captain Larken ... did not turn a hair, but merely added that if the sea state on 19 May looked at all possible he would give it a try by landing craft, but that the light jackstay method could and would be made to work. His Executive Officer, Commander John Kelly, quickly got to work to have every available space turned out so that troops would have somewhere to stretch out, preferably under cover. Feeding these extra men would also be a problem, but not one to defeat Kelly or* Fearless.

Commander John Kelly and Commodore Mike Clapp with members of 40 Commando on the night of the landings at San Carlos.

On 20 May and after meeting up with the Carrier Battle Group, *Fearless* and her entourage entered the self-declared Total Exclusion Zone 'for operations to recapture the Falkland Islands'. Outside, the weather was foul from the Argentinian air and sub-surface points of view and thus perfect for the British approach to the Amphibious Operations Area. Inside the 600 or so Marines of 40 Commando swamped every last available space including the wardroom which was turned into a dormitory, as were most passageways. The whole ship was now on action messing with long lines of men shuffling towards distribution points, clutching mess tins and mugs while side-stepping sleeping bodies.

Although there was no doubt that the assault was 'On', the executive order had yet to be given from London. The date of the landings (should they be approved) had been chosen for some days yet the actual timings were altered once or twice to take account of last-minute intelligence. It was not until about 1115 on 20 May – less than twenty-four hours before the planned assault – that the code word *Palpas* was received and with it came considerable relief that the waiting was over: the weeks of planning and uncertainty would end in action.

That night, and in clearing weather, HMS *Fearless* led the Amphibious Task Group through the northern entrance of Falkland Island Sound and came to her anchor a few cables west of Chancho Point – the southern entrance to San Carlos Waters – in the earliest hours of 21 May 1982. In the Amphibious Operations Room the well-practised procedures for such events had been under way for some time. Concentrated into this small space was information on every man and piece of equipment in the Amphibious Task Force, its landing order, its destination, even plans for its, or his, safe removal if hit or wounded. Into all this were dovetailed further plans for surface, subsurface, air and electronic warfare. Intelligence from a variety of obscure and secret sources was being fed in almost continuously, assessed, processed, disseminated and reacted upon. Seldom in recent British military history had so much information, and so many hopes, been concentrated into such a small space.

It would not be over-dramatizing the event to suggest that the aspirations of the whole nation were at that moment focused onto HMS *Fearless* and the shoulders of the two amphibious commanders – a Royal Marines Brigadier and a Royal Navy Commodore – standing calmly in the middle of that cluttered room. For the next few, tense hours the eyes of the nation, and through them, in many respects, those of the whole of the western world (and not a few of the eastern bloc) would be turned towards *Fearless*'s Amphibious Operations Room, its decisions and reactions. Like it or not – and it was, in the world order of things, a minor military operation – the successful landings were of vital importance not only to the Islanders but to the principles of freedom, and they were about to be conducted against odds considered unacceptable even with the correct ships.

All did not go quite according to plan in *Fearless* for while the escorting frigates and destroyers – with the noble HMS *Ardent* in the vanguard – took up their allotted anti-air, anti-surface and anti-submarine screens and with others beginning the preliminary naval gunfire bombardment, her ballast pumps chose that moment, of all moments, to sulk. This 'bubble in the host' – compounded by the slow entrance into the Sound thanks to the earlier thick weather and radar 'silence' – seemed set to ensure a delay of at least one hour onto the first beach.

The original plan had been for *Fearless*'s four LCUs, with 40 Commando embarked, to lead those of *Intrepid* with 2 Para embarked, in one long line ahead – for fear of the mine threat – down the west edge of San Carlos Waters to land their troops either side of Little Rincon with the Paras to the south and thus closer to their final destination on Sussex Mountain. *Foxtrot One*, under the command of Colour Sergeant Michael 'Connie' Francis was to have been the lead craft in this assault but the lead craft had been changed to *Intrepid*'s *Tango One* carrying 2 Para in order that the initial landings would be staggered by ten minutes to save confusion if there had been an enemy between the two separate landing points. 2 Para also had the furthest approach march ahead of them. In command and navigating this slow, vulnerable and unarmed flotilla was the newly appointed Officer Commanding the Task Force Landing Craft Squadron,[348] accompanied by Colonel Seccombe, Royal Marines, the Deputy Brigade Commander, on board should events get out of hand. Radio silence was in force but if the enemy intervened Tom Seccombe's direct contact with the Brigadier would have been invaluable.

Eventually the snake of craft crossed the Line of Departure about fifty minutes late and so, instead of steaming at 6 knots, skirting the edge of the kelp banks, full speed straight down the middle of the loch was ordered by the Landing Craft Commander. Thus it was *Intrepid*'s *Tango One* under the command of Colour Sergeant Barrie Davies[349] that landed the first men ashore from 2 Para at 0715 GMT[350] to begin the repossession of the islands. Ten minutes later Michael Francis in his *Foxtrot One* landed the first man of 40 Commando to the north of Little Rincon.

As part of the second wave, *Fearless*'s LCUs, now joined by her four LCVPs and this time led by the Landing Craft Commander in Colour Sergeant Brian Johnston's *Foxtrot Four*, then landed 3 Para and two light tanks of the Blues and Royals in the Sand Bay area to the west of Port San Carlos. In broad daylight the ships of the Amphibious Task Group began anchoring in San Carlos Waters with *Fearless* as far south as depths would allow. It was also time for the Argentinian Air Force to wake up and this it did with the first of numerous air-strikes that would continue almost unabated through daylight hours (and not a few night time ones as well) over the next weeks. Having completed the last scheduled wave of the day and picked up a section of the SBS, *Fearless*'s LCUs – as did those from *Intrepid* after they had landed 45 Commando at Ajax Bay – began their return home but, while steaming south alongside the comparative safety of the cliffs of Doctor's Point, they were ordered to stop, in the case of *Fearless*'s LCUs, by a brief radio message: 'Ship is under air attack. Lie off. Will call you in when convenient.'

Throughout that first day of repossession *Fearless* and the other ships in San Carlos Waters and Falkland Sound came under repeated air attack, resulting in considerable damage to a number of

HMS *Fearless* LCMs resting at San Carlos.

Air Raid Warning Red in San Carlos Waters.

escorts and the loss, after a fine and lengthy fight, of HMS *Ardent* commanded by Commander Alan West.[351]

Jeremy Larken's war diary written as events unfolded gives a previously unseen insight of minute-by-minute events. Of interest, are the Commanding Officer's personal comments which were added down the right hand margin but included here in the text:

> *21 May:*
> *1016Z. Hands to action stations. As programmed (the ship is) to be ready for air attacks at dawn. Landing operations going well.*
> *1200. Air raid warning red.*
> *1247. Two Pucara attacking* Canberra.
> *1329. Under missile attack from Mirage. Engaged Seacat.*
> *1342. Mirage closing – hostiles at 180° 20′ and inbound.*
> *1411. One Mirage splashed and one A4. Another A4.* Argonaut, *minor damage with four casualties. One Pucara splashed. Attacks are* not *being pressed home.*
> *1802. Fire Ardent. Doesn't look good.*
> *1817. Ardent has been overwhelmed and will shortly be abandoned.*
> *2238. A tremendous day of resolute (and in some ships no doubt heroic) deeds. The aim has been sustained. The enemy has unquestionably lost too many aircraft to continue sustained operations at this sort of level … we have lost one fine frigate … there is however no doubt where victory lies – provided our national nerve is sustained.*

Dusk of that first day in San Carlos Waters came as a relief: the landings had gone better than hoped and major air attacks were not expected to continue after dusk. There had been casualties:

190

two light helicopters shot down; *Ardent* sunk: *Argonaut* and *Antrim* badly damaged; *Brilliant* hit by sixteen 30-mm cannon shells that had caused casualties and *Broadsword* likewise. The only two unscathed frigates were *Plymouth* and *Yarmouth*; nevertheless as Captain Kit Layman in HMS *Argonaut* was to write:

If the history of the Royal Navy is a good guide, ships are there to be used and therefore to be risked. The Royal Navy has never minded losing a few ships in the knowledge that warfare is a risk taking business. Hitler, Mussolini and Anaya hated losing ships and withdrew them and,

Bofors gunner AB Ron Moody being congratulated by the Captain.

in extreme cases, scuttled them rather than have them sunk. The amphibious assessment was that the job could be done. It was done and the losses acceptable.[352]

Later, Jeremy Larken wrote:

After the first assault wave just before dawn, we knew it was going to be a long day. We knew we would be attacked by the Argentine Air Force and on that first day there were 72 planes attacking a force of some 12 to 15 ships. A burst of cannon fire wounded some of our gun crew. The others remained at their posts and continued firing while our medical team moved in and took away the injured.

D-Day at Ajax Bay.

Battle damage.

The next day brought fewer interruptions from enemy aircraft – and those were offshore – allowing the offload to continue at a pace while operational damage was repaired or at least contained. Along with other ships' companies those on board *Fearless* could barely believe their luck but it was true and by the second dusk much had been achieved. There was, though, one task that did directly affect *Fearless* and that was the predicament facing HMS *Argonaut*, then anchored off the north-east shore of San Carlos Waters, unable to move or fight. Three LCUs were dispatched to offer any assistance that might be appropriate. Slowly and during an air attack, the crippled Leander class frigate was nudged south, under the protection of the rest of the fleet, while on board extreme valour was being exercised to stabilize two unexploded bombs.

With perfect weather for offensive air operations over the next days, the Argentinian Air Force obliged and, among other partial successes, succeeded in damaging Commander Nick Tobin's[353] HMS *Antelope* with two unexploded, 1,000 pound bombs . Later that evening, 23 May, one of the bombs exploded while being defused, killing one and wounding another of the Army's bomb disposal team. With the subsequent fire taking hold, Captain Larken decided that the only chance of saving the frigate was to tow her onto a beach so, while hasty plans were being drawn up, two LCUs were dispatched as fire-fighters and lifeboats. *Foxtrot One* commanded by Michael Francis[354] and *Foxtrot Four* with Colour Sergeant Brian Johnston lay alongside *Antelope* plying their fire hoses and accepting survivors but the situation was quickly becoming so dangerous that *Foxtrot One*, once she was full of survivors, steamed back towards *Fearless* while Brian Johnston was ordered to retire himself for fear that the second bomb would 'cook-off'. However, as

Battle damage.

Sandbagged machine-gun post on upper deck abaft the bridge.

there were still men on board the stricken frigate he ignored the Flagship's orders until the last man had been embarked – a total of well over 100. The second bomb exploded very soon afterwards.

LCUs towing in HMS *Argonaut*.

Yet the crew of *Foxtrot Four* did not stop helping survivors. Simon Bloomfield, an LMEM(M) in HMS *Antelope*, was later to write:[355]

> *That landing craft came alongside* Antelope *when we were bombed and rescued us: along with the rest of the crew they put themselves in danger to get us off. Once we were in* Fearless, *Dusty (LMEM(M) David Miller – Foxtrot Four's stoker) made sure myself and another shipmate were OK and gave us clothing as we only had the overalls we were dressed in. He also gave us cash to keep us going. It was with extreme shock that while I was on survivors' leave I learnt of not only his death but that of the rest of the landing craft crew. The moment I read of it in the* Daily Mail *will live with me for the rest of my life.*

At least one other of *Fearless*'s landing craft was involved in the rescue of *Antelope*'s crew. LCVP *Foxtrot Seven*, under the command of Corporal Alan White, Royal Marines, saved forty-one of the ship's company, an act that was to earn him the Task Force Commander's Commendation. With other LCVPs, *Foxtrot Seven* was later employed as a minesweeper in the entrance to Salvador Waters.

The next was another full day and one that was to get worse before it got better. A number of ships were harbouring unexploded bombs, there were problems with support helicopter operations and 42 Commando needed moving back from the east of Port San Carlos to within a more easily defended perimeter. *Fearless*'s war diary and her Commanding Officer's comments only hint at her personal problems after she had been hit by cannon shells:

> 24 May
> *All very exciting – we have been blooded. S(M) McLeod with severed calf muscle. Casevac'd to Ajax Bay. Doctor says it can be stitched together.*

In all four men were wounded[356] but, apart from the luckless S(M) McLeod, they were treated on board.

Off Hauf in 1966 it had been jellyfish, off San Carlos in 1982 it was krill[357] as Jeremy Larken's Night Order Book demonstrates:

> 23/24 May at San Carlos: *Power – starboard at 5 minutes notice. Krill blocks cooling.*
> 26/27 May at San Carlos: *The krill war continues.*

In between towing frigates and rescuing survivors all landing craft from both LPDs were employed non-stop in ship to shore movement of men and stores yet, unlike helicopters, there were no spare pilots to take over during what otherwise should have been rest periods. The coxswains began to hallucinate but it was not until the intervention of the Officer Commanding the Task Force Landing Craft Squadron that periods of rest were inserted into the off-load programmes; even so when the odd 'funnies' were injected they tended to be at the expense of rest as little was allowed to interfere with the build-up of supplies ashore.

By now all landing craft had been brought under one command of the newly formed Task Force Landing Craft Squadron, whose headquarters were set up ashore, adjacent to 2 Para's landing beach and Brigade HQ, under the control of Major Roger Dillon[358] with Corporal 'Taff' Williams[359] as his signaller. Between them these two would undertake a task that would eventually require a total of two officers and five NCOs. It was from here that the daily and nightly tasks were coordinated to meet the Brigadier's requirements of stores ashore while matching the availability of all landing and raiding craft.

One such task, alluded to earlier, was to collect Lieutenant Colonel Nick Vaux's[360] 42 Commando from the east of Salt Point, up the San Carlos River, and deliver it back to Port San Carlos settlement using landing craft from both *Fearless* and *Intrepid*. The men could have 'yomped'[361] but by far the quickest method, on the assumption that the depths were suitable, was to use landing craft. The only chart available was one that had been hastily surveyed onto a scrap of tracing paper by Ewen Southby-Tailyour[362] some years before and so at last light on 24 May *Foxtrot Four* and *Tango One* began this tortuous journey along a stretch of waterway never previously visited by craft of this size. At one point the lead craft, *Foxtrot Four*, ran aground but was towed off stern-first by *Tango One* while the previously unknown shoal was pencilled onto the rough chart. Two round trips were required but well before dawn 42 Commando had been repositioned.

Jeremy Larken's war diary:

> *25 May*
> Coventry *lost – sunk*
> Atlantic Conveyor *hit. A bad day. Glad to have something to do overnight to take our minds off it all – SBS insertion.*

Another incident that day that again included *Foxtrot Four* – quickly establishing a reputation for being at the forefront of the action – occurred after an enemy pilot ejected close to *Fearless*. Lieutenant Ricardo Lucero was plucked from the water by Brian Johnston's crew and, with a broken knee, was soon under the care of the ship's sickbay.

The SBS insertion, mentioned by Jeremy Larken in his war diary, had begun on the evening of 25 May when *Fearless* sailed for Salvador waters, in which it had been decided to establish a Special Forces Forward Operating Base. Earlier, HMS *Yarmouth* had failed to land the SBS due to appalling weather on this open, north-facing coast so it was now *Fearless*'s turn. The target was Green Island, across the isthmus from Port Louis and Berkeley Sound, and while it meant the ship steaming throughout much of the night it was probably a welcome break, emotionally if not physically, from San Carlos Waters.

Lieutenant Ricardo Lucero is carried to the sick bay from *Foxtrot Four* after ejecting.

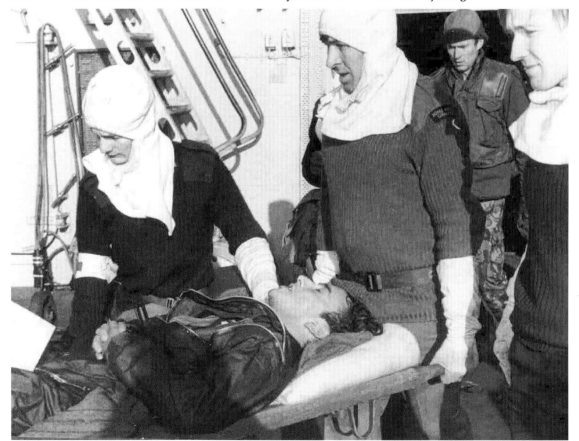

Jeremy Larken's war diary:

26 May
0000. Ready for approach to Salvador for SBS insertion
0335. Three Rigid Reading Craft away after one swamped in dock.

Most special forces insertions – especially into the outer islands and West Falkland – were undertaken by a frigate but not so this night as HMS *Plymouth* was conducting an observed shoot onto Argentine positions in the Fox Bay area. By dawn on 26 May all ships were back in San Carlos Waters but, unfortunately, so was the bulk of the Commando Brigade. Following the loss of the *Atlantic Conveyor* with the majority of the Task Force's Chinook helicopters it was clear that the Brigade would have to walk to Stanley and orders to initiate that evolution, plus an assault on Darwin and Goose Green, were given. On the 28th *Fearless* steamed eastwards to refuel and collect Major General Jeremy Moore[363] and his staff from HMS *Antrim* before rendezvousing with *Hermes*. All went well and the amphibious flagship was anchored back in San Carlos Waters before dawn on 30 May, where, very obviously to the relief of the newly embarked General, news of 2 Para's victory at Goose Green and the securing of Douglas and Teal Inlet settlements by 45 Commando and 3 Para respectively, was received.

Thankful for the brief respite – although there was some guilt at leaving 'bomb alley' – *Fearless*'s ship's company was back in action with a vengeance as a quote from Mike Clapp's book suggests:

John MacGregor's[364] engineering team were flat-out helping with unexploded bombs and repairing damage ... Fearless's (men) appeared almost everywhere, assisting in some often small, but nevertheless important, operation. There was a magnificent atmosphere of determination and enterprise.

With the arrival of the Divisional Commander and the advance elements of the Army's 5 Brigade, *Fearless* was now home to an entirely different Embarked Force and, in some respects, her duties changed as well: particularly in the Communications Department. At this time the Commodore, knowing that *Fearless* represented a high value target to the enemy, ordered *Intrepid* to replicate as much as possible the situation in *Fearless*'s operations rooms, so that should the former have to be abandoned, the staff could, with ease, take up where they left off by using the latter's, similar, facilities.

One worry was the reported possibility of a land-launched Exocet attack from Pebble Island as the ships passed in and out of Falkland Islands Sound: Jeremy Larken's Night Order Book:

2/3 June at sea. . . . Off Pebble Island. Possibility of Exocet attack. . . . Defence is: launch Chaff D,[365] turn away to put threat on starboard quarter using maximum revolutions to accelerate turn. Essential launch flash is observed therefore two Gun Direction Platform lookouts do nothing but watch on bearing of Pebble Island.

Ashore, the Commando Brigade consolidated its position along the northern, or left, flank and began the task of investing Stanley from that direction. The Army brigade continued to offload into San Carlos while starting its approach along the southern flank via Goose Green. Unfortunately it was this operation, not always conducted with the full knowledge of the Divisional Commander, that was to lead to both LPDs being put at considerable risk, to say nothing of the Brigade itself.

Events over this period have been covered extensively elsewhere and so will not be revisited here other than in a purely *Fearless* context. After much 'to-ing' and 'fro-ing' the Commodore's final plan had HMS *Intrepid* lifting the Scots Guards to the entrance of Choiseul Sound via Lively Sound from where her LCUs would deliver them direct to the tiny beach at Bluff Cove. The same journey was planned for the following night with the Welsh Guards embarked in the same LPD.

Y Turret.

Intrepid floated out her landing craft – led by Barrie Davies in *Tango One*, with Ewen Southby-Tailyour embarked as navigator – to the south-west of Lively Island at 0430Z on 6 June before returning with her escorting frigate to the comparative sanctity of San Carlos Waters. She left behind the Scots Guards facing a hideous, seven hour journey – instead of the expected two hours – that was to include gale force winds from ahead, star shells and artillery or mortar fire. This small flotilla was equally badly frightened by the unexpected appearance of two frigates, under the control of the Carrier Battle Group, despite assurances having been made to the Commodore Amphibious Warfare – and passed to the Officer Commanding Task Force Landing Craft Squadron – that no such ships would be in the area while the move was taking place. Nor had the frigates' Commanding Officers' been briefed by their own Flag Officer of the landing craft presence; each, therefore, thought that the other might have been enemy. This flouting of de-confliction agreements nearly led to what might have been the worst blue-on-blue disaster of the war and was only averted by a single word flashed by a pin-point red light from the lead frigate which read simply, 'Friend'. Ewen Southby-Tailyour's reply was, 'To which side?' Nevertheless, to any Argentinian watching on a radar or even from a far hill, it must have been obvious what was afoot.

For the second night's insertion of the Welsh Guards, Jeremy Larken, who had been due to take *Fearless* to sea for refuelling but who had heard of his sister ship's reluctance to go further east than Lively Sound, promised the Commodore that, if allowed, he would launch his landing craft as close to Bluff Cove as he possibly could and certainly in the area where the Scots Guards should have started their LCU journey – south of Elephant Island. The Commodore agreed.

What neither Jeremy Larken nor the Commodore were to know was that various outside factors, including the weather and the improper commandeering of *Intrepid*'s landing craft at Bluff Cove by a Parachute Regiment officer, would prevent those vessels from making the rendezvous. Thus, on arrival at the launching position originally ordained by the Commodore, only half of the Battalion could be dispatched towards its destination. The other half had to return to San Carlos Water to be lifted forwards in the RFA *Sir Galahad*. It was these Welsh Guardsmen who were still on board the RFA off Fitzroy settlement on 8 June when she – and *Sir Tristram* – were bombed.

Of the two *Fearless* LCUs that remained in the area – *Foxtrot One* and *Foxtrot Four* – the former was involved in the courageous rescue of survivors from both *Sir Galahad* and *Sir Tristram* while the latter had, earlier, been dispatched to Goose Green to collect 5 Brigade's communications vehicles. Ignoring the orders to wait till dusk, Brian Johnston,[366] knowing the imperatives of the hour, sailed back as soon as his craft was laden. During the afternoon of that day – 8 June – four A-4B Skyhawks, heading along Choiseul Sound, launched their attack on *Foxtrot Four* one mile due south of Johnson's Island, with cannon and bombs, scoring a direct hit on the stern and wheelhouse, killing six crewmen. The LCU remained afloat long enough for the survivors to send a distress signal which was picked up by the Falkland Island Company coaster, *Monsunen*, now under Royal Navy command. She rescued the fourteen survivors and took the sinking landing craft in tow but this was abandoned to allow *Foxtrot Four* to drift 'on a course of 190° in a slowly sinking condition'. It is believed she sank two hours later. What is certain is that she took with her 5 Brigade's communications equipment. Within minutes of the attack two Royal Navy Harriers had intercepted the Skyhawks and shot down three. The fourth aircraft of the flight was later seen to crash. After the war Charles Howard was to interview *Foxtrot Four*'s crewman, Marine 'Tich' Cruden, and pieced together this description in June 1999:

> As they flew low up Choiseul Sound at approximately 1615, one of the Skyhawks that had not used her bombs saw Foxtrot Four *and scored a lucky hit with a single 500lb bomb on the LCU's stern, blowing off the engine room.*
>
> *Of the embarked army signallers, one was injured, not gravely. Of the eight crew,[367] five were killed instantly. Two survived. Marine Quigley[368] was on the wheel, and was blown into the water. He swam back, and clambered over the stern. The crew accommodation now had burning fuel oil slopping around in it. Marine Cruden was there, about to go on watch. He suffered eye injuries (rendering him temporarily blind), burns and imbedded debris, which troubles him still. Just above deck level in the accommodation, there is a hole through which the ramp and vehicle recovery wire runs from the well deck to the winch. Normally it is about nine inches across by six inches high, but it had been enlarged by the blast of the bomb. Marine Cruden, unable to see, his hair and clothes on fire, managed to crawl through this aperture, and fell into the well deck, where in his own words: 'The Army put me out with a fire extinguisher.'*
>
> *His burns were not too deep, and his hair grew back. Marine Jim Quigley and the signallers also put the oil fire out.*
>
> Foxtrot Four *had acquired some captured Argentinian weaponry in Goose Green, so Jim Quigley tried to bring a rocket launcher to bear on the Skyhawk as it turned to re-attack but the Royal Signals Captain, the senior officer present, ordered him not to fire, but to run up a white flag.[369] The Skyhawk left them alone. A charitable interpretation is that the Army Captain was not acquainted with the Royal Navy's philosophy of continuing the fight.*
>
> *Marine 'Griff' Griffin, another crewman, died of his injuries while Marines Jim Quigley and 'Tich' Cruden plus the Army signallers were struggling to get him out of the accommodation.*

The last known photograph of *Foxtrot Four* with Marine Jim Quigley.

One of the radios in the signallers' Land Rovers was used to call for help, though unknown to the people in Foxtrot Four, *the action had also been observed and reported by the Combat Air Patrol aircraft but all available resources were then on rescue operations involving HMS* Plymouth *and the two LSLs.*

Harrier on deck in San Carlos. Note latest Flyco.

The Commodore, responsible for the movement and supply of stores along both flanks, received an initial report that *Sir Tristram*, while seriously if not mortally wounded, still held stores and ammunition destined for the Divisional attack on the hills surrounding Stanley so Jeremy Larken was tasked to send his Marine Engineer Officer, two RFA officers and five naval ratings to carry out a survey and inventory. They were also to search for crypto material and collect personal effects before any unauthorized removal was made. A bonus for *Fearless*'s inspection team in their unpleasant duty was the discovery of the wine store: a sample bottle was slightly mulled but consumed with no ill effects. A rather more militarily-significant passage in the MEO's report stated that the ship herself was salvageable but that in the meantime she could be useful as a prisoner of war ship with 300 good bunks and a massive amount of undamaged space on the vehicle deck.

Although the war was now noticeably reaching the 'end game' in the British favour no chances were being taken. Jeremy Larken's Night Order Book:

> *5/6 June at San Carlos: Remain underway at slow speed to avoid likelihood of swimmers. . . . Be careful not to proceed south as far as* Antelope *wreck.*
>
> *11/12 June at San Carlos: Ship at full buoyancy. Carry out Operation Awkward including reversal of engines in opposition ahead and astern at 30 rpm. Threat: air attack – they are working on it. High level bombing most likely. Try to point up and down the loch without straining the anchor too much. . . . Anchor buoyed in case of having to cut and run.*

On 14 May the Argentinians surrendered to Major General Jeremy Moore who swiftly moved his headquarters ashore to Government House, leaving his deputy with a skeleton staff on board. As there was still uncertainty how far the surrender extended, *Fearless* remained in San Carlos until the air threat had been demonstrably reduced. Jeremy Larken wrote in his war diary:

> *A day which started poorly became transferred into one of tidings of great joy.*

But he also wrote in his Night Order Book:

> *Seaboat to patrol between ship and shore dropping 4–5 scare charges per hour.*

There was one final task for the ship and that was the acceptance on board of Major General Menendez, the Argentinian Falkland Island Commander, and three of his henchmen as prisoners of war; the General himself being accommodated, under Royal Marine guard, in the quarters recently vacated by Jeremy Moore. He remained sulking until arrangements were made for him to be returned whence he came.

On 16 June *Fearless* at last made her way to Port William, the outer port of Stanley Harbour, where in due course, the Commodore and his staff moved ashore, allowing the ship, for the first time since the beginning of April, to 'do her own thing' and begin to unwind; although members of her crew joined teams from other ships, as well as Marines and Paratroopers to clear the revolting detritus of a defeated and ill-disciplined Army from the streets, gardens and houses of this once quiet backwater.

Another task willingly but wearily accepted by *Fearless* was that of running a harbour boat routine for the numerous ships, military and civilian, that were congregating in the inner and outer harbours – such has always been the lot of an LPD's landing craft.

During this period, and while looking for remnants of Argentinian resistance and downed pilots across the outer island, HMS *Avenger* and her Lynx helicopter searched for signs of *Foxtrot Four*: sadly there were none and her final resting place and that of her gallant crew remains a mystery.

Prize crew led by Lieutenant Ian Craik on board the ex-Argentine Navy *Yehuin*.

Fearless, with a tear-inducing gap in her dock, sailed for home on 23 June but before clearing McBride Head she was, for some now-forgotten reason, summoned back by a flash signal at 0300Z and with that little hiccup solved she was finally cleared for departure on the 25th. It was a journey of introspection and relaxation with a suitable crossing-the-line ceremony that had not seemed appropriate on the journey south. Jeremy Larken's Night Order Book instructions began to take on a more relaxed air:

> *25 June at Sea: Homeward bound! Ship in defence watches, darkened and silent.*[370] *A good lookout is essential with the ship in the silent state –* Europic Ferry *may be following and she goes quite fast. . . .*

Throughout this journey *Foxtrot Four* and her missing crew were seldom out of people's minds – and not just those of *Fearless*'s own ship's company. David Lord, whose squadron aircraft had mostly deployed from *Fearless*, wrote:[371]

> *On the way home we made a concerted effort to raise funds for the families of men killed in* Foxtrot Four, *culminating in a grand village fête as we steamed through the tropics. The Captain, Jeremy Larken, and his partner – the ship's youngest sailor dressed in appropriate female attire including lipstick, a wig, silk headscarf and a rather fetching twin set (emerging from a war zone is grand testimony to the indefatigable nature of Jack, perhaps the owner had escape and evasion in mind) –*

played host as a village squire and her ladyship. The flight deck swarmed with sailors, marines and airmen dressed in an odd assortment of clothing, some of it female, a lot of it highly original peasant garb, all cheering on their shipmates thronging the bring-and-buy stalls, playing human slot machines, betting on horses, village stocks etc. The day's joviality was underlain by an unspoken awareness that Foxtrot Four was not coming home with us and by personal remembrances of the conflict they had survived. It was a significant and cathartic event for the whole ship's company.

As a backdrop to the fayre on the flight deck sat four Sea Kings of 846 Squadron, flanked by two diminutive splashguards. These were two Agusta A109 helicopters that the CO 846 (Simon Thornewill, a test pilot[372]) and Lieutenant Pete Rainey[373] (another test pilot) had liberated in pristine condition from Port Stanley. The enemy had equipped these two aircraft as gunships but, to the best of my knowledge, their weaponry had not been used in anger.[374]

HMS *Intrepid*, among other ships across the amphibious fleet, also held fundraising events for *Foxtrot Four*. Bombardier Nick Jones returning with his unit, 79 Kirkee Commando Battery, remembers:[375]

While returning in Intrepid *we, and the ship's company, held various 'whip rounds' for the dependants of those killed in* Foxtrot Four. *One such event was the auctioning of a three course evening meal for four in the main galley. Each time a bid was made a concession was asked for. Soon it became a two horse race with four men from 2K1 mess deck (79 Bty) and a ship's company mess-deck. My comrades eventually won the bidding by each paying £100, a lot of money in those days. During the bidding they had secured the services of the Commanding Officer, who read out the menu, the Executive Officer who unwrapped and lit their cigars and the RSM and BSM who waited on them. They were shown to their table and were allowed to wear civilian clothes for the first time in three months. The ships Amphibious Detachment came over and thanked them for their generosity as did the ship's company mess-deck that they had been bidding against. The names of the men were Lance Bombardier Ken Rae, Lance Bombardier Fred Gardner, Gunner Leon (Buster) Brown and Gunner Tony (Benny) Duce.*

When *Foxtrot Four* was replaced she was named *Foxtrot Juliet* in honour of Brian Johnston and his crew and that name has been carried on into *Fearless*'s own replacement: a decision that has also become a tradition, for when HMS *Ocean* lost a landing craft crewman, Marine Christopher Maddison, during the second Gulf War, his landing craft was similarly renamed. David Lord has more memories of the journey home:

Throughout our Falklands embarkation in Fearless, *we had pleaded with the wardroom's Chief Petty Officer Cook to serve up a Chicago-style, deep-dish, pizza for 846 Squadron. The pizza request started as a joke, and then both sides of the main galley/wardroom divide adopted the plea as a sort of unifying banter. Our requests met with gruff rebuttals for weeks on end. Then, just before we entered the south west approaches 846 Squadron was presented at dinner with a drip tray – a polished aluminium affair from a Sea King engineering pack. Filling this 4 foot by 3 foot drip tray was a succulent deep-dish pizza. I cannot imagine how the Chef obtained the makings with all the trimmings but we recognized the tribute the galley staff had paid us and responded with liquid offerings from the bar – a small event, but it is such small events that distinguish happy ships from the rest.* Fearless *was a very happy ship, and we Junglies felt that she was ours, at least for a little while.*

Fearless anchored briefly at Ascension Island before continuing her journey in company with *Intrepid*, arriving in Plymouth to offload the embarked force on 13 July. His Royal Highness Prince Philip spent over an hour on board talking to as many members of the ship's company as time

The welcome home party.

allowed. The next day the two LPDs entered their home port, Portsmouth: *Fearless* had been away for ninety-nine days.

Perhaps, unusually, the last word on *Fearless*'s deployment comes from an aviator, David Lord again. He speaks from a Fleet Air Arm point of view but it would not be difficult to put his words into the mouths of other members of the various Embarked Forces that the ship carried between April and July:

> Fearless *in the Falklands was tremendously well-served by her officers and crew. Theirs was a collective competency that made up for the slow rate of fire of her 1940's-vintage Bofors and the often-outpaced Seacat missiles. The ship's Executive Officer, John Kelly, was promoted to Captain while the Task Force deployed and we addressed him as the Vice Captain. He had opened up the entire ship's resources to assist 846 Squadron in its tasking ashore.*

A much-needed Assisted Maintenance Period followed, running concurrently with a combined Easter and summer leave, boosted by two weeks for war service. By 3 September *Fearless* was ready to take part in Exercise NORTHERN WEDDING, a visit to Newcastle, and the autumn Dartmouth Training Ship cruise to the Mediterranean. Being an LPD, her life was quickly back to normal.

Gibraltar was the first port of call but this time the visit coincided with the change of Governors and so General Sir William and Lady Jackson embarked for a passage to Naples that began with a full ceremonial departure from the Rock. *Fearless* was home for Christmas, via a final run ashore at Brest.

Arrival in Portsmouth from the South Atlantic.

Spring of 1983 brought a standard West Indies Dartmouth Training Cruise – although there was nothing standard about the trip up the Mississippi River to New Orleans for the Mardi Gras in company with HMS *Zulu*, then commanded by Commander Sym Taylor who, ten years later, would be *Fearless*'s fourteenth Commanding Officer. As she steamed westward across the Atlantic, *Fearless* and her 'jack-of-all-trades reputation' had preceded her arrival, for a message was received from the British Virgin Islands Government stating that it would be most grateful for assistance.

Help was needed to dispose of a sunken, 3-ton crane, whose jib was sticking up out of Cane Gardens Bay; to re-hang the church bells; to adjust the Post Office clock and to blow up some coral restricting the entrance to Paraquita Bay. The MEO, Commander John Mcgregor, led 'the first wave' into Tortola with four divers under Lieutenant Peter Mason and Surgeon Lieutenant Colin Priestland; explosives expertise was supplied by Lieutenant Commander Philip Moore and Chief Petty Officer Dave Crees, while a tractor team under Sergeant Colin Byetheway and volunteers from the Mechanical Engineer Department formed the nucleus of this 'demolition banyan'.

Captain Jeremy Larken says farewell in Plymouth Sound.

CMECH Neil Cooper, MEA Ted Bailey and MEA Mick Harston fixed the bells and the clock and the entrance to Paraquita Bay was deepened from 4 feet to 7 feet 6 inches, allowing it to be used as a hurricane shelter for yachts ... and that is flexibility!

After a visit to Freeport in the Grand Bahamas, and what was recognized to be the second best run ashore after New Orleans, *Fearless* arrived in Plymouth on 4 March, in time for another role change and a new Commanding Officer.

Fittingly for a submariner, Jeremy Larken was taken ashore in an LCVP rigged with a mock-up of the fin and rudder of a nuclear submarine – the former painted with symbols representing aircraft 'splashed' and operations undertaken.

Chapter Thirteen

Captain R. Trussell, Royal Navy

Tenth Commanding Officer
1983–1984

Norwegian Arctic, Baltic, Mediterranean

HMS *Fearless* was Captain Roger Trussell's third command after the submarines *Onyx* and *Conqueror*. He retired in 1989 as Director, UK Defence Commitments Staff and writes:

On taking command of HMS Fearless *on 4 March 1983 I was conscious that it would be just as challenging as command of a nuclear submarine. However it was different in two respects; in the former the challenge was to exploit speed, endurance and concealment, in the latter to exploit versatility, the space onboard and visibility. In both cases the busy past and future programmes of these vessels indicated the desire of HMG and the RN to get value for the taxpayers' money. In* Fearless's *case this was achieved by allocating her two alternating roles, normally but not always conducted at separate times.*

This pattern of operating was altered for a period at the end of 1983 by a deployment to Cyprus and the Lebanese coast for Operation

Captain Roger Trussell.

OFFCUT. *The ship was to be ready to evacuate the small British Force in Beirut and any remaining Britons during November, December and January 1984. At the start of this deployment the ship's company gave her the nickname HMS* Martini *with the matching motto of* Any time, Any Place, Any Where, *followed soon after by the introduction of the Weekly Martini ship's newspaper: typically scurrilous, ingenious, at times risqué but invariably intended to be amusing.*

To return to March 1983 it was a revelation to witness the transformation of the ship in a few hours from training ship to the amphibious role with a new Captain and COMAW and staff, sundry helicopters and vehicles embarked for Northern Norway and Exercise COLD WINTER. Some humorists commented that there was logic in appointing another submariner in command of a ship that could partially submerge, though having two propellers was complicating matters a bit.

Anybody monitoring the conduct of this exercise would have been in no doubt about the importance the UK attached to such winter training. The number of warships including HMS Hermes *and Ships Taken Up From Trade, our passage northwards through the inner leads and day and night landings were surely proof of our serious intent, albeit a defensive one.*

The exercise allowed time for a few hours break off Harstad where we dined local civilian and military dignitaries. They were quick to pay tribute to our efforts to stiffen their defences and their resolve.

One comment in particular should be highlighted. At the end of Exercise COLD WINTER 1983 Major General Arne Rosnes, commanding 6 Norwegian Division stated that:

The key to the successful defence of Norway lies in this area – a unique fortress built by nature – and where it is essential to learn how to survive in the Arctic conditions. The British are 'top' and are more trained in this tough area than others. The Falklands campaign has proved to be a confirmatory school solution of the tactics used and the ability to operate in a harsh climate – on exactly the lines Northern Norway demands.

Praise indeed, for the General believed, as did his British colleagues, that Norwegian training helped immeasurably to win the Falklands War while, conversely, he also believed that the reverse was true. He was, of course, referring to sea as well as ground forces. Roger Trussell continues:

Three weeks later, back in Portsmouth after a very rough Force 9 passage with a crowded flight deck of helicopters, I felt we were once more prepared for our primary role. . . .

A one month Assisted Maintenance Period gave time to change 20 per cent of the ship's company and to prepare for the Dartmouth Training Squadron role in the Baltic.

The biggest problem was being able to give the time to trainees whether for conning the ship, coastal navigation, seaboats or seamanship.

The ports we visited – Malmo, Aarhus, Helsinki and Hamburg – would be the envy of most cruise ships. We capitalized on our visibility by arriving with Guard and Band paraded and the Upper Deck manned, followed by liaison officers meetings, calls on local dignitaries, return calls and formal luncheons. An evening cocktail party for 100 or more guests would precede a Beating Retreat ceremony. This time it was not possible to obtain our favourite Royal Marine Band of FOF3 but we were fortunate to be able to borrow The RAF Scotland Pipe Band and the Band of the Royal Hussars from Germany, both of whom helped to fly the flag well. Days in harbour were punctuated with multiple visitor activities involving most members of the ship's company as hosts. In Helsinki there were seven large events in one day when the ingenuity of the officers and men excelled as they revelled in their role as ambassadors.

The balance in this programme came from transits of the West Coast of Scotland and weapon training in the Moray Firth including Seacat firings and the disembarkation of the 4th Assault Squadron to Fort George to practise their skills. Our efforts paid off with the award of the Fleet Seacat Trophy the following year and a contented Assault Squadron. More balance with a Sunday liaison visit to Gordonstoun School, flight-deck games for students and a lunch for the school Governors.

September 1983 began with weapon and warfare training at Portland and a 24 hour demonstration of the ship's capabilities for Michael Heseltine, the Secretary of State for Defence accompanied by his PPS and escorted by Admiral Sir John Fieldhouse and Richard Mottram, a senior MOD civil servant. COMAW and Brigadier Martin Garrod[376] were co-hosting the visit with me. The future of amphibious warfare was still far from assured with no decisions yet made about replacements for Fearless *and* Intrepid *so the visit was important though relatively low key. Accordingly we attended carefully to our visitors to the extent in my case of arranging for a mix of heavy and light armour to be embarked from a beach near Bovington Army camp. In the course of our serious discussions Mottram, in his devil's advocate way, asked how we could justify the Carribean DTS deployment in January and February when we were meant to be protecting the Northern Flank. I replied that we took the precaution of deploying 45 Cdo by air to Norway for winter training prior to our arrival as part of the finale to the COLD WINTER exercises and we had a dual role to perform. I completed my presentation by saying that the ship was a really flexible tool for the government. None of us knew at the time of the forthcoming Beirut task.*

From Portland we shot north for the September amphibious exercise in the Danish islands, picking up 45 Cdo and COMAW en route. As a team we were able to demonstrate our commitment to defence in that region in a similar way to our north Norway activity using helicopters and landing craft by day and night and fraternising with the Danish defence community in Copenhagen. We returned to anchor off Rosyth to conduct the role change, taking onboard the officers under training prior to a short visit to Portland.

Our stay there was unexpectedly delayed for a few days to make good repairs to the ship's bows with a concrete plug following an early morning collision with the German merchant ship MV Gerhard. *The best that can be said about this incident was that our speed was 6 knots in thick fog at fog stations. In spite of a 4 day board of enquiry and later a 7 day court-martial we never established details of the other ships contribution to the collision. Suffice to say that the United States Navy Captain who said that a collision in the morning can ruin your whole day made a gross understatement.*

Board of Enquiry over, repairs completed and a visit to Casablanca cancelled, we made the most of the Mediterranean and its weather for training. Visits to Palermo, Cyprus, Naples and Gibraltar competed with the Baltic for giving young officers a taste of life at sea and in harbour. Cyprus in particular was ideal for training afloat and ashore for everybody and made all the better by the influence and hospitality of the Commander British Forces, Major General Sir Desmond and Lady Langley.

There was nothing run of the mill about our experiences in Palermo and Naples. Some of the cocktail party guests were escorted onboard by 'gentlemen' carrying what looked like 'violin' cases and in Naples we were encouraged by the Italians to arm Royal Marine upper-deck guards with instructions to shoot in the event of trouble from Red Guards during the cocktail party and Beating the Retreat. It was a novel way to greet guests with our own armed guards. British Naval Attaché Rome, Commander Hugh Orme, had a hard time acting as my interpreter when we called on the Sicilian equivalent of a Lord Lieutenant, in this case the ex-head of the Italian Secret Service. I commented that we had something in common with 'the rabbi who scored a hole in one on the sabbath' in that we had to stay 'mum' about our knowledge and experiences. The

Mayor of Naples confided that he had a short expectation of life due to the Mafioso. Such intimate conversations were invariably witnessed by the duty Midshipman 'doggie'[377] – another translation difficulty – who attended most official calls with me.

We left Gibraltar only to pass by nine days later having disembarked the Officers Under Training in Portsmouth and stored for patrolling off Lebanon with 846 Squadron helicopters.

By coincidence – or was it – *Fearless* relieved HMSs *Glamorgan* and *Brazen* as a ship reprieved from a death sentence on the same day that Hansard recorded a debate on the Royal Navy – 29 November 1983:

Mr Stanley (Cons) (Col 451): ... We plan therefore to maintain (these ships) in service for the foreseeable future.

MV *Gerhard*'s port side after the collision.

Mr Ashdown (Alliance) (Col 467): I hope the Minister will come clean on what the Government will do to replace (these ships). The decision will determine the future existence or non-existence of the Royal Marines. It is impossible to conceive a Royal Marine force unless it has the (ships and craft) to do the job.

Roger Trussell:

We were able to put our versatility to good use in a variety of ways. In Beirut the engineering department improved the basic services of the dilapidated building in which BRITFORLEB[378] were accommodated and we evacuated a touring civilian pianist who could have passed for an Arab but proved his credentials with a classical concert performance on the wardroom honky tonk piano. At sea the ship's company entertained the British Press Corps from Beirut on Christmas Eve and, later, a United States Navy contingent from USS Guam, part of the huge United States fleet assembled off Lebanon. Although we felt a bit out of sight from the United Kingdom and most men had not seen their families since August, it was clear that we were not forgotten. We were visited by FOF3, the Fleet Legal Adviser, a forces entertainment team, appeared on television and radio in the UK and had so-called 'stand off periods' at anchor to enable people to go ashore.

Christmas Day in a crowded, junior rates' mess deck. Captain Roger Trussell in cap.

Ratings certainly know how to extract humour from any situation and how to enjoy Christmas day at sea. In similar vein, James Oliver, the Commander, showed his versatility in leading me on mess deck rounds with him in Arab dress and me in square rig as Bosun's Mate with the youngest sailor, Steward Des Cathbert as Deputy Captain. Throughout we were accompanied by Father Christmas, alias Chief Petty Officer Steward Ron Sadler who was also the subject of a weight-guessing competition which raised £81 for the Blood Cancer Research Group at the Royal Infirmary, Worcestershire. All that piping practice at Dartmouth finally paid off.

During Fearless's *time on patrol, A Squadron, Queen's Dragoon Guards were relieved by 'A' Squadron 16/5 Lancers shortly after which the ship was host to a Combined Services Entertainment show – a concert party – which entertained nearly 500 sailors and soldiers in the tank deck. The ship also took groups of men for 'rest and recuperation' in Cyprus and accepted, in return, four Chelsea pensioners whose combined age was 297 years. Over Christmas, the ship received what her company liked to think was, at ninety feet, the longest Christmas card in the world. This had been sent by the* Fearless *Cub Scout Pack of Longleat whose return present was a photograph of their card draped around the stern of the flight deck. A Christmas Cake competition was won by Cook Taff Davies, a carol service was held on board and there was an extra ration of beer, a tot of rum and mince pies.*

We rejoiced to return to Portsmouth on 20 January 1984 and to be greeted by staff members of C-in-C Fleet and FOF3. Most of us had not been home for 5 months.

An extract from Roger Trussell's Report of Proceedings[379] explains the aim of Operation OFFCUT:

To implement any of a range of options ordered by the MOD. These options were to embark for their own safety on a temporary, daily or permanent basis, a part or all of the British contingent of approximately 134 troops in Beirut. A secondary task was to provide logistic support for the contingent and to provide recreational facilities for off-duty personnel. Operational Control for HMS Fearless *was given to Major General Sir Desmond Langley KCVO, MBE the Commander British Forces Cyprus. . . .*

One unusual task was the LCU delivery of a load of . . . rockets for Hunter aircraft of the Lebanese Air Force to the port of Jounieh (north of Beirut). . . .

On 4 December (we were warned of) the threat of a Libyan submarine in retaliation for USAF bombing Syrian Forces in the Lebanon. . . .

To go back, briefly, in time: *Fearless* had arrived in Portsmouth from her Mediterranean tour on 18 November with her ship's company, rather naturally, looking forward to Christmas leave. Instead they were given under two days to re-store for Operation OFFCUT as the support ship for British forces operating in the Lebanon.

At that time British troops formed part of a multi-national peacekeeping force which had been operational since December 1982. Royal Navy participation included a refuelling stop for RAF Chinooks flying between Lebanon and Cyprus while the LCUs ferried the heavier stores between Akrotiri in Cyprus and Jounieh, ten miles north of Beirut on the Lebanese mainland. This was not an easy, 130 mile passage: on one occasion bad weather required them to take station within feet of the starboard quarter of their escorting frigate, HMS *Achilles*.

Much of the work undertaken involved improving living conditions and security for the troops ashore based at Hadeth, to the south-east of Beirut. Although not, strictly, part of *Fearless*'s story it is interesting to note that although the British soldiers did not get involved in Lebanon's gun battles, they could fire in self defence, if necessary, under a 'yellow card' system similar to that used in Northern Ireland. As a result the British contingent was the only one not to suffer casualties and an extract from the *Daily Telegraph* of 1 December 1983 explains why:

According to Major Boissand of A Squadron Queen's Dragoon Guards, 'It says something for the discipline and attitude of our soldiers that although we have been here since February we have not had to open fire, although on many occasions we have come under fire. . . . We believe that by not firing ourselves, we will do more good than getting involved in the battles. We are not here for that. If we run into a fight between other groups, we use our communications to report it. For example we may round a corner and find a gunfight raging. One of those involved in such a battle might fire at us on sight but when you consider that the age of some of these people is 13 or 14 and that they are not under strict military discipline, it is not surprising that they get carried away a bit sometimes.'

Not for the first time – nor the last – superlative British discipline in the field was in marked contrast to that of other nations who shoot first and ask questions later: a policy that has no place in peacekeeping.

On 10 January *Fearless*'s relief, RFA *Reliant*, appeared on cue off Akrotiri: the handover was completed and the next day a course set for Gibraltar where she stopped for a few hours' Christmas-rabbit-run before arriving at Portsmouth on 20 January. Roger Trussell continues:

The five week Assisted Maintenance Period was dominated by three weeks well earned leave for most. In the case of myself and three officers we had to endure a lengthy court-martial of more than a week as a result of the minor collision back in September. It was unusual as these things go because I elected for our trial to be held simultaneously in order to save time. I chose to plead guilty based on an Admiral's

The Septic 7 entertain the junior rates in their dining hall.

advice received years earlier that in that way justice can be seen to have been done but this decision disappointed my two excellent defenders. The net result was a reprimand for me, the Officer of the Watch and the Navigator. The Operations Officer was acquitted, as was the Navigator subsequently on appeal.

One year after taking command it was at last possible to have four full days of training with the assistance of FOST's Staff at Portland before the resumption of amphibious training in Norway. This time it was a major NATO exercise with US carriers and marines and our own amphibious staffs and 45 Cdo. The amphibious message was vividly transmitted to John Stanley the Minister for the Armed Forces who gamely witnessed at first hand helicopter operations in near white-out conditions and a night penetration of the inner leads near Tromso by landing craft. He distinguished himself by finding time to buy ice cream cones for himself and some members of the ship's company. Canvassing – or is it leadership? – takes many forms.

By comparison the second amphibious exercise in September in Danish waters was a minor affair with landings off Kalunburg and Moen. These were conducted with customary vigour by the UK side which was then echoed by a dodge-the-helicopter, low flying display by the Royal Danish Air Force in Moen Bay which was reminiscent of San Carlos to Falkland veterans.

Sunday Divisions at sea.

While in Newcastle we embarked the hardware for a British Trade Exhibition we were to hold in Copenhagen and Stockholm. This had been the brainchild of James Mellon, our Ambassador in Denmark and myself when we had met informally a year earlier in Aarhus. It certainly brought an added dimension to a port visit using the available space in the near empty tank deck and helped the Embassy to show off British manufacturing. One immediate result was the placing of an estimated £5 million orders.

In Helsinki, the second trade exhibition concentrated on Jaguar cars with less immediate visible trade benefits.[380] However we did leave all the cars ashore before departing to collect the four LCUs off Fallbaden. They had just had the time of their lives on a navigation and hearts and minds transit across Sweden from Gothenburg to Norkopping via Jonkopping. Throughout they had been greeted by many surprised Swedes including a few less surprised, but well prepared, CND campaigners. This incursion by friendly unarmed Royal Marines was much more appreciated than the recent Soviet submarine intrusion to their coastal waters.

The crossing of Sweden by the four landing craft was in reply to an invitation to attend the 700th anniversary celebrations of the town of Jonkopping in the middle of southern Sweden, at the foot of Lake Vattern. Captain Rob Need, the Officer Commanding Amphibious Detachment, accompanied by Commander Chris Childs (the ship's MEO acting as the Commanding Officer's representative) led this flotilla from Copenhagen to Gothenburg before entering the Swedish canals. Roger Trussell again:

LCUs descending locks while transiting Sweden between Gothenburg and Norkopping.

The craft were faced with the daunting prospect of negotiating the restricted width of the locks and sections of the canal where, in places, there were only six inches to spare with the craft having to be manually warped round the bends.

The British Ambassador, Sir Donald Murray – an ex-marine himself[381] – joined the craft for the final approach to Jonkopping, where more than 1,000 people had gathered to give them a great welcome.

Three days and nights of official and informal celebrations followed which taxed the stamina of all who made the trip. There was also great warmth as the craft returned to the ship, with groups at every lock and village to see the spectacle. Some hitched a ride between locks, while some of the Marines jogged or cycled along the towpaths.

A last stop was made at Soderkopping, at the eastern end of the canal, before the Squadron reluctantly locked out into the Baltic to re-dock into Fearless *at Stockholm.*

Still with the OUTs onboard we took part in a Joint Maritime Course with elements of COMAW's and HQ 3Cdo Brigade's staff onboard in preparation for a tri-service VIP visit headed by Admiral Staveley, C-in-C Fleet, and his Army and RAF opposite numbers. These gentlemen spent a day on board as we manoeuvred off Cape Wrath.

On our return from Danish waters we role changed in Devonport and embarked a range of British Army fighting vehicles which were to be our national contribution to Defendory 1984 *Expo in Athens – and shown off, additionally, in Istanbul and Algiers. For these events we had a professional Defence Sales team onboard and for Algiers we were reinforced by the Deputy Director for Military Assistance Overseas, Commodore Parry.*

By tradition no effort is spared trying to squeeze as much as possible into ships' programmes. For example on this deployment we held a Remembrance Service, wreath laying and divisions off Gallipoli when transiting the Dardanelles.

Roger Trussell – as have others – raised the perennial discussion about large ships versus small ships for training purposes:

As for the DTS role, it was the subject of much debate and a number of MOD papers for several years. I have no doubt that small ships, if you can spare them, are more suitable for the training of young officers and giving them a taste of life in the type of ships that they will be joining.

In the summer of 1984 an article by Midshipman M.J. Toy appeared in the *Britannia Magazine* offering a junior officer's point of view under the headline '*Fearless* or frigates – Dartmouth Training Ship or Squadron' that voiced opinions similar to those of his recent Commanding Officer:[382]

I have experienced both the Frigate Squadron and HMS Fearless *fulfilling the role. Officers Under Training will explain from a strategic view the advantage of being spread between three or four units, although training staff are also more thinly spread. An advantage of a number of units travelling together is that evolutions can be regularly carried out between them.* Fearless *herself and her machinery and equipment are not typical of today's fleet and this does not make her ideal for first experience at sea.*

It is known that (Midshipmen Under Training) will scrub, polish and chip, and are encouraged to do so. I agree that (we) should perform such tasks, but the difference was noted between the Frigate Squadron and Fearless. *A cleaning job, or indeed any job where assistance was required would, in the frigate, be done alongside the ship's company. In* Fearless, *Officers Under Training were sent off to chip or scrub by themselves, thus being denied the opportunity to chat with, and learn from, the ship's company. Although this is a generalization, Officers Under Training in* Fearless *were definitely more used than trained on occasions.*

Another young officer, Sub Lieutenant P. T. Hickson, noted:

> *The DTS package is divided up into 8 training period weeks comprising one week each of Seamanship, Supply and Administration, Navigation, Operations and Warfare, Officer Training Department, Marine Engineering and Weapons Engineering. The majority of the training period time is spent in the Portakabin and occasionally working part of ship in that particular department.*
>
> *In addition to this there were other things to do to keep the Officers Under Training happy. Our first port of call was Barbados. . . . We docked in Bridgetown in the morning and work began in earnest for the cocktail party that same evening. I was looking forward to the party as I was to be a steward and thought this would be an opportunity to mingle with all the guests but to my horror I found that at the last minute I had been put into the pot wash. So my first night in the Caribbean was spent up to my elbows in water, washing glasses.*
>
> *I am fully aware that DTS is not designed to be a pleasure cruise, and I never expected it to be. Of all the aims the most important one to me was to experience the conditions in which the sailor has to live and work.*

The arguments have been rehearsed before, and while everyone agreed that the Dartmouth Training Squadron was preferable to a single ship others have argued that without this additional role for the LPDs, the amphibious capability would have been lost. This had been a political not a naval decision (in the sense that it was forced upon the Navy by government financial constraints) which shows Richard Mottram's devil's advocacy – mentioned above by Roger Trussell – at its most devious. Roger Trussell ends his summary:

> *The ship was ready for maintenance, and the ship's company for leave while my HODs and I prepared for the change of command.*

He then added:

> *I have not mentioned the contribution to the whole team effort made by all Heads of Department including the Chaplain and PMO. No mention either of Mr Keung and his enigmatic Chinese laundry men, the HODs London taxi and so on.*

Chapter Fourteen

Captain P.G.J. Murison, Royal Navy

Eleventh Commanding Officer
1984–1985
Later, Commodore

West Indies, Norwegian Arctic, Baltic

Captain Peter Murison had earlier commanded the Ghanaian Navy Ship *Elmina*,[383] HMS *Eskimo* and was later Captain Fishery Protection. After *Fearless* he commanded HMS *Challenger*. He retired in 1991 as Director of Naval Officer's Appointments (X):[384]

Captain Peter Murison.

My feelings on assuming command of this great ship (the tallest in the Fleet!) must be very similar to those of my predecessors and successors. I remember, at the start and through-out the seven month Commission, feeling a sense of enormous pride, anticipation and sheer good fortune. Pride, simply because **Fearless** *was a proud ship, and what Commanding Officer is not proud of his command? Anticipation, because much of what we did was totally new to me, and good fortune because I was supported by first rate Heads of Departments and officers and an extremely professional and willing ship's company.*

My time in command may be divided into three phases. Firstly, leading the Dartmouth Training Squadron in the Caribbean, secondly in an amphibious role in Norway and thirdly showing the flag in the Baltic – weren't we lucky!

I sailed from Plymouth as Captain DTS on 8 January 1985, with the Officers Under Training embarked, in company with HMSs Glamorgan, Arrow *and RFA* Green Rover. *We anchored off Ponta Delgada in the Azores on the 13th for stores and mail, but also to transfer the Wessex helicopter from the tank deck to the flight deck – no easy achievement in a heavy swell.*

Arrow *and* Green Rover *having been detached on 19 January, we arrived at Barbados on 23rd where FOF2 (now Admiral of the Fleet Sir Ben Bathurst) flew his Flag in* Fearless *and where he inspected Divisions of the OUTs who were most impressive. On, then to Tortola in the British Virgin Islands to land working parties to provide assistance to the local community ably led by the MEO (Cdr Chris Childs) and the Amphibious Operations Officer (Major Andrew Eames, RM). I flew ashore to witness another aspect of the versatility for which* Fearless *was famed. It never ceases to amaze me the number of varying tasks at which the sailor can excel. All involved could take great satisfaction from a job well done.*

The highlight of our visit to Martinique was a Beat Retreat by the Royal Marine Band on the Flight Deck following a cocktail party for what seemed like the whole of the local French population. The Band, as usual, were quite superb and moved many of the French guests to emotional tears. What a proud moment for me.

On passage to Mayport, Florida we embarked FOF3 (Vice Admiral Sir Dicky Fitch – sadly no longer with us) from Grand Turk. A seven day maintenance period in Mayport was followed by passage to Ponta Delgada for fuel and thence to Plymouth for a role change on 7 March. So ended the first phase of this commission and I hope the OUTs will have learnt from it and enjoyed it. They certainly worked hard and played hard as I and my chums had in Triumph under Varyl Cargill Begg (who we regarded as one above God)! Sadly I don't suppose many of them will have the same opportunity to serve in some of the more exotic parts of the world as we did.

During March we took part in COLD WINTER 85, and PURPLE WAVE. COLD WINTER with 3 Commando Brigade, Royal Marines, embarked was a real eye-opener to me involving rehearsals and drills in Trondheimsleia, opposed transits to Vestfjorden and support of the land forces in the Amphibious Operations Area at the head of Lyngenfjord. It was here that we were visited by members of the House of Commons Defence Committee (Edward Leigh, Ken McGinnis, Robin James and David Woodhead), all of whom were suitably impressed.

FOF2 inspects Sunday Divisions in Barbados.

Three memories stick in my mind. The first was, when weighing anchor in the vicinity of Trondheim in a howling gale and blizzard, the capstan seized with the anchor about three fathoms below the waterline. We virtually sailed down the Fjord while the Commander (James Oliver) and his team attempted to free it. Much to my relief, after about an hour, they were able to complete weighing. An anxious moment!

The second was when I went aft to see how things were going, and to my amazement I found no less than ten helicopters on the Flight Deck with two Sea Kings returning due to nil visibility! One landed on the side of the fjord and the other landed on and when the weather improved, returned to Invincible. *A tight squeeze!*

Finally, witnessing the whole ship evolution of landing the personnel, vehicles, stores and all the paraphernalia associated with an amphibious landing, by helicopter, LCUs and LCVPs, was a memorable experience. All with the most stunning scenery at the head of Lyngenfiord. On a lighter note, I recall taking a turn round the Flight Deck at first light and watching a very aged Norwegian fisherman in a small boat landing a good sized cod. He indicated that he would like to give it to me, and in return I gave him a few packets of cigarettes. COMAW (John Garnier[385]), the Brigadier, 3 Commando Brigade (Henry Beverley[386]) and I had the fish for lunch and it was quite the best I have ever eaten.

We returned to Portsmouth on 29 March via Exercise PURPLE WAVE for a maintenance period and seasonal leave and where the ship's company received a well deserved accolade from COMAW:

'It has been a great pleasure to fly my broad pennant in Fearless *during exercises COLD WINTER and PURPLE WAVE. All departments have demonstrated high standards of professionalism which, combined with the ready cooperation and good humour of all your people, made a valuable contribution to the success of these two busy and complex exercises.'*

A visit to Rosyth to provide the venue for Admiral Sir Nicholas Hunt's farewell official reception as FOSNI. Nick Hunt always did things with tremendous style, and this was no exception. However, our arrival and departure time provided the Navigating Officer with the standard Dryad exam question; namely, when could we pass under the Forth Bridge with a sufficient safety margin above and below. The answer, 0530!

The 6 May saw us in Oslo for the 40th Anniversary of Liberation Day with FOF3 embarked. Two 21-gun salutes were given on arrival, one national and one to HM King Olav V, before we secured alongside Akershus Fortress. There was a full programme of moving ceremonies and services to mark the occasion including an audience with HM the King and visits to the ship by many dignitaries: the Norwegian Prime Minister (Kare Isaachsen Willoch) HM Ambassador to Norway (Sir William Bentley), and members of the War Veterans Association. One highlight of the visit was the handing over of three condemned cells to the Akershus Resistance Museum; I was standing next to one Veteran who was due to be shot on the morning of liberation. This ceremony was followed by a Government reception at Akershus in the presence of Crown Prince Harald. Altogether a very memorable and educational visit and once again Fearless *came up trumps.*

There followed a transit of the Great Belt and the Baltic for a visit to Helsinki where we received extremely generous hospitality from the Finns and HM Ambassador (Mr Brooke Turner). The Band of the King's Own Scottish Borderers (embarked in Fearless*) performed at a number of functions including Beat Retreat as they had in Oslo. Another very successful visit. During the transits to and from Helsinki we received a fair amount of attention from intelligence gatherers, though what they hoped to learn I was at a loss to know. However they did provide interest and amusement for the ship's company.*

Our final visit was to Newcastle, at the request of the ship's company, as their most popular place for the paying off dance. This was enormously successful and we were all rather reluctant to take our

Band of the King's Own Scottish Borderers.

departure. The passage up the river was interesting in that half way up we had to turn and make a sternboard for about two miles. I think we were the last big ship to get that far up the river due to lack of use and subsequent silting.

Back to Portsmouth and a final day at sea on 29 May for a Families Day and Staff College Sea Day. Unusually, we were able to meet up with Intrepid *commanded by one of my oldest friends, Anthony Provest, for a heaving line transfer. This gave me particular pleasure because, since I outranked him by six months, I was able to take charge of him for the one and only time! Also in the programme was a light jackstay transfer with* Pheobe *commanded by Jonathan Band my ex PWO(A) in* Eskimo *and now Admiral Sir Jonathan Band (First Sea Lord). There was a lack of volunteers to be transferred by jackstay, so I volunteered my wife much to the consternation of our young children!*

The incident that I will never forget occurred while entering harbour for the last time. We had passed the Outer Spit Buoy and were therefore committed to the Channel. No outbound traffic had been reported, so imagine my concern when I saw the cross-channel ferry passing the Round Tower, outbound. He did keep outside the channel to the west, but his speed was such that he suffered shallow water effect and took a violent sheer to port across my bows; not the sort of thing I wanted with FOF3 embarked and over a thousand people on board. There was only one thing for it, 'Starboard 30. Full astern'. The engine room responded as I knew they would and a collision was averted, but it did cost me a bottle of champagne to those who were so quick to react.

I have tried some twenty years on to portray Fearless *in all her roles. In her long and illustrious career, she has served the Royal Navy and the country well. If I have omitted any detail or the mention of the many characters who made up a first class ship's company, I apologize, but I am sure they would all wish to join me in wishing her successor, HMS* Albion, *happy sailing.*

Peter Murison assumed command on 11 December 1984 and was soon involved in a typical piece of *Fearless* flexibility when, as he mentions briefly, the ship was required to lend a hand to the

CO's wife in jackstay transfer.

Hearts and minds in Tortola. Clearing Cane Garden Bay Beach.

people of Tortola in the British Virgin Islands while she moved on to Martinique. This was quite an undertaking with 132 members of the ship's company and trainees landed for four days to undertake a number of tasks in support of the Civil Community.

Duties included the disposal of a sunken motor vessel, a bulldozer, derelict cars and the redecoration of a school for handicapped children. First a large area of scrubland and jungle at Cane Garden Bay, the main camp site, had to be cleared but this was easier ordered than executed, for the working party encountered giant spiders, hornets' nests and a wide variety of near impenetrable flora and fauna. Nevertheless, CPOMEA (H) Sloane and CMEA (P) Blakely led the assault on a large derelict bulldozer with their acetylene cutting equipment, helped by the Amphibious Beach Unit and its heavy lifting gear while the removal of the sunken motor vessel *Maudelle* took rather more ingenuity. Involving 1,500 man-hours it was the longest single task but, conversely, offered the most valuable experience for the ship's divers who do not often practise their underwater demolitions and explosives expertise. The modernization of Fort Charlotte Children's Centre at Roadtown was also a lengthy if less complicated task, mainly undertaken by the ship's embarked apprentices who, to mark the re-opening, organized and financed a small welcome-back party for the children.

The ship was rewarded with the use of a private beach for a banyan on Peter Island near Tortola after she had returned from Martinique to collect the shore party. To say thank you for the thank you, as it were, *Fearless* entertained numerous locals on board over two days before sailing for Grand Turk, Florida, the Azores – in company with HMS *Glamorgan* – and Portsmouth.

It had not all been hard work for two of *Fearless*'s company – LRO(T) Mark Rutley and JS(M) Tony Harmer – had joined Robin Knox-Johnston[387] in his sixty foot catamaran, *British Airways*, for a 322 mile cruise to Tortola where three more members – LS David Preece, Marine Chris Chisholm and MEA App Kevin Bowler – signed-on for a further 943 miles to Freeport in the Bahamas.

With March 1985 came the ritual role change and Exercise PURPLE WAVE in north Norway. Easter leave swallowed up most of April before an amusing four days in Oslo celebrating the 40th anniversary of Liberation Day with Flag Officer Third Flotilla embarked. For her stay in Norway's capital she had embarked 220 trainees, plus a detachment from 845 Naval Air Squadron and the band of the King's Own Scottish Borderers. The Officers Under Training formed a guard of honour at the British cemetery during a wreath laying ceremony and the King of Norway was saluted as he passed *Fearless* on his way to a commemorative Service of the Martyrs of the Occupation.

Back in Portsmouth and determined to end the commission on a high note, on 29 May *Fearless* embarked more than 1,350 families and guests, including staff officers on a Sea Day visit plus the Flag Officer Third Flotilla, Vice Admiral Fitch, his wife and son. The *Fearless* Cubs of the 15th Long Eaton Sea Scout Group were also on board and able to witness their new liaison ship, *Intrepid*, in a

Full up on top.

Full Astern Starboard!

series of close quarter manoeuvres. The younger sister had recently completed her amphibious work-up and was ready to take over the operational and training roles. In fact this had been an opportunity for the Royal Navy to show off in front of Members of Parliament and foreign dignitaries as well, of course, as its own families. Other ships taking part in this display were HMS *Invincible* – flying the flag of Flag Officer First Flotilla – and HMSs *Glamorgan*, *Phoebe* and *Nottingham*.

At the end of the day *Fearless* broke away to enter Portsmouth while streaming her paying-off pennant. The next day, 30 May, in the words of the official diary, she 'commenced rundown to full de-humidification'. The Commission's end had nearly been more final than planned for, as Peter Murison mentions, the near collision with a ferry could have brought *Fearless*'s life to a premature close: the photograph paints a more vivid picture than can any words.

It was now *Intrepid*'s turn to take up the duties as the United Kingdom's only LPD and Dartmouth Training Ship.

By mid July the remaining ship's company of just fifty had moved ashore to HMS *Nelson* and Captain Murison had – on the 19th – handed over to the ship's Senior Officer, Lieutenant Commander Barber.

Chapter Fifteen

Refit
1985–1990
Portsmouth, Devonport

Fearless's major refit began, effectively, on 30 May 1985 although her non-operational date and reversion to thirty days' notice did not begin until 17 June.

Three years later, in July 1988, she was towed to Devonport where the bulk of the work was undertaken at a cost of just over £50 million. Apart from the normal overhaul of all machinery and hull fittings – including considerable modernization of the main galley – she would be fitted with two Vulcan Phalanx close-in, air defence systems each capable of firing 3,000 rounds per minute and two BMarc guns each capable of firing 600 rounds per minute. She would retain her Seacat missile systems and her bridge-wing Bofors while, below, the operations rooms would be updated with a Plessey command system, the military communications improved and a computerized message handling system installed. Further aft, the flight deck was to be strengthened to operate Sea King helicopters – some years after it had first done so.

In November 1989 *Fearless* left dry dock and the next month her new ship's company was able to move on board.

The only 'domestic' event of note that took place during *Fearless*'s absence from fleet duties was the abolition of the wardroom wine chit, an event lamented in verse by Major Ted Troubridge,[388] Royal Marines – a member of a famous naval family:

> *Thoughts on reading DCI RN 65/86 Wine Chits – Form S1828 (U).*
> *Paragraph 1: As the result of a cost-cutting exercise CS(REP S) is currently unable to continue to print form S1828 (Wine Chit).*

> *Oh Navy Board, what have you done,*
> *To thus deliberate*
> *On the imminent extinction of*
> *Form S1828.*

> *Its simple unpretentiousness,*
> *Its faintly buffish hue,*
> *It served its purpose well, and could*
> *Continue so to do.*

> *But you, Sirs, in your wisdom,*
> *You have put the scalpel in.*
> *No more of 2/3rds whisky,*
> *Farewell to 1/3rd gin.*

> *And those of us, the thirsty,*
> *Who may come from near or far,*
> *For but an hour of quiet*
> *Conversation at the bar,*

Will wonder what has happened
As we cast our eyes around,
To find that S1828
Is nowhere to be found!

And are you overlooking that,
Whenever did arise
A need for other uses for
Its handy shape and size?

Like scribbling down the number
Of that very pretty Wren,
And nurturing the hope of
One day seeing her again.

Or even calculating
(In an argument with the 'D')
The course and speed and fuel required
To get from A to B.

Or (dare I say) a wager,
Or perhaps an IOU,
Or a game of noughts and crosses,
(When there's nothing else to do).

But no, Sirs, you've decided.
You have struck your mortal blow.
You had to save a frigate, so
The Chit Book had to go.

The most significant international event during *Fearless*'s refit was the ending of the Cold War, but if her ship's company thought they were in for an easier time they would be proved wrong – often.

Meanwhile by 1986 at Foxhill Bath and in the offices – among many others – of DORSEA,[389] CGRM and the Procurement Executive a team had assembled as part of Director General Surface Ships (Amphibious Group) to assess the responses from industry to a Government invitation to tender for a new LPD (or for the 'SLEPing'[390] of the current two) a new LPH and new LSLs plus all their smaller, supporting craft. It was the beginning of a long and tortuous gestation towards the birth of HMSs *Ocean*, *Albion* and *Bulwark* and the RFAs[391] *Largs Bay*, *Lyme Bay*, *Mounts Bay* and *Cardigan Bay*.[392]

Chapter Sixteen

Captain S.R. Meyer, Royal Navy

Twelfth Commanding Officer
1990–1991
Later, Rear Admiral

Norwegian Arctic, West Indies, Mediterranean, Black Sea

Captain Stephen Meyer had previously commanded the Sultan of Oman's SNV *Al Mansur*[393] followed by HMSs *Bildeston, Galatea* and *Liverpool*. After *Fearless* he commanded *Illustrious* and was to retire from the Royal Navy in 2002 as Chief of Staff to the Permanent Joint Headquarters. Stephen Meyer writes:

Ordered to Devonport post-haste to take command of HMS Fearless *in February 1990:*

'*No time for Commanding Officer designate courses, old boy,* Fearless *is due back at sea within a fortnight of you joining.*'

I found the Old Lady still deeply ensconced in dry-dock, with little signs of her refit ever ending. Thus began a hugely frustrating struggle to get her back to sea.

I was blessed in taking over a fantastic ship's company, whose exceptional morale seemed oblivious to the steady stream of setbacks in those months. But then there were the triumphs, small steps along the road to sea: floating in the basin; moving on board (no more accommodation charges); moving out of the basin to the sea wall (no more shore-side heads!); raising steam; basin trials and then, at last, to sea.

Captain Stephen Meyer and Marine Steve Westwood; Commando Medallist and later Colour Sergeant on COMATG's staff.

The day we were due, finally, to sail for sea trials dawned clear and bright. However a snag in flashing up meant that one boiler was not available. Commander (E), the indefatigable Mike Bleby, thought that it could be sorted that day, but not in time for the tidal window. Conventional wisdom was clear that it would be utterly foolhardy to sail for sea trials on just one boiler, after so many years alongside. We sailed.

That day, the ship came to life again. As we cleared the breakwater at Guzz, everyone onboard could feel the change; there was a sense of euphoria in the air as the ghosts of the dockyard were laid to rest. The second boiler was fixed in record time and other faults evaporated – Fearless *was back in business.*

The next few weeks can be recalled in a series of cameos: steering gear trials at high speed off the breakwater, when the rudder jammed hard to port, resulting in two 360 degree turns before we could stop; the exhilaration of winding up to our first full power run; taking her alongside in Devonport for the first time without tugs; firing our new weapon systems; and, finally, docking down to embark our main armament, the LCUs.

After a cold, wet and miserable work-up in December and January, we were at last declared operational and sailed for a foreshortened winter deployment. The few weeks we spent in the north honed our amphibious skills and re-established Fearless in her rightful role. By the time we sailed south for Easter, we felt at home in the LPDs' traditional stomping ground of Norway.

Our summer deployment was to the Caribbean. As a result of Sea King IVs being required for Op Haven in Northern Iraq, we were going to deploy without any helicopters. However, after much begging, borrowing and blackmail, we eventually rounded up one Sea King II and a number of Army Air Corps Lynx and Gazelles,[394] the Army crews having had little experience of flying outside Germany, let alone from a deck in the Caribbean! Nevertheless, with a Company of 42 Commando, under the command of Major John Rose,[395] embarked, we set off across the Atlantic.

A pleasant crossing, including a mid-Atlantic hands-to-bathe from the dock, was interrupted by a dramatic rescue. After a radio call for assistance, the PMO, Surgeon Commander John Turner, was transferred by gemini to a small yacht where a 12-year old French boy, Briag Courteaux, was found to be suffering with advanced stomach cancer. Recovering the boy and his mother to Fearless, and leaving his father to sail on alone, we turned at best speed towards Bermuda. After 3 days, with our medical team working desperately to stabilize Briag's condition, we eventually launched the Sea King at

Main vehicle deck loaded for operations. Looking aft.

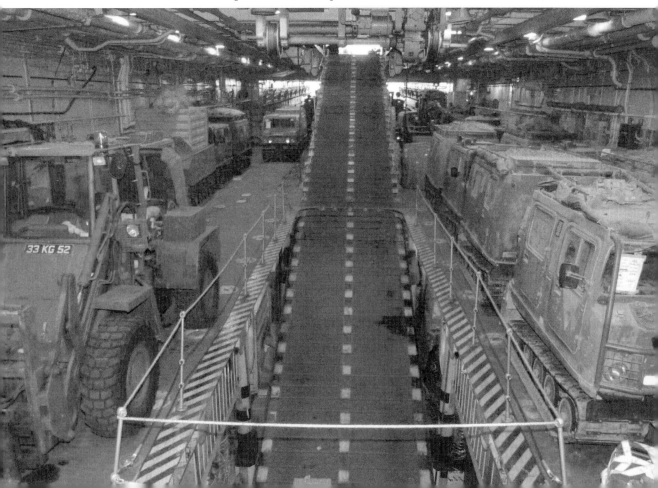

absolute maximum range to land Briag on the island. He was immediately flown on to the USA for surgery. The wonderful corollary to the incident was that, a year later, John Turner and I joined Briag and his parents in Paris for a dinner to celebrate his 'all-clear' from the cancer.

The deployment was all that a Caribbean deployment should be. After a longer than expected crossing, we decided to get everyone ashore as early as possible to let their hair down. The Governor of the British Virgin Islands allowed us take over a quiet beach for a day, for 'amphibious training'. At dawn all landing craft and helicopters hit the beach simultaneously. Fully camouflaged, the Company from 42 Commando raced ashore, followed immediately out of the landing craft by the ship's chefs in banyan shirts, carrying the barbecues! With half the ship's company ashore for the morning and half for the afternoon, we soon got into the West Indies mindset.

Exercises in and visits to half a dozen other islands over the next few weeks made for a perfect balance of work and play. Again, fragments from the recesses of one's mind: with the Dutch in Aruba and Curacao; an incursion into Venezuelan air space, when the Sea King crew mistook South America for a small island; entering and leaving Montego Bay with no tugs available (quote from the pilot who had promised us tugs: 'There's no tugs in Montego Bay – we was only kiddin' you, man'); towing a hulk off a beach in Dominica at the request of the local Prime Minister, and blowing the bottom out of it to sink it as a reef for divers then finally heading home, leaving a small party of Royals ashore in Grenada to shore up the beleaguered Prime Minister.

Summer leave saw an earth shattering change to Fearless *– the arrival of female crew members. Having been planned to become 'mixed' the previous year,[396] the introduction was delayed by a hitch in numbers going through training. The sole exception to this was Lieutenant Kate Pope,[397] who bravely was, for much of the year, the only woman among the 700 or so men onboard. Now a further 60 WRNS joined the ship's company. Despite much wailing and gnashing of teeth in some quarters, the whole process went extremely smoothly and, if anything, improved the efficiency and morale of the ship.*

That summer we assumed the role of the Captain of the Dartmouth Training Squadron. With DTS staff and a multi-national group of trainees embarked, and a different flight from the Army Air Corps as our aviation component, we sailed for an autumn deployment to the Mediterranean and the Black Sea. Visits to Gibraltar and Naples were followed by the most memorable visit many of us have ever made, Sevastopol.

Reading between the lines of Stephen Meyer's Report of Proceedings[398] and interpolating various notes from the Crimea visit:

Through anti-sub netting. First ever visit since 1947. Decidedly eerie – poor weather, uncertain welcome – after the escorting Grisha Class patrol craft declined to lead Fearless *through the gap. Pilot joined inside the harbour.*

Back to Stephen Meyer's general résumé:

Arriving just weeks after Gorbachev had been held prisoner in a dacha outside the city, and Yeltsin had stormed the Russian parliament, the atmosphere was electric. History was all around us, with unforgettable visits to Yalta, to the scene of the Charge of the Light Brigade, to Cathcart's Hill and to Balaclava. Openness was the order of the day, with eager Brits being allowed to photograph the new Beluga submarine, and climb over modern military aircraft, and the Russians being shown around the Ops Room and MCO of Fearless. *The hospitality of the local populace was overwhelming, as was the vodka! All too soon the visit was over, but the band played on; the Dartmouth band, which had joined us in Sevastopol, held a memorable concert on the Vehicle Deck, while the ship was on passage across the Black Sea to Constanta, in the recently liberated Romania.*

From Constanta, Fearless *was dispatched at best speed to the Adriatic, where Dubrovnik was under attack by the besieging Serb forces. En route we brushed up on weapon drills and various other*

Entering Sevastopol 1991 with Grisha class patrol craft as escort.

operational skills, whilst our Russian speakers urgently scoured the library for books on Serbo-Croat! Sitting in defence watches just outside territorial waters, it was terribly frustrating to watch the night sky lit up by shells pouring into the city, where we knew many refugees to be trapped. However no intervention was to be authorized, and so we proceeded on to Venice, Palermo, Cadiz and home.

Within days of returning to Pompey, the Dartmouth Training Squadron was disbanded, and I handed over my wonderful Command.

This was a varied and exciting two years in the life of Fearless. *Dragging her back to sea after so long alongside, and seeing the Old Lady come back to life, was hugely satisfying. Then to have three very different, but equally rewarding, deployments in the course of a single year is something that few could hope to experience. We were very fortunate. But most of all, we were fortunate with whom we served in this commission.* Fearless *always had the reputation of being a happy ship; I would like to think that was never more true than in 1990–1991.*

What Stephen Meyer did not know when he took command was that *Fearless* was not a fortnight away from sea but over half a year! On his arrival, the ship had spent two years in Devonport Dockyard and, by the time she finally sailed, it was nearly five years on from her decommissioning. The refit package at Devonport dockyard had been the longest since the completion there of the carrier HMS *Invincible* and, in common with previous experiences, it, too, proved challenging: that *Fearless* sailed at all says more for the patient hard work of her Ship's Company rather than that of others. Many of the crew, as was another custom, had come straight from *Intrepid*, via a short tour ashore, bringing with them the necessary experience in all departments. As it was, Stephen Meyer had to wait almost exactly seven months after assuming command before he could issue the order to 'Ring on main engines' in early September 1990.

The re-commissioning was conducted in Portsmouth on 9 November 1990 and, as the Commanding Officer has explained,[399] paradoxically it was Plymouth's Flag Officer that 'did the honours'.

To help us get out of dockyard hands, we had made Alan[400] and Gillian Grose (he had been Flag Officer, Third Flotilla and was then Flag Officer, Plymouth) semi-official sponsors of the ship, as our official sponsor, Lady Hull, was by this time too frail. It worked. With FO Plymouth now asking for daily progress reports on our refit, things had speeded up dramatically!

In keeping with tradition, Mrs Erica Meyer and Ordinary Seaman JS Martin – at seventeen years old the youngest member of the ship's company – together cut the commissioning cake. On 12 November the ship sailed for a six-day shakedown period, one day of which was spent with families on board. On this day, in what might now have been considered a tradition, the two LPDs carried out a brief period of manoeuvres. Their next and last meeting at sea was to be in January 1991 following which *Intrepid* would be paid off for good, although her services were to be required for the next decade as a source of spares for her elder sister.

The usual checks and inspections followed with the added spur that *Fearless* was placed on seven days' notice for Operation GRANBY in the Gulf following Iraq's invasion of Kuwait but, sadly for the ship's company after so long in refit and preparation, the ship would not be required. Instead with Commodore Peter Grindal embarked as COMAW, she returned to her usual stamping ground of north Norway which included a first passage under the Tjelsund Bridge – with just inches to spare – thanks to another refit alteration when her mast had been reduced by twelve feet. Otherwise it was business as normal in the Arctic.

Captain Stephen Meyer entertains his SNCOs of 4 ASRM. Standing L. to R. Sergeant Stan Stancliffe, unknown, Sergeant Mick Sellen, Captain Simon Guyer, C/Sergeant Stokes Worral, unknown sergeant, Sergeant Steve Burke, Sergeant Stan Fitzpatrick. Seated L. to R. unknown, unknown, Major Mike Woolley, Captain Meyer, WO2 Dave Oates, C/Sergeant Stu Thompson.

Fearless beneath the Tjelsund Bridge (near Harstad) – but only after her mast had been shortened by twelve feet.

Back into a familiar routine, visits to Portsmouth for a sons-at-sea day and, after a brief stop at Harwich, and following a newly established affiliation, she anchored off Scarborough.

For some, the highlight of the Scarborough visit was the arrival on board of Miss Tamara Harwood, who was unanimously voted Miss *Fearless*. Her Coronation, thanks to members of the Royal Navy Amateur Radio Society attracted worldwide attention.

On 15 May *Fearless* sailed for the Caribbean. During the Atlantic passage she was diverted, as Stephen Meyer recounts above, for a life-saving rendezvous with a French yacht. Immediately on arrival in the British Virgin Islands the ship launched a dawn assault onto Beef Island and in record time established an operations base ashore. Once again in familiar waters but without the Dartmouth Training Ship role *Fearless* took part in a number of military exercises, although perhaps the most interesting was the salvaging, and then sinking, of a 150 ton coaster, the *Ile de Serk*, which had taken part in the 1940 evacuation from Dunkirk. The beginning of the end for this brave little ship occurred in 1988 when she had been driven ashore during a gale, close to the town of Rousseau in Dominica. With *Fearless* in the area the authorities had called for help in finding the coaster 'a more fitting home'. This call was heeded on 22 June when the hulk was stabilized and made watertight before being dug out from her penultimate resting place. Members of the Public Works Department and prisoners from the local jail, all under the guidance of Lieutenant Commander Graham Binningsley, carried out this unpleasant task.

The dig took four days then, using a 600 foot towing hawser *Fearless* began to tug but, at the same time, had to keep close to the shore despite shallow water, an awkward current and the wind adding to the difficulties: the LCUs helped in the positioning process. Eventually the *Ile de Serk* heeled to starboard then, having 'left one or two bits behind', began inching seawards.

Towing off the *Ile de Serk* on the shore to the right. LCUs keeping *Fearless* in the deep-water channel.

The large crowd roared out their appreciation, echoed by *Fearless*'s ship's company lining the upper deck. The LCUs then took over the tow for the four mile passage into deeper water while a demolition team led by the DWEO, Lieutenant Commander Neville Radbourne, placed charges around the coaster's hull. To make sure she sank, Royal Marines from *Fearless*'s 4th Assault Squadron fired four Carl Gustav anti-tank missiles, and the *Ile de Serk* went down, bows first, within a minute.

Fearless's operational duties did not end there, for between 23 and 26 June she took part in Operation SUMMER BREEZE, a drug interdiction operation off Puerto Rico. The Virgin Islands and St Johns, Antigua, were visited before the return across the Atlantic, during which she called at the Azores for a final rabbit run and on 11 July secured to Charlie Buoy in Plymouth Sound.

Stephen Meyer mentioned his ship's next visit – to Crimea. This was the first visit by a British warship for well over forty years with considerable diplomatic and military effort put into making it the undoubted success that it was: a success not only at international level but, in the words of Leading Seaman Steve Dermott, at a level which counted nearly as much:

> *It's an amazing place. There were 14 of us. We had a two course meal, bottles of wine, vodka and champagne. The bill for the lot came to £4. It's a great run ashore despite the only items in a local toy shop being plastic buckets.*

For this vital occasion *Fearless* had embarked the British Ambassador, Sir Roderick Braithwaite, and had flown the flag of Rear Admiral Bruce Richardson, Flag Officer First Flotilla. After leaving Sevastopol the Admiral commented:

The Soviets opened up their warships, their aircraft, their homes and their hearts to us. Mutual understanding is the objective on both sides. From the very minute that we arrived we experienced the warmth of the welcome of the people.

Surprise, however, was a two-way commodity for some Russians were convinced that the one lady ship's officer, the lady officer cadets under training[401] and the Wrens, were on board merely as concubines, while the Chaplain was clearly the ships 'political officer'. The *Sebastopol Press* also had its views on the visit as one of its correspondents, A. Bushuyev, commented:

The wet gloomy weather which has followed the long sunny summer spell has not, it seems, dampened the spirits of the British sailors who are here on an official visit in the Royal Naval landing ship HMS Fearless.... *It is 45 years since a British sailor has set foot on Sebastopol soil. On the Chaplain's cabin door, journalists read the following inscription:* The most beautiful thing a person can do is to forgive. *These words sum up precisely the aim of the visit: peace, friendship and kindness.*

Fearless returned home via a number of Mediterranean visits including – briefly – being stood-by to evacuate British Nationals from the Dubrovnik area of Croatia. An Assisted Maintenance Period began on 8 December 1991 and Captain Stephen Meyer left on the 18th.

It would be difficult not to end this period of her life without highlighting the dichotomy within the government. On one hand it was becoming increasingly clear that *Intrepid* was unlikely to sail again and yet a Government Minister was quoted as saying at this time: 'The amphibious capability is of increasing utility in peace, crisis and conflict.'

Meanwhile at Foxhill, Bath, in the Director General Surface Ships', Amphibious Group office, the interminable business of procuring replacement LPDs ground slowly on.[402] It would be another twelve years before a new LPD would be operational.

Chapter Seventeen

Captain S. Moore, Royal Navy

Thirteenth Commanding Officer
1991–1993
Later, Rear Admiral, CB

Norwegian Arctic, Mediterranean, Home Waters

Captain Simon Moore had previously commanded HMSs *Walkerton*, *Rhyl* and *Berwick* and was to retire in 2000 as Assistant Chief of Defence Staff (Operations). Simon Moore summed up his time in command thus:

Captain Simon Moore.

There is something special about maturity, especially for the female sex: a lady's elegance will still turn more heads than a 21 year old displaying her midriff and Ella Fitzgerald still sings better than Kylie or Britney. And so it is with ships. In December 1991, when I took command, Fearless was already mature; she had had a splendid history and I was delighted that we were going to have an ongoing relationship.

The early 1990s were a funny time – suddenly there was no Soviet threat but the world still didn't look any safer. The Navy was just as busy as ever while the politicians and the strategists tried to figure out why we were needed. And so I was told in no uncertain terms that my job was to keep a lady of some maturity running while the amphibious case was agreed and the politicians, the Treasury and the military realized that we really did represent an essential, force-multiplying capability.

So my 20 months in command were perhaps a less exciting period than some in the history of Fearless. We didn't fight any wars; we didn't embrace any startling changes; we didn't hit the headlines. But we did everything we had to do; we made some big improvements to the state of the ship; we became increasingly efficient at our operational job; and we enjoyed the huge satisfaction of keeping an old ship going. And, as the most gratifying result of all of this, we were members of a happy ship's company. Perhaps that sounds rather smug but it is the proper introduction to the very strongest element in the ship's success, which (as always) was her people.

Everything that Fearless did was as a result of human effort. To take just a few examples: the sheer ability to move through the water depended on unremitting effort from the ME department; the efficiency of amphibious operations needed the skill and tenacity of the Assault Squadron. Air operations only happened because we had a Flight Deck crew who would work on in the open whatever the weather.

Other ships pressed buttons or were run by computer programmes but we did it all ourselves. And even the various modern equipment that we had, like the message processing and the Operations Room systems, seemed to need even more hands-on maintenance than their manual predecessors.

And we had the ship's company to provide all those needs – and they seemed to enjoy themselves as well. The problem now is that there were so many characters that it would be impossible to mention them all. But I cannot forget the Leading Cook who looked like an extra from Easy Rider; *the Wren who would stand in the eyes of the ship to check that the mast would pass under the bridges in the Norwegian fjords; or the WO (MAA) who had seen it all before and knew exactly how it should be handled. And then there were the happenings that the Captain knew nothing about like the 'sporting' activities of the RM Drivers' Mess; or how the LCU crews impressed the cruise ship passengers in Rhodes; or the runs ashore of the junior officers – including the Lieutenant who in his day job was my super-efficient secretary.*

So what did we do? Well, we deployed to a JMC and then to Norway for a Teamwork exercise in the late winter of 1992. The ship seemed to know her way round the inner leads and fjords better than the Navigating Officer. As I had previously been the SOO to the Commodore Amphibious Warfare, I knew the ground pretty well too but the frequently appalling weather, the demands of flying and boat operations in the Arctic, and the strain of a continual visitor programme meant that life was never quiet. Then after Easter, we deployed to the Mediterranean for a warm weather repeat of the winter deployment. We worked with the French out of Toulon for some time and got on well with them both afloat and ashore – although I never heard exactly what the Stokers did in St Tropez, I have a pretty good idea.

But the ship needed a big DED to keep her going and that then occupied the autumn and early winter of 1992/93. Of all the maintenance completed and improvements made, perhaps the most significant

Arctic exercises. LCU in Lavangan Fjord.

Children's party cooks.

was the fitting of a sewage disposal system – an enormous undertaking in an old hull. Eventually it was done and we sailed again for trials and to Portland to work up. The 1993 summer started with exercises and demonstrations around the UK before another short deployment to the Mediterranean, which included an eye opening visit to Haifa. Then home again and suddenly for me it was all over and in July I handed over command to Captain Sym Taylor.

There is nothing in Naval life so spare as a former Commanding Officer. Luckily for me, I went on to other exciting appointments but each time I sailed from Portsmouth in a Brittany Ferry I would look across at L10 in her usual berth on the end of Fountain Lake Jetty and remember happily the fun and thrill of commanding a mature lady.

It is difficult to add anything to Simon Moore's narrative for, as he said, nothing out of the ordinary occurred. Indeed this unusual state of affairs is reflected in the lack of paper cuttings for this period while even her official diary contains little more than a succession of exercises and visits. She did manage to anchor off Scarborough for two days where, as always with that hospitable town, sporting and social activities vied for participants from among the ship's company.

Other highlights included a five-day visit to Rhodes and, of more military importance, embarking two companies of French *Commandos Marine* and elements of the Italian San Marco Group before sailing in company with the French Ship *Orage*[403] for exercises in Corsica and the Perpignan area of France while being supported by two carrier groups.

In passing through Gibraltar it is interesting to note that Simon Moore's 4th Assault Squadron, Royal Marines, 'trounced' a team of US Navy Seals in the Top of the Rock Race.

The ship's Blue Beret Platoon.

Even VIP visitors – usually a highlight of her life – were few and very far between; the most notable being that of the Secretary of State for Defence, Malcolm Rifkind, on 16 July 1992, who watched an amphibious demonstration off Browndown in the Solent.

In this respect, of course, and in her Commanding Officer's words, *Fearless* did everything that was expected of her without fuss.

Captain Simon Moore's last night on board coincided with his ship's Summer Ball in Portsmouth dockyard on 30 July 1993.

Chapter Eighteen

Captain A.J.S. Taylor, Royal Navy

Fourteenth Commanding Officer
1993–1995
Later, Commodore, CBE

Northern Europe, Home Waters, West Indies

Captain Sym Taylor had previously commanded a requisitioned tug, the *Clare*, in Hong Kong to deal with a sudden influx of illegal immigrants and, later, HMS *Zulu*. He retired from the Royal Navy in 1999 as Commander British Forces, Gibraltar to become Chief Executive of the Disposal Services Agency responsible, among other tasks, for *Fearless*'s future – or lack of it.[404] He had also been the Executive Officer of HMS *Intrepid* between 1987 and 1988 and writes:

Captain Sym Taylor and AB(M) Billy Milward cut the birthday cake.

> I have given some thought to the memorable moments of my time in command and in no particular order they include:
>
> Two deployments to North Norway and operating the ship to the very limit. I recall the OOW 'panic alarm' sounding in my night cabin at 0200 – on rushing up to the Bridge I discovered that the OOW, ably assisted by the Second Navigator, had managed to put the ship one cable off a lee shore with a hard 70 knots pushing us even closer. Judicious use of 'Starboard 35 and revolutions for 15 knots', even though the ship was deep, did the trick.

> Commemorating the 50th Anniversary, to the very second, on the beaches of Normandy. We had a number of D-Day veterans embarked and they joined the Assault Squadron craft for the re-enactment. BBC's Kate Adie was embarked throughout and she became a great favourite with the wardroom.

> Taking an Embarked Force to the Caribbean for eight weeks (without COMAW or his staff). We put the Royal Marines Embarked Force ashore for four weeks jungle training in Guyana: while they were doing their business the ship conducted a range of other activities. For the first five days we put several hundred ship's company ashore into Georgetown to offer support to the people of this poor country. All sorts of activities were conducted. We refurbished, redecorated, rewired and restored an old persons home, taught the Guyana Defence Force all sorts of skills – ranging from field work, through musician training (we had the FOSNI[405] RM Band embarked – they also played in the main thoroughfare of Georgetown) to teaching them how to play rugby. The dentist and his assistant were sent up country

Wardroom laid for the Trafalgar Night dinner.

with a Gazelle helicopter and in five days treated huge numbers of people; he removed over one thousand teeth in the process. We had a medical team detached with another Gazelle to offer treatment and advice in remote areas. Finally, we detached two separate teams to provide permanent potable water supplies to remote villages. These teams installed pumps, storage facilities and the associated pipework to make this possible. At the same time, two ex-East German patrol craft were docked down onboard for a thorough refit.[406] The refit involved engine overhaul, rewiring and restoration of the craft's facilities. All this was accomplished while Fearless *remained 20 miles off the mouth of the Demerara River as we were too deep to enter harbour and there was no secure anchorage. The result was the award of the Wilkinson Sword of Peace to* Fearless *for humanitarian aid to the people of Guyana.*

As an aside, during our Caribbean deployment, we were concurrently tasked to act as West Indies Guardship (WIGS) allowing Fleet to re-task the intended frigate elsewhere. As I had previously been the NA/DA Caribbean, I insisted that Fearless *remove the Combined Operations funnel badges and replace them with the 'Yellow Bird' badge of the old West Indies Squadron. This was accomplished by AMEO doing some instructive and entertaining abseiling down the outboard side of the funnels! What fun!*

During a JMC, negotiating the Sound of Sleat and the Kyles of Lochalsh immediately before the construction of the Skye Bridge closed it to frigates and above. Fearless *was the last ship through and the Navigating Officer had to check daily with the bridge authorities to see if there was room for us to pass. In the event, the bridge projected across the narrows at our bridge wing level and we had thirty feet or so on either side. A huge crowd watched us pass through.*

At anchor in West Loch Roag (west coast of Lewis) for amphibious rehearsals with the wind speed off the top of the scale of the anemometer. To avoid dragging it was necessary to have revolutions for 14 knots rung on – all very exciting!

Other moments come to mind – entertaining the President of Guyana, his entire Cabinet, the Commissioner of Police and the British High Commissioner to lunch whilst at sea. We received them using four Gazelles, fired a gun salute, paraded a Guard and Band and generally did a cracking job entirely underway! And then there was the Distex where we completely overwhelmed FOST with three Sea King IVs, 8 landing craft, 2 Michigan tractors and the threatened use of the BARV!

And then the time I took the ship alongside without the use of tugs – the harbour pilot, who had received the usual full brief, at le moment critique *whispered in my ear that the time was now right for the bow thruster to be put 'hard to port'!*

I will always remember the poignant commemoration service conducted every year on the anniversary of the loss of Foxtrot Four – *what a good move to call the fourth LCU* Foxtrot Juliet.

Sym Taylor took command at the end of July and the beginning of a month of assisted maintenance. He was luckier than many Commanding Officers for his ship was in full commission having just worked up with Portuguese Naval forces and 42 Commando in the Mediterranean and Portugal. Nevertheless it was the ship's turn to attend three weeks of Portland training and all the pressures that that involved. A brief amphibious training exercise with the Dutch and a visit to Rotterdam in November preceded a Base Assisted Maintenance Period and Christmas leave.

With an unlikely prescience, the final exercise at Portland included the Disaster Exercise mentioned by Sym Taylor and a Non-Combatant Evacuation Operation from a simulated Caribbean tourist spot called Norsip. To add realism, the civilian roles were played by nearly 300 assorted Wrens, Royal Marines and sixth formers, with their teachers, from local schools. Immediately following this the ship conducted an extended inspection involving overnight amphibious operations off Warbarrow Bay – the whole package receiving significant national media attention. Sym Taylor's subsequent Report of Proceedings[407] deserves quoting:

During the second half of November Fearless *deployed to the Netherlands to exercise with the Royal Netherlands Marine Corps. Following the cancellation of a number of NATO exercises during 1993, the Netherlands element of the United Kingdom Netherlands Amphibious Group had been unable to get to sea for any amphibious training, and this two-week package not only helped to redress the balance, but also gave the Dutch authorities a unique opportunity to visit an LPD in her working environment. This is particularly relevant, as the Royal Netherlands Navy is building an amphibious transport ship, and whilst the Dutch Marines have a core of amphibious experience, the Navy has, until now, ignored it.*

Just before Christmas leave the ship's company celebrated the 30th anniversary of her launch with a suitably decorated birthday cake sliced by Captain Sym Taylor and AB(M) 'Milly' Milward who, at eighteen years, was, in his own words on the *Fearless* website: 'The youngest and best looking gunner on board – had two good drafts '92 to '94 and '96 to '98. 3P2 Mess was the party Mess. . . .'

The New Year, 1994, saw another milestone in naval weapons systems and perhaps it was relevant that the second longest serving ship in the Royal Navy (the longest being HMS *Victory*) should have conducted the last firing of the Seacat missile. The missile hit the towed aerial target proving that despite age it could still be effective – much as might have been said about the launch platform.

Otherwise 'business as usual' was the order of the day while the Commando Logistic Regiment had the ship to itself in February for a useful exercise across beaches in the Cromarty Firth area; including the rare beaching of not one, but two LSLs.

Exercise ROYAL DAWN at the end of February and beginning of March, was particularly interesting for it included Dutch and French forces and had been preceded by much-needed training for the Amphibious Operations Room's Supporting Arms Coordination Centre. Operational control of surface combatants, fixed wing ground attack aircraft, attack helicopters and numerous firing serials by 29 Commando Regiment, Royal Artillery were practised.

The culmination of this intensive training period was a combined raid by Special Forces and 45 Commando, Royal Marines, in the Loch Ewe area. Held in appalling weather conditions this, as

Under new management. Lieutenant Conor McCormack and Lieutenant Neil Wraith on watch.

might be expected, proved the best training for, not only the men on the ground, but for the Command and Control routines exercised by the ship.

After Easter leave and a brief training period conducted from Gibraltar with French, German and Spanish ships and forces, and immediately before a passage to Guyana in the West Indies, *Fearless* played a major role in the 50th anniversary of the D-Day landings in Normandy.

Embarked for three days were ten members of the LST and Landing Craft Association led by their Chairman, Lieutenant Commander Roy Ellis RD RNR, whose son had been a Midshipman on board for the Queen's Silver Jubilee Review of the Fleet in 1977. For some it was the first time they had been to sea in a Royal Navy ship since the days of hammocks.

Six members of Richmond Rugby Football Club also joined *Fearless* but they, rather ill-advisedly and after considerable drinks, boasted of their physical fitness to a lady officer. The unimpressed – and unnamed – Lieutenant Commander challenged George Daily, a second row forward, plus his companions, to a dawn run around the flight deck. At 0600 the next morning Mr Daily appeared, to find the lady officer completing her umpteenth lap while the rest of the rugby team were in such a dreadful state that they were unable even to make breakfast.

Following the Fleet Review by Her Majesty the Queen – which involved manning the side, a 42-gun salute from HMS *Illustrious* and cheering HMY *Britannia* – an LCVP embarked fourteen national flags of the participating nations from Southsea beach. *Fearless* weighed at 1445 to proceed in company with about sixty other ships – merchant, civilian and military, sixteen of which were British warships – for Arromanches where she anchored off Gold Beach at 2230. Just before 0525 (GMT) on 6 June 1994 the LCVPs conducted what was called in the schedule *An H Hour Sail Past* ending with the landing of the Participating Nations' standards on Gold Beach at the precise time of the original landings. One veteran in an LCU was afforded the privilege of lowering his ramp onto the very beach he had previously seen fifty years before and ordering 'Out troops!' As the ramp touched French sand, HMS *Edinburgh* fired a 21-gun salute. Kate Adie, then the BBC's Chief News Correspondent, was moved to write:[408]

> *Everyone wonders what it must be like in the moments before battle begins. I had a brief experience in the first Gulf War, but nothing compares to the feelings of those who crossed the channel to France in 1944 on the D-Day operation.*
>
> *Fifty years on, I stood among the men who were reliving that day. A leaden sky, but a smooth sea, and a group of men absolutely silent, staring ahead as* Fearless *ploughed towards the French coastline.*
>
> *They'd been invited on board as part of the commemorations, and it has to be said that* Fearless *was probably the nearest Royal Navy ship afloat in age to the ships which made the original crossing. I've never seen so much polished brass – and that was just the engine room.*
>
> *There were three days of ceremonies, the first one memorable for me as I impersonated a totally drowned rat standing outside Portsmouth's Guildhall in a permanent downpour for an eternity, while seventeen Heads of State and other grand folk headed into the warmth for a banquet. We hacks stood on the pavement in driving rain and ate a Pompeyburger, only perking up when a minor royal went straight into a huge puddle, having decided to wave to a non-existent crowd.*
>
> *Brilliant sunshine the next morning, and a day filled with everything that could fly or sail past Southsea Common.* Illustrious *appeared to be about to come up the beach, a Swordfish buzzed about, and a lot of Czechs who apparently didn't speak a lot of English whizzed around in Migs.* Britannia *made an entrance, Concorde shot by, and a lone Lancaster headed out to drop poppies mid-Channel.*
>
> *That evening, we were aboard* Fearless, *confirming the BBC belief – and hope – that the Royal Navy has a special vat of gin and tonic where other more unimaginative navies have fuel. The veterans had a wonderful time, many of them fascinated by the sight of female sailors at sea! There were tales of the Normandy landings, and just a little whisper of apprehension as the ship set off – a tiny sense that the next morning would bring back a flood of memories, many of which had been quietly stowed for half a century.*
>
> *On deck the next morning, it was an extraordinary sight as we neared the coast. The crew moved around quietly, getting the Marine's LCUs ready and shepherding some of the less nimble gentlemen into them. The engines growled, and we set off for the shore; there was not a word spoken, just a few hands gripping the rails and steadying themselves as we bumped into shallower waters. We looked back, and* Fearless *loomed up like a protective guardian, her crew lined up and still. I would not venture to imagine what was going through the veterans' minds, except to say that even as the spray fizzed across the LCU, the expressions on the faces of the men next to me told it all: eyes narrowed, lips were compressed.*
>
> *They all said afterwards that they were not thinking of the moment they leaped into the water under German gunfire, but of those who jumped with them, who had not survived to cross the Channel with* Fearless *that day.*

Fearless was alongside Fountain Lake Jetty at 1330, 7 June, preparing to sail on the 9th for the West Indies – via a brief stop at Plymouth. An extract from Sym Taylor's Report of Proceedings[409] explains why:

> Fearless *sailed from Plymouth for duties as West Indies Guard Ship (WIGS) on 9 June 1994 with E Company Group, Royal Marines, embarked: formed for this deployment principally from the Commando Logistic Regiment with elements of 3 Brigade Air Squadron, 539 Assault Squadron, Royal Marines,*[410] *45 Commando, 3 Commando Brigade Signal Squadron, 131 Independent Commando Squadron, Royal Electrical and Mechanical Engineers (TA) and one or two smaller units.*

As it was to turn out, almost everything about this deployment was new or unusual and included what was described at the time as one of the most ambitious aid projects to be carried out by a Royal Navy ship in the region for many years: best introduced by an extract from Sym Taylor's Report of Proceedings[411]:

> *The passage to Guyana was conducted without refuelling while the period was utilized preparing for the embarkation of two Guyana Coast Guard craft and sorting out aid equipment donated by numerous Ministry of Defence establishments, aid agencies and British companies. Much equipment purchased by the Guyana Defence Force (GDF) in the United Kingdom was also embarked and was catalogued and checked during the passage.*

This also included large quantities of uniforms for both organizations and the wherewithal for refitting two of the Coast Guard's patrol boats in *Fearless*'s dock as well as a number of redundant vehicles for the GDF and machine tools for the Coast Guard.

Immediately on arrival off the Essequibo River on 22 June E Company was landed from sixteen miles offshore due to heavy silting of the river estuary history and the prevailing weather conditions as Sym Taylor was to emphasize:

> *Adverse weather, poorly surveyed waters and an 18 hour transit for the landing craft to Makouria Jungle Training Camp all conspired to make the offload more difficult and time-consuming. While the reasons for the lack of embarked Sea King IV helicopters are well understood, there is no doubt that the effectiveness of* Fearless *and the embarked force was much reduced throughout these amphibious operations.*

539 Squadron hovercraft on the Essequibo river.

Meanwhile the ship sailed for Chaguaramas, Trinidad, with an Embarked Force of a Royal Marines band and Guyana Defence Force personnel who were introduced, on passage, to amphibious drills. She had also loaded two Coast Guard craft; one each in an LCU. On 10 July *Fearless* arrived back off the Essequibo River, from exercising with Trinidad and Tobago forces, to recover the Company and begin the major projects for which she would receive the Wilkinson Sword of Peace:[412]

> *Approximately 100 of the ship's company went ashore daily (10–15 July) to assist with aid projects for the civil community. A number of projects were undertaken including the refurbishment of an old peoples' home (the Gentle Ladies Home) the re-establishment of fresh water supply to a village within the interior of Guyana, a dental treatment programme during which over 1,000 teeth were extracted in a four day period and an immunization programme for the local South American Indian population. Of all the aid projects the refurbishment of the Gentle Ladies Home proved the most satisfying to the ship's company with real improvements to the quality of life being made for residents.*

PO Les Pearce and POWEM Muzz Murray led this team to become local heroes in much the same way as Surgeon Commander Stuart Allison and Surgeon Lieutenant Commander (D) Adrian Jordan and their staff:

> *The most far reaching and ambitious of the projects were those carried out by the medical and dental teams. Between them the teams visited many of the larger settlements within the interior of the country, the first time some of these people had ever seen anyone with medical training. Not all of the requests for assistance could be fully met and, in some cases, only partial assistance could be given but even this was very welcome.*

45 foot Guyana patrol craft under repair in an LCU.

Another team, led by Sub Lieutenant Kenny Macauley and an Australian exchange officer, Lieutenant Commander Steve Woodall, reached settlements thirty miles inland with water storage equipment and pumps.

> *The two Coast Guard craft embarked were returned having been fully refitted onboard and checked for seaworthiness. Training was given to Guyana Coast Guard personnel in the running and operation of a planned maintenance system for the craft. A POMEA also assisted in the establishment of an outboard motor workshop for the Guyana Coast Guard.*
>
> *The ship hosted a cocktail party ashore at the British High Commissioner's Residence which was very well attended. As the ship remained underway 15–20 miles offshore (in international waters) throughout the visit it was not possible to open the ship to visitors, however a large number of Guyana Defence Force were entertained onboard.*
>
> *The visit proved to be most successful during which strong links have been established between the UK and Guyana with much good publicity being gained. The President of Guyana, the Prime Minister, Foreign Minister and British High Commission attended lunch onboard on 13 July, a Guard and Band were paraded. Dr Jagan made a wholly complimentary speech when he praised the UK and thanked* Fearless *for the specific areas of support offered to Guyana in their difficult period of transition to democracy.*

Sym Taylor later wrote:[413]

> *The President, Dr Jagan, was a super chap who recalled that he was jailed then exiled by the British Government[414] immediately before Independence in 1963. He told me that he never expected to be honoured in this way in an HM ship.*

Fearless returned to Trinidad for more training with the Trinidad and Tobago Defence Force but her duties as the West Indies Guard ship were far from over[415]:

> *Approval was sought and obtained by BRITDEFAD Bridgetown for* Fearless *to conduct anti-marijuana agricultural surveys on passage north towards Puerto Rico. On sailing from Trinidad on 25 July the embarked helicopters, with local police representatives onboard, conducted surveys of the islands of Union, Canouan, Nayreax, Tobago Cays, St Vincent, Grenada and Montserrat. These surveys proved most successful with upwards of 15,000 marijuana plants being located for future destruction.*
>
> Fearless *paid a brief visit to Montserrat during which (the Commanding Officer) called on the Governor, Mr Frank Savage, as well as the Chief Minister of Montserrat, who subsequently conducted a brief visit to the ship. The Governor took passage on board overnight to San Juan, Puerto Rico, where he was briefed on the US view of anti narcotics activities in the Eastern Caribbean. Elements of Coy Gp RM landed at Roosevelt Roads, Puerto Rico and conducted a live firing exercise on local ranges. 4 ASRM conducted a most valuable four-day landing craft Navex from Roosevelt Roads to Tortola, British Virgin Islands.*

The ship then enjoyed a two-day visit to San Juan but despite numerous attempts to organize a series of exercises with either US or Puerto Rican National Guard forces, this proved impossible because of local holidays and other commitments so: 'Maximum use was made of the excellent recreational facilities to be found in San Juan ... ' including, no doubt and once again, the delights – and joys – of the Black Angus. *Fearless*'s final visit was to Tortola during carnival week, followed by Bermuda for the hand over of her West Indies duties to HMS *Broadsword*. She arrived in Portsmouth, having offloaded her Embarked Force in Plymouth Sound, on 19 August 1994, straight into a long-anticipated Families' Day.

Leading Seaman 'Buck' Taylor receiving his 'Blue' from Captain Sym Taylor.

Interestingly, and in contrast to a number of other Commanding Officers before and since, Sym Taylor was able to conclude this Report of Proceedings[416] with, among others, the following positive comments:

> *The encouraging features of the deployment were the much improved reliability of the landing craft and serviceability and robustness of the ship's propulsion machinery. . . . The most significant shortfall was the lack of embarked support helicopters.*

A few months later, and in a narrow Norwegian fjord, he might have regretted his views on the reliability of his ship's propulsion machinery when there was, on 15 February and during Exercise GREEN WADER:[417]

> *A 'total steam failure' in Laerdalsfjord! We were steaming at 10 knots up the fjord when we lost one boiler, the other was swiftly cross-connected but at this point we were approaching a particularly narrow part of the fjord and it seemed to be sensible to reverse course and seek more sea room. Good decision! Within five minutes or so the flame went out in the second boiler! The options were limited – we had three cables clear water in any direction and with 15 knots of wind, we were slowly edging onshore with the closest point of an approaching hazard at 1.5 cables. As anchoring was not an option (water too deep!) and as all the landing craft had been detached (except one LCVP) there was little we could do other than await the best efforts of the ME Dept. The single LCVP was launched and it did*

what it could to push against the prevailing wind. The RMAS tug which had been detached from Rosyth for the duration of the Winter deployment was unserviceable so our only other hope was HMS Roebuck – some 14 miles away (one hour, or so).

Roebuck was ordered to prepare for towing aft. In the meantime the Buffer[418] offered to rig an awning to act as a sail – but this was hardly helpful as all that would have been achieved would be greater leeway towards the shore. The fjord sides were steep-to so there was no danger of grounding – we would have made a rather heavy alongside. All available fenders were prepared. However after an hour or so, Commander (E) advised that he had steam available in one boiler and I could use 30 revolutions to crawl in the right direction. All was well! After the obligatory investigation, it was discovered that the loss of both boilers was attributed to water in the fuel caused by a perforated dieso pipe which penetrated a ballast tank. The real mistake was the fact that both boilers were being fed from the same fuel tank. Heads rolled (in a nice way) and this mistake was never repeated in my time.

It was time for an Assisted Maintenance Period which began on 13 March and ended effectively, on completion of Easter leave, coinciding with the arrival of a new Commanding Officer on 11 April.

Chapter Nineteen

Captain R.A.I. McLean, OBE, Royal Navy

Fifteenth Commanding Officer
1995–1996
Later, Vice Admiral, CB, OBE

Mediterranean, West Indies, United States, Home Waters

Captain Rory McLean commanded the mine-sweepers HMSs *Lewiston* and *Upton* then the frigates *Jupiter* and *Charybdis*. After *Fearless* he commanded the aircraft carrier *Invincible*. He writes from his position as Deputy Chief of Defence Staff (Health):

Captain Rory McLean.

As with others before me, my time in command was dominated by three things – engineering and maintenance, quality of people and the enormous flexibility that is amphibiousity; all inextricably linked and yet separate.

My first command experience in amphibious warfare was a major NATO exercise off Sicily called DESTINED GLORY. In all, twenty-one ships from twelve nations, together with over 6,000 marines of all descriptions gathered for a 3 week trial of strength. Typically the planning had been exhaustive and the execution nothing short of miraculous. We assembled in a bay for the familiar 'conferences' that epitomize amphibious warfare. Best part of the first day was just getting command teams to Fearless *and returning them! Day two was dominated by sending my communicator by boat to all ships to let them know what frequencies we were using! What followed thereafter was a huge acceleration in cooperation that moulded a disparate team of ships and military formations into a truly formed body able to execute a complex 'ship to target' series of manoeuvres that exceeded our wildest dreams. Just as well because, unknown to the participants, we were already nominated as the multi-national contingency force for a NATO OPLAN to conduct an administrative or fighting withdrawal of UN/NATO troops from Bosnia in the event of a serious escalation following Srebinica. That this was not required was a relief but at least we were ready. I would not have believed such integration of military effort and international cooperation possible in such a short time.*

Setting sail for UK after three weeks of glorious weather we needed to make a fast transit. With the glass falling and a forecast of gales ahead we made best speed. However, only 12 hours later we were heading directly into a classic Mediterranean gale and by midnight were facing winds of about Force 8/9 and a typically very short, sharp and violent sea. Slowed to barely 5 knots, by the forenoon watch it was clear progress was going to be very slow. At 1100 hrs a chilling pipe went out – Flood, Flood, Flood. Flood in the After Boiler Room etc.

As if by instinct I knew this was serious. I went to my cabin to await developments. Itching to know what was really going on, I nevertheless bit my tongue and waited. A few more 'pipes' later and after what appeared an agonising wait, the MEO appeared. Grasping a bucket to allow him to be seasick with at least some dignity he started to explain. By now the ship was virtually hove-to but the vertical acceleration as we succumbed to huge seas was certainly taking its toll.

The main circulation pipe had gone in the after boiler room. For the uninitiated, this is a huge pipe (some 8 feet in diameter) which scoops seawater to provide cooling for the steam system. A stoker doing rounds of the boiler room noticed a dramatic jet of water emerging from a joint in the main 'circ'. Raising the alarm he attacked the problem with our old friend – the soft wood wedge! Ramming it in merely made the situation worse as the corroded metal collapsed and the hole became even bigger. Soon it was the size of a football and the machinery space was seriously filling up – the water level was now well above the plates! What followed can be summed up as 'classic **Fearless***'. The whole team sprang into action – the two ballast pumps could cope – or would they (given their notorious unreliability)? With the chance that we could lose the compartment, the MEO advised that we had to shore up the whole space. There is nothing which sends a chill round a ship's company more than having to shore up a cavern as vast as a boiler room for real. Everyone in the ship knew the situation was becoming serious. We turned beam on to the sea and for eight more hours rolled almost uncontrollably to the shelter of Palma harbour.*

Lucky for us, the pumps did just control the situation, but nevertheless we did complete the shoring as a precaution. Just before arriving in Palma I went to see the site for myself. The MEO had told me the situation was under control! Arriving at the scene it looked anything but and resembled a Second World War John Mills movie! Stokers soaked from head to foot, water spraying everywhere but, smiles all round – they had cracked it! Forty-eight hours later we had effected a 'concrete' repair and were heading back to UK as if nothing had happened!

Undoubtedly the highlight of my time in command centred on a six-month deployment to the USA and the Caribbean which I think serves to demonstrate the flexibility of maritime forces in expeditionary operations. As ever, we were trying to emerge from the inevitable Extended Maintenance Period which so dominated **Fearless**'s *later life and which was already running four months late!*

The deployment date was absolutely critical to achieving C-in-C Fleet's commitment to the major exercise PURPLE STAR: the largest UK/US exercise since real operations during the Second World War. The UK contribution involved the largest number of RN/RFA and STUFT shipping ever assembled for an exercise and included a carrier group and an amphibious task force centred around **Fearless**. *Indeed we were scheduled to lead the whole UK/US Amphibious contribution. It was nip and tuck whether* **Fearless** *would be ready – C-in-C FLEET was facing serious embarrassment and, with the decision whether to replace* **Fearless** *still hanging in the balance, our attendance was crucial.*

Over the last weeks of the extended DED I saw the whole ship's company and indeed the contractor pull out all the stops in a manner nothing short of miraculous. Walking through the machinery spaces three weeks before the new Ready for Sea date it was almost impossible to believe they could be put back together in time. Pipes and machinery were strewn everywhere – hundreds of people were beavering away in a seemingly uncoordinated way – holes were still being cut in the ship's side as shipping routes for yet more machinery returning from overhaul ashore. C-in-C FLEET was phoning up daily seeking my personal reassurance that we would be ready. He got that reassurance and on the due date we sailed – don't ask me how but it was the classic manifestation of the excellence of a ship's company motivated by a common aim – and a Caribbean deployment!

We made it and the exercise was an unqualified success. Michael Portillo[419] visited and, having created some entertaining 'theatre' to sell the amphibious case, he approved the replacement of Fearless *with* Albion *and* Bulwark. *I will not dwell on the details save to say that amphibious doctrine has survived and yet again stood the test of time. And on a personal note, I have never seen so many ships, aircraft, landing craft and amphibious troops in my life concentrated in one place and probably never will again. The projection of power from the sea, deep inland was proven as almost never before in modern times.*

The Caribbean deployment with four LSLs and the Armilla patrol frigate and tanker was largely routine, company-level exercises all over the Caribbean. What made it remarkable for me was that almost weekly it was punctuated with unforeseen incidents of varying degrees which yet again proved to me the value of having RN ships deployed world wide, and the quality of 'Fearless' *type people for whom no challenge was too great. Long range search and rescue was a matter of routine – and on one occasion in a highly coordinated operation we rescued a sailor who had been wrecked at sea and floating in a life raft for 14 days without water.*

Drug interdiction operations interspersed with humanitarian relief to several islands became the norm including the volcano eruption on Montserrat. Restoring power, water and fuel supplies as well as repairing schools, coastguard vessels were a weekly occurrence. We could not have achieved so much without the Chief Tiff's, Chief Stoker and the Chippies' come-in-handy stores! The ingenuity and innovation of the whole ship's company – male and female, ashore and afloat plus the embarked Royal Marines – was superb.

The culmination of the deployment was GREEN FEVER, a major disaster relief exercise in Belize conducted in real time with 400 expats, Mayan villagers and the OPERATION RALEIGH team playing out their planned roles as actors over the jungle exercise areas.

The whole force was distributed around the Caribbean. A telex came to me in Martinque, as the Operational Commander, that there had been a major earthquake in South Belize. The corrupt Government in North Belize was paying no attention. Hundreds of British dependents were at risk – what do we do? The usual 'command estimate' followed and, in real time, the whole force was activated to arrive in South Belize seven days later.

Without wishing to bore readers we had a plan which centred on setting up a 'receiving centre' at a specific place where we could 'interview' refugees and assess the situation, with a view to evacuation and follow on action.

We picked up the whole force en route to Belize. Given the coral reefs we could only get to within 10 miles of the landing point. Another little challenge! As Fearless *made her way to anchor, the echo sounder suddenly showed the depth decreasing rapidly and in such an alarming manner that we had to go full astern – it reached 20 metres and then deepened – the danger had passed and we anchored. In mild curiosity (heart still in mouth) we converted a landing craft (LVCP) to the survey role and discovered a 'coral' pinnacle which was completely un-surveyed and whose apex was the size of a tennis court. When investigated by the ships divers it did, indeed, turn out to be an uncharted 'pinnacle' which could have ruined our day.*

Furthermore, as an exercise in diplomacy we were asked by the Foreign Office to anchor (for real) in a position mid-way, in a half mile piece of sea disputed by both Guatemala and UK. The idea (from a FCO perspective) was to invite the Guatemalans aboard for lunch to see if they would notice. On arrival and during drinks on the bridge they did. But it was all done in such a good spirit that they took no serious offence. Our national claim was re-established!

The exercise was probably one of the best organized I have ever experienced. The landing craft crept ashore, squeezing through the coral reefs with only feet to spare and we set up the 'receiving station' close to the landing point using existing infrastructure.

Hordes of locals (all recruited by the exercise staff) made for a highly realistic start – all born actors! Trying to establish order out of chaos the Royal Marines painstakingly put together an assessment. Interviewing the many displaced personnel provided a picture of complete devastation and dislocation over several hundreds of miles. Over time, we were able to stabilize the local area and send out search parties for the rest – by vehicle and by helicopter, deep into the jungle. But as with all good exercises the situation deteriorated into rape and pillaging in the local area and developed into a real battle inland as the British Ambassador was captured by looters and local militants. Again, the detail is irrelevant, merely to say that this was the most realistic disaster relief training I have ever encountered in near real time (four weeks) and the ingenuity of the Royal Marines and ship's company was once again put fully to the test and not found wanting. In addition, the role of women in such operations was proved and writ large.

Finally, after a return to UK on astro-navigation alone we come to the most poignant and sad experience I have ever had in any command. We were off Portland Bill in the evening. The Worshipful Company of Brewers were aboard for a liaison visit. I hosted a dinner in the Commodore's Dining Cabin and selections of the ship's company were helping me entertain. Amongst those was the Weapons Electrical Officer, Brian McClenaghan: the life and soul of any party and an excellent ambassador on these occasions. Dinner was over around 2200 and the XO and Brian took our guests on a tour of the ship and then back to the wardroom. I retired for the night.

In the twilight of sleep I was aroused by the Chief Medical Attendant saying 'Sir, the WEO is dying.' I could hardly comprehend what he was telling me. 'We'll try to keep him alive' – and he vanished. I rushed to the Bridge to see the XO, illuminated by red lights, on the phone to the Coast Guard seeking a SAR helicopter.

Sitting in my chair assessing the situation, suddenly the bridge lights progressively dimmed – we had lost a boiler. The XO explained that the WEO had, unusually, retired early and at nearly midnight had presented to the PMO, in his cabin, complaining of feeling unwell – he was ashen and grey. The wardroom fire party took him to the Sickbay where everyone made frantic efforts to save him from the heart attack he had clearly suffered.

We needed to get him ashore but with no helicopters of our own, the Coast Guard rescue SAR helicopter was the only answer. Saddened by the event but content that all was in hand, I sat there on the bridge in almost complete silence. Secondary power had been provided and we had some lighting. Suddenly I became aware of a presence behind me. It was the PMO who said in hushed tones, 'Sir, I'm sorry but we have lost Brian' and at that precise point the second boiler failed and we lost everything – power, electricity – and were drifting, completely helpless, in the Portland race. We rigged emergency Flight Deck lighting to allow the arrival of the Bristow SAR helicopter. It landed and took Brian's body ashore. A devastating experience.

The next morning, after a night of interminable signals, I had to break the news of Brian's death to the ship's company: we were such a close band of brothers that this was perhaps the most difficult peacetime task I have ever had to do. Wallowing in a heavy swell and also in sorrow we were eventually rescued by tugs and taken to Portsmouth. An undignified entry seemed a fitting end to a tragic set of circumstances. Again, the resilience of the ship's company, both in technical and human adversity, shone through: I was saddened but so proud of them.

Brian was given a full military funeral as befitted a man who had, in a previous job, looked after so many bereaved families as XO of HMS Drake. Seeing my ship's company – men and women alike – mount a funeral of that nature will live with me forever.

As Rory McLean understates, he was thrown into the deep end with Commodore Paul Cantor on board for Exercise DESTINED GLORY during the early weeks of May: an exercise that culminated in a mammoth four-beach, night landing onto the coast of Sardinia. If that was not initiation enough, *Fearless* obligingly waited until the journey home – in a gale – to present her team with the flood mentioned in Rory McLean's opening paragraphs. She was diverted to Palma but eventually reached Portsmouth and an emergency docking.

A visit to Rosyth for one of the tri-annual, international JMC exercises which this time included the Commando Logistic Regiment, the annual memorial on 8 June for the crew of *Foxtrot Four* and a Families' Day off Spithead preceded a six-month, scheduled Extended Docking and Essential Defects period in Portsmouth Naval Base's D Lock, which she entered on 3 July.

This period was billed as the longest work package undertaken by the Fleet Maintenance and Repair Organization since warship refits ended in Portsmouth in 1991 and was designed to keep *Fearless* in service until the twenty-first century. In practice it turned out to be a huge challenge to the FMRO for not only was it necessary to renew ten miles of cabling but the main galley and laundry were converted from steam to electric. 1,250 new pipes were fitted along with 4,500 electrical components. Over 1,000 sub-contracts were placed, mostly with local firms often working in sub-zero temperatures.

So serious were some of the problems that there were fears that *Fearless* would be unable to take part in a major United States exercise, PURPLE STAR which had been planned for some years. The discovery that a complete bulkhead was missing through corrosion moved the *Daily Telegraph* to declare, 'Rusty ship may halt US Manoeuvres'. The newspaper went on to comment that, as the Navy's only command and control ship for amphibious operations, *Fearless* was vital to the success of the exercise and ended with the gloomy news that: 'Orders for two replacement assault ships have been delayed because of protracted negotiations with VSEL,[420] the builders. . . .'

As fast as one defect was recognized and rectified others appeared to crop up, the situation not helped by a sudden and freak fire in a boiler economizer. For their skill and bravery while attending to this problem, CPOMEMs Ron Renshaw and Malcolm George were awarded Commendations by the Commander-in-Chief Fleet, Admiral Sir Peter Abbott.

Finally, despite other gloomy predictions, *Fearless* was ready for sea, allowing the order for a 'cold move' to Fountain Lake Jetty to be given on 8 January 1996.

Most of February was spent undergoing Harbour Acceptance Trials, a period alleviated by Ceremonial Divisions on 5 February during which the Wilkinson Sword of Peace was presented. The principal guest of honour was, naturally, Captain Sym Taylor.

March was another month of trials and rectification which also included a total steam failure on the 12th, coinciding, as mentioned by Rory McLean, with the death of the Weapons Electrical Officer. If *Fearless* had ever been considered a lucky ship – which, by and large, she was – this was one of the black periods in her life.

On 24 March she was able to cut loose from Portsmouth and head westwards for staff sea checks and amphibious training until the 15th when she moored to D Buoy in Plymouth Sound to load her Embarked Force for Exercises PURPLE STAR, CARIBEX 96, CARIBBEAN FURY and GREEN FEVER. Of the four, the latter was the most interesting for it involved the large-scale evacuation following an earthquake, civil unrest and an outbreak of disease in Belize outlined earlier. This most realistic exercise involved elements of 3 Commando Brigade and about 2,000 locally-serving British personnel and troops of the Belize Defence Force. Three hundred volunteers, many of whom had never seen a warship or helicopter made up the willing and excited 'evacuees'. Lieutenant Commander Alan George, *Fearless*'s Aviation Officer commented:

Ashore, the marines of 42 Commando and 4th Assault Squadron and some members of the ship's company deployed with their vehicles into an area of about 800 square kilometres. Their job was to reach children, families and elderly people then escort them to an evacuation centre area. Helicopters provided the only means of transport for evacuees and groups because of flooding rivers and broken bridges. High temperatures, mountainous terrain and thunderstorms tested the helicopter crews to the full, often operating out of small jungle clearings. After registration and additional medical aid, helicopters and landing craft moved the evacuees to Fearless *and the RFA* Sir Geraint. *If dealing with these evacuees was not enough, the Task Force had to face many diverse challenges, people being taken hostage, people missing in dense jungle, looting, rape and bereavement. The whole exercise was witnessed by senior officials from neighbouring South American countries but nothing could have been more rewarding than the smiles on the faces of the young children.*

However PURPLE STAR was the main international, military attraction which, from the British point of view, included amphibious assaults on the beaches of North Carolina alongside the US Marine Corps. Unhappily, this phase was marred by a mid-air collision of US helicopters; nevertheless 50,000 British and American service personnel took part in the largest mobilization of Anglo-American forces since the Gulf War of 1991. The exercise lasted for twenty-five days at the end of which the American commander, Vice Admiral Clark, commented:

The men and women of the United Kingdom Task Group distinguished themselves in the most complex combined joint operation in recent history.... They brought considerable expertise to the exercise and we are all the better for it.... Above, on and under the sea, (their) war-fighting skills were magnificent....

This busy deployment ended on 14 July when *Fearless* sailed for Plymouth from Fort Lauderdale. The passage was uneventful apart from assisting in the unsuccessful search for a man overboard from the MV *Adelia Maria* in the Atlantic and for the fact that the ship was navigated solely by sextant.

On board were two lady officers, Lieutenant Caroline Mason, Royal Navy, and Lieutenant Nicola Cullen, Royal Navy, and a mess-deck of lady ABs and Leading Hands.

Nicky Cullen, who served on board between November 1995 and December 1996, is the only lady officer[421] to have written about her experiences in *Fearless*:[422]

Nicky Cullen. Officer of the watch during her sextant-rendezvous with RFA *Fort Grange*.

I joined the wardroom in 1995, five years after women were allowed to sea. Caroline Mason was one of the section MEOs. There were about four Lieutenant engineers with each having a section to look after – boilers, electrics, landing craft and ballast (I think – don't quote me!)[423] and about twenty-five other females, mostly ABs and Leading Hands working in all sections – warfare, stewards, engineers, stores accountants, met forecasters.

Both Caroline and I were Divisional Officers to the girls. I had three in my Division – all cracking lasses! Having two female officers on board certainly did help the girls – they had someone to talk to about 'things' and the Commanding Officer and Executive Officer had us to bounce ideas and regulations off – and we brought a bit of decorum to the female fraternity. We had a few wild girls who enjoyed the Royal Marine company! We didn't have many female senior rates – only one Regulator and you don't really want to go and chat to a service female policewoman!

It should have been a daunting experience, being one of about 27 females in a ship's company of 385, however I don't think any of us gave it a second thought: except, perhaps, when the Embarked Forces looked at us as though we were from another planet!

The Appointer[424] came to see all the Junior Warfare Officers who were nearing completion of their professional course at HMS Dryad *in the October of 1995. After giving the lads the bad news about who had been 'pinged' to join submarines, he allocated the rest of the jobs on offer. I was nominated to join* Fearless. *'Poor you, you won't be going anywhere after the major fire' or 'You'll just be alongside in that rust bucket' were some of the comments. Little did they know that they would join their fishery protection boats and bob around the 'oggin' in the winter storms in the South West Approaches while I would be sunning myself in the Caribbean in the only ship in the Fleet that managed to achieve all her deployment commitments, including arriving and departing from port on time – quite an achievement for the old lady and a testament to the dedication and TLC from the ship's company.*

My first and lasting memory of being a complement officer was the difference an additional stripe made to a 'snotty's' single one! I joined the ship at the end of November, and over Christmas leave was promoted to Lieutenant. It was noticeable immediately – the increase in respect that I gained from the ship's company but also the added responsibility that I now had as a Lieutenant! I could no longer shrug my shoulders and feign ignorance as a Subbie!

During a passage from Plymouth to Portsmouth tragedy struck – our WEO, Lt Cdr Brian McClenaghan, suffered a heart attack one evening and died. I was asleep at the time of his death, trying to get a few zzzs before going up for the Middle Watch. However I was aware that something had

Exercise PURPLE STAR. Flight deck (originally the upper vehicle deck) in proper use by a Sea King.

Onslow Beach during Exercise PURPLE STAR.

happened – the air conditioning had shut down and the ship went eerily quiet. Both flames had gone out in the boilers and we had lost all power. It was as though the ship knew that Brian had died. Again, the ship's company pulled together to get the old girl up and running – it took eight hours and we drifted in the tide off Portland Bill, tugs standing by in case we stood into danger. Once alongside in Portsmouth preparations were made for a full military funeral.

We all rallied around after Brian's death and continued preparations for Exercise PURPLE STAR. After embarking troops in Plymouth Sound we sailed on a murky April morning for sunnier climes. There was much press and political interest in our participation, mainly focussed on highlighting perceived weaknesses in the Fleet capability and the fact that Fearless *was a rust-bucket with huge holes in her bulkheads! Despite this, Vice Admiral Vernon Clark USN who directed Exercise PURPLE STAR gave his verdict that our amphibious task group was 'magnificent'. We were fully worked up; our contribution was very well received at all levels and many people were extremely complimentary on the part we played.*

With that feather in our caps and a buoyant mood running through the ship's company we headed for our next exercise, CARIBEX 96, where 42 Commando Royal Marines were working with local Caribbean Defence Groups, prior to carrying out a Commando Group Exercise in Belize. While on passage, during the space of five days, we twice flew to the rescue of seaman casualties. The first call came after a 1,600 tonne Danish merchant vessel, the Elizabeth Boy, *alerted the US Coast Guard that it had recovered two people clinging to the wreck of a speedboat close to Puerto Rico. One was already dead; the other had extreme dehydration after being adrift for 18 days. Three others were missing.* Fearless, *being 400 miles from the scene was contacted and we headed towards* Elizabeth Boy.

A Sea King was dispatched when 200 miles off, in the dark, and the doctor, Surgeon Commander Adrian Baker was winched down to stabilize the critically ill man. The helicopter then refuelled and took Alexander Johnie to Curacao hospital.

Five days later we were called to ferry a seriously injured man from MV Lee Francis *to hospital in Trinidad – he had been hit by a flailing wire and had cuts to his wrists and abdomen.*

Again, with very positive PR for Fearless *and the RN, we set sail for Belize for the final amphibious exercise of the deployment. R 'n R was due for the ship's company and in consultation with Fleet Visits Coordinator, the Commanding Officer made it possible for us to visit Cancun in Mexico. Who was Visit Liaison Officer? Lucky me! I chose my visit team and since we were to be the first ever RN warship to visit this luxury resort we were landed early and drove up through Belize to the area. On arrival we spent 4 days recce'ing the hotels, beaches and cultural entertainments for the ship's company! Seriously though, the British Military Attaché and the British Ambassador certainly pulled out all the stops to ensure that the inaugural visit of an RN warship was as successful as possible.*

One of my greatest personal achievements was mastering the art of astro navigation! In order to gain my Ocean Navigation Certificate, I needed to produce a set of sun sights and star sights and plot our position. The Navigating Officer set all the bridge watch keepers a challenge – to get the ship from Fort Lauderdale, Florida to the South West Approaches (off the Isles of Scilly). I was also nominated to plan and execute the passage plan, using my astro fixes to alter course and vary the speed as required to make our rendezvous with RFA Fort Grange *for refuelling. It seemed like a mammoth task, especially when we weren't allowed to cheat because the Navigator blanked out the GPS displays! The Commanding Officer was often seen in the back of one of the Sea Kings on the flight deck in the evening, scribbling down the GPS position from the set in the cab and checking our astro positions to make sure we weren't widely off course! The day of reckoning came when we actually had to RV with the RFA – I am pleased to say that my fixes put us off track by only 1.5 nautical miles. Not bad considering that we had just crossed a major ocean using a navigation method which is now seen as a black art by the younger watch keeping generation!*

I feel very privileged to have worked for the Commanding Officer Captain Rory McLean and the Navigator, Lieutenant Commander Steve Hopper: masters of their own specializations. The knowledge that I gained from their teaching has stood me in great stead ever since and now I am teaching the future Landing Craft crews of the various Assault Squadrons!

I have very fond memories of HMS Fearless *– even though conditions onboard weren't the best: stifling temperatures in the heat, cramped accommodation and fellow mess companions of the 6 legged variety (although I never actually saw any). Everyone that I have met who has served in the old girl all talk about her with affection and we all share that bond. What other ship will ever instil such emotion?*

Rory McLean's time in command drew to a close but not before the winter months had been filled with a logistic exercise off Browndown, a passage to Rotterdam – including a dinner for the Ambassador – and visits to Cardiff, Middlesbrough and Scarborough.

On 10 December 1996 Rory McLean took leave of *Fearless*, having begun the planning cycle for a Far East deployment and a stand-by role during the handing back of Hong Kong to China.

Chapter Twenty

Captain M.S. Williams, Royal Navy

Sixteenth Commanding Officer
1996–1998
Later, Commodore, CBE

Far East, Mediterranean, Home Waters

Captain Malcolm Williams's earlier commands had been HMSs *Andromeda* and *Scylla*; he retired as Commodore, Naval Officer Appointments in 2003 and writes:

I took command of HMS Fearless *on 10 December 1996 and on 14 January we slipped from South Railway jetty to the sound of the Royal Yacht's band, for OCEAN WAVE '97, a seven month deployment to the Far East covering the hand-over of Hong Kong to China. We embarked 40 Commando, Royal Marines, under the command of Lieutenant Colonel Jim Dutton,[425] their Elephant mascot, elements of 845 and 846 Naval Air Squadrons and headed via Greece to Suez in company with those amphibious Knights, the RFAs, Sir Geraint, Sir Percivale and Sir Galahad: described as 'biscuit tins with attitude' in any but the calmest of seas.*

The amazing magic tricks of the Gully Gully men at Port Said introduced the many novices in our crew and the Embarked Force to the East while a record 581 sailors and marines visited the Pyramids – not without incident but that

Captain Malcolm Williams with Paul Ingle, IBF World Champion boxer from Scarborough.

is another story! From Suez to Djibouti and then on to Goa for our first real break not least from the mess deck temperatures of over 90°F, and there we received a visit from the First Sea Lord, Admiral Sir Jock Slater. On 27 February we embarked COMAW[426] and headed into the South China Sea and where better else to hold a kite flying competition, but despite demonstrations of incredible scientific ingenuity it was won by a plastic bag!

At Brunei we poured 40 Commando ashore into the jungle and left 4 ASRM, with their Landing Craft, training Brunei soldiers in the art of amphibious warfare – an important early lesson was having

258

to adjust the landing depths to their shorter stature – while we visited Kota Kinabalu. On 14 March we crossed the line with the traditional ceremonies under the keen eye of Chief Spittlehouse as King Neptune and Chief Keeling as his Judge – not a shred of compassion was shown. On 16 March we berthed at Sembawang for a longer break which included a swimming gala won by the stokers and much expenditure on electrical goods.

Then it was back to Brunei for Exercise SETIA KAWAN II.[427] On 6 April CGRM[428] visited; one of 909 souls on board that night in preparation for D-Day when 4 ASRM, 845 NAS and 846 NAS landed over 450 troops across the beach. During the two week exercise our chefs prepared over 35,000 meals while POMEM 'Hattie' Jacques announced that he had consumed more than 1,000 cups of tea since leaving the UK.

With the backload completed we sailed for Singapore and a three week maintenance period during which some wives and friends were able to fly out to join us while many of the 'single' ship's company took the opportunity to travel widely.

Throwing the Terror Club duty manager into the pool was not a good move but a wardroom highlight of the visit was 40 Commando, Royal Marines' Regimental dinner at Raffles[429] to celebrate their return to Singapore after 26 years. On 14 May we slipped from Sembawang and headed for the east coast of Malaysia and an amphibious exercise with the 4th Royal Malay Regiment. The following day a snake was discovered in one of the helicopters; I have never seen aviators move so quickly, nor for that matter in such numbers.

The landings on the evening of 23 May were conducted in radio silence and without lights. Watching the helicopter crews ferrying the guns and stores ashore was an awe inspiring sight which was covered by Mark Austin from ITN and Andrew Gillighan from the Sunday Telegraph. *After a brief visit to Kuantan in Malaysia on 31 May we sailed for Brunei, pausing en route to pay our respects to the men of HMS* Repulse *and HMS* Prince of Wales *before rendezvousing with our trusty Knights, RFAs* Sir Geraint *and* Sir Galahad *at Kota Kinabalu and then proceeding to Manila. WOMEA Newell and a team of volunteers repainted the inside of a dilapidated Cheshire Home to the wonder of its cheerful occupants who showed such an indomitable spirit. The rest of us enjoyed the delights of the Philippines including the Hobbit House; an enterprising bar run and staffed by dwarfs.*

On 20 June we sailed in company with HMS Illustrious *and with the Brigade Commander, Brigadier Tony Milton,[430] embarked to lurk in the South China Sea while the hand-over of Hong Kong was in progress. The closest we got was 64 miles but on the night of 30 June we had our own celebrations, a dinner in the Commodore's Dining Cabin and at midnight a meeting of the newly formed Old China Hands Officers Association to toast the event.*

The following day we rendezvoused with the Royal Yacht and manned and cheered ship for the Prince of Wales. Afterwards we were delighted to be ordered to 'Splice the Mainbrace'.

Returning to Singapore we disembarked 40 Commando after the longest embarked military force deployment since the 1970s and on 7 July sailed for home against the SW Monsoon, crossing the line again on 10 July. After wrestling with an economizer leak in temperatures of 140° F on 20 July in the northern Red Sea we rendezvoused with the Royal Yacht and RFA Olna *to conduct the last multi-steamship replenishment in the history of the Royal Navy. After a brief visit to Haifa during which most of the ship's company visited some of the biblical sites, we arrived off Plymouth on 3 August, embarked fifty-five sons and daughters and proceeded up channel to anchor off Browndown at 2232 on the evening of 3 August after 202 days away and 26,886 miles. It was a singular achievement for the thirty-four year old lady of the sea. In July alone* Fearless *had steamed 8,981 miles, more than in any other single month since she was commissioned. The following morning we entered Pompey in whites, dressed overall in honour of the Queen Mother's birthday and berthed to the strains of* Jurassic Park *– a reflection of the age of the ship or its Captain or both – and a memorable greeting from families and friends.*

Then into a major maintenance period until December during which, with characteristic irony, the air conditioning plant was replaced (after our tropical deployment) in preparation for a winter in Norway! A slight problem with the dimensions of the new stern gate[431] led to a delay in our readiness but on 16 January we returned to sea and to Plymouth for our work-up. My ship's company were magnificent and successfully completed training with a 'Very Satisfactory' report which was rounded off by the news that CCMEA Bromfield, and CPOMEM Wilson were to be promoted to Warrant Officer.

Surfing across the Norwegian Sea we crossed the Arctic Circle at 0205 on 23 February and embarked the Commodore and the Brigade Commander, 42 Commando Royal Marines and 1 Battalion Royal Netherlands Marine Corps for Exercise COLD WINTER. With the birds flying backwards in 70 knot winds and zero visibility it was exhilarating in the fjords. On 1 March with the back-load completed we were off again, this time to the Atlantic seaboard of France and Spain for the major NATO Exercise, STRONG RESOLVE. After a rough passage we arrived in Quiberon Bay to be greeted by our French counterpart FNS Foudre.[432] Swell created some of the worst conditions I had seen in the dock and, again, could only applaud the skill with which the 4 Assault Squadron coxswains handled their landing craft – like seasoned rodeo riders.

This was a period of 'Distinguished Visitor Warfare' as we played host to a succession of visitors and not without some amusement. The sight of six, soaked French 4 Star officers[433] disembarking in our dock from a perilously wet ride in the Foudre's Landing Craft remains with me still – they were not amused; but we had offered them the use of our LCU!

On 15 March we hosted the North Atlantic Council embarking, among others, SACLANT, Admiral Gehman, and SACEUR, General Wesley Clerk. Dr John Reid, Minister for the Armed Forces also visited us. More memorable however was having prime fillet steak with the Amphibious Beach Unit – how they managed to eat so well under any conditions is one of life's great and enjoyable mysteries.

After assaulting the Spanish coast, a visit to Lisbon and the Supply and Secretariat Department's Mess Dinner in the Bay of Biscay – calm for once – we arrived in Portsmouth on 30 March having steamed 9,402 miles since Christmas. During Easter Leave 1,000 ft of the sacrificial batter boarding in the dock was replaced – a measure of how appalling the weather had been – and the flight deck was made Night Vision compatible – a first in the Royal Navy.

We sailed on 21 April for Exercise DESTINED GLORY 98. First, to Flushing to embark 12 Company of 1 Battalion RNLMC (in thick fog just to keep the Navigator up to the mark) and then to Plymouth to embark 45 Commando, Royal Marines commanded by Lieutenant Colonel Jerry Thomas. On 2 May we entered the Mediterranean and then two of my Marine Engineers came to see me – always in pairs when there's bad news, and there was: the 'fridges had failed! After a few hasty signals we entered Cartagena on 4 May and with the help of the whole ship's company and 45 Commando de-stored several tons and £35,000 worth of food in 2 hours.

We sailed with 2 'chilcons' on the flight deck and rendezvoused with the international force of 21 ships as planned, and a magnificent sight it was too. We hosted a BBC 9 o'clock news team who initially made some disparaging remarks about the 'old rust bucket' but after a few hours on board they left with a completely different view of a spirited old lady who was still doing the business and was anything but rusty. A memorable event during the landings was our chefs providing 250 baguettes to a battalion of ravenous French Marine Infantry whose own caterers had let them down.

After the exercise a visit to Barcelona and then Plymouth to embark 70 ship's company fathers and the Master and Liverymen of The Worshipful Company of Brewers for the passage to Pompey. On 13 July it was back to sea for a visit to our affiliated town of Scarborough with Councillors embarked for the passage.

Scarborough's hospitality was second to none, aptly summed up by our veteran visitor, Chief Hummel, who was heard to remark, 'Every time I come here I do more and remember less'. On 22 July

A sign of the times. HMS *Fearless*'s netball team captained by 'Flo' Farley.

we anchored at Spithead and embarked 400 friendly souls for a Families Day, poignant for me, my last day at sea in command after 46,663 miles, 18 port visits and 38 replenishments.

When I walked through the tank deck and the dock and shook hands with my ship's company it was one of the saddest yet proudest moments of my career. What memories abide with me? The annual memorial service for the crew of LCU Foxtrot Four; the village fete and BBQs on the Flight deck; our bow cutting through a calm tropical sea on a moonlit night; the Dodgy Hodgy music show on Sunday mornings; the warmth of the Scarborough and the Brewers' affiliations; temperatures in the machinery spaces and on the mess decks; entering Pompey in whites; the crowded and darkened Tank Deck before an assault; the throaty roar of the BARV's Merlin (Fearless's tank); manoeuvring into an LCU; Landing Craft thrashing about in the dock and the helicopters ferrying the guns ashore but above all my memory is of a resilient ship's company who rose to every challenge and who were a privilege to command.

Malcolm Williams assumed command four weeks before his ship was to make her first visit to Port Said for thirty-one years. On leaving Portsmouth, two days were spent in the Channel shaking down before collecting from Plymouth Sound a section of RRC and hovercraft from 539 Assault Squadron as well as 40 Commando. A brief stop was made at Piraeus before heading for Egypt and a meeting with the only other steam-driven surface ship in the Royal Navy – HMY *Britannia*.

Along with her accompanying RFAs this was to be the largest amphibious passage through the Suez Canal for twenty-five years and was marked by visits to Egypt's ancient monuments while others satisfied themselves spotting the Black Shouldered Kite, together with five other regional bird species, along the canal's banks. More masochistic teams from three ships rowed the equivalent length of the canal on rowing machines – a marathon won by RFA *Sir Galahad* with a distance of 106.5 nautical miles.

The amphibious task group was part of Operation OCEAN WAVE, under the command of Rear Admiral Alan West,[434] flying his flag in the aircraft carrier HMS *Illustrious*. Throughout the following seven months in the Middle and Far East *Fearless* would, at any one stage, also operate with HMSs *Gloucester, Beaver, Chatham, Iron Duke* and *Richmond* as well as the nuclear powered submarines *Trenchant* and *Trafalgar*. The survey ship, HMS *Herald* accompanied the force. Ashore, the forces would include 45 Commando under Lieutenant Colonel Rob Fry[435] which arrived in the Far East at the end of March and Sea King helicopters from 845 and 846 Naval Air Squadrons and Gazelles from 847 Naval Air Squadron.[436]

Before leaving the mainland of Africa for the breadth of the Indian Ocean – via Goa – *Fearless* put her Embarked Force ashore at Djibouti for fitness training and acclimatization: it is here that the French Foreign Legion maintains a training base on the understanding – much as the Royal Marines use north Norway – that if you can operate in such a high temperature then you should be able to do so with ease elsewhere in the tropics.

The Court of King Neptune.

This deployment was of particular interest to the embarked military forces as HMS *Illustrious* carried four GR7 Harriers from 1 Squadron RAF: the first time in recent years that front-line, ground attack aircraft had been carried at sea with their own front-line support. For the Commando Brigade this two-commando deployment back to the heat of the jungle from the Norwegian Arctic was the first for a quarter of a century but during the intervening years small deployments had been undertaken while individuals retained their jungle skills through 'in theatre' courses.[437] Now it was time to put these latent skills to the test during SETIA KAWAN in a free-play exercise that ranged across two thirds of Brunei and which involved conventional and guerrilla warfare and offensive and defensive tactics. The main opposition was formed from the 2nd Battalion of the Royal Gurkha Rifles and elements of the 3rd Battalion, The Royal Brunei Army – serious opponents indeed through the jungles and swamps.

The test was severe with temperatures as high as 95 degrees Fahrenheit by day but the exercise was considered a success and reaffirmed the operational capability of amphibious forces as a key contributor to the United Kingdom's Rapid Deployment Force.

High temperatures were not just the bane of the troops in the jungle as Malcolm Williams says:[438]

> It has been quite a shock for people to come out here and find out what it was like in the majority of ships 20 or 25 years ago. We have done what we can by installing stand-alone air-conditioning in as many mess-decks as possible and have been getting progressively used to the heat, but I have great admiration for the way my ship's company have coped with the accommodation down below.

Temperatures in the main engine rooms could reach as high as 140 degrees F making a return to an 85 degrees F mess-deck comparatively pleasant! Nevertheless the 170 strong Engineering Department coped with this while also producing up to 200 tonnes of fresh water a day for cold drinks and showers.

Exercise MUKA WAVE followed off the east coast of Malaysia and on 15 June in company with *Illustrious*, *Fearless* visited Manila for four days before the whole Task Force reconvened in the South China Sea in time for the hand-over of Hong Kong and the New Territories to China on the evening of 30 June 1997. Although trouble was not expected it was a convenient excuse to have such a large task force in the Far East after such a long time.

Happily, the events in Hong Kong passed off peacefully – if sadly – allowing the Royal Yacht *Britannia* with his Royal Highness the Prince of Wales embarked to steam between two lines formed by Rear Admiral Alan West's task group in international waters: each ship manned the side and gave three cheers. The Prince's response, at the end of a congratulatory signal, was to order the main brace to be spliced and, that order having been executed, the Task Group split: *Illustrious* and her team for Australia; *Chatham* and the Hong Kong Squadron for Manila and *Fearless* and two of the Knights for Singapore from where 40 Commando flew to South Africa while their home for the previous months headed westwards for Portsmouth which she reached on 4 August after seven and a half months away. A three-month refit awaited.

For some years continuing government prevarication had delayed the placing of orders for the replacement LPDs and although the contract had at last been signed in July 1996 it was obvious that *Fearless* would have to continue in service longer than originally planned. Apart from the inevitable mechanical maintenance needed after such a time abroad, a major defect had arisen with the stern gate. Corrosion, too, continued to play its part with *The Times* newspaper reporting that she was 'Too rusty to return to sea'. This was an exaggeration as her hull was – and remained to the end – fully seaworthy and, as *Intrepid* was close by, it was easy to cannibalize younger equipment and fittings.

Farewell to Hong Kong.

With her life clearly nowhere near at an end, other enhancements and additions were made. For example under the headline 'Flight deck crew are no longer in the dark' the *Navy News* announced that *Fearless* was the first warship in the world '… to take advantage of a breakthrough in technology'. During this refit the ship's flight deck lights were fitted with a revolutionary filter that made them almost invisible to pilots using night vision goggles, new air conditioning units were installed, communications equipment upgraded and a 1007 radar fitted.

By 19 February 1998 and after all the usual sea trials, checks and inspections, *Fearless* was ready for Exercises GREEN WINTER and COLD WINTER 98 and crossed the Arctic Circle on 23 February. For the ship, the older hands and her Embarked Force, these were pretty standard northern flank reinforcement exercises although much of the weather was worse than usual with driving blizzards. It was, therefore, with some relief that the next exercise, STRONG RESOLVE – billed as the 'largest NATO exercise ever held' – took place in March off the west coasts of mainland Europe yet, although warmer, the weather was little better. The exercise itself, though, did have a different feel to it as it was designed to test NATO's response to crisis situations occurring in two geographical regions at the same time. To achieve this, considerable realism was exercised on the part of both the enemy and NATO naval and marine forces.

Following a brief return to Portsmouth, Exercise DESTINED GLORY took place in May off the Spanish coasts where *Fearless* was able to cross-operate with USS *Wasp*[439] but more importantly with the Italian LPD MM *San Marco*.[440]

Fearless returned to Portsmouth on 4 June – via a 'fathers at sea day' off Plymouth – to spend July in home waters, including a visit to Scarborough, and then, having safely placed his ship in Portsmouth's 3 Basin, Malcolm Williams's time in command came to an end on 20 August 1998.

Chapter Twenty-One

Captain J.R. Fanshawe, Royal Navy

Seventeenth Commanding Officer
1998–2000
Later, Commodore, CBE

European Waters, Mediterranean, Black Sea

Captain James Fanshawe had earlier commanded HMSs *Hurworth* and *Cleopatra*. He retired in 2005 as Commodore Devonport Flotilla and writes:

Driving towards Fearless *on the morning of 25 August 1998, just prior to taking command, I remember thinking that I could have tucked my first command,* Hurworth, *into the dock. She seemed immense berthed alongside in Portsmouth, looking extremely smart in preparation for the International Festival of the Sea '98, which was the first commitment after I joined. Tens of thousands of visitors streamed on board and there is no doubt that she was a highlight of the Festival. I spent most of the weekend with a growing sense of pride as I met many of the people who were prepared to queue*

Captain James Fanshawe with his victorious cooks. Chef Williams on the right.

for hours to set foot into a ship with such a rich history. Well over 30 years old by then, readers will have already dipped into the various events which had made her so famous around the world. To meet a number of former members of the ship's company only served to reinforce the spirit of the ship that hit you the moment you reached the top of the gangway.

I sailed for the first time on 2 September to another high profile event, this time in Rotterdam for World Harbour Days. Once again we were besieged with people keen to have a look around. My main memory of that visit was arranging a champagne breakfast to say goodbye to the outgoing Commodore Amphibious Task Group, Commodore Paul Stone. I had enjoyed a fabulous dinner the night before in a Michelin-starred restaurant with a charming Dutch couple, where we sat at a table next to the chef's preparation area. At one point I saw him cutting up some meat and frying it in very hot fat. I asked him what he was cooking and, grinning from ear to ear, he replied with one word: 'Balls'! They turned out to be sliced sheep's testicles and delicious. I returned to the ship with a clear plastic doggy bag containing three of these delicacies, which I left in my fridge overnight, prior to instructing the chef how to cook them for breakfast.

At 0745 the following morning, the Commander, Ross Thorburn, made an impeccable report that all was well. I asked him whether he and the HODs had enjoyed themselves that night and it soon became obvious that they had when he told me that they had only returned onboard together 15 minutes earlier. We had a splendid breakfast but, as spirits were just beginning to flag, I asked my new set of HODs

Royal Marines rustling sheep.

whether they had enjoyed their food. In unison, they replied that it was all delicious. Only history will relate who was the last man out when I told them what they had actually eaten with their eggs and bacon! It is fair to say that the Engineer, Iain Whitehorn, the Pusser, Simon Airey, the Doctor, Seamus Greer, the AOO, Jeremy Parker, the WEO, Neil Skinner, and the Chaplain, Charles Howard, watched much more carefully what they were eating after that!

By the end of 1998 we had added an amphibious element to JMC 983 during which we frightened a NATO submarine that had sneaked into Loch Eribol for a rest; this was my only contribution to ASW in the LPD. It was in this beautiful Loch that I learnt the real utility of LCVPs and saw the ingenuity and powers of persuasion of Royal Marines. Lord Clarke's son, James, asked if we would move some of his sheep from an island to the mainland to prevent them becoming marooned during the winter. This was successfully achieved in the end while at least the sheep kept their dignity intact.

Ship-handling in Fearless *was always rather a hit and miss affair as she tended to have a life of her own, particularly going astern. This was never more obvious than backing into the SSBN berth in Faslane in horrendous weather at the end of the JMC. Thank God for English speaking tug drivers.*

Taking the Commando Logistics Regiment to Holland for their annual LOGEX in November 1998 had its highs and lows. These started in Eemshaven where the tug skippers most certainly did not speak English. The Navigator, Duncan Foster, eventually gave up worrying where exactly they wanted the ship to berth; his morale was only restored after he had had a lengthy discussion with his Oz cousins who make beer. About the only high was the invitation to join the wardroom for a TV supper in dressing gowns and slippers where we sat and watched the first ever edition of Thunderbirds *and a variety of other TV classics.*

Back in Portsmouth for a Base Assisted Maintenance Period, the ship was struck by tragedy in December when RO Carl Meagher died onboard. It was a very sad event and touched us all, especially those who attended his funeral, including his best friend, RO Howie Howcroft.

Having finally prised the ship off our home berth, Fountain Lake Jetty 4, on 13 April 1999, there was great disappointment that the planned deployment to the States was cancelled. Instead of hitting the beaches of Carolina we took Wales by storm and piled Commandos into Castlemartin. However, it turned into a very successful training period and prepared us well for the autumn deployment to the Mediterranean for Exercise ARGONAUT 99.

I was extremely lucky to be host during much of my time to Commodore Niall Kilgour, Commander Amphibious Task Group, and Brigadier David Wilson,[441] *Commander 3 Commando Brigade. They were always a pleasure to have onboard and our friendship spread throughout the two embarked staffs and the ship's wardroom, which was extremely well led by the Commander, Ian Beaumont. It was a very happy period for us all and we were determined to get the most out of our three months together in the Med.*

This was dominated by Exercise BRIGHT STAR off Egypt and three visits in the Black Sea. I could provide lurid details of foreign embarked troops but diplomacy hints that this might be better left untold. You must have taught me something, Niall, after all these years! Patio Paradise, the deck outside my cabin, certainly became a Centre of Gravity during a very long three weeks swinging round the anchor in Arabs Gulf. I will never forget my night under the stars with David Wilson learning how to navigate south by extending a line joining the tips of a crescent moon. We woke up apparently in the middle of nowhere only to discover that the Captain of Ocean, *Scott Lidbetter, and the Commanding Officer of 40 Commando, John Rose,*[442] *were camped a mere 100 metres away on the other side of a sandy bump which seemed miles away in the darkness.*

During this period we provided the platform for the first ever military visit by the newly appointed Secretary of State for Defence, the Right Hon. Geoff Hoon. I vividly recall the look on his face when we produced his old school friend, Iain Whitehorn (Cdr E), out of the Engineer's Workshop. It was most impressive that he not only remembered him but produced a photo of the two of them in the Nottingham High School Under-15 Netball team on his return to UK which he persuaded the Editor of the MOD magazine, Focus, *to print.*

At the end of this Exercise I was privileged to conduct a moment of Naval history, the last ever steam-from-steam RAS when we took fuel from RFA Olna *on 3 November 1999.*

The Black Sea visits were spectacular, capped by a return visit for **Fearless** *to Sevastopol. In fact the only hint of where we were to berth before arriving was a photo taken of the ship alongside during the previous visit in 1991. The chart was delivered by the pilot, which would have been fine had the visibility not been less than 50 metres at the time. We crept towards the berth and only realized we were getting close when we heard the Ukrainian band playing on the jetty. This was the only time in my life I have ever given a Royal Marines band the order to stop playing and my navigator, Adam Egeland-Jensen, was extremely grateful I did. His skill that day should certainly not go unmentioned.*

The visit was an extraordinary experience for us all. Standing on the top of the heights looking down on the apparently flat area where the Charge of the Light Brigade took place gives you no idea how different the ground looks when you come down to the Valley of Death. The weather dominated our week alongside and culminated in the air temperature plunging to minus 15°C. We left unable to see the sea surface under what the Met pundits call Arctic Sea Smoke. It was an eerie feeling. The return trip through the Bosporus in daylight made me only too glad that it was dark when we went north at 'Full speed please, Captain'.

Food was a notable highlight throughout my time onboard. As in every ship, the standard of catering was phenomenally high, largely as a result of the talents of the three Chief Cooks, Jacko Jackson, Vince Cottam and Banjo West. These three epitomized what is great about all our people. Not only were they great chefs but they were into every aspect of general life onboard. They nurtured many of the younger chefs to star in a variety of Salons Culinaire *and were the morale barometers around the ship making sure that the voracious appetites of Royal Marines were fully satisfied. In addition, they raised*

Evening 'race meeting' on the flight deck.

thousands of pounds for charity in various events. How Banjo West[443] made it to our home town of Scarborough on the back of a tandem from Portsmouth so quickly is still a mystery, but it certainly raised a lot of money!

I coaxed Fearless *back into Portsmouth for my last time on 14 December 1999. As always, the Marine Engineers had one last surprise. I had become accustomed to steaming around with 2 black balls bent on in case of breakdown. However, the 'Ready for Sea' report by Cdr (E) that day left the Chief Admiralty Pilot and I somewhat perplexed as we prepared to steam alongside from our anchorage at Spithead. We were told that the rudders would respond to whatever the Quartermaster did but that there would be no visual indication that anything was happening on the Bridge or in the Wheelhouse. Nevertheless, apparently, all would be well as there would be an Engineer Officer in the Tiller Flat to tell us what was actually happening. I held my breath as we made the long turn to port towards Outer Spit Buoy and even more so when we tried to steady on the northerly leg. Commander (E) was right, it all worked and I saw once more the skill of the Engineers, but this is definitely not something I would recommend in normal circumstances!*

I often used to reflect both on the ship's past and on earlier amphibious operations. I particularly remember a moving visit by members of the Landing Craft Association who had all been present at the landings on D-Day. Listening to them talk late into the night over several whiskies brought home the spirit of all those who have been involved in amphibious warfare, particularly the true grit and understated humility of the men who landed in Normandy in 1944.

Like the other Commanding Officers, I have a special place in my heart for Fearless *and all those with whom I served on board, both Royal Navy and Royal Marines. As always, it is the people who make the Navy so effective and so much fun. I could not possibly list them all but they were all totally dedicated and, in their individual ways, made their own contributions to ensure that* Fearless *was ready to enter the 21st Century. Many had served several times in the ship and there was a great sense of belonging to a unique community which bonded us all together.*

Finally, it was most encouraging that a revitalized amphibious capability was beginning to emerge, with the LPD working alongside Ocean *and her Tailored Air Group, other warships and the RFAs in integrated Task Groups. Much operational progress had been made and it was encouraging that so many had been able to develop their professional skills on board, while having the opportunity to enjoy themselves in various parts of the world.*

James Fanshawe took over command in No. 3 Basin, Portsmouth Dockyard three days before the International Festival of the Sea[444] – an event which plunged him into the social and public side of *Fearless*'s life before one day at sea and when she did sail it was for Rotterdam and another social extravaganza – World Harbour Days.[445] In his personal diary – rather than the ship's diary – James Fanshawe noted that on 2 September *Fearless*:

Sailed to Spithead 9 anchorage – FIRST DEPARTURE – SHE MOVES.

He also took the opportunity to take a brief passage in a LCVP and LCU and then spent an hour of ship-handling prior to his first foreign visit. 'Set off up channel – great to be back at sea.'

The ship-handling practice had been a wise precaution as *Fearless*'s rendezvous with the Royal Netherlands Navy's new LPD *Rotterdam*[446] was an awkward one in poor visibility which he described as: 'Frightening.[447] Followed by a murky passage up river Maas with a very nice pilot.'

The new Commanding Officer's first amphibious training period was held in the Forth area in mid-September but this was nothing out of the ordinary to an elderly LPD: what was unusual and which gave great pleasure throughout the ship were the results of the *Salon Culinaire* held at Aldershot between the 22 and 24 September. The star of the show was undoubtedly Chef Williams who won a Gold Medal and three Silver as well as £100 for the Hygiene Prize. CPO Ck Vince

Cottam also won a Gold and Chef Brown a Certificate of Merit. In a ship where living conditions on the lower deck had been pretty basic from the day of her launch, good food was always a redeeming feature – now in her twilight years the skill of her cooks was rewarded.

Joint Maritime Course exercises in the north of Scotland beckoned and having entertained His Royal Highness Prince Michael of Kent on board in his capacity as Rear Admiral of the RNR – and who wisely disembarked before the passage around Cape Wrath – *Fearless* again exercised with her foreign cousin MS *Rotterdam*. Prince Michael was moved to write:[448]

> *It was the first time I had ever been involved in anything like a Joint Maritime Course or seen the mechanics of an amphibious landing, my eyes were opened to the intricacies of it all. It is perfectly fascinating. (I was particularly impressed) to see to what extent the Reservists are now integrated into the Navy and how valuable their contribution has become. You and your officers went out of your way to look after us all and we had the most exciting time.* Fearless *provided vintage hospitality which was greatly appreciated. I do hope the rest of the exercise went well. I must say I thought of you steaming up towards Cape Wrath and was not entirely sorry to have disembarked! With all my grateful thanks again for showing me, at least, a new side to life in the Navy. It was an excellent show.*

Off the west coast and at the Cape Wrath live firing area, the exercises developed into what was described as the largest peacetime exercise off north-west Scotland with vessels from most west European countries, the United States and Canada taking part. As might have been expected, the local population had something to say and Janice MacLean, Secretary of Wester Loch Community Council is quoted:[449]

> *It was a wonderful experience to come aboard* Fearless. *The officers explained what was going on to clarify things a bit more. We didn't disagree with them even before this!*

The future was creeping this side of the horizon as HMS *Ocean* had now joined the fleet for her first exercise – AURORA – off the south Devon coast in May, but *Ocean* was not a command ship nor could she carry armour so *Fearless* would continue to be responsible for these aspects for some years yet. To drive this point home, both ships were placed on standby to support NATO forces in Kosovo but between 4 and 8 June *Fearless* went to Hamburg – and her ship's company to the Reeperbahn – instead.

In a brief change of tempo, on 9 June, and while on passage back to Portsmouth, Sergeant N.S. Bartlett, the coxswain of *Foxtrot Juliet*, held a *Foxtrot Four* Memorial Service on the flight deck with formal invitations issued for a buffet lunch afterwards, on board his own LCU.

The German visit had been long-planned, as had been *Fearless*'s involvement in Exercise ARGONAUT 99[450] of which BRIGHT STAR, hosted by Egypt, was a phase; nevertheless to allow for the possibility of operations in the Adriatic *Fearless* sailed six weeks early – on 17 August – for the Mediterranean and Exercise NORTHERN APPROACHES. Working alongside – and against – Turkish infantry in the Syros Bay area was a revelation for her Embarked Force while a major earthquake inland caused a diversion when nearly 100 of the ship's company gave blood.

BRIGHT STAR, between 10 and 31 October, involved landings close to the site of the Second World War's Battle of El Alamein for which *Fearless* embarked Egyptian armour; but the most important national outcome of this mammoth exercise[451] was the debut of the British Amphibious Readiness Group which could now, with the emergence of a designed-for-role LPH, begin to take shape. It was, too, the largest international gathering of western forces since the earlier Gulf War and, significantly, involved a major Arab player – Egypt.

The Secretary of State for Defence, Geoff Hoon visited and, on watching the Royal Navy in action for his first time, declared of *Ocean* and *Fearless* respectively: 'I came away very impressed having seen the newest and the most experienced of naval vessels.'

Ceremonial sunset on the flight deck.

Ship's seaboat. Final replacement for the original whalers. Captain James Fanshawe at the helm.

At 'Endex' *Fearless* was detached to Sevastopol – now becoming a fixture on the 'must see list' – for a visit which not only included Partnership for Peace Exercises with Bulgarian and Romanian forces and for which the Commandant General Royal Marines[452] and a Royal Marine Band were embarked, but also a set-piece amphibious assault for the benefit of Ukraine: the runs ashore also helped with PfP relations. Temperatures in Egypt had been in the high 80 degrees F range while those in Sevastopol were as low as 5 degrees F.

Apart from the joys of cheap food and drink commented on after an earlier visit[453] there was another reason for celebration when it was announced that MEM Andrew Skyner had won the top prize in the Royal Navy/Royal Marines Sport Lottery. He was presented with his cheque by the Commander-in-Chief Fleet[454] shortly before this visit where, no doubt, the £3,000 went a very long way.

Fearless's journey home included six days in Lisbon and a brief stop in Mevagissey Bay to shelter from bad weather before her Commanding Officer considered it safe to enter Plymouth Sound. She moored to Charlie Buoy on 12 December 1999.

James Fanshawe handed over his command in Portsmouth on 6 January 2000. On return from BRIGHT STAR he had summed up his time in command thus:

> *It's been an outstanding success and great fun. There's been a nice balance between all the things that the Royal Navy is good at. We have had a marvellous opportunity to train and improve our amphibious capability and we've certainly achieved that.*

Chapter Twenty-Two

Captain C.J. Parry, Royal Navy

Eighteenth Commanding Officer
2000–2001
Later, Rear Admiral, CBE

Home Waters, Mediterranean

Captain Chris Parry had earlier commanded HMS *Gloucester* and was later appointed Commodore Amphibious Task Group. At the time of writing he was serving as Director General of the Joint Doctrine and Concepts Centre. Chris Parry believed that at this stage of *Fearless*'s life people will have a good feel for what the ship was about so he chose to concentrate on the major event of his time in command and, in doing so, hoped to highlight much that was good about the ship.

Captain Chris Parry.

Fire at sea – 2 November 2000. They say that you develop a sixth sense in command, which manifests itself just before something is about to happen. Well …

As Flagship of the Amphibious Task Group, we had sailed early from an enjoyable run-ashore in Antalya in Turkey after Exercise DESTINED GLORY in order to support the United Kingdom's Government efforts to stabilize Sierra Leone in what subsequently became Operation SILKMAN. We had enjoyed a first-class exercise and the ship had performed extremely well in both her command and her Landing Platform Dock roles. We had the staff of COMATG onboard, but not the Commodore himself, and a full load of embarked military forces. During the night of 1/2 November 2000, the rest of the Task Group had joined from various port visits, although Ocean *still had 20 miles to run to rejoin as the incident happened.*

At about 0515, we were some 150 miles west of Crete when I was dimly aware in my bunk of the distinctive whirr of someone cueing the main Broadcast and the faint, unmistakable sound of a distant voice checking with someone what he should say. 'What's going on here?' I thought, rapidly emerging from sleep. Although I could not distinguish what was being said, there was sufficient urgency in the voice to have me out of my bunk instantly and into the action working dress clothing that we always wore at sea when on operations or exercises. Seconds later, I heard the main broadcast alarm tone and a breathless, excited voice from HQ1 shout 'Fire! Fire! Fire! Fire in the Aft Machinery Space!'

Immediately, I rushed to the bridge, arriving in time to hear the Officer of the Watch calling me on my intercom to tell me that there was a fire! Thanking him for his consideration, I then ordered that, if the ship had to go to Emergency Stations, I would want the ship's company and Embarked Force to muster on the fo'c's'le rather than the Flight Deck, as I might need to operate helicopters and, in any case, I did not want my ship's company sitting on top of the seat of the fire. Quickly, I went down as far as I could, amid people rushing to their places of duty, donning Fearnought suits and breaking out fire-fighting equipment, to the level above where the fire had been reported. There were hoses everywhere and the area was closed down, but already very hot in the high ambient heat of the Mediterranean climate. I made my way to HQ1, received an early situation report from the Damage Control Team, including the fact that there had been three personnel in the compartment, and told Commander (E) that if the fire had not definitely been extinguished within 10 minutes, I would want to use the steam-drenching system. I returned to the bridge and looking aft saw black, thick smoke pouring out of the starboard funnel and rising high into the sky.

What had happened? Two duty watch ratings, MEM Edwards and MEM Weir and a young officer had been on the lower level of the Aft Machinery Space and were conducting a routine filter change on a fuel pump. On the upper level were POMEM Harris and LMEM Holwell. During the filter change, a spray of pressurized fuel made contact with a hot surface and ignited dramatically. Despite gallant attempts to put out the fire locally, the intensity of the heat and the thick smoke forced the personnel from the compartment and made the adjacent After Machinery Control Room immediately untenable. Before they departed, the team took action to shut down the after unit. The foam proportionators were then discharged into the lower part of the compartment, but, as this did not seem to have an immediate effect on the smoke pouring out of the starboard funnel, and there were indications that there might be a secondary fire in the compartment, the steam drench system was operated for 30 minutes. Meanwhile, by 0550, we had thankfully accounted for all personnel, standby assistance had been sought from Ocean *and RFA* Sir Bedivere, *which lay off the starboard side at 500 yards, and the integrity of the remaining ship's systems confirmed, most notably the remaining, critical Forward Propulsion Unit.*

At this point, the situation appeared to stabilize, but the plume of smoke continued to emerge from the funnel and we were concerned that there was a secondary furnace fire in the boiler or that the After Machinery Space boundary to the boiler had been breached. In fact, although we did not know at the time, the tripping mechanism for the aft system had failed or had been damaged by the fire when the Chief of the Watch, CPOMEA Emerson, had shut down the unit and fuel was still being admitted to the furnace under gravity resulting in incomplete combustion. Once the service tanks were drained down, the fire diminished, but it then appeared that a further fire had started in the economizer, caused probably (as we later found out) by the passage of combustion products up the funnel.

While all this was going on, my command team and I were trying to find out what was causing the continuing stream of smoke out of the funnel (on the basis of 'no smoke without fire') and maintain morale and momentum. I spent a lot of time moving around the ship, but returned often to the port bridge wing to check on the smoke emissions and to give myself time to think. Trying to sort out what was going on, we even wondered whether we might have to abandon ship and had the LCVPs lowered to deck level while other preparations were also made – just in case. In order to ensure that spurious messages did not proliferate from the ship, we imposed total control on all external communications circuits, although I maintained a secure open circuit with Northwood Headquarters to tell them what was going on and to ensure that we had access to the best advice. It was fortunate that we were out of mobile phone range.

A couple of mental images particularly stick in my mind. At one stage, after about an hour of all this, I was looking down at all those of my people on the fo'c'sle who were not involved in the fire-fighting and thought how much I could do with a cup of tea. Not much chance, I thought, but if I feel like that, so must everyone else! Thirty minutes later we had flashed the galley up, with the Senior Rates cooking, serving and distributing (the Junior Rates were all boundary cooling and providing first aid parties) and had given the whole ship's company and Embarked Force a hot drink and a bacon/sausage sandwich. It is amazing how the act of munching a bacon sandwich always forces the face into a smile!

The second image was when I went down to speak to the first of my re-entry teams before their descent into the abyss that was the Aft Machinery Space at that stage. All around me men and women – Officers, Senior and Junior Rates, Royal Marines, NAAFI personnel, all mucking in – were going purposefully about their business without fuss, full of spirit and demonstrating an obvious desire to get the job done well. It was the Royal Navy – its training, its ethos and above all its people – at its unbeatable best.

It is perhaps worth saying that we could not ascertain the cause of these continuing fires at the time, but, as the boundary temperatures from the original fire had dropped and as I was keen to maintain my people's momentum, I decided that we should re-enter the After Machinery Space. In any case, the day was getting progressively hotter and, with ventilation stopped, it would be an under-statement to say that the prospect for each 15-person re-entry team, in full Fearnought rig and man-handling three 240 feet lengths of hose down and along 3 decks, was not an appealing one. We prepared two teams and, led by POMEM Teague, the first re-entry team entered the Aft Machinery Space. The team immediately began to cool down the extremely hot compartment, but soon became drenched in fire-fighting water and steam rising off hot components. This aspect caused considerable discomfort and, together with the high ambient temperature, the tiring nature of the task and the time they had already spent in Fearnought suits, soon led to heat exhaustion in some. This team was replaced by a second team led this time by POMEM Hainey, who found working conditions similarly arduous and they had in turn to give way to a third team led by POMEM Jacques, which finally stabilized and regained control of the compartment.

Nobody could remember the last time that steam-drenching had been used at sea and we had all been brought up to believe that the action would significantly damage any compartment on which it was used. When I finally went to the compartment myself, I was surprised, amid the obvious damage, especially that caused to lagging and plastic items by the fire and smoke, how little the compartment had been affected by the steam-drench. The ship herself, built along traditional lines and having seen so much during a long, distinguished career, simply seemed to shrug her shoulders after quite a heavy blow and (literally) moved on.

We had started the re-entry at about 0750 and the compartment was fully regained by 0930. Once we had dealt with the economizer fire by putting water into the funnel, we were able to get under way on our remaining unit and shaft. We then spent our time looking after our people who had been affected by heat exhaustion, smoke inhalation or the unfamiliar experience and made certain our families and friends knew that everyone was safe. I gave interviews to two local radio stations in the Portsmouth area (and to BBC Radio Yorkshire for our excellent affiliated town, Scarborough) to reassure families and friends as well as making sure that only authoritative information about the incident was released – by Fearless.

When we approached Malta, we temporarily re-embarked the Commodore and told him our story. I had decided that Fearless *could not, without risk and a full survey of the damage, go to Sierra Leone. We transferred the Commodore and his staff and our Embarked Military Force to* Ocean *and made our way to Grand Harbour for a technical assessment, the inevitable Board of Inquiry and the genuine tonic of a truly memorable run-ashore with my excellent ship's company. Then we made it all the way back to Portsmouth without further incident on the single, trusty remaining shaft.*

What were my feelings about it all? Like most of my people, I was disappointed that the ATG Flagship did not go to Sierra Leone for the operation. I had always known, from our time together up until that point, that I had a great ship's company who were up for anything that the violence of the sea, the enemy and anything or anyone else could throw at them. There were 657 heroes on the ship that day in November. For me, the response of my men and women to this major fire, with its innumerable, but familiar individual and collective acts of real character, courage and resourcefulness, together with the journey back to Portsmouth (which was a minor triumph in itself), continues as a rich seam of treasured memories and as a source of great pride today. Good old Fearless!

This was the second fire on board since Chris Parry took command on 6 January 2000. On 26th of that month and while in deep refit, sparks from a dockyard welding torch had ignited a small fire in the after machinery space that, although quickly extinguished by a Petty Officer, resulted in five members of the ship's company and two dockyard workers being treated for smoke inhalation.

Fearless was in dockyard hands when the new Commanding Officer took over and, due to the continuing absence of her replacement, he was given six months to complete a refit originally scheduled for rather longer.

We were set a tall order, to prepare the ship to rejoin the fleet in half the time most ships have. The ship's company have worked miracles over the last few weeks and the result is a tribute to their efforts. We are now ready for our forthcoming deployment and going out to do what we do best.

And what *Fearless* did best included a visit to Scarborough in August, after two months of trials and training. Before leaving Portsmouth members of Scarborough's Borough Council, the Rugby Club and Sea Cadet Unit arrived on board for the passage up the North Sea. On arrival, the ship anchored offshore from where her landing craft ferried more than 4,000 visitors. It was as good a way as any to loose the chains of a dockyard refit.

Main galley.

Ocean and *Fearless* were now a team – as intended – and so on 16 September with 42 Commando embarked and in company with HMS *Northumberland*, the UKATG headed south once more. The first exercise, for which they were joined by *Fearless*'s foreign cousin, *Rotterdam*, took place around Gibraltar. It was then on to Malta to re-establish relations with old haunts that stretched back to her first commission and, those desires having been satisfied, she continued eastwards for Turkish waters and Saros Bay – again – to take part in Exercise DESTINED GLORY 2000.

While resting in Antalya on 29 October, orders were received for *Fearless* and *Ocean*, plus their attendant RFAs, to sail, with 42 Commando re-embarked, for United Nations peacekeeping duties in Sierra Leone. *Fearless* sailed two days later for Operation SILKMAN, as the deployment would be known, but two further days into this operational tour the fire broke out that has been described by her Commanding Officer.

The Commodore transferred his Flag to *Ocean* along with his staff and equipment plus numerous stores that *Fearless* no longer needed: a cross-decking that was conducted by boats and helicopters. Flying operations started at 1000 and were not completed until 2200 that night after seventy-five helicopter lifts and numerous LCVP and LCU transfers – a remarkable feat by the whole ship's company, especially as heavy, cumbersome, communications equipment had also to be unbolted and shipped across. This was a task that could take two days alongside Fountain Lake Jetty but which was conducted in twenty-four hours at sea. Three Sea Kings were also transferred and volunteers called for to supplement the relatively small ship's company in *Ocean* but:[455]

> *The experience of serving in HMS* Ocean *is one that* Fearless*'s ship's company have chosen to forget. After the transfer* Fearless *headed for Malta where we all enjoyed a 'howler' of a run ashore.*

Ship's Operations Room after the 1985–1990 refit.

But even the journey home on one engine was not without its additional drama for, while steaming north across the Bay of Biscay, urgent medical attention was needed on board a Spanish trawler about 120 nautical miles west of Ushant. HMS *Montrose*, the Fleet Ready Escort Ship, was ordered south from Portsmouth. Her Lynx helicopter then picked up *Fearless*'s medical officer, Surgeon Lieutenant Commander Duncan Blair, and rendezvoused with the trawler wallowing in heavy seas, high winds and pitch darkness.

With immense difficulty on the part of the aircrew[456] and the doctor, the patient was lifted-off by high-wire transfer and taken to *Fearless* where he was stabilized before being flown on to Derriford Hospital in Plymouth. Duncan Blair was later awarded a Commander-in-Chief's Commendation.

On 16 November *Fearless* made her unscheduled return to Portsmouth. Shortly afterwards, and probably unnoticed by the ship's company, the Secretary of State for Defence announced that an exercise involving seventeen warships of the Royal Navy would take place off Oman in September and October 2001: its code name would be SAIF SAREEA, the Arabic for SWIFT SWORD.

Inevitably it was decision time again for *Fearless*'s future. This unplanned and costly maintenance period, coming so soon after an expensive six-month refit, was encouraging many to believe that she had, in reality, reached the end of her life. Increasingly expensive to run she might have been but, of more importance, the country also needed a credible amphibious capability and so the decision was made to deploy *Fearless* for another two years – to 2003. A hull and boiler survey was carried out – the boilers had exceeded their twenty year design life by sixteen years – resulting in a decision to replace all their tubing.

Unfortunately for Captain Chris Parry, though, another would have the privilege of being her last Commanding Officer and so he was obliged to hand over *Fearless* on 4 April 2001.

Chapter Twenty-Three

Captain T.A. Cunningham, Royal Navy

Nineteenth Commanding Officer
2001–2002
Later, Commodore

Mediterranean, Gulf

Captain Tom Cunningham had earlier commanded HMS *Gloucester* and, at the time of writing, was serving as Director of the Naval Staff in the Ministry of Defence.

In 1999, although I knew much about Fearless *from her reputation, I was one of a small group of Naval Officers that had very little real experience of the ship. In fact, slightly less than 4 hours experience in total and that gained only by dining on board with a friend who was the XO in 1995. It was a somewhat intimidating, but nonetheless pleasant, surprise therefore to be informed by the Naval Assistant that I was destined to take command of the Mighty Lion. Almost everyone that I knew in the Navy claimed to have painted at least some part of her during their sea training and had assured me that it was only their own painting efforts that held together that particular part of the ship.*

I took command on a bright spring day in April 2001 when my predecessor glowed with enthusiasm and promised me that Fearless *would be unlike, and better than, any ship I had ever experienced. I quickly formed four very striking first impressions:*

Captain Tom Cunningham at a *Foxtrot Four* **service.**

First, there was a real sense of pride in the ship. Although this was undoubtedly due in part to her illustrious history it was also associated closely and most recently with the major engine room fire of the previous autumn. The fire had had a notable effect on everyone on board whereby the shock of the potentially catastrophic consequences was matched by a real pride in the impressive fire-fighting effort. A dangerous situation had been handled with great skill and courage and everybody knew it.

Second, this pride was bolstered by an almost stubborn independence of mind. This seemed to be a reaction to the widely held belief that Fearless *was always broken and never went to sea. I was informed quickly and emphatically that everything would work very well indeed if it was not routinely taken apart to establish why it had not yet broken.*

Third, there was an extraordinary loyalty to the ship, unlike anything else I had ever experienced. In that first week I met individuals who had over 15 years cumulative service in Fearless, *large groups who had transferred en masse from the steam-driven Royal Yacht and young sailors who delighted in the atmosphere and the challenge and registered no dissatisfaction with the terribly austere accommodation. I was amazed by the amount of tender care expended unstintingly on a grand, but undeniably old, lady. We were her last suitors and guardians and it was up to us to see her graciously into the sunset with her reputation intact.*

And fourth, probably as a result of the previous three, the ship had a compelling sense of identity and team spirit. Fearless *was absolutely 'all of one company' with an exceptional spirit both in and between each mess and each department.*

Pride, independence of mind, loyalty and team spirit are not a bad hand to be dealt to a new Commanding Officer. However, they were all needed and proven on only my second day in command when Captain Stuart Rule, our very popular Royal Marines diving officer, died in a diving accident under the ship. It was a terribly traumatic time for everyone but particularly of course for Stuart's wife, Zoë and his family. It also rocked the ship. The characteristics identified above meant that the impact was sorely felt. However, they also meant that there was a resilience and spirit whereby people supported both one another and Zoë who was also well known on board.

That resilience and determination was also being drawn upon heavily by the repair work in the engine room. We were falling behind schedule and the impact was particularly unattractive. In the autumn we were to deploy on the major joint training exercise in Oman, SAIF SAREEA. Unless we could complete BOST before summer leave we would have to complete that training after the FOST summer break and miss deploying with the rest of the Group. This had very painful implications for our deployment programme.

The problems of rebuilding the engine room were exacerbated by the detection of a significant crack in the steam drum. The feasibility of the demanding welding repairs required had to be demonstrated on another steam drum. We had to prove both the ability of the welder to effect the difficult repair without further damaging the drum and the effectiveness of the repair technique. Once the feasibility was proven the welding repair was performed on the in situ *steam drum. Then new improved non-destructive testing techniques were applied to test the effectiveness of the repair and these techniques identified further, previously unseen cracks. This was terrible news.*

However, it was difficult to assess what these newly developed techniques were telling us about a steam drum that had been cast over 40 years previously. A huge amount of expert discussion ensued. Eventually it was decided that the cracks were probably old and in any case currently so small that it would be safe to operate the boiler. However, another inspection would be required within weeks to confirm that the cracks were not growing. Throughout all of this the engineers were rebuilding and dismantling repeatedly as opinions changed. They were also addressing huge problems with the turbo alternators that cut short our already short sea trials period and required yet another dismantling of the engine room.

The pressure on the engineers was immense. I have never known a group of individuals to work longer hours, day after day without weekend breaks, for such a long period. The implications for those involved and their families were undeniably severe and the consensus off the ship was that we had passed the point both of the achievable and of the sustainable. This was not the view on board where, again, stubborn independence and pride prevailed. Setback after setback was countered with ingenuity, risk management and even more hard work. This brought us up to within 24 hours of the last possible moment when we could have sailed for Staff Sea Check in time to allow the minimum acceptable number of days training before the FOST closed period. That 24 hours allowed us the luxury of a 'work up'; the shortest I have ever heard of!

Given the lack of work up time, the last RN 'steam' Staff Sea Check, conducted unusually on a Friday, went surprisingly well; that is to say 'satisfactory'. This hugely significant achievement was in no small way due to the enormous reservoir of experience in the ship. We were on track but, with no weekends or spare days in the 14 day programme, there was absolutely no room for slippage. It was a fantastic experience to see the ship fight through this enormous challenge and we reached the final day on track to complete training before the closed period. On that final Thursday, FOST, Rear Admiral 'Sandy' Backus who had, coincidentally, commanded the last steam frigate squadron, flew his Flag as we conducted the last RN steam ship RAS at OST. It would be very difficult to convey the sense of elation and satisfaction as we steamed east that evening for Portsmouth and leave.

In August we sailed at the head of the Amphibious Task Group with COMATG and 3 Commando Brigade Staffs and elements of the Brigade embarked for amphibious work up. We then deployed, at last, for SAIF SAREEA, in accordance with the plan.

The subsequent critical change to our deployment was as a result of the events of 11 September 2001. We were off Turkey working with the Turkish Marines when the images of the Twin Towers attacks appeared on television. Henceforth, during our Suez Canal transit and in the Amphibious Operating Area for SAIF SAREEA, force protection was a major issue. However, although we knew that this would change the nature of our deployment we first had to enter Aksaz, Turkey to have the boiler checked before we could continue the deployment at all. Thankfully, it passed with the previously identified cracks now categorized by a wide audience of academic and technical experts as casting imperfections from the processes used over 40 years previously.

SAIF SAREEA was a tremendous success and, although we did not know it at the start, was to provide excellent preparation for our Royal Marines who were soon to deploy to Afghanistan. What we also did not know at the time was that after the exercise we would not return home as planned for Christmas. Instead we were tasked to remain in theatre as part of Operation VERITAS and operations in Afghanistan.

After the initial personal disappointments it became apparent that this could be a novel situation even for a lady as experienced as Fearless. *We embarked seven helicopters of the Joint Helicopter Command from Salalah to look after while the carrier was detached elsewhere. We then went to Diego Garcia to give the Royal Marines a break after 6 weeks in the desert and before they would be ready to go into Afghanistan. This trip allowed the aviators time to work-up their procedures by which we could safely fly from the now rather packed environment of the Flight Deck. Then we returned to the Gulf area to transfer the Marines for their continuing adventures.*

Meanwhile, COMUKMARFOR, Rear Admiral James Burnell-Nugent,[457] now in Bahrain as Deputy Coalition Maritime Component Commander, spotted that Fearless *was ideally suited to conduct United Nations Security Council Resolutions anti-smuggling and boarding operations in the North Arabian Gulf or NAG. We arrived in the Northern Area Gulf with our 7 helicopters and 8 landing craft and immediately and unsurprisingly dominated the boarding activities there. It was great employment for the ship and gave everybody, including the Air Group and the Landing Craft Squadron, a real and often exciting task.*

We departed the theatre in February 2002 after conducting a high profile amphibious exercise with the newly formed UAE Marine Force in some very shallow waters. On our way out of the Gulf we transferred our unusually large Air Group, to whom we had become very attached over the previous 3 months. Together, we had amassed a lot of flying hours from a cramped flight deck in difficult circumstances that had demanded high levels of professionalism and coordination from all concerned.

Although one might normally expect the return from a busy deployment to be fairly routine this had never been destined to be a routine deployment. We were being kept informed of the continuing difficulties in prioritizing the demands on the ship's maintenance budget. There was much discussion of what maintenance was necessary to run Fearless *on safely for the final year of her planned life. That final year was very dear to the ship and had been an important part of the incentive to complete the boiler repair the previous year. It would include a farewell tour of the UK and a final visit to the Netherlands Amphibious Forces with whom* Fearless *had a very long, close association.*

This discussion resurrected the argument that the ship would work better if she was not routinely dissected. The fact that since leaving Portsmouth for Staff Sea Check back in July 2001 she had operated almost without a murmur for 8 months continuously seemed to add some support to that argument. In fact, it was not only the main propulsion that worked. Fearless *had experienced extraordinarily high levels of availability from all of her systems throughout the deployment; due largely I am sure to the depth of experience and expertise on board. Unfortunately we already had direct experience that managing 40 year old boilers in a modern Health and Safety climate was difficult. Duty of care demanded that we conducted at least some checking of the state of the system and this was going to be expensive. Also, HMS* Albion *was looming close and it appeared that she would be available soon to replace* Fearless. *The conclusion was almost inevitable. Accepting a small gap in capability between* Fearless *and* Albion *would allow money[458] to be diverted to keeping ships at sea that otherwise might be unsupportable. We were told in Barcelona that on our return to Portsmouth* Fearless *would immediately begin the process of paying off. This was not welcome news and risked taking the shine off what should have been a triumphant homecoming after a very successful final out of area deployment.*

Again, personal disappointments were soon swept aside. The loss of the farewell tour may have been felt sorely but it would not detract from our duties as the final guardians of the grand old lady's reputation. We looked to planning the ship's final entry to Portsmouth. In some ways this was an appropriate note on which to make her exit from the stage. At 37 years of age she was returning from a seven month deployment including active service operations during which she had performed immaculately. It would be hard to find a better high on which she could make her departure.

Then Tom Cunningham added:

This perhaps should have been unsurprising in a ship whose 'joint' credentials preceded the Permanent Joint HQ by decades.

As so often before, a new Commanding Officer joined in the middle of the refit with no apparent, firm end in sight. Tom Cunningham was no exception and on 4 April 2001 had an unenviable task immediately ahead of him, as a paraphrasing of a paper compiled by one of his ship's company explains:[459]

Repairs took longer than planned and during April and May we never quite knew when we would be sailing. In the end we sailed at the beginning of July for a 10-day safety package at FOST and three weeks summer leave.

The FOST time was essential as there had been a large number of crew changes including a new Commanding Officer, XO and many of the key management team. As the deployment grew closer and the ship prepared for what everyone expected to be a FOST nightmare the ship's company initially thought the CO and XO were 'little Hitlers' but, in fact their leadership and direction proved well justified. FOST expected the ship to turn up with a poor attitude, not ready for training and also very rusty from having been six months alongside. This was not the case: we were fully focused, ready for training and – thanks to the leadership which we all began to appreciate – certainly not rusty, physically or emotionally. During the initial Operational Sea Checks it became apparent to the FOST staff that what we wanted was more and so the training programme was juggled to allow for extra complex serials to be incorporated.

New, flush-hulled Schottle high volume, low pressure pump jets.

Apart from aspects within the ship herself, a significant change had also occurred with her LCUs. Following earlier trials six of the Royal Marines' LCUs – including *Fearless*'s four – were now propelled by the Schottle, flush-hulled, high-volume, low pressure pump jets and renamed LCU Mk 9Ss.

Fearless sailed for her last deployment – and, unknowingly, for her last operation – on 20 August 2001. A brief stop was made in Plymouth Sound to collect elements of 40 Commando Royal Marines, a Royal Marine Band and the 'new' COMATG, Commodore Jamie Miller.[460] The periodic, in-house series of amphibious training packages – Exercise GREEN WADER – were held off the beaches of Braunton Sands and then, much to everyone's relief, the ship was cleared for deployment with the Fleet Task Group and ARGONAUT 01.

The first run ashore was in Cadiz on 2 September and it was during the official cocktail party here that the incident described so graphically by the Ship's Master at Arms – Kevin Williams in Annex C – took place.

Putting that incident behind her, the ship sailed for Turkey and a series of amphibious landing exercises before entering Marmaris harbour. News of the 11 September New York bombings reached the ship, naturally and instantly causing widespread speculation of a programme change. Most of the ARGONAUT 01 attendees met at the entrance to the Suez Canal: a gathering of sixteen Royal Navy and RFA vessels making up the largest deployment of United Kingdom ships since the Falklands War. Security in the canal was tight with the Egyptians providing an overt presence on both sides and, apart from a stoker accidentally firing a round into the bank, the transit was trouble-free, although the ship was at instant readiness for full action stations.

Transiting the Suez Canal en route, eventually, for the northern Gulf area.

One of *Fearless*'s enduring problems was her air conditioning as Tom Cunningham's ship's company was about to find out. The passage through the Red Sea was notable for the first hot weather encountered when it became apparent that the ventilation was not up to the job without modification. The lateral-thinking Chief Petty Officer in charge, adjusted fans and cut holes in trunking to improve the venturi effect and removed a squashed baseball cap that was stopping 50 per cent of the airflow through the Ship's Operations Room vent. Mess decks, inevitably, had their problems with temperatures hovering around 104 degrees F. Apart from the anticipation of cooler weather *Fearless* approached the *Bab el Mendab* with some trepidation:[461]

> *There had been reports of possible attacks by small boats armed with guns, rockets and man-portable weapons but* Fearless *went through in the dark followed by a fishing vessel which came too close for comfort: otherwise there were no incidents apart from less than complimentary language on the VHF.*

The land phase of Exercise SAIF SAREEA had been four years in the planning and was designed to test every facet of expeditionary warfare including logistic back-up direct from the United Kingdom. Much of *Fearless*'s time was spent at anchor while her Embarked Force operated with the Omanis yet most thoughts were directed elsewhere, a fact emphasized when, halfway through the exercise, 40 Commando was told it would be re-deploying to Afghanistan.

The US bombing campaign in Afghanistan began on 7 October after which no Middle East port was considered safe for coalition forces. *Fearless*, as did other ships, reverted to defence watches but on 27 October she was re-tasked to support Operation ORACLE. The next day 40 Commando began re-embarking for a rest period prior to conducting 'real' operations.[462]

King Neptune's arrival for his final court on board HMS *Fearless* while en route for Diego Garcia.

Fearless's rest period was held on the American-occupied, British-owned island of Diego Garcia and was, from all accounts and despite the absence of women[463] considered better value than Goa might have been.

The only incident of note was when the oldest Able Seaman in the Royal Navy, Noel Whatley, an avid aircraft spotter, was arrested – for spotting aircraft. Both the Commodore and the Commanding Officer came to his defence so convincingly that a formal invitation to visit the base and its bombers was issued with Noel Whatley chief among the invitees.

Towards the end of November, it was decided to send HMS *Ocean* home for much-needed maintenance and then for her to return in March to relieve both *Fearless* and *Illustrious*. Until that

Able Seaman Noel Whatley (fourth from left) at Diego Garcia with Commodore Miller and Captain Cunningham.

decision, many in *Fearless* had expected their ship to be released in time for Christmas but instead they headed for Dubai and three weeks alongside, where some took the opportunity to fly out their wives or girlfriends.

Throughout January and February *Fearless* carried out Maritime Interception Operations in support of UN Security Council Resolution 986 by conducting non-compliant boardings for which she formed two teams. A third team, named the Health and Comfort Team, visited all ships detained in the Northern Area Gulf to ensure that they had sufficient fuel to exist while 'outside authorities' decide what to do with them. Often this team was able to transfer up to 10 tons of fresh water from an LCU.

Although *Fearless*'s time on station just missed the qualifying period for a campaign medal for her crew, it was unanimously agreed that her contribution to this operation was outstanding and summed up by Rear Admiral James Burnell-Nugent when he wrote of her role:[464]

> HMS Fearless *was the flagship of COMATG in the Task Group which sailed from the UK in August 2001 under the banner of ARGONAUT 2001. I was the Task Group Commander, with HMS* Illustrious *as my flagship. We consisted of 8,000 men and women, 24 ships, 2 SSNs, 15 Harriers, 35 Helicopters and 9 units from 3 Cdo Bde – 40 commands altogether.*
>
> *The centrepiece of the deployment was originally Exercise SAIF SAREEA II – a combined joint exercise in Oman to demonstrate the key elements of the UK Joint Rapid Reaction Force. Additionally, visits to 27 countries were planned. The Amphibious Group consisted of HMS* Fearless, *HMS* Ocean, *RFA* Sir Tristram, *RFA* Sir Bedivere, *RFA* Sir Galahad, *RFA* Sir Percivale, *RFA* Fort Rosalie *and RFA* Fort Austin *with 3 Cdo Bde HQ, 40 Cdo Gp, Cdo Log Reg, 59 Sqn RE, 539 ASRM, 845 NAS, 846 NAS and 847 NAS embarked.*

By early September the Task Group was spread between Malta and the Red Sea. The slowest (mine-hunters) were at the front, the Amphibious Task Group off Cyprus and Turkey and the fastest (Illustrious) at the rear (Malta). On 11 September it all changed – although the 'life must go on' mantra meant that Ex SAIF SAREEA II was untouched in principle, but in practice was greatly amended to allow for substantially increased force protection issues and that some staffs (including the exercise Distaff!) and units were withdrawn. We found ourselves in the extraordinary position of being in the exercise (Fearless just offshore Oman) on 7 October when two of the supposedly participating SSNs were in fact firing Tomahawk Cruise Missiles against the Taliban in Afghanistan. Operation VERITAS was underway.

As SAIF SAREEA drew to a close at the end of October, the UK Government announced that some units would remain in the Gulf region for Operation VERITAS. These were Illustrious, Fearless, Southampton, Cornwall, Sir Tristram, Sir Percivale, Fort Victoria, Fort Rosalie, Bayleaf, Brambleleaf *and* Diligence. *Two hundred Commandos from 40 Cdo remained in* Fearless; *all other units returned direct to the UK. So much for visiting twenty-seven countries!*

After a massive amount of cross-decking (during VIP Sea Days) we were in the right configuration for the Task Group to split. Our first operational tasking involved some Special Forces operations into Afghanistan from Illustrious – *by now converted to a LPH. The 200 Marines from 40 Cdo embarked in* Illustrious, *leaving* Fearless *and the remainder of the ATG with no operational tasking. We anticipated that some would soon arrive – and indeed it did – but a break for the ATG was urgently needed, especially with such an open ended commitment. Suggestions of Mombasa or the Seychelles were greeted with derision by the UK spin doctors – so Diego Garcia it had to be.*

Extraordinary start to an operation – identified by The Times *under the banner headline 'Hoon Muddle over Marines' when, in fact, the Marines were preparing to go into Afghanistan in great secrecy.*

The Gulf. UAE forces enjoying a cool landing.

Apart from the somewhat localized delights of Diego Garcia, Fearless *must have had a rather dull time for most of November – mainly spent arranging and re-arranging continuation training. The next call was to provide a Company in Kabul just before Christmas to accompany the formation of an interim administration for Afghanistan. I was informed by the PJHQ one day that there was no requirement for the Royal Marines to cover this task; 24 hours later the Royal Marines (re-embarked in* Fearless*) were 'a rank outsider'; 24 hours after that I was directed to deliver a Company (minus some elements) to Kabul within 48 hours. As you might imagine, no problem for* Fearless *with 40 Cdo who had been pirouetting across the Arabian Sea between Pakistan and Oman as we found the optimum insertion route.*

This left Tom Cunningham in Fearless*, COMATG disembarked, with little to do over Christmas and into the New Year. So, obvious choice, use her general seamanship skills and embarked aviation capability as a contribution to UN sanctions enforcement against Iraq in the Northern Gulf. Had it not been over Christmas we would never have achieved this. Fortunately with the MOD B Team being more adventurous than the A Team (who were on leave), we did. Maritime Interdiction Operations (MIOPS) it was to be. The bug was anthrax. As the A Team returned from leave on the first Monday in 2002, they noticed that 7 days' notice had not been given to the ship's company of* Fearless *before she was moving to the Northern Gulf. Fair cop – 48 hour delay!*

Fearless *thus made her final operational contribution. In Area COMISKEY, just south of Iraq/Iran territorial waters, visiting and inspecting suspected smugglers mustered into a holding area by the coalition interdiction force. And she did it admirably. The combination of high skills in traditional seamanship, aviation assets and landing craft gave her just the right portfolio of capabilities to do this important work. I doubt if it had ever been done so well.*

But come the end of January we had run out of sensible employment for her and C-in-C Fleet wanted her back in UK to pave the way for the acceptance into service of HMS Albion. Guess what – Albion two years late and no sooner had Fearless *got back to UK when we deployed 3 Bde HQ and a Commando Group into Afghanistan. My plan was to keep* Fearless *east of Suez until her disposal and never return her to the UK. But it was not to be.*

So, what do I think overall? The six months that Fearless *was under my command she showed the most remarkable versatility, agility, diversity of capability and imagination. There was nothing she could not turn her hand to and did so with excellence. Her ship's company were a remarkable assemblage of talent – in no way imprisoned by the primary role of the ship – and brimming with deep leadership talents. Size, sustainability and skill at all levels made her an immensely capable ship in so many fields.*

The spooky thing is that these are just the qualities we are looking for in our future platforms that will make up the so-called Versatile Maritime Force.

So, in my book, HMS Fearless *was not yesterday's ship but a tangible glimpse of the characteristics we need from our people and their ships, now and in the future.*

Long before he wrote the above appraisal of *Fearless*'s overall contribution Admiral Burnell-Nugent sent the following signal to the ship as she was preparing for home and retirement:

1. AS YOU PREPARE TO DEPART THE ORACLE JOA AND CONTINUE ON PASSAGE TO THE UK I WISH TO CONVEY MY SINCERE AND GRATEFUL THANKS TO YOUR SHIPS COMPANY FOR THEIR ACHIEVEMENTS SINCE DEPARTING THE UK LAST AUG.

2. FEARLESS RENOWNED FLEXIBILITY AND ADAPTABILITY HAS BEEN MOST EVIDENT. SWINGING FROM SAIF SAREEA TASKING TO CONTINGENCY OPERATIONS, CULMINATING IN A MOST SUCCESSFUL PERIOD OF MIOPS AND AN EXCELLENT EXERCISE SEA DAGGER II.

3. THE WAY YOUR TEAM RESPONDED TO THE SHORT NOTICE REQUEST FROM COMUSNAVCENT FOR MIOPS ASSISTANCE WAS PARTICULARLY IMPRESSIVE. ADDITIONALLY IT DID NOT GO UNNOTICED THAT FOR THE LAST TWO MONTHS YOU HAD MORE AIRCRAFT EMBARKED THAN THE LPH.

4. I HAVE EVERY ADMIRATION FOR THE DEDICATION AND PROFESSIONALISM SHOWN BY YOUR SHIPS COMPANY AND NUMEROUS OTHER GROUPS YOU EMBARKED IN MAINTAINING AND OPERATING SUCH A VERSATILE SHIP AT SUCH A HIGH STATE OF TEMPO AND FLEXIBILITY.

5. SAFE HOMEWARD PASSAGE AND ENJOY YOUR WELL EARNED REST.

6. BZ[465]

And, on the day *Fearless* left the Gulf she received the following signal from *Illustrious*:

221605Z FEB 02

FROM CO ILLUSTRIOUS FOR CO FEARLESS

1. AFTER A LONG AND VARIED DEPLOYMENT TOGETHER IT IS TIME TO BID YOU A FOND FAREWELL. YOUR RETURN HOME IS THE CULMINATION OF AN EXTREMELY SUCCESSFUL TOUR THAT HAS INCLUDED SIGNIFICANT CONTRIBUTIONS TO HIGH PROFILE EXERCISES, DEFENCE DIPLOMACY AND OPERATIONS IN THE NORTHERN GULF.

2. YOUR SUCCESS IS ALL THE MORE NOTE WORTHY WHEN THE UNCERTAINTY OF THE SUMMER 01 PROGRAMME AND RUSHED PREPARATION FOR OST AND WADER ARE TAKEN INTO ACCOUNT. IT IS TESTIMONY TO THE HARD WORK AND UNIQUE SPIRIT THAT EXISTS IN FEARLESS THAT YOU HAVE ACHIEVED SO MUCH.

3. I AND THE TEAM IN ILLUSTRIOUS HAVE LOOKED ON IN ADMIRATION AND I'M VERY GRATEFUL TO YOU FOR ALL YOUR GOOD WORKS. ENJOY YOUR WELL-DESERVED REST ON RETURN TO UK. I WISH YOU A SAFE AND SPEEDY PASSAGE.

Everybody on board knew that *Fearless* was returning home to be 'put down' and while most were saddened by this inevitable decision, no one was surprised, indeed the surprise had always been that she had lasted so long – and that due to the dedication of her specialist crew some of whom had, over recent years, been invited to extend their time just to keep the Royal Navy's last surface steamship, steaming. In fact she could have soldiered on until HMS *Albion* was accepted into the fleet and could have enjoyed her farewell tour of the United Kingdom and Northern Ireland – and Holland – and, while doing so, repay so much kindness.

The passage home would have been uneventful but for the announcement during her very last foreign visit – to Barcelona – that she would not remain operational until the arrival of HMS *Albion*. As both Tom Cunningham and Kevin Williams[466] (the last WOMAA) have said, the disappointment was acute and thus the Spanish run ashore even more poignant – and wild!

Fearless had a heart – a soul – a Ship's Company. The Government's decision to, effectively, force the Navy Board to deny a loyal crew – late home from an unscheduled war – a promised last chance to show off their ship to their home towns, was not only seen as being financially driven (*Fearless* was, as Tom Cunningham states, in good mechanical order) but it was also a decision that was socially and operationally misunderstood at the lower levels of the naval service.

Fearless sailed from a Spanish port for the final leg of her long career on 11 March 2002 with strict orders not to call in at Gibraltar as her previous port of call had been Barcelona. Consequently, when needing to land a compassionate case she had to loiter miles offshore in the darkness at 0300 on the 13 March; such was the cravenness of the MOD's political masters.

Ladies 'charity' photograph on the flight deck.

Many newspapers picked up the story with *The Times* of 8 March 2002 stating, 'Navy's oldest warship steams off to scrap heap' above a measured piece, parts of which stated:

> *Yesterday's announcement (about* Fearless) *comes after last week's disclosure that the Navy's carrier-borne Sea Harriers are to be withdrawn from service between 2004 and 2006, removing the main air defence capability from Britain's three aircraft carriers.... The shadow Defence Secretary said, 'this (*Fearless's *demise) is yet another defence cut ... which looks like a Defence Review by stealth'.*

It is right that *Fearless's* last arrival into her home port – into any port – on 18 March 2002 is told in her Commanding Officer's own words:

> *Back home, there was enormous interest in the final entry into Portsmouth of a ship whose name was synonymous with the Falklands Campaign and which had been in service for nearly 40 years. We were told to expect a huge reception party.*
>
> *Yet again, fate played a hand. On the morning of the entry it was obvious that the weather was far from ideal. While at anchor in driving rain off Spithead the westerly wind increased to over 40 knots. Insufficient though to prevent the Deputy Commander in Chief coming on board to welcome us home and then to depart again via a very wet boat transfer. Fortunately we had managed to embark the pilot earlier that day and had discussed the various options for the entry. The Harbourmaster had made 4 tugs available to assist and we agreed a plan to cope with 35 knots of wind blowing us directly onto the berth. Then, in 45 knots of wind, we tried to weigh anchor to be ready for the forecast reduction in windspeed. This proved extremely difficult because of the ship's tendency to sail dramatically on the wind whenever any tension came on the cable. The Buffer was rightly concerned with the weight that this was placing on the cable and the weather was too rough for a tug to come out of the harbour to assist. We were beginning to contemplate the reception party on the jetty being pounded by the weather while we sat at anchor all day at Spithead. Options for breaking the cable were being discussed when*

Final alongside.

suddenly and inexplicably we managed to haul sufficient cable that the sailing phenomenon stopped. Now underway we considered again the options and, with the wind indicating nearly 50 knots in the Solent and gusting 30 to 40 in the harbour, we began our entry.

We had a good plan. We had assessed all of the risks and we were content, if not actually thrilled, with the situation. However, the Ship appeared somewhat less than content. In the high winds she was extremely reluctant to follow her helm and therefore difficult to manoeuvre through the channels, requiring robust use of power as encouragement. Nobody had expected her to bow out willingly but this lack of cooperation was not proving helpful. Eventually we entered the harbour[467] to be greeted by a ferocious wind of over 40 knots and a large, brave, windswept and bedraggled welcome party along the seafront, on the castle and on the jetty. The Royal Marine band played on bravely but could barely be heard above the storm. The decommissioning pennant[468] pulled the stub mast away from the superstructure and gave rope burns to the communicators who tried to grab it. It was then grabbed and held by members of the crew at Procedure Alpha. They, in turn, were grabbed by their colleagues when particularly severe gusts tried to lift them airborne with the pennant. Meanwhile, we steered upwind towards Haslar Creek to connect the tugs when one of the 2 more powerful tugs had an engine failure. This was a fun morning!

Eventually we came alongside. Sadly and with due ceremony, using a human chain of marine engineers, we passed the final 'Finished with Main Engines ...'

... with the 'milometer' reading just about 749,000 nautical miles.

The final ship's company.

I left the Ship soon after we returned from leave. Summoned to the Ministry and into a busy job that had me out of the country for the final de-commissioning celebrations which were all handled by my Executive Officer, Brian Warren, who took over as Commanding Officer on my departure. I recalled the delightful letter that I received from Fearless's *first Captain, Hugh Corbett, when I assumed command. He had commented that it was poignant for the first and last Captains to be in touch. I had responded that although nobody could challenge his claim to be the first Captain there were already those who had wrongly claimed to be the last.*

I had a tremendous fourteen months in command of Fearless. *It was hectic, challenging and at times just tough. But it was always hugely enjoyable and that was invariably because of the people. The Ship was just full of tremendously powerful characters; too many to list but I will never forget them. And nothing ever changed those first impressions I had formed on taking command: pride, independence of mind, loyalty and team spirit.*

We really did have the feeling that, together, we could do anything and it just doesn't get any better than that.

A month later *Hansard* recorded the following question and answer:

Written answers for 18 April 2002:

Mr. Jenkin: To ask the Secretary of State for Defence what savings will be made from the early withdrawal of HMS Fearless. *[49765]*

Mr. Ingram:[469] *The earlier than previously planned withdrawal of HMS* Fearless *will accrue savings of at least £2 million. This will be achieved by cancelling a previously programmed assisted maintenance period and through the reduction in operating costs. Moreover, HMS* Fearless *is nearly 37 years old and so in poor material condition. The unique nature of much of her machinery such as boilers and steam plant make repairs and maintenance difficult and it is highly probable that further un-programmed and potentially costly work would have been required to maintain her at the previously assumed readiness state.*

But all she wanted to do was steam around the UK saying 'Goodbye' and 'Thank You' … and prevent an amphibious-command capability gap during the most important, complicated and opposed amphibious landings for almost exactly twenty years: across Iraq's Al Faw peninsula during the opening ground operations of the Second Gulf War.

Chapter Twenty-Four

Commander B.H. Warren, OBE, Royal Navy

Twentieth Commanding Officer
2002
Later, Captain

Portsmouth Dockyard

Commander Brian Warren's first command had been the offshore patrol vessel HMS *Orkney*: he was appointed as *Fearless*'s last Commanding Officer on 12 May 2002, destined not to take her to sea but to, in effect, put her to sleep. He writes from his position as Assistant Director Defence Public Relations (Royal Navy):

Commander Brian Warren.

HMS Fearless*'s Farewell Celebrations: Initially, the Lion's Last Roar was to take the form of a full Decommissioning Ceremony and a Ship's Company Ball in the Autumn of 2002, following her return from SAIF SAREEA II. Regrettably, circumstances dictated otherwise and the uncertainties of the final operational deployment in support of operations in Afghanistan, together with the unforeseen short notice announcement of her early retirement, inevitably altered both the nature and timetable for the planned decommissioning activities. Disappointed but not disheartened, the serving officers were forced to de-tune the scale of the planned activities but, undeterred, arranged to stage two smaller functions in order to capture as many people as possible and ensure that a full cohort of ex* Fearless *shipmates could share in those last fond memories. In the event,* Fearless *hosted an official Cocktail Party on 20 June 2002 to say farewell, followed by a luncheon on 27 Jun 2002 for previous Commanding Officers as part of the Golden Jubilee celebrations.*

The Farewell Cocktail Party: This was particularly well supported despite the shorter notice, and was a poignant but thoroughly enjoyable event with attendance from serving members spanning her full history to add to the sense of occasion and give their last farewell. In accordance with tradition, the Cocktail Party was held on the 30 mm Deck (forward Seacat Deck for the older members), but owing to the impressive and unprecedented support, the celebrations soon spilled onto the foc'sle. One hundred and twenty distinguished guests graced the Last Commission Wardroom, consisting of ex-officers and their partners representing all branches in her long, inspirational and impressive history. The 'Fearless First Commission Club' was led by Rear Admiral J. Carhill OBE, with the 'Falklands Club' headed by Rear Admiral Larken's wife, Wendy Larken. The event was also well attended by previous COMAWs, COMATGs and Commanding Officers.

The final party drew to a close with the very last Ceremonial Sunset on board courtesy of the band from the Royal Marine School of Music. Major General A.A. Milton[470] (then COMAMPHIBFOR) took the salute, flanked by Rear Admiral A.K. Backus OBE (then Fleet COS (W)) and Rear Admiral N.S.R. Kilgour (previous COMATG and then Fleet COS(OPS)) on either side.

Golden Jubilee: Fearless *officers were not involved in the Naval Base Golden Jubilee Celebrations and therefore took the opportunity to entertain previous Commanding Officers and their partners for the day. Luncheon in the wardroom was followed by a visit to MV* Triton *(the trial ship for the multi-hull Future Surface Combatant), which then sailed around Portsmouth Harbour providing an excellent view of proceedings. Fortuitously, the 'theme' of the display was amphibious warfare and the distinguished group of Commanding Officers were able to witness new equipment and methods that had not been available to them in their own* Fearless *days. It was undoubtedly an auspicious day, and provided a welcome opportunity for those Commanding Officers who had been unable to attend the Cocktail Party, the chance to say their individual farewells.*

The ship was very quietly decommissioned with the lowering of her Jack and Ensign at sunset on the 31 July 2002.

The very last serving officers have formed a Fearless Last Commission Club *following in the fine footsteps of the ship's* First Commission Falklands Club. *A very successful inaugural dinner took place at the Old Naval Academy in November 2003, with plans for an annual event in hand.*

Brian Warren ended his piece with three recollections:

Did you know that one sailor in my time was so patriotic towards the ship that he had the ship's pennant number tattooed across his stomach just below his navel. Because he wriggled so much 'L10' came out as 'LID' – dedication or what!

Secondly:

After some 65 days plus at sea in the Indian Ocean (Sep–Nov 2001), Fearless *made a very welcome stop alongside in Diego Garcia. Although this was deemed an 'operational' visit, as is custom, Commodore Miller (embarked COMATG) considered it entirely appropriate that some of the local dignitaries be invited to a small lunch party on board, in this case, they were all US military personnel. The well rehearsed routine, was disrupted by an immense tropical downpour earlier in the morning. Commodore Miller was looking forward to hosting his pre-lunch drinks party on the Captain's private 'balcony', a location which offered guests both an unrivalled position and an alluring ambience. The Commodore's natural optimism prevailed and with precious little time to spare to make alternative arrangements, I was dispatched to establish what conditions were like for myself. Not surprisingly, most of the recent rainfall had collected in the awning where it was creating more than an unsightly 'bulge'. As I am an unusually tall chap, I was able to size up the situation in a trice and realized that with some deft manhandling it was probably possible to build up enough momentum to expel the offending ton of water!*

Without a moment's hesitation, using my arms stretched above my head acting as sort of tent-poles, I set about manoeuvring the bulk of rainwater athwartships along the awning until, with a final almighty shove, I sent it cascading over the port side access ladder. However, my satisfaction was short-lived as the disappearing waterfall elicited a shrill shriek of surprise from somewhere below. I was confronted by a sopping wet Commodore ascending the same ladder having borne the full brunt of the unexpected water cascade and now engulfed in helpless laughter. Astonished and both horrified and completely overwhelmed by the humour of the situation, I could only join in the laughter. Eventually, I recovered enough to offer a strenuous apology and we both retired to our respective cabins to compose ourselves for the lunchtime event.

In my subsequent correspondence with the Commodore over the years he never fails to remind me of this event in his salutation. . . . 'Dear taut awning'. I, of course, learned a very valuable lesson: 'never tilt at an awning without offering a warning!'

And finally:

Before taking command, I had the privilege of serving Captain Tom 'TC' Cunningham as his Executive officer for over 12 months, supported by the extraordinarily talented WO MAA Kevin 'Taff' Williams to keep me on the straight and narrow. Some would say that I complemented Captain Tom perfectly and together we represented something of a remarkable partnership. In fact this Executive tripartite prided itself on humour, fair-mindedness and hard work. The ship's company were undoubtedly worked hard but no matter how demanding the task or how difficult the conditions, they came to realize that their efforts were never taken for granted but recognized and always appreciated.

A case in point concerned every sailor's pet hate – my rounds of mess deck, heads and bathrooms! Cleaning ship is a contentious issue at the best of times, but in an old ship the conditions suffered during this particular extended 2001–2002 deployment – acute fresh water shortages and internal ship temperatures often exceeding the external extremes – were a potential minefield of pent up exasperation.

The Ship's Company were worked ragged for their FOST work-up in June 2001 but surprised the Staff with outstanding results in terms of presentation and cleanliness. The problem was how to maintain these standards on deployment.

Mindful of the delicacy of the situation, but nevertheless determined to keep the Mighty Lion *sparkling, I (having recently come from FOST myself), together with Taff Williams put our grey cells to work and came up with a cunning plan. Masters of diplomacy and negotiation, we brokered an unprecented arrangement which we hoped would be both viable and acceptable to all parties. With Captain Cunningham's full blessing a sliding scale of 'rounds' was introduced into each of the ship's compartments: if a mess/heads/bathroom/passageway etc. met the highest standards of cleanliness and hygiene one week, it was exempt 'standing rounds' the following week, providing that standards were maintained, thus discriminating sailors could be released from the seemingly endless and universally onerous 'rounds routine'. Simple but highly effective: very soon the whole ship's company rose to the challenge with alacrity.*

The next step was to offer the ship's company 'double or quits'; the buzz quickly got around and within a week or so barely any sailors or marines were standing 'normal rounds', and my evening routine with the WOMAA turned to a real pleasure. This allowed more time to talk to the 'lads and girls' and only a quick cursory check of the other areas to ensure standards hadn't slipped. And so it continued in this fashion to the end.

The 'cunning plan' was an audacious move but proved to be an outstanding success, illustrating in the process just how adaptable and innovative the Fearless *team could be in difficult and demanding times.*

Chapter Twenty-Five

The End and the Future
2002 Onwards

Fearless was taken in hand by Lieutenant Bob Lane, Royal Navy – the Officer in Charge, Disposal and Reserve Ships Organization – on 24 October 2002 on which date she lost the prefix 'Her Majesty's Ship', became a Disposal List ship and was officially classified as 'a hulk' alongside 3 Berth in 3 Basin, Portsmouth Dockyard.

Commodore Sym Taylor – *Fearless*'s fourteenth Commanding Officer and now Chief Executive of the Disposal Services Agency – wrote:[471]

> *We very nearly sold* Fearless *to an overseas navy for further service but the deal fell through at the final stages when an economic crisis occurred causing the Defence budget to be frozen.*

Bell and Battle Honours Board in the safe keeping of Scarborough City.

There was an option for Fearless to replace Rame Head as a special training vessel. I would not wish to go into details of the actual task – but you will know what I mean! Sadly the costs of retention were deemed to be too great.

Fearless (and Intrepid) are likely to be sold for scrap, however there are a number of complications. UK has ratified an OECD Convention on the export of hazardous waste and as ships being sold for scrap are considered to be in this category we have a new raft of environmental legislation to consider before we can make the sale. Where we stand at present is that we have tendered both ships for sale for scrap and received nearly 40 firm bids. . . . What is going to happen is that the receipts that we could have expected (and scrap steel is at a very high level at present) will become a cost to the MOD and the Taxpayer. If this makes little sense to you – you will be re-assured that I think similarly! Both ships are likely to remain in Portsmouth for the foreseeable future.

I have walked around both ships in the past year and between decks both are really in quite amazing condition – you would feel quite at home! The upper decks, as you would imagine are deteriorating and already look unloved!

A little later Sym Taylor wrote again:

You may be interested to know that we still have a potential buyer for Fearless – a well known pub group are seriously considering purchasing the ship and converting her to become a backpackers' hostel and night club venue. Everything depends on them getting approval for a suitable berth in London. Although this all sounds pie in the sky – they are sufficiently serious to be spending money on a detailed survey of the ship! Anything would be better than paying someone to scrap the ship – current environmental legislation has turned what used to be a receipt for scrap into a cost!

Fearless and Intrepid awaiting their fate. Fareham Creek, 2005.

On retirement *Fearless*'s landing craft were also placed on the disposal list although an earlier LCVP, *Foxtrot Seven* – in which Corporal Alan White rescued forty-one men from HMS *Antelope* – had, in 1986, been donated to the Royal Marines Museum at Southsea. The LCU *Foxtrot Three* was sold to a private company in the west of Scotland and was last heard of, with a crane fitted, transporting lorries between the islands.

In the meantime, Colin Waite – a retired Royal Marine – opened a website,[472] devoted to preserving not only memories of service in both *Fearless* and *Intrepid* but to saving *Fearless* herself. Following the tsunami on Boxing Day 2004 he posted the following:

> It has been a bad start for 2005 in the Far East with what has to be the worst natural disaster on record. This has led to one organization setting up an ambitious plan to put Fearless *back to sea as a humanitarian relief ship. Should* Fearless *be the chosen vessel and all goes through there will be a need for crew so if you need another memory I will keep you posted as to what happens next.*

Not all want to see *Fearless* saved but this is more for fear of a much loved matriarch slowly dying through lack of affection, than because they were never in love with her. It is best, some reckon, that she is saved ignominy and quickly put to rest. Others think differently.

As this biography goes to the publishers in early 2006, her future remains unresolved: but whatever that future or lack of it may be and for whatever reasons – affectionate or otherwise – she will not be forgotten.

Annex A

Executive Officer
Commander David Joel, Royal Navy
1971–1973

Some New Heavies

Cdr. David Joel left for DNAP and passed over to Cdr John Lock one LPD, three shore-side heads and 257 unsold copies of the Last Commission Book.

Commander David Joel hands over to his successor.

When I joined *Fearless* as the Commander in October 1971, I found that, after her sixth year in commission, she was looking a little tired, both inside and out. Within the accommodation areas the decks were stained and messy, while externally there were rust streaks down the sides, making them very difficult to clean. The problem inside was that the ship's company and Embarked Forces took their meals in the magnificent dining halls adjacent to the galleys, but had got into the habit of taking their hot drinks away with them to their places of work. In a seaway, therefore, a lot of drinks were spilt. I had come from the Director of Naval Equipment at Bath and my confederates there were itching to use some new devices for 'housekeeping' in a big ship. On my request, *Fearless* was provided with the new wet/dry suck machines, which washed and cleaned the floors, plus the polishing machines which used new types of long-lasting shiny polish. Soon the ship shone and that was evident to her company.

Embarked Forces always created problems. When the Adjutant and RSM from the King's Regiment arrived one day they both had hobnailed boots, which they stamped on my decks every time they said 'Sir'. I was horrified and banned such boots; all joining regiments had to wear rubber soles.

Externally the decks were also a problem, for all the ' beading' around the upper decks, of which *Fearless* had five tiers, was allowing water to leak beneath it, causing great rust runs down the

300

vertical structures and ship's side. It was a huge problem, for the beading could not easily be re-bedded with white lead paste; it would have cost a fortune and have taken months to do in a dockyard. After consultation with a firm in Portsmouth we bought thousands of feet of what looked like adhesive chewing gum. It came in 50ft rolls, one inch wide. The seamen, led by the Commander and Bosun,[473] then applied this gum on the bottom edges of the beading, pressing it down both inside and out. This caused great amusement as we did it. Then it was painted shipside grey outside and green deck colour inside. The beading, previously varnished, was painted a pine coloured yellow. It looked good and it worked to perfection. When *Fearless* was in Reserve some twenty-five years later, I inspected the beading closely. To my surprise the 'chewing gum' was still intact with no rust stains. Beat that.

The Fairy Huntress. There were lots of these in the Navy; smart little 23ft Captain's or Flag Officer's 'barges'. The engineers at Bath had governed them down so that their planing hull was ineffective. Their design speed was 25 but they only did about 15 knots. Boats were one of my many tasks at DNE, so I demanded that *Fearless's Huntress* be up-rated to her design speed. Furious arguments arose, but I won and the result was only too apparent. I drove her myself all around the Greek Islands and at Malta, usually with the Bosun as crew and my run ashore oppo.

There came the day of our sea inspection at Rosyth. The *Huntress* was sent in early to pick up the Admiral and the Admiral was early too, he not knowing we had such a lovely speedboat. The ship was closed down at Action Stations ready for sea. To my horror I looked out of my scuttle to see the *Huntress* flash by with FOCAS embarked. He was 15 minutes early. I phoned the Captain who was not fully dressed and he said 'For God's sake Commander, delay his arrival to the bridge'. I raced down to the gangway just in time.

Admiral to me: 'Where is your Captain?'

'He awaits you on the bridge, Sir'.

'Why?'

'We are at Action Stations Sir'.

I then led him round the long way via the forecastle deck, to enter by the front door as it were. The door clips were tightly fastened, but as I undid them the man inside quickly did them up again. However a loud shout fixed him. We were in and quickly to the bridge where the Captain met the Admiral – just in time! We passed the inspection with colours flying.

The *Huntress* was much talked about and one day the Wessex Flight CO challenged me to a race between his helo and the boat. The race was to deliver a message to HMS *Intrepid* anchored about 1,500 yds away. I had implored my Captain to anchor closer (say 1,000 yds), but he was adamant. The race had to start and finish from *Fearless's* wardroom. The *Huntress* had to be at deck level and the helo blades spread but cold. Before the pilot could leave the helo the blades had to have stopped rotating. The race started – everybody taking sides. The helo overtook us just short of *Intrepid*. I thought we were doomed but raced back and was hoisted. The pilot beat me to the wardroom by thirty seconds. The champagne was shared, but it did show that the *Huntress*, over short journeys, was quicker and far cheaper than the helo. Honours were even.

The Chinese and Mahjong. A leading steward (Chinese) looked after me. He was superb, faultless at anticipating any potential disasters. He was clever, the leading mahjong player in the ship. The Chinese are great gamblers and sometimes I received complaints from mess-decks above about the noise of the players and the interminable clatter of the mahjong ivory pieces. My leading steward sent more money home to Hong Kong than his pay, simply because he always won. He was good looking and spoke English well. He also had an English driving licence having passed his test in Plymouth. Admirable indeed. But, for a small sum, he agreed several times to pass the test again for his chums, using their names. This worked very well about eight times, but on the ninth one of the examiners recognized him and he went before the Magistrates' Court. Magistrates asked, 'Why do you break the law and pass tests for other people?'. He replied, 'Well Sir, Englishmen say all Chinamen look alike so there is no problem'. This amused the Bench and he received a summary fine. He was thought a hero, and he was.

HMS *Glamorgan* and Trafalgar Night 1972. We had our Trafalgar Night at sea and the next day arrived in Grand Harbour, Valetta, to find HMS *Glamorgan* ('Glamorous Organ') secured to a buoy. Rumour had it that they were to have their 'Night' that evening. I knew their Captain well; he was the most senior captain afloat in the Royal Navy and was soon to be promoted to Rear Admiral. I had just turned in at about 2330, when I heard a commotion outside my door. It was flung open by an enlivened Surgeon Lieutenant in white mess dress, with others behind him. Instantly I recognized him as the Captain of *Glamorgan*. He greeted me with affection. We were raided! I grabbed my phone, called the Commander (S) requesting all officers to the wardroom. We all assembled two decks down, the *Fearless* officers in pyjamas, the 'Organs' in mess kit, and held one hell of a party. Our doctor played a trombone, so it was all delightfully noisy but well away from the ship's company. Around 0200 Tom Baird said he had gone up three decks to visit my Captain, who had sent him away and slept on. I paid little attention and the party went on until dawn, when we poured our guests into one of the assault craft at deck level and lowered them into the sea. The RM coxswain was ordered to accelerate hard; the guests all fell into the bottom of the craft amid cheers and a lusty farewell.

Next morning, after colours, my Captain took me aside and said 'I really must demand that you take better control of the wardroom. Last night most ghastly noises went on all night. And do you know, a drunken Surgeon Lieutenant shook me and asked if I wanted to buy a battleship'. He was very angry. After further deprecating discussions, I said to him, 'Did you know who the Surgeon Lieutenant was?' 'Of course I didn't' he replied. I told him it was Tom Baird, Captain of *Glamorgan*. He was shattered. 'Oh what can I do? I haven't called on him, and he is the most senior captain afloat, and the senior officer in the harbour.' I said that Tom had invited me to breakfast at 0830, perhaps he would like me to take a note to him. So that is what happened. I arrived in the DLG by boat and had a champagne breakfast with Tom, who sent a signal to *Fearless*: 'Last night I was entertained with all the old world custom of Trafalgar Night and I thank you all for the courtesy of entertaining me and my officers – yes do please call at your convenience.' All was well that ended very well indeed. My Captain eventually became the Second Sea Lord while Captain Baird a Knighted Vice Admiral as Flag Officer Scotland and Northern Ireland. I remained a Commander.

Chaplain
The Reverend John Oliver, Royal Navy
Later, OBE

A burnt child receiving a present from HMS *Fearless*. **The Reverend John Oliver on the left.**

It is difficult to write adequately on the role of the Chaplain in HMS *Fearless* in a short article so this is only a sketch. As in other appointments in the Royal Navy the Chaplain's primary task is the conduct of Divine Worship. He is also required to be the 'friend and adviser' of all on board. This means making himself available to every individual regardless of rank or status, giving him the unique privilege of being able to visit every part of ship. If he is to care for his people properly he is called to deal with the 'whole man' by playing an active role in seeking to ensure a good quality of life for all within the confines of a floating home, away from normal family life. Different Chaplains have different ways of approaching their tasks and operating under the authority of different captains so any account is a subjective one.

In the absence of a permanent Chapel, worship on board *Fearless* was conducted in any suitable space: on weekdays a daily service of Holy Communion was held in an office space while for the main Sunday service a dining hall or space on the upper deck was used. There was a compartment known as the Chapel on 02 deck with 'ecclesiastical' wooden chairs but it also doubled as the Naval Staff Office. Since worship involves the offering of the life of the ship the Chaplain must be involved in that life. In my own case this meant serving on the Ship's Welfare Committee, many hours of mess-deck and part-of-ship visiting, organizing indoor games competitions, teaching periods with Midshipmen under training and, above all, being available for individual calls for help or advice.

Some welfare problems could take much time – with just two brief anecdotes serving as examples. During Exercise NORTHERN MERGER a signal was received requiring the urgent return home of a rating whose wife was seriously ill. To ensure his speedy recovery to the United Kingdom a Sea King helicopter was called to lift him to Esjberg in Denmark en route for a civilian flight. To ensure that all went smoothly the Chaplain – myself – was to accompany him as far as the airport. With no notice, and straight from the middle of an exercise, I left the ship in action working dress and without any money. I saw him to his flight and only then discovered that no arrangements had been made to pick me up. I went to the control tower to get in touch with the ship but after several abortive attempts using all the military links available a member of the staff used an ordinary land line and got straight through. I was instructed to make contact with the Danish Army who hosted me in the field that night from where I was eventually picked up by a Royal Marine helicopter whose pilot had no idea where *Fearless* was – and nor should he have known as he was based ashore. However, he did manage to find HMS *Bulwark* from where, 30 hours after leaving, I flew to *Fearless*. But at least the rating was back home in time. On another occasion, in Antigua, a young sailor got himself into prison after an alcohol-fuelled folly and so I spent most of my time on that visit seeing him and liaising with the prison authorities.

Welfare matters of another kind were more congenial. Most ships have a pet charity for each commission and in *Fearless* we adopted the children's burns unit based in Royal Naval Hospital, Stonehouse.[474] The Welfare Committee organized fund-raising events and with the proceeds purchased play items for the children, some of whom came from homes with little material possessions and even less affection. One child had severe burns through child abuse. Our visits to the hospital were always greeted with joy and sailors and Royal Marines are always especially caring for children in need.

Another example of the extra duties sometimes given to an embarked Chaplain manifested itself when I was asked by my Commanding Officer – John Rumble – to organize a Sons-At-Sea day. This turned out, in practice, to be a dress rehearsal for a visit by Princess Margaret and her two children. In response to the general invitation eighteen youngsters were embarked at Plymouth and landed at Portsmouth two days later. I had to organize a daily programme which made sure that they were 'kept out of mischief' and with the unstinting help from all departments the youngsters had a good time. They were divided between different messes each night and the sailors and Midshipmen ensured a more or less happy stay – some of them were not enamoured with the confines of their messdeck bedrooms!

I was also involved in children's parties and these form an almost essential part of life in HM Ships. At home we assisted at the Christmas party of the children's ward I have mentioned but on board preference was given to disadvantaged children and the sight of their happy faces was always a rich reward for the Herculean efforts of members of the ship's company.

The Chaplain was, in *Fearless* – and throughout today's fleet – not only the Chaplain for the ship but the representative of the English Church wherever the ship may go. This involves visiting and liaising with the local church which, sometimes, could throw up unexpected hazards. When *Fearless* was off Long Island in the British Virgin Islands the Chaplain was offered transport ashore by one of the LCAs during their landing exercises. He was assured that it would be a 'dry' landing

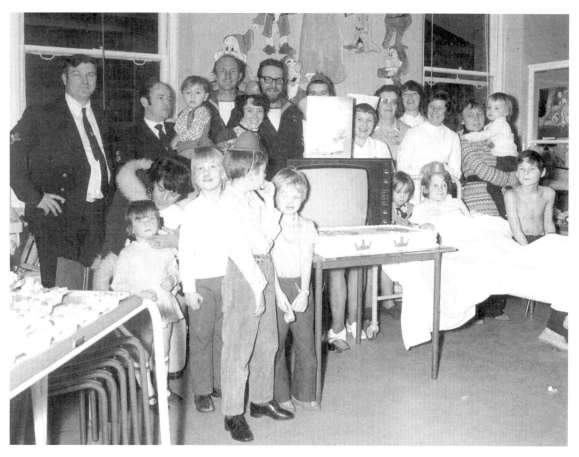

Burnt children's ward, Royal Naval Hospital, Stonehouse.

so I was in full clerical rig. When invited to disembark I did so into two feet of good salt water much to the amusement not only of the 'Royals' but the local priest who just happened to be watching. A sense of humour is a necessary part of that 'clerical rig'! On that occasion I was able to take a service in a local school and the wetting was worth the while.

During her time as the Dartmouth Training Ship, *Fearless*'s Chaplain held regular Chaplain's Hours with small groups of Midshipmen. The subjects for discussion were chosen by each group and while often lively were constructive and moved beyond the confines of things merely nautical. Muslim Midshipmen had their own group and were happy to spend time with a Christian Minister. For them the question of food was of importance and, as a result of their complaint that rations at Dartmouth always seemed to include pork sausages, was heeded. A useful side benefit!

Although the ship's Chaplain, my remit included the families at home and so whenever we returned to our home port there were baptisms to be arranged, homes to be visited on pastoral matters and weddings to be conducted. Having to christen seven babies at one service was one of the many highlights of my ministry in the ship – a fairly noisy but very happy occasion.

In many ways the most difficult part of the Chaplain's ministry in any ship concerns his status. Although he lives in the wardroom he must not be identified as a 'ranking' officer and for that reason his uniform bears no distinguishing badge of office and is, simply, the unadorned reefer jacket of a naval officer. His cap badge is similar in style to an officer's but is black with only the outline edged with gold wire. Although uniform was and is required for certain occasions more than often I worked in civilian clergyman's rig. Regulations state that 'he should be accorded the respect owing to his position'. Such respect has to be earned – it doesn't just happen. If he is perceived as an authoritative figure he could easily cease to have credible authority as a priest. On the other hand if he tries to be 'one of the lads' he easily loses respect. He must be himself.

The framework of all his relationships is his daily discipline of prayer and worship. It is this that enables him, through whatever personal gifts he has, to seek to represent the God he serves to the men he serves, and the men he serves to the God he serves. No one on board *Fearless* had a greater privilege and I was a lucky man.

Annex C

Master at Arms
Warrant Officer First Class Kevin Williams MBE

L. to R. The last MAA, Kevin Williams, Lieutenant Commander Stillwell-Cox, Captain Cunningham, unknown MP, CPO Kev Garner, Commodore Miller, unknown Midshipman, unknown MP, Commander Warren, Lieutenant Commander Berry, CWEM Steve Rule, CMEM Walker.

My first encounter with *Fearless* was in late 1973 for a few days' sea familiarization training as a boy seaman. I subsequently joined her in November 1999 until Aug 02 as the WO1 (MAA). It was the finest appointment I have had in my thirty-two-year career and my final appointment at sea. I could not have served anywhere better and if she were still in commission I would still be there today. Receiving the MBE in the Queen's Birthday Honours in Jun 03, on recommendation from Commodore Millar, Captain Cunningham and Commander Warren was an award I was privileged to receive on behalf of all the wonderful people of *Fearless*. A most fitting tribute to round off my career.

There were so many fine people serving on board during my appointment, I apologize now for not mentioning each and every one of them. They all deserve my sincerest thanks for their dedication and support for a job well done. I would like to say a personal thank you to my staff RPO Justin Newbury, RPO Fiona Wright and LReg Dave McCracken. Also a special mention to WOMEA Ken Kealing MBE, Steve (Canteen Manager), Cpl George Summers, LS Scouse Gwilliam, POMEM Tony Teague, CPOMEM Dave Delaney, Cpl Billy Graham, AB Noel Whatley, Lt Cdr Craig Jones, Lt Cdr Ken Aitken, WWTR Tracey Poultney, all Departmental Coordinators and Cpls/LHOMs and Capt Stuart Rule RM who sadly died in a tragic diving accident at Fountain Lake Jetty, Portsmouth Naval Base.

I remember shedding a tear with Captain Tom Cunningham in his cabin when they announced that *Fearless* would pay off on return from our extended deployment in March 2002; much earlier than expected and leaving the United Kingdom without an amphibious capability. Can you imagine how the ship's company felt? Glad and relieved that the deployment was coming to an end, but sad and apprehensive of the uncertainty of the ship decommissioning.

The majority of the engineers had only been extended in the Service because of their expertise in the running of *Fearless*, many of whom had served in her in excess of ten years and in some cases this was their third or fourth draft to the ship.

These people were extremely skilled. If something went wrong mechanically, and if we had not robbed it from our sister ship or could not get it off the shelf, it would have to be hand made. In many cases this meant making it on board. I often walked past the Engineers' workshop late in the evening to see the lathes turning and another piece of equipment undergoing repair or manufacture. I am sure without their skills we may well have spent hours not underway.

The seamen on board did not opt to transfer to the Warfare Branch, therefore *Fearless* was their one and only sea billet. You can imagine the anxiety that these people felt. I had Able Seaman Noel Whatley, who had served twenty-two years in the Royal Navy and had been granted a two-year extension of service, on board. His sole job was to process, compact and store all the gash in three large chacons in the Lower Vehicle Deck until we could land it ashore. On most occasions 100 personnel for two hours would be required for this mammoth evolution. Whatley's dedication to the long hours in a very unpleasant work environment (the heat and smell of rotting food etc. was indescribable) was recognized by all. He richly deserved two Commanding Officer's prizes for his outstanding contribution. However, this was no substitute for the uncertainty of his remaining time in the Service.

The people of *Fearless* are what made the ship. They were fantastic in every sense. The majority of disciplinary cases were of a minor nature and I put this down to an older average age of the ship's company and their pride of serving in *Fearless*. The ethos was 'work hard and play hard' and most adopted this without question! The camaraderie was second to none. Even though she was a very old lady – 1950's technology and living conditions were deplorable – everyone accepted their lot. Let's face it, the majority of the CPOs lived in a 40-man mess-deck, likewise did the POs and the JRs of similar sizes without any recreational space within the mess-deck. I clearly remember some of the female members asking me where they could stow all their civilian clothing, uniform and personal items including make-up and hair dryers etc. because their lockers were the old style and were much smaller than they had been used to on the newer and more modern ships. They soon learnt the difference between what was necessary and what was desirable! The ship and its routines were run much like the old style navy and it was a well-tuned engine. When I first joined the ship I was frequently reminded by the 'old hands' that the routines worked well and they pleaded with me not to change things. I accepted that it would be a pointless exercise to upset them by bringing the ship into the twenty-first century!

The embarked personnel enjoyed their time with us and they preferred *Fearless* rather than *Ocean*. *Ocean* was too impersonal, accommodation was a one rather large open plan space and they could never keep themselves fit because the upper deck was out of bounds for the majority of time because of helicopter operations. Although *Fearless* was old they were all accommodated in small mess-decks with televisions, VCRs and a beer fridge! The food was good and the homemade bread was excellent. Additionally, the upperdeck was in bounds 95 per cent of the time for them to carry out their fitness routine. *Fearless* knew how to look after her guests, whether Embarked Forces or others.

In my time on board I served with two Commodores (COMATG) three Captains and two Commanders (XOs). All had their own very different personalities and commanded in their own style. Commodore Kilgour[475] and Captain Fanshawe were a team that liked a drink and socializing with all. Captain Fanshawe always introduced himself on the ship's main broadcast as the 'Cruise Director'! He once entered my office to inform me that the quality of the print of Daily

Orders was sub-standard. I informed him that the printer had seen better days and there was no money in the pot for a replacement. He then instructed me to un-plug the printer, which I did, he then picked it up and I followed him out on to the port waist where he threw the printer over the side and into the sea. He then turned to me and said 'See the Supply Officer for a new one!'

Commodore Miller was a little eccentric and enjoyed hiding his toy soldiers in the Captain's Day Cabin! On completion of Captain's Requestmen/Defaulters he would tell me that his toy soldiers had informed him what had taken place! He referred to me on the ship's main broadcast as 'War Dog Williams' or as his 'Welsh Fusilier'. He was humorous, well liked, respected and was a people's person, a man's man. Captain Parry was teetotal but still enjoyed socializing. He loved his rugby and the Royals. He may even have been a Royal Marine in a previous life! He did not always see eye to eye with Commodore Kilgour especially over whether to anchor or to complete dock operations underway! Captain Cunningham and Commander Warren were a great team and were here, there and everywhere. They wanted to know everything about their people and they remembered every little detail about them. They were humorous, well liked and respected. They listened and wanted others' views before making their final decision. They definitely made life a little easier on board especially during the last and very demanding extended deployment, post the 9/11 attack. I value their qualities and friendship.

As the senior Non Commissioned Officer on board my position as disciplinarian, administrator and coordinator, combined with many aspects of a ratings' welfare in which I had personal involvement, made me an invaluable link between the Command and the ship's company as: Whole Ship Coordinator; Regulating Staff Officer (Senior Service Policeman); Assistant Security Officer; Assistant Education Officer; Between Decks Officer; Senior Customs Officer and Mail Officer.

As any Seagoing Regulator will tell you, the evolution of mustering and accounting for spare hands for any given emergency is a slick procedure that is trained for with regular monotony. It's an evolution not to be taken lightly, for when a real emergency occurs, the procedure operates as it should; men and women are accounted for and manpower is provided to where it is needed by the Command. Enter the laundrymen.... A collective group of Chinese and Gurkhas of strong moral fibre, but who possess a distinct dislike for fresh air, and the participation in Emergency Stations! Prizing these individuals out of the depths of *Fearless*'s laundry facility was at best difficult, and at worst physically impossible.

'FOST? Who are they?'

'A Training Organization, which is of no concern to them.'

'What's more important, a not so pressed shirt or Emergency Stations?'

You can see the dilemma for the Regulating Petty Officer orchestrating the evolution. Tired of bearing the brunt of those in 'Green Jackets', who innocently ask 'Doesn't *Fearless* have Laundry Staff', the RPO allocated a specific job to a young rating to attend the laundry on commencement of the evolution. His instructions were simple, shout, scream and intimidate until said laundrymen arrive on the flight deck. If this failed (and it generally did), provide written confirmation of named laundrymen working in their facility. FOST Staff would quip 'I want laundrymen in lifejackets'. These comments were always met with the reply 'If you want them, go and get them, it's not your shirts they're going to wreck if you piss them off!' This well known scenario is played out on many ships, and it would be fair to say the Regulator always played second fiddle to the will of the laundrymen.

The year is 2000 and the *Mighty Lion* is now in the Mediterranean, having just left the port of Antalya, Turkey bound for the war torn shores of Sierra Leone. At about 0510 in the morning the General Alarm sounds. Sailors and Marines pause to register for a few moments before leaping into action and moving swiftly towards their respective emergency station. Every member of the ship's company has a sense that this is the real deal, so they move with a sense of purpose and true professionalism. The RPO attends the flight deck to start mustering the spare hands. As he moves from the port waist, the flight deck is obscured by a thick acrid black smoke; he moves through it and is relieved to see squads of spare hands fell in by department, being mustered by their trusty coordinators. Within nine minutes, much quicker than the FOST bogey time, all hands are mustered, and the flight deck is reported as correct to the WO (MAA) on the bridge.

It is at this juncture that the RPO feels a tug at his shirt. . . . 'Boss all laundrymen on deck, when we get off?' Turning he sees the No.1 laundryman (an ex-Warrant Officer Gurkha), armed with rucksack of belongings and wearing his already inflated lifejacket.

Imagine a freshly made cup of tea and the peace and tranquillity surrounding the Petty Officer of the Watch on deck drinking it on the upper deck before 'call the hands' in the sun drenched Gulf of Oman. Enter a Short Engagement Seaman (SE(S)) who resembled 'Private Pile' from the motion picture *Full Metal Jacket*. After scanning the horizon the DPO's attention turned to the stern of the ship to observe the SE(S) running towards the port quarter of the flight deck at speed. Without pausing or slowing down young 'Private Pile' jumped over the side and started swimming. Poised with disbelief, the DPO started to move towards the upper deck tannoy to report the incident to the Bridge, while the Chief of the Flight Deck launched a Perry Buoy. A Man Overboard procedure occurred and 'Private Pile' was duly recovered.

With the rating ensconced in the sickbay and medical checks completed the WO (MAA) went for a chat! A man not easily lost for words, he was bewildered by the reply of young SE(S), when asked why he had jumped over board. 'I just fancied a swim Sir; I was a bit hot you see!' An opinion was quickly formed that the young SE(S) needed recuperation in the UK!

HMS *Fearless*, being such an old lady, needed plenty of tender loving care. This typically took place at her Base Port of Portsmouth, usually for six or seven months of the year! The ship's company were used to the domestic disruptions during maintenance periods and adapted well to the hardships encountered: closed heads, poor heating, no hot water, ad hoc showering facilities and dust and grime all adding to the enjoyment of life. Most affected were the male members of the ship's company, who were scarred for life by observing the daily ritual of the dressing-gown clad Senior Rate Wrens going for their morning showers and constitutionals! The gangway staff got used to seeing the frightening sight of them waddling across the flight deck to the port side gantry and came to know the sight well: even able to set their watches by the precision of the morning waddle!

The ship's company of HMS *Fearless* was definitely blessed with characters. These individuals made life all the more pleasant. Humour came in various forms, maybe a joke here and there, or the reciting of a humorous anecdote by an individual that always claimed he was there. Whole Ship Flight and Vehicle Deck functions were always well supported and a great success. Participants often turned up in fancy dress, and it is universally known that Royal Marines like cross-dressing (or was that dressing up)! One such SNCO from 4 ASRM (we'll save his blushes) had made a considerable effort for one of the many functions. Observed departing one of the Junior Rate Wrens messes by the RPO who was on rounds, he was stopped. Wearing a sleeveless denim jacket, pink tutu, plastic Roman centurion's helmet, combat boots and carrying a plastic sword, did not unnerve the RPO at all. 'Where have you been?' the RPO asked. The SNCO replied 'I've been to the onboard beauty salon and had my toenails professionally painted!' Looking at his feet, the RPO duly noted the toecaps of his combat boots had been cut away revealing toes painted in a very fine shade of pink that matched the tutu!

Being normal practice the DPO was conducting his Middle Watch Rounds at approximately 0200. These rounds were not a quick affair due to the large quantity of compartments and messes he had to visit. *Fearless* had been at sea for some weeks and he was used to walking in to darkened messes and listening to the tunes of snoring sailors. On this particular morning the DPO had the company of a Young Officer (YO) whom he had collected from HQ1. It was turning out to be an uneventful set of rounds, everyone where they should be, no illicit drinking or high seas frolics were taking place. Only the RM messes to go. Sign off the rounds log in HQ1 and bed! The first mess (2C1) deserted, not a bootneck in bed! Sensing something not quite right the DPO and his eager assistant, who had suddenly come to life, moved to 2C2 mess and opened the door. All of the lights were out, but a bright multi-coloured glow faded in and out in a phase of about five seconds. On the bright phase you could see clearly, with vision greatly reduced when the glow was phased out. Bewildered by this light show and keen to seek out the source and locate the missing booties from 2C1, the DPO and YO moved through the mess, entering the mess square as the light phased out to a dim glow. Realizing that they were not alone (fifty booties just can't sit quietly, no matter how hard they try) the lights phased bright. Confronting the DPO was Charlie Section booties sat and standing in every conceivable space, beer in hand and wide grins on faces, erupting with laughter – and all stark naked except for headgear, flying helmets, hardhats, space helmets, Roman centurion helmets, cowboy hats and an array of wigs. Even Elvis's quiff was in the building!

'Should I go and get the XO now?' asked the YO.

'I'm sure that will please him a whole lot' replied the DPO.

As the mess light came on the DPO noted a myriad of Christmas tree lights criss-crossed across the deckhead (bloody ingenious these bootnecks)! Singling out the mess corporal, illuminating the errors of his ways and what corrective action was required, the DPO departed the mess to complete his rounds. On checking Charlie Section messes a short while later, all booties were snoring like babies, the mess was squared away, gash ditched and the beer fridges were locked! The YO they tell me is okay, still serving, but comes out in a nervous rash every time a man wearing green winks at him!

The XO[476] had conceived a brilliant plan for the CTP on 2 September 2001 in Cadiz. Accordingly the commanding officers from the adjacent ships in the Task Group arrived shortly before 7 p.m. for pre-action calibration drinks with the embarked Flag. Their officers arrived just after 7 p.m., and with the other host officers congregated in the wardroom for a quick sharpener and briefing from the XO himself. So far so good.

Guests arrive, pipes, bugles, whistles, salutes and fanfares smartly dispensed as and where appropriate. Amazing precision stuff, all personnel present, correct and immaculate in whites, with smart car door openers, a small Royal Marines Guard at the bottom of the gangway and a posse of eager YOs to escort guests to the drinks area on the for'ard deck under the crisp and taut awning, where hosts were ready to pounce in their dozens. More than a hundred guests turned up on this beautiful, balmy evening, and were generously and most ably hosted by the Task Group officers.

The VIPs took their positions, whereupon the band marched on, the guard marched on, and the ceremonial ensign lowering team took their position under the ensign staff – each with great precision and even greater panache, ready for the sunset ceremony.

However, undeterred by this, enter Billy, three sheets to the wind from his run ashore, spoiling for a fight and absolutely determined that no-one, not even the Queen's Guard, was going to stop him getting back to his mess-deck pit for some much needed zzzzeds.

Now, XO senses trouble and dispatches the OOD2 to intercept him at the bottom of the gangway and then, shielding the fortunately-small-in-stature Admiral's view of the affray with his not inconsiderable bulk, XO then sends reinforcements in the form of the DCO. This tactic proved effective, albeit momentarily, and the XO breathed a sigh of relief and the band played on.

Five pleasurable minutes passed and the sense of peace, the rhythm of the bass drum and enjoyment was next disturbed by the ominous sound of the blues and twos sirens ready to escort the VIPs home. The following is a loose extract from a report sent to higher authorities.

At this juncture, Billy (let's call him that to preserve anonymity)[477] departed the bottom of the brow. A short while later Billy was seen attempting to climb the head rope and he then, losing his grip as he swung precariously from the line, fell into the harbour. At this moment Leading Seaman Harry (name changed), who was returning from his own run ashore, dived, from not too inconsiderable height, into the harbour to assist Billy.

Alas no rescue award for LS Harry for Billy was quite indignant at the suggestion that he required assistance. He made his feelings clear to LS Harry and in the mêlée of thrashing arms and legs interrupted by gargles of energetic explanation, poor LS Harry ended up the worse of the two and with more than just his pride dented. Witnessing this whole affair and sensing impending disaster, Chief Petty Officer Mick (name changed), with great presence of mind, raced from the fo'c'sle to the port waist for a Perry buoy. Then, with more enthusiasm than accuracy, hurled it over the side to aid the flailing swimmers. Instead of landing conveniently near his intended targets, the Perry buoy, almost like a Frisbee, arced gracefully towards the jetty. Among the audience that had been drawn to this little affray watching the events unfold was an elderly holiday maker based on a nearby cruise liner who was out for a stroll with his wife. Fortunately, this expensive and important life-saving device was spared from damage, when its fall towards the concrete was cushioned by the chest of the elderly gentleman, who by the way, also suffered from angina. This poor gentleman, for his troubles, then promptly collapsed. Enter now the PMO. In the middle of a tear jerking, moving and dramatic ceremonial sunset, the medical team less than surreptitiously made their way past the VIP guests and clattered down the brow to attend the felled spectator. The finale 'Last Post' was synchronized and accompanied beautifully by more blues and twos; this time it was an ambulance to take away the forlorn casualty. Subsequent inquiries are ongoing regarding medical costs, ambulance charges and the expensive cruise liner holiday which the gentleman had unfortunately missed while incapacitated in hospital.

Billy, meanwhile, was clearly enjoying himself, having embarked on a lazy breaststroke across the darkened harbour. A slow panic now began to ensue as it slowly dawned on everyone that he might drown. The duty watch was now scrambled, boats deployed and searchlights and signal lamps blazed over the water. Despite all this activity he cheerfully evaded the efforts of the first harbour pilot boat and, managing to dodge other incoming vessels, he eventually reached the bow of a large cruise liner moored on the far side. Spookily, this was the very ship from whence the injured spectator had walked. After a short period taking the evening air, while standing on the bulbous bow of the ship, he resumed his swim. By this time, the ship's seaboat had reached the scene and a merry chase ensued during which there were several more occasions when he was feared drowned. Fortunately, after 1 hour and 20 minutes, with the strains of 'Hearts of Oak' long gone and all guests clear, a somewhat bedraggled Billy was brought back on board. He was still fully clad but, predictably, had lost his ID card.

It did not take long for the PMO and DCO to determine that Billy had had one or two sherbets too many and he passed the remainder of the evening under the 'protective supervision' of 4 mess mates! Strangely, the film crew seemed to have covered very little of the flight deck ceremony, appearing to find the nocturnal swim far more newsworthy.[478]

We cannot begin to tell of the tumultuous emotions that assailed the beleaguered XO that evening, suffice to say he did not go ashore on completion, but eventually went to his cabin and rested after a very stiff G&T at about midnight, to mull over a busy session of investigation, recrimination and explanations which would inevitably start early the next day.

Detachment Sergeant Major
Warrant Officer Second Class Barrie Knight, Royal Marines

Warrant Officer 2 Barrie Knight briefs HRH Prince Philip on the return of HMS *Fearless* from the South Atlantic.

I was walking across the flight deck of *Fearless*, in the Portsmouth Naval Base thinking of Easter leave and then on to Hamburg. I remembered the newspapers were full of stories of the Argentinian invasion of the Falkland Islands. At that moment the Captain came up the gangway three steps at a time and said, 'Mr Knight, we are at four days' notice to sail, we are going south!'

I put my brain into overdrive and remembered all the things that needed to be done. I made lots of notes very quickly: next of kin forms, first aid courses, respirator tests, all personnel to have first field dressings, anti flash gear available and spare sets on LCUs and LCVPs. All ranks must know at least three ways of getting from their mess-deck to the flight deck or to the side of the ship, they must be able to do this by day and night and wearing gas masks. I had remembered an incident on a US aircraft carrier when eighty men died from smoke inhalation because they only knew one way out from their mess-deck. I resolved to make sure this wouldn't happen in *Fearless*.

Escape hatches in messes must be free from paint and easy to open. A few years ago ratings died when trapped under the escape hatch because it had been sealed by paint. ID discs must be worn at all times and able to be read. I must train ranks on GPMG drills and aircraft recognition, some evening instruction would be necessary to cover this. Scuttle covers must be checked and free from paint on the clips. First Field Dressings must be taped onto bulkheads and above doors, to be readily available. Copies of next of kin forms to be held in the office and also the Captain's office – and so the list went on.

The next few days were a hive of activity: loading stores of all kinds and never clearing the backlog of lorries from the jetty, ammunition of all types and boxes and boxes of tinned food.

Personnel on leave return, and the Embarked Force comes on board. We sailed on Monday 6 April 1982 and what a send off Portsmouth gave us. In one of the houses on the port side a lady was standing in her window naked from the waist up, the marines on 03 deck thought this was very good and so did I. It kept us all interested!

I asked if anyone had ever fired at fast moving aircraft and the answer came back as a resounding 'No'. I had to start teaching very quickly, I couldn't just say 'Lead!' I had actually fired GPMGs at drone aircraft on Salisbury Plain many times; however we only ever managed to hit one! This was therefore, a sobering thought as we had fired 64,000 rounds on four courses and hit almost nothing.

We started test firing of GPMGs on the lench poles. In order to do this, the Royal Marines' galley party became upper deck gun crews. It took time to enable them to fire bursts of fifty rounds and to understand the point of aim and the beaten zone. After practice their confidence improved and so did their gun drills. I was very pleased with them but the real test was still to come.

Tensions began to grow in a quiet sort of way after leaving Ascension Island and we embarked 40 Commando from *Canberra*. I put one company in the wardroom, the others in the Chiefs' Mess and Dining Hall. This was a very good time seeing old friends and they settled in quickly.

I asked the Captain if Phalanx Cannon with ammo, could be dropped to us by air from Ascension Island as these were rapid firing with a range of two miles. I knew they had been fitted to Vulcan bombers but alas I was told they were no longer available, having been sold on. So as usual we had to make do! By this time I was now able to use four GPMGS situated on 03 deck, which were able to fire over the flight deck.

I went to the 40 Commando briefing and they were happy with all the work that had been done for them. They were ready to go! I could see the huge amount of kit being carried by each man and I asked the Bridge if any members of the crew could help the Commandos down the ladders on their excursion to the vehicle decks. The help offered was superb, every spare man on board turned out to assist.

While the Commandos were loading we could hear the firing on Fanning Head keeping everybody alert, for it was no longer a drill! As dawn came up it was time for all upper deck guns to be manned. I watched, as guns were uncovered, trays and weapons checked and belts of 3,000 rounds loaded. Steel helmets and flak jacks on, a first aid box by the funnel. All guns were now manned until dark. Tension was at a high point searching for the first enemy plane to come down San Carlos Water. I heard 'Enemy planes at forty miles and closing'. I saw them and cried 'Aim below them, they are coming straight at us and downwards, watch your tracer, fire bursts of fifty or more'. The battle passed and all was quiet for a short while then another wave came in and the battle commenced again. This time the young marines were ready for them and gave a good fight. The gunners quickly gained in confidence and I was pleased to see their reactions quicken as they fired long bursts whilst watching the beaten zone in the sky. By the end of that first day the marines on the guns were nearly knee deep in empty cylinders and were exhausted. They had learnt a lot. Now they had to clean the guns and re-supply ammunition. I noticed they looked after their guns just as if they were looking after their own mother. Great care was taken of each and every piece. They had grown up today and were doing what they had joined the Corps to do.

The upper deck gun crews were given soya bread at midday and tea, while on their positions, served to them by a small Naval Rating. This task quickly became jinxed as it seemed every time he appeared, all hell would break loose, then he could be seen on all fours dragging a large paper sack and a kettle across the deck. His head, covered in sweat, would come up over the sandbags and a voice would say 'Lunch', and then quickly disappear back down again. We liked him a lot and used to laugh about it, once the shooting had stopped.

On 23 May HMS *Antelope* took a direct hit and at 2020 the UXB exploded and the ship caught fire. The crew were rescued by LCU and LCVPs. They were brought to HMS *Fearless* and the Master at Arms and myself began to muster names of the crew as they came into the vehicle decks. Some were suffering from shock and had difficulty in remembering their names but others helped them and we rang around the messes to see what spare beds were available. If we were told five we asked if they could take seven or eight, they all did: no one refused. All the Senior Rates went to the Sergeants' Mess as I knew it to be almost empty. The bar was opened and Sergeant Woolhead served coffee.

The question being asked time and time again was, had we got the whole crew on board? I raced off and with the aid of the Master at Arms we had mustered all of them by midnight. I went back to the Sergeants' Mess and told them the good news; I thought they would then go to sleep but instead, they all cheered like mad and started drinking at a rapid rate, making sure I joined in too. I rang the Commander and told him the situation. He said to let them go on and write off the cost. I went to sleep just after two a.m. and was up again by six o'clock. I went to see HMS *Antelope* slip sadly beneath the waves with not a word said by anyone watching.

HMS *Argonaut* was hit by two bombs and towed back into San Carlos Water by the LCUs from HMS *Fearless*: this was surely a sight to see, little LCUs pulling and pushing a great big war ship. The next day as one of the naval engineers was working off a Carley Float, repairing the side of the ship, we went to Air Raid Warning Red at which time the personnel holding his lines let go and went to Action Stations. There was a bit of a swell and a wind that day which caught hold of the Carley Float and off the engineer floated down San Carlos Water. One or two bombs were seen to explode in close proximity to his float. I imagine this must have frightened him considerably for a lone figure could be seen with arms flailing lest we forgot to pick him up!

Back on deck an Argentine jet exploded above the ship and all of the gun positions were covered in pieces of canopy, steel and alloy: the sandbags did their job and saved lives. We were very lucky that there were no fatalities. In the heat of the battle it was difficult to work out who had hit the plane and who had seen exactly what had happened. The pilot ejected and was captured by *Fearless*. We cleaned up the decks as best we could and the battle recommenced.

By now I now had to carry a full list of all ranks on board and in the evening the first job was to sit with the Master at Arms and bring the list up to date. This took quite some time because of the landings on deck and SBS and SAS turning up at all hours. A water sterilization team also came on board and I put them to sleep in the vehicle decks. They were supposed to go ashore next day but I was busy and we took them to sea with us. I was elsewhere the following day and forgot them again so I told the Corporal to ask the Bridge to contact me the very next day to remind me to drop them. However it was another four days before I managed finally to get them ashore. They said being below decks during a bombing attack was a terrible thing to sit through, they had never been in ships before. I laughed and shook hands with them as they left; they were pleased to go.

The Captain asked me to go ashore with the Chief GI to look at 20-mm cannon which were at Goose Green, then fly them back to the ships so they could be used on board for defence. The guns were new and looked to be very good. We had taken the Captain's Secretary with us because all the instructions were in German and he was able to read the language. However, the area had not been cleared of mines so we needed to move in single file. While working on the gun the Secretary wandered away from us and picked up one of the weapons, idly he pressed the trigger and let off a burst of fire. We all jumped ten feet in the air and promised to kill him if he touched anything else again!

A Sea King helicopter arrived late that afternoon with a crew all very smart and clean dressed in their flying suits. I asked them to lift the gun to *Fearless*. They queried the weight, we were all tired, dirty and in no mood for discussion so just told them to 'Lift it'. We also loaded the cab with

20-mm ammo, which they were none too pleased about either. They returned and shut down the engine but again we asked them to take another gun plus ammunition, which they did. It was only then we found out that they were anti-submarine crew, so were not used to these sorts of excursions and this was their first day on the job: they were good at it by the next day.

The following day, back in Goose Green again, was spent lifting guns and helping the Paras get 35-mm cannon working: as we walked back to the helicopter pad with the RSM of the Paras a loud explosion happened some 200 metres away: we hit the deck at speed. Large pieces of shrapnel flew in all directions and we could see that the ammo dump had exploded. Bodies were everywhere, one man was seen to be ablaze and having had his legs blown off. Mercifully, the RSM was able to assist him and he died without further pain. We stood up and tried to help where else we could but it was just mess all around, my marine who worked long with me said, 'Sir, if I get out of this alive I will live my life every minute of everyday'. I said that was a very good idea and we returned to the ship, dirty, tired and subdued, thinking what a week it had been.

A lighter memory of that week was of a small boy at Goose Green who was given his first bread roll for three weeks. It was covered with a thick layer of butter topped with about an inch of strawberry jam. When he put the sandwich to his mouth all that could be seen above the jam were a pair of dancing eyes and a mop of hair as he took his first bite. The Paras, Gurkhas, Marines and Navy watched and walked away with a new spring in their stride for they had made someone's day at last.

One day Corporal Draper called me to the office saying a parcel had arrived for the Detachment from the manufacturer of Kellogg's corn flakes. I opened it and found inside Mars bars, Bounty bars, chocolate biscuits and all sorts of goodies which were packed on top of loads of pairs of ladies knickers in all shapes and sizes, many complete with a lipstick message. One such message read 'You may be lonely, but I am with you'. Word quickly got round and a queue formed along the passage. One of the young Marines picked up a pair of the knickers and stretched them over his steel helmet, they fitted perfectly with the leg holes just above his ears. This soon caught on and the Gun Crews could be seen with coloured heads. I have to say, however, the larger sized pairs did look terrible and were soon rejected. Later on a very senior officer could not believe his eyes at seeing so much colour on tin hats and was lost for words when told what they were.

The 8 June was a very sad day for all of us. Two aircraft attacked LCU *Foxtrot Four* and the crew were killed with the exception of two. I went to the Sergeants' Mess to reflect on the loss. They however, would have wanted us to fight on, so I resolved to do just that, with every tool available and every man on board. Next day I looked at the gun crews, and stretcher-bearers and it seemed they all had a steely look in their eyes and fingers never far away from triggers: it seemed everyone had had the same thoughts. The Captain asked if I thought he should speak to the Detachment. I said 'No, they are all busy and want to get on with the job at hand'. He agreed.

One night I had a phone call to say that prisoners had come on board and would I go to the vehicle decks and sort them out. I arrived to see ten Argentinian prisoners lying on the deck with their hands tied behind their backs with parachute cord. Their hands were swollen and they were in some pain. At this time Marines arrived to take over the guard duties. I also noticed one of the prisoners was very well dressed in a new combat suit and he appeared to be listening to what we said. I told him to get to his feet and informed him that they were prisoners on board HMS *Fearless*, to which he replied that *Fearless* has been sunk and where were the rest of his men? I told him I didn't know where his men were but would find out and reassured him that he was indeed on board HMS *Fearless*. He complained that his men were in pain from the tight ropes on their wrists. I said I had seen that already and I requested permission to take them off. I told him anyone trying to escape or reach a hatch cover would be shot, boots had to be removed and legs crossed at all times. They were all searched again to make sure there were no hidden weapons and then food was to be brought to them. I found out this man was an officer and he demanded a cabin of his own under the Geneva Convention. I told him this was not possible and they were to stay where they were until tomorrow.

About this time mail arrived on board and I was at a loss to understand why there were eight bags of the stuff for the Detachment. It soon became clear when we found out that one of my Marines had written to the newspapers asking for a pen friend. I think half of England had replied. Every marine had ten letters or more and it became the order of the day to sort them into 'eligibles'. The older ladies' photos were given to the Sergeant Major and I will admit to having a look and some of the girls appeared to be very nice. Soon a 'Gronks' board was erected which got bigger by the day as the mail kept coming. This board was to be a great help to us later on.

Bombs; and a very near miss to the bows of the ship and very close to the forward mess decks. The blast came through the bulkhead and badly frightened two marines in the mess at the time who were both blown off their bunks.

Back on guns at first light, but we now have 'Y' Turret: one 20-mm Rhinemetall twin barrel AA gun. A super bit of kit with a range of over two miles and able to fire 800 rounds per minute of mixed tracer and high explosive. This was great. The next day we decided to test fire 'Y' turret and all the ships around were informed. However, I forgot to tell the flight deck crew and they were pushing a Sea King at the moment when the gun let off 300 rounds. We were not top of the pops that day.

I remember one very cold dark night when all the guns were covered and it was time to grab a bite to eat. Going below, the Junior Ranks' Dining Hall had been commandeered to take the casualties from *Sir Galahad*. The burn cases were terrible to see; nothing had prepared us for those sights. They had clothing melted into their skins, heads so swollen due to water trying to protect the brain. They no longer looked like men. All were in dire pain. There was little any of us could do except give what comfort we could. The Commander came down to see and was shaken by the black swollen heads. It was a learning curve for us all. I went back to the Sergeants' Mess and found it empty: I lay down and tried to sleep as I was back on the guns at first light. In came an LMA as this was now a stand-by sickbay. And so the war went on.

The final assault on Port Stanley began. 3 Commando Brigade captured the high ground to the north of the capital in a night attack. 5 Infantry Brigade took the south of the capital also at night and Major General Moore accepted the surrender at 23:59 on 14 June 1982 after which I went on board HMS *Intrepid* to see if the ship would agree to have a collection for the crew of *Foxtrot Four*. The Commander said they would be pleased to help in any way possible.

On 17 June, *Fearless* moved by night to Port Stanley and anchored in Port William Harbour. On 20th we all went to a Memorial Service in Port Stanley. The Cathedral was full, for the time had now come to slow down, reflect and give thanks. Quite a few tears were shed that day. Afterwards I made my way through the extensive damage and back to the jetty and saw that the Union Jack was once again flying over Government House. The free world tells us that freedom is worth fighting for and that you do not miss it until you have lost it but by then it can be too late to regain.

On 25 June at 2200 we set sail for the UK and for the first time in three months I slept with my boots off. It was nice but seemed very strange.

During this time the ship held a concert to raise money for the next-of-kin of those who were killed. The whole ship took part and the flight deck was seen to be full of stalls. The Detachment 'Gronks' board (spoken about earlier) which by now was eight feet high and thirty feet long containing some 300 photographs and addresses of prospective pen friends was on display at ten pence to walk round. This art gallery was never empty!

We continued north and arrived in Plymouth Sound on 13 July 1982. HRH Prince Philip came on board and was very interested in our 20-mm cannon. He asked if they were German? I told him 'Yes', but explained that the Captain's Secretary could speak the language and had translated so that a team of four had managed to get almost ten guns firing again. He thought that was a job well done. The Commander from HMS *Intrepid* came on board and handed me a cheque for £11,000 pounds raised by the ship's collection for the next of kin of the men who had been killed in *Foxtrot Four*. I was overwhelmed and have to admit to having had a lump in my throat at that moment. It was a magnificent effort made by our sister ship. I was lost for words. God bless them.

We disembarked the Embarked Force and then sailed for Portsmouth where we arrived on 14 July to a tumultuous reception; unbelievable. However on the Bridge the Captain, Commander, the Padre and myself were deep in thought. The task, which lay ahead of us, was not a happy one for we were to meet the families of the men who were killed. I thought this was going to be a long day for us all, but much longer for them. The Captain's wife accompanied the next-of-kin up the gangway and I escorted them to the wardroom. We had cleared the route in readiness.

I had served in Borneo when we had men killed, in the Middle East and in Aden. We had some killed in Northern Ireland, but this time it had been my men, from my mess, and from my ship. I was uptight and full of trepidation. We did all we could to answer their questions and tell them what they wanted to know. It was indeed a long day for us all, but I was touched by the quiet dignity they all showed.

This war had been a team effort and each and every person was a vital part of the ship's company. The war had bonded men together and made life long friends that would never change. The good humour and the will to get on with the job showed at all times and I was proud of my Detachment. They gave kind, friendly support to all ships and all beaches, to prisoners, to casualties, embarking forces, to everyone. It was an episode that none of us who were there will ever forget.

And so I went on leave. My wife said we were to go on holiday to Switzerland and I drove to the hotel and arrived in the dark. We got up next morning and went to breakfast. We were just seated in the dining room when two Swiss jet aircraft flew overhead fast and quite low. They had taken off from a nearby airfield. I think I was seen to jump at least a foot out of my chair. The lady owner, who was standing close by, quietly said to me, 'I think you may have just come back from the Falkland Islands?' I gave a small smile and nodded. That evening, a large bottle of champagne was left in our room.

We drank to absent friends.

Commodore Amphibious Warfare
Commodore A.J.G. Miller, CBE, Royal Navy

Commodore Jamie Miller flanked by Captain Tom Cunningham, Brigadier Roger Lane and the Amphibious Task Group Commanding Officers of SAIF SAREEA II.

Commodore Jamie Miller was COMAW or COMATG embarked in *Fearless* during 2001 and 2002. He had the undoubted privilege of being the last Commodore to fly his Broad Pennant in *Fearless*, fortuitously during her last operation, and offers these reflections in a series of jottings:

Some Mighty Lion *jottings from the General's notebook: nickname 'General' gained as Commander/ Executive Officer of* Ark Royal *1993–1994 when I ran a fairly taut ship to avoid 'women at sea' issues.*

Provenance – COMATG – Commander Amphibious Task Group as they now call COMAW. Some intimate asides of Fearless *operationally: quasi compared to Operation CORPORATE but nevertheless most demanding for the* Mighty Lion*, period August 2001 to May 2002. Cameo memories/thoughts as follows:*

First met her 1970 when a Midshipman in Cavalier *and I visited for a Danish amphibious landing. Next, Corpus Christie 1976 – temporary flag ship for my boss CINCFLEET – I was Flags.*[479]

Then – 25/26 May 1982 – as a Coventry *survivor, passing through a completely darkened tank deck, save for very dim red lighting, being transported from* Broadsword *who had picked a lot of us up and via* Fearless*'s Foxtrot Four, later Foxtrot Juliet, to RFA Fort Austin. I will never forget Foxtrot Four's 2nd Coxswain*[480] *going one-handed up the ladder to* Fort Austin*'s clearway carrying two battered survival suits, cardboard boxes containing all the odds and ends from our pockets; letters, oily* *soaked, from waves etc. because* Fort Austin's *Chief Officer, quite rightly in a decided hurry to clear the anchorage after four days in Bomb Alley, would not send down a line. Later,* Foxtrot Four, *Colour Sergeant Johnston, three of his Royal Marines and LMEM Miller and MEA(P) James were dead.*

Much later, in Cadiz Sep 01, en route to the Gulf I got to know Fearless's *RO Miller. He was eleven when his elder brother in* Foxtrot Four *was killed. He joined because of his brother's death and found a welcoming home in the LPD.*

So I have an intimate connection with Fearless *from 1982. In her twilight I was very honoured to be at a final farewell in the tank deck when we remembered* Foxtrot Four *and Colour Sergeant Johnston and his crew; Mrs Johnston present.*

Fearless *Middle East 2001–2002 snapshots: en route to Exercise SAIF SAREEA II – Amphibious wading with Turks – two very stoic but cheerful Turkish Admirals, seasick in LCU after a fine* Fearless *'band of brothers' lunch. As we returned on board, met with news of a light aircraft colliding with the Twin Towers which led to 11 September aftermath and a late return home for the* Mighty Lion *in May 2002. Intensified security, a move to secure Turkish Naval Base at Ahsez as we planned the move onwards of the amphibious caravanserai,* Fearless, Ocean, Southampton, Nottingham, Monmouth, Sir Tristram, Sir Galahad, Sir Bedivere, Sir Percivale, Fort Rosalie, Fort Austin, Bayleaf, Oakleaf, Roebuck *and STUFT,* MV Tor Anglia. *A fire during this, and fusses over boiler state which was sadly later used as an excuse to pay her off early, out of turn as a savings measure. Much calm and a huge sense of purpose from all on board, huge talent and wealth of experience pervaded – thanks to longevity of service on board and a 1950s/1960s sense of devotion and decorum. As we wended our way onto Masirah, Oman, this kernel of excellence in the Flagship meant that we were able to dispatch 'Fix it' parties to any unit: to fix the Type 42's SCOT Comms or to help the beleaguered small ME party on* Fort Rosalie *clear, over four days, dead jellyfish from the main circs and intakes.*

Fearless *was the best, my jewel, my focal point to engender active, vibrant links between disparate communities – Embarked Military Force to Assault Squadron to ships companies to Merchant Navy; STUFT to United Arab Emirates to Oman to Kuwait and USN allies.*

With the Lion's vibrancy and huge enthusiasm to do everything at 100 per cent understated excellence we were able to kindle a true Nelsonic type of Band of Brothers feeling – Brigade: Roger Lane, Gordon Messenger COS, Will Taylor D/COS, David Capewell CO 40 CDO, Tim Chicken 45 CDO, Paul Ashe CO 29 etc. (all discerning observers!) used to remark that the blue/local relations – due to different programmes had somehow gone misty, now they were hugely alive and positive. This stood me personally in great stead in 2003 off Iraq. Different Flagship, now Ark Royal, *but same people, same players in the main and we did well together thanks to that original* Fearless *fusion.*

Off Masirah, the Bay, Ghubbat Sarat, Ras Al Madrabiah in October 2001 – Exercise WADER and landings – basic stuff, old lessons re-learnt, jelly fish into intakes, just same as WEO's father had experienced off Aden in 1967 – where they used scare charges to blast them away. No longer available! Again essential for real live ops in OP TELIC Iraq 2003.

Terrorist attack threat increasing, a need to dispatch 40 Cdo elements discreetly to Afghanistan with world's media on us. Exercise RED BREAK the post SAIF SAREEA II R & R package for Brigade cancelled by me and instead of R & R we had to find somewhere quiet to dispatch 40 Cdo local elements discretely. I knew Diego Garcia so we went there with Sir Tristram, *1,400 matelots and Marines with 5,300 USN/USAF. B1s and B52s surreally taking off over us in the lagoon to bomb Afghanistan. Essential we did not 'over relax' and blow relations with USN –* Fearless's *people just immaculate, we had an excellent fun – free US T-shirts and umbrellas for all.* Royal *went off quietly for war fighting – all content.*

Amphib Ex UAE – Feb/Mar 2002. Again 40 Cdo embarked, Fearless *and a couple of LSLs with UAE landing craft – we went the extra mile to embrace and welcome our UAE friends – joint cliff assaults, UAE command elements dining and messing in Commodore/Brigadier's dining room etc. As such, this, Exercise SEA DAGGER 2002 was most successful on Pol/Mil terms, genuine, warm friendships and relationships kindled – even Sheikh M.B.Z. – Mohammed bin Zayed invited me, Roger Lane, and the most sterling, redoubtable Flag Captain, Tom Cunningham (even Gordon Messenger too I recall! – now CO 40 Cdo, late COS Bde) to a very personal lunch ashore.*

All good stuff and was to prove its weight in gold when I was to have to use/borrow UAE training grounds in February 2003 for essential rehearsals prior to the Iraq amphibious operations. Again all due to the Fearless *effect and her people.*

Fearless *has been home to thirty-seven years of COMAWs/CQMATGs, EMFs, and ships companies, been a hero in the Falkland's campaign, ferried me in* Foxtrot Four *to safety, and provided magnificent support and command to generations of Amphibious Task Groups – all done with huge style, efficiency and warmth: well, it was certainly like that when I had the pleasure to fly my Broad Pennant in the* Mighty Lion. *I am very proud to have been the last COMATG with her –* Fearless *was a Flagship with huge heart. As with my Indian Army father's provenance, in the Urdu or Pushtu* lingua franca *of stamping grounds in Wazuristan and Afghanistan close to 40 Commando's stamping ground in late 2001:*

Shabash. Bahadur bundobast – or: Bravo. It's been a grand affair.

Annex F

Brigade Commander
HMS *Fearless* at War
Major General J.H.A. Thompson, CB, OBE

When as Commander 3 Commando Brigade, I arrived in *Fearless* by helicopter in rolling banks of low cloud off Portland in the late afternoon of 6 April 1982, I was embarking in a ship with which I was thoroughly familiar. Only eight years had passed since, as Brigade Major (Chief of Staff), I had carried out numerous deployments in *Fearless* and her sister ship *Intrepid* over a period of two years intensive exercises and training. Now I was about to go to war in her.

In this time of uncertainty, it was comforting to reflect, that I knew the ship so well, especially her procedures for fulfilling her amphibious role, as well as being totally 'at home' with her command, communications, and control systems for an amphibious operation, including their limitations. Fighting a war is complex enough, without the added burden of doing so in an unfamiliar environment. There was an added bonus: Captain Jeremy Larken, a very experienced

Brigadier Thompson on 23 May 1982 in San Carlos.

submariner, was a man of boundless enthusiasm and determined that *Fearless* would live up to her lifelong reputation as a 'can do' ship. Commander John Kelly, her Executive Officer, was another in the same mould, as well as being one of the most experienced 'junglie' helicopter pilots in the Navy. With me was Commodore Mike Clapp, who would command all the landing ships, merchant ships taken up from trade (STUFT), and escorts supporting the amphibious phase of the war. He was an experienced aviator and ship CO, and firm believer in the amphibious role, unlike the majority of naval officers at the time. This was the 'first team', and it was good to be part of it.

The only unfamiliar sight as we entered the door into the superstructure by Flyco and passed the aircrew briefing room, was a double layer of compo ration boxes on the deck in every passageway throughout the ship. Jeremy had stored *Fearless* like a submarine bound for a long patrol. Being tall, he had to walk bent almost double, being rather shorter, I was spared this discomfort.

The Brigade Commander's cabin in the *Fearless* is spacious and, with day cabin and en suite heads and bathroom, is a palace compared with every other accommodation space in the ship, except for the Commodore's and the Captain's. The space was to be put to good use during the voyage south. Here I could hold meetings with my two principal staff officers: Major John Chester, the Brigade Major and his logistic opposite number, Gerry Wells-Cole, the Deputy Assistant Adjutant & Quartermaster General (DAA & QMG), their 1982 titles (now respectively Chief of Staff and Deputy Chief of Staff). We met each day for 'morning prayers' as we called them, before going on to a wider staff briefing. Almost every day I met my artillery regiment CO, Lieutenant Colonel Mike Holroyd-Smith and Major Roddy Macdonald my engineer squadron commander, who constituted what I called the 'R' Group, (R for Rover). We had worked together for a year or so, and, once ashore, by 'roving' the operational area together, going forward to see for ourselves, were able to get to grips with the situation quickly and start the planning process going with minimum loss of time and fuss. My 'R' Group during the voyage down, although for obvious reasons we did no 'roving', included Major Ewen Southby-Tailyour, whose encyclopaedic knowledge of the Falklands, including sea approaches and beaches was invaluable.

The Commodore's dining cabin was rapidly converted into a briefing room for the joint Amphibious and Landing Force staffs. The need for such a space had either not been foreseen or had been ignored when the LPDs were designed. On peacetime exercises, briefings had been held in the Amphibious Operations Room (AOR). But its layout made it far from ideal as a space in which to brief a crowd of staff officers, or visitors. Once operations began, such events would be a distraction from the business of command and control of a brigade operation. The designated Brigade Intelligence Office, adjacent to the AOR, was about the size of large broom cupboard, another relic of the low priority accorded to intelligence in peacetime. Eventually, the Captain agreed to relinquish half of Wardroom Two as an intelligence office, and the brigade intelligence staff were at last able to work properly producing excellent results. It is interesting that Vice Admiral Sturdee, on passage to the Falklands in 1914 to hunt von Spee, found it necessary to convert his day cabin in his flagship, the battle cruiser *Invincible*, into an intelligence office.

Well before the changes outlined above had been made, the staffs settled in to the planning routine that would continue until the landings on 21 May took place, and *Fearless* proved to be a good ship in which to work, as she always had in the past. The co-location of the Commodore, myself, and our respective staffs enabled planning to proceed reasonably smoothly with both of us on hand to resolve points of disagreement.

Also located in *Fearless* were the CO of 22 SAS and OC of the SBS. Most of the SAS and SBS were embarked in *Hermes*, with the rest of the Carrier Battle Group, to begin with up to several thousand miles away, and seldom less than 200 miles from *Fearless*. The outline Advance Force tasks were agreed between the Commodore and myself, followed by summoning the relevant CO/OC for discussion and advice if required. Once the Commodore or I had confirmed the task, the requirement would be sent by signal to the Carrier Battle Group Commander in *Hermes* for implementation. It was then up to his staff in conjunction with the relevant special force commanders, helicopter COs, and captains of ships to plan and implement the insertion and extraction of the force concerned in detail.

The plan for the landing at San Carlos having been made jointly by the Commodore and me, it was approved by the Task Force Commander, Admiral Sir John Fieldhouse, based in Northwood, just north of London. On 13 May 1982, the wardroom in *Fearless* was the setting for the pre-landing Brigade Orders Group at which I gave my orders to the assembled commanding officers of the eight major and fifteen minor units of the 3 Commando Brigade; we were about to undertake the first major all-British amphibious operation since the Second World War. Five days later, the wardroom, stripped of furniture, was the home for a rifle company of 40 Commando, who with the remainder of the Commando had been cross-decked from the liner *Canberra*. The ship having already been at overload, was now at 'super' overload, with some 800 more men on board than her design allowed for. Troops slept wherever they could find space, including the tank deck and in the LCUs. The ship's company of *Fearless* did everything to make them welcome, and she more than lived up to her 'can do' reputation. With so many mouths to feed we were all on 'action' messing: soup or stew served in one's mug, with bread rolls.

The Commodore's staff had promised that D minus 1, the long approach to the Falklands, would be the 'longest day', with the ever-present threat of Argentine air and submarine attack. I spent some of that day on *Fearless*'s bridge, watching the force steaming towards the AOA, or rather that part of the force that I could see through the thick 'clag' that mercifully shielded us from the attentions of the Argentine Air Force. There were lighter moments, such as *Canberra* being caught ditching gash, and being ordered by *Fearless* signalling by lamp, to desist at once.

At midnight on D-1/D-Day, as we approached Falkland Sound, the AOR was manned by the staffs. At this stage there was very little left for me to do, until the actual landings started, so I went up to the compass platform and watched the bombardment of Fanning Head by *Antrim*, before going to the tank deck to chat to the men of 40 Commando as they embarked in the LCUs which were to take them ashore at Blue Beach from the amphibious anchorage in Falkland Sound outside San Carlos Water.

The only decision required before daylight, was not to change any of the timings, including postponing H-Hour, to take account of delays to the landing schedule caused by problems with the transfer of 2nd Battalion the Parachute Regiment (2 PARA) from the ferry *Norland* to LCUs alongside. The solution, which had the full support of the Commodore, was to let it roll.

The delays caused by snags encountered by the loading of the first wave (40 Commando and 2 PARA), resulted in the second wave (45 Commando and 3 PARA) being landed in daylight instead of in darkness. With the onset of day, the amphibious ships, including *Fearless*, weighed and proceeded to anchorages inside San Carlos Water. At this stage a problem familiar to me from exercises arose. The more powerful maritime radios blocked out signals from the obsolescent landing force radios which shared antennae, so communications from Brigade HQ to our units varied from very poor to non-existent. Sorting out the problem began right after H-Hour, when radio silence under which the Brigade net had been for the previous two weeks or so was lifted, but time was required to iron out the snags. So, as usual, I would spend most of the first day in the highly unsatisfactory position for a commander of being unable to communicate with my units. Poor communications were almost certainly responsible for the loss of two of my Gazelles, with three aircrew killed and one badly injured.

The solution to poor communications was to go and see for myself, which I did by Scout flown by my Light Aircraft Squadron Commander, Major Cameron.[481] Our departure from *Fearless* was delayed by air raids, but by mid-afternoon, I had a good picture of what was going on and where my units were. As usual, my Tactical Headquarters was landed to provide a 'foot on the ground', should I wish to command from ashore during the first day. I decided to land Main Headquarters that night, and transfer ashore at first light. There was talk of *Fearless* putting to sea from time to time, and I had no intention of being carted off in her, with my Brigade ashore.

Furthermore, given the intensity of the air attacks, I did not wish my headquarters vehicles and radios to end up on the bottom of San Carlos Water. The move ashore was made no earlier than it would have been had we been on exercise. The LPD was an admirable ship from which to command the landing, but less so as a Headquarters for a land battle. The physical barrier of the water gap, coupled with the need for the ship to be positioned to carry out its other important function of operating landing craft, made the business of command slow and extremely frustrating. The frustration included having to launch and recover by helicopter from a deck that one did not control, which was frequently closed by air attack, causing one to spend far too much time hanging around. At night the fastest, and usually only way, between the beach and *Fearless*, was a long flog by raiding craft. Once my Brigade was ashore, my place was with them. On board *Fearless* I felt remote from, and out of touch with my brigade, and uneasy in consequence.

Notwithstanding the imperfections of the landing force radio circuits on D-Day, the command and control of amphibious ship-shore movement was smoothly conducted, and could not have been exercised from another ship. Without the LPD's capability to dock-down and launch large landing craft no substantial landing of troops and equipment could have been achieved. *Fearless* provided an effective combined headquarters for the Commodore's and my staffs during the long, seven week, planning phase and the first day of operations. There is no doubt that without *Fearless*, and her sister ship, *Intrepid*, the amphibious operation to retake the Falkland Islands would have been impossible. My comment about communications problems, are not a criticism of *Fearless*. They were well known and were not corrected many years before because of treasury parsimony in particular, and lack of interest in amphibious operations in the Ministry of Defence in general.

I look back on my time in *Fearless* with great affection. She, her Captain and ship's company were not just *Fearless* but *peerless*.

Annex G

Brigade Major
HMS *Fearless* in Peacetime
Major General J.H.A. Thompson CB, OBE

With the staff of Headquarters 3 Commando Brigade, I joined *Fearless* in Gibraltar in April 1972. The bulk of the Brigade Headquarters & Signal Squadron with all the vehicles, radios and other kit needed to set up the Headquarters ashore had embarked in Portsmouth, and were there to greet us. Ahead of us was a busy programme of training in the Eastern Mediterranean, culminating in DAWN PATROL, a large NATO Maritime and Amphibious Exercise. I had been Brigade Major (Chief of Staff), for about two months, and this was my first big exercise. It was a test, not only for me, but also for the headquarters as a whole. We were to command *and* run Exercise DAWN PATROL, the first time a British Headquarters had done so. Under command were our own 42 Commando, a USMC Marine Amphibious Unit (equivalent to a battle group), the Italian San Marco Battalion (Italian Marines), and Greek Marines. The Commodore Amphibious Warfare (COMAW) and his staff were responsible for running the maritime part of the exercise.

Under Secretary of State of the Army 1971–1972, Geoffrey Johnson Smith and Major Julian Thompson.

I had to learn my way around *Fearless*, not only the Amphibious Operations Room (AOR), which it would be my responsibility to run, but also how the ship functioned to support an amphibious landing. The Brigade Commander, Pat Ovens, was to join us in Cyprus, along with Commodore Gus Halliday (COMAW) and his staff. So I, and the staff had a perfect opportunity to run through procedures and carry out CPXs without distractions during the passage to Cyprus. It soon became evident that *Fearless* was a happy, 'can do' ship under her captain Simon Cassels, and what better place to spend the spring than in the sunny Med. The familiarization with the amphibious side of the ship's organization was carried out under the guidance of an old friend, Captain Ewen Southby-Tailyour, the Officer Commanding Amphibious Detachment (OCAD).

Our time in Cyprus was taken up with practising the landing of the Headquarters over a beach and deploying to the training area. This involved waterproofing the vehicles and trailers, setting up the headquarters, and going through the procedures for shifting command ashore; all new to me, and some of the staff. Here Pat Ovens joined us. As a subaltern he had won a Military Cross with 41 Commando in Korea fighting with the 1st US Marine Division, and raiding the coast. Consequently he was highly regarded by the USMC, which was to stand the Brigade Headquarters in good stead over the days ahead, when we 'pepped up' some of the hallowed procedures of NATO's southern flank.

Soon we joined up with the rest of the Exercise Task Force, and began to learn how NATO conducted its business. Most of our soldiering had been done in the Far and Middle East, and much of what we encountered was strange; beginning with the Pre-Sail Conference, a necessary procedure, but as conducted on NATO exercises, a talking shop without structure. The staff of 3 Commando Brigade took note and determined that such events would be run better in future.

The briefing for the forthcoming exercise was my responsibility to stage-manage. It was held in *Fearless*'s wardroom, and conducted as a proper Orders Group, as I, and my GSO 3 Operations, Malcolm Hunt,[482] had been taught at the Army Staff College, Camberley, including the entrance of the Brigade Commander and COMAW to a silent room, with all standing to attention. The brevity of the occasion clearly took some of the 'allied members' by surprise, having resigned themselves to enduring a complete afternoon of 'waffle'; the whole business took thirty minutes.

The exercise in Greece went well, and due in no small part to *Fearless*, the two British Headquarters acquitted themselves well. Our American liaison officers, accustomed to the sophisticated equipment in their two headquarters ships, the *Mount Whitney* and *Blue Ridge*, were amazed that a relatively simple communications set-up could actually support a command and control system that worked better than theirs. There were lighter moments such as when Captain Southby-Tailyour fitted the Beach Armoured Recovery Vehicle (BARV) with a gun (a piece of drainpipe), which drew admiring comments from our allies. One evening, Southby-Tailyour took the BARV along the road from one of the beaches to the local Greek restaurant; surely the first time the BARV has ever been used for a 'run ashore'.

Further exercises over the next year cemented the good relations between the Commando Brigade Headquarters and *Fearless*. A short affair in the Orkneys was a precursor to a long NATO exercise in Norway. The action was so fast moving, and covered so much of the long coastline, that the Brigade Headquarters never got ashore. By the time Main HQ was landed and set up, the exercise 'play' had moved some fifty miles north up the coast. One night, two companies of 45 Commando were inserted behind 'enemy' lines by *Fearless*'s LCUs. Captain Ewen Southby-Tailyour came up with a brilliant plan to 'spoof' the enemy radars by rafting up the LCUs to make a bigger target and simulate a Norwegian coaster. It worked, and the 'enemy' were suitably taken by surprise. The use of LCUs, primarily designed to carry vehicles and armour, to take in troops by night was innovative and was to be repeated less than ten years later in the Falklands in somewhat different circumstances.

My last exercise involving *Fearless* during my time as Brigade Major was in Corsica, involving 41 Commando and the *2ème Régiment Étranger Parachutiste*. It was sad to say goodbye to her as we headed for home by air, and she went for a well-deserved port visit. The exercises in my second year as Brigade Major were in *Intrepid*, not the same at all. Someone in the Navy Department had decided that the LPDs should double up as Dartmouth Training Ships (DTS), with priority given to that role over amphibious training. The anti-amphibiousity gang in the Royal Navy were very much in the ascendant; they would only be put back in their boxes by the events of 1982, and it would take almost another decade after that before the lids were firmly nailed over them. The new role for the LPDs meant that not only would the Officers Under Training, or OUTs (their bizarre acronym), take much of the accommodation, but in addition portakabins were erected on the superstructure as navigational classrooms. Most irritating of all, a large proportion of the ship's programme was devoted to coastal passages, to allow the young 'gentlemen' (there were no women OUTs in those days), to brush up on their coastal navigation. Add to this numerous port visits to coach the aforesaid 'young gentlemen' in the social skills demanded by another high priority mission of those days, throwing a cocktail party, and the time left for amphibious training was meagre. We yearned for the good old days with *Fearless*.

Annex H

Brigade Air Squadron
(The Light Helicopter Perspective)
Major R.I.S. Hawkins, Royal Marines

In Chapter Twelve, Lieutenant Commander Peter Lord explained what life could be like for a Naval Air Squadron operating troop lift helicopters. In 1969 Lieutenant Richard Hawkins, Royal Marines, commanded a flight of Sioux helicopters during a Mediterranean deployment, with a Battle Group based on 45 Commando, Royal Marines, embarked:

Lieutenant Richard Hawkins.

In her thirty-seven years in commission HMS Fearless played host to a remarkable number and variety of light helicopters of many nationalities and services. Most of these visits were brief, required little logistic support and made few demands on the ship's Aviation Department.

Hosting helicopters for lengthy deployments, mainly from 3 Commando Brigade Air Squadron was a very different matter.

In view of the vital need for RM light helicopters to deploy and operate from the LPDs over the years it is interesting to note that Fearless's sea trials in 1966 barely included any intensive work with Army or RM light helicopters, either Scouts or Siouxs. Perhaps this was not surprising when the original ships layout named the flight deck the Upper Vehicle Deck! But this was to change as soon as Fearless arrived in the Far East in February 1967 when she started operating with the Air Troops of 40 and 42 Commandos in earnest and with whom the first set of SOPs were developed.

When Fearless arrived off Aden on 31 October she received a constant steam of visitors from the Commando Sioux, including those of 42 Commando who had now disembarked to RAF Khormaksar to join the Air Troop of 45 Commando. On 21 November 1967, the 3 Siouxs of 45's Air Troop were embarked to take passage back to the UK. For this the aircraft were manhandled down the ramp (with a 1/3 incline) to the vehicle deck, with four inches of 'headroom' to spare. On arrival in Plymouth Sound a month later the helicopters were flown ashore, their last flight as they then went straight to the scrap heap!

In 1969 two Sioux of 45 Commando and two Wessex of 845 NAS were embarked for a three month Company Group deployment to the Mediterranean. This was the first of many Embarked Force deployments of varying lengths over the subsequent fifteen years. These often included helicopter detachments of the Brigade Air Squadron operating Scouts, Siouxs and their replacements of Lynx and Gazelle. In February 1998 during an amphibious exercise off Spain Fearless operated two Sea Kings,

328

two Gazelles and two Lynx – all competing for the two spots. This gave the Aviation Department ample opportunity to play the daily game of Flight Deck chess at championship level. For this game, maximum points could be scored for moving the most number of helicopters with as many unqualified people as possible, at night, in foul weather conditions – and then having to move them back again. This was one of the ways for Flyco to get his own back for the mud which the aircraft brought on board on their skids.

In the Falklands war, **Fearless** sailed for Ascension with three Scouts embarked, which with the balance of 3 Commando Brigade Air Squadron were subsequently deployed around the remainder of the amphibious shipping for the onward leg to the Falklands. There **Fearless** provided support of every nature to the Squadron which in turn played a critical role in all phases of the campaign.

Initially technical support for the RM Flights was provided from the Fleet Air Arm. In 1998 they were replaced by technicians from the REME who became well versed in the ways of **Fearless's** aviators. The Brigade Air Squadron monthly report said in 1973: 'The REME have always had an interesting time on board and have to protect the aircraft and other equipment from corrosion and from sailors!'

However they rapidly took on nautical airs and received many strange looks on their return to Middle Wallop when they asked directions to the 'heads' and went for a 'run ashore'!

Corrosion was a continuing battle. The aircraft and their associated equipment were not designed for a life of constant exposure to sea water, salt spray and funnel smoke. On the deployment of Montforterbeek Flight to Norway in 1972, the Sioux secured to the flight deck endured a Force 9 gale and the ship rolling at 35 degrees. Flight deck chess had a more serious side as the light helicopters were delicate creatures compared with the Troop Lift Wessex and Sea Kings, and the confines of the vehicle decks and flight deck took their toll from constant, often heavy handed, ground handling. The naval rates couldn't resist fiddling with all the pointy bits which protrude from military helicopters to 'see if they would break off'. They usually did.

Uniquely for helicopters in the Amphibious Force, the Siouxs used AVGAS, and in the first commission **Fearless** had no AVGAS tanks. This created a refueling problem for deployments of any length, resolved by the carriage of 40 gallon drums of fuel on the flight deck ditching ramp. Understandably these measures were undertaken with a degree of reluctance due to the high fire hazard. Water contamination in both ships and aircraft fuel systems was a constant risk, with potentially disastrous consequences.

Despite the compatibility issues from an operating standpoint, relationships between the embarked flights and the Aviation Department remained excellent: summed up by a Brunei Flight report after a Norway deployment in 1972: 'HMS **Fearless's** Air Department gave the usual efficient and cooperative support to the Flight throughout the whole exercise.'

HMS *Intrepid*
1967–1991

HMS *Intrepid* with HMS *Fearless* beyond, 29 May 1985.

Motto: *Cela va sans dire* – That goes without saying.

Battle Honours:

Lagos	1759
Quiberon Bay	1759
Havana	1762
St Kitts	1782
Martinique	1794
Zeebrugge	1918
Atlantic	1939–41
Dunkirk	1940
Bismarck Action	1941
Norway	1941–42
Malta Convoys	1942
Arctic	1941–43
Aegean	1943
Sicily	1943
Salerno	1943
Falkland Islands	1982

Commanding Officers:

Captain J.A.R. Troup DSC RN	1966
Captain J.H.F. Eberle RN	1968
Captain W.D.M. Staveley RN	1970
Captain J.F. Kidd RN	1972
Captain N.J.S. Hunt MVO RN	1974
Captain D.H. Morse RN	1978
Captain P.G.V. Dingemans RN	1980
Captain A.G.M.A. Provest RN	1985
Captain P.K. Haddacks RN	1986
Captain J.C.L. Wright OBE RN	1988
Captain R.A.Y. Bridges RN	1989

HMS *Intrepid*'s life was not quite as long nor as intensive as her elder sister's: it was also her unfortunate duty, towards the end, to be cannibalized to keep *Fearless* operational. Nevertheless it is worth reiterating the point made in the Introduction that most comments reflecting on the flexibility and 'can do' attitude of one ship refer to the other: after all, and particularly in the Engineering Department and the Assault Squadron, many of the same people simply moved from one ship to the other, such was the specialist nature of their work.

Annex J

Albion and *Bulwark*

HMS *Albion*

To understand the genesis of the replacements for HMSs *Fearless* and *Intrepid* it is necessary to go back to the 1983 Defence White Paper which stated:

> *We remain committed to the maintenance of strong and flexible naval forces equipped with modern weapons, sensors and aircraft capable of playing a major part in NATO's maritime defence effort in the Eastern Atlantic and Channel, and of deploying world-wide in support of our interests and those of our Allies outside the Alliance area. These forces include the Royal Marines, whose special expertise and versatility make them particularly valuable for tasks both within and beyond the NATO area.*

After the Falklands War the Chiefs of Staff agreed that the United Kingdom should retain an amphibious fleet large enough to lift the fighting elements of a Commando Brigade; the remainder – mostly logistics – would be deployed in ships taken up from trade (STUFT) – an acceptable and cost effective option practised by a number of sophisticated amphibious forces. The fighting element to be carried in specialist ships was assessed as being: 3,913 troops; 1,262 vehicles; 42 helicopters (24 medium support and 18 light attack); 664 short tons of stores; 16 landing craft; 8 Mexeflotes. The agreed specialist shipping to be procured was to be two LPDs; two LPHs and six LSLs.

The Chiefs of Staff statement was reinforced by Mr George Younger,[483] the Secretary of State for Defence on 9 December 1986 when he said:

> *Her Majesty's Government has decided to retain an amphibious capability in the longer term ... and we look forward to rebuilding or extending the life of the present ships.... In parallel with this work we shall also address the means of providing helicopter lift, including the concept of an Aviation Support Ship.... The old ships will be retained until we have new ones ready to take their place. Yes, I can give*

that assurance. The expected life of Intrepid *and* Fearless *stretches into the mid 1990s and that should give us ample time to work out the best method of replacing them. It is our intention that the new or refurbished ships will be ready by the mid 1990s when the present ships reach the end of their useful lives.*

In fact the first LPD took almost exactly twenty years from concept to commission thanks to prevarication, reduction in capabilities, more money, less money and hugely-confused Procurement Executive indecisions over 'new ships or re-built ships'. The first of the hundreds of problems and vissisitudes were well covered in *Navy International* of November/December 1993 and written by the author.

Eventually, the first steel was cut for HMS *Albion* by BAE Systems of Barrow in November 1997 with unit fabrication beginning three months later. Her keel was laid down on 22 May 1998 and she was launched on 9 March 2001. She was handed over to the Royal Navy at Devonport on 4 April 2003 and commissioned on 19 June.

HMS *Bulwark* was laid down on 27 January 2000, and launched on 15 November 2001. At that time she was scheduled to commence sea trials in February 2003 but additional delays to her completion due to the priority given to HMS *Albion* meant that the date slipped to late 2003. She was commissioned on 28 April 2005. They are believed to have cost £359m (*Albion*) and £272m (*Bulwark*).

Displacement: 18,500 tonnes (full load)
Docked down: 21,500 tonnes (approx)
Length: 176 m
Flight deck: 2 spots; 64 m long
Beam: 25.6 m waterline, 28.9 m max
Draught: 7.1 m
Speed: 20 knots
Range: 7,000 nm at 18 knots
Complement: 325
Sensors: 2 × Kelvin Hughes 1007 Radars Type 966 Surveillance Radar
Armament: 2 × Goalkeeper Close In Weapon System (CIWS), Seagnat Decoy System
UAT Electronic Warfare System, 2 × 20 mm close range guns, 4 × Machine Gun positions
Propulsion: 2 × 6.25 MW and 2 × 1.56 MW diesel generators driving two AC motors through twin shafts and a bowthrust unit, all operating at 6.6KV. RNs first integrated Full Electric propulsion ships.
Military Lift: Embarked Military Personnel (EMF) 305 troops, with an overload of a further 405. Vehicle deck capacity for up to six tanks or around 30 armoured all-terrain tracked carriers. Floodable dock, with the capacity to take either four utility landing craft (each capable of carrying a Challenger 2 tank). Four smaller landing craft on davits, each capable of carrying 35 troops.

Two-spot 64 m flight deck able to take medium support helicopters and stow a third. Deck is capable of taking a Chinook. The *Albion* design does not have a hangar.

LCU Mk 10

The design and build contract for ten Mk 10 LCUs was placed with BAeSEMA (now part of BAE Systems)[484] at Glasgow in May 1998. The craft were to be built by Ailsa-Troon in their shipyard on the Clyde under a £20 million sub-contract, however the yard went in to liquidation after delivering the first two. In November 2000 the contract for the remaining eight craft was re-awarded to BAE Systems Govan at a revised cost to the MOD of £30 million. Each LCU is 29.8 m in length and displaces about 170 tonnes light, 240 tonnes fully laden. Typical payloads include a main battle tank such as the Challenger Mk II; or four High Vehicle Equivalents, or 120 troops and two over-snow vehicles; or a matrix of equipment and vehicles.

LCVP Mk 5

The LCVP Mk 5 is constructed of aluminium and is expected to have a service life of about twenty years. The LCVPs have a maximum loaded displacement of 25 tonnes. They are 15.5 m long and have a breadth of 4.2 m. They have a top speed of 25 knots and a range of 210 nautical miles at 18 knots. They are crewed by three Royal Marines and can carry 35 men and 2 tons of equipment or two light trucks or one Viking All Terrain Armoured Personnel Carrier.

Notes

1 *Fearless and Intrepid* by Neil McCart, Fan Publications 2003.
2 Later Admiral Sir James, KCB, CBE, ADC. Commander in Chief Fleet. Still serving.
3 See Lord Lewin's foreword to Michael Clapp's book *Amphibious Assault Falklands*, Leo Cooper, 1996.
4 The Commander bluntly told the Admiral's Chief of Staff, a senior captain, to get off the ship after he called seeking evidence against the Commanding Officer.
5 See Chapter Twenty-Five.
6 Then commanding HMS *Argonaut*. Later Rear Admiral, CB, DSO, LVO.
7 See Chapter Twelve.
8 English language edition first published in the UK by Conway Maritime Press in 1990.
9 Captain B.C. Watson RN to Rear Admiral R.M. Colvin, 22 February 1936.
10 *History of Combined Operations Organisation 1940–1945*. Amphibious Warfare Headquarters. London. 1956.
11 Ibid.
12 Later General Sir Alan, KCB.
13 *History of Combined Operations Organisation 1940–1945*. Amphibious Warfare Headquarters. London. 1956.
14 RM Archive: 2/14/1.
15 Inter Service Training paper 35 dated 30 June 1939.
16 The USN had started converting a 'missile submarine' (USS *Greyback*) into a troop carrier in 1957 capable of carrying seven embarked force officers and sixty enlisted men plus landing craft or swimmer delivery vehicles (SDVs), later known in the US as SEAL delivery vehicles, while retaining her conventional attack capability.
17 See Chapter One.
18 Major General Moulton, as MGRM Portsmouth, had foreseen the use of the LPH prior to Suez (an operation that certainly strengthened his case) and had given presentations to all the Staff Colleges on the use of ship-launched helicopter assaults.
19 CB, DSO, OBE. General Moulton had flown with the Fleet Air Arm before the Second World War, commanded 48 (Royal Marine) Commando in Normandy and Holland in 1944, 4 Commando Brigade in 1945 and 3 Commando Brigade from 1952 to 1954. He was Chief of Amphibious Warfare from 1957 to 1961.
20 Sidgwick and Jackson, 2000.
21 A term that had been reached only after a number of others had been suggested and rejected. The term 'dock' was not, in the terminology of the twentieth century 'sexy' enough as it was considered that men would prefer to serve in a ship rather than a dock.
22 Known irreverently but accurately as a Large Slow Target.
23 This is as written: no speed was specified at the time.
24 Two vehicles abreast in each of the four of the LCMs, and two LCMs abreast decided the width of the dock and thus, in loose terms, the width and length of the ship.
25 Later to become LCUs (utility) to bring their definition in line with NATO standards. Further development of the same craft continue until the roll-through Mk Xs were procured for the next generation of LPDs.
26 No. 92/62 dated 25 July 1962.
27 The MOD's words.
28 Landing Ship Assault.
29 'D' is for 1942 – first year of production; U: body style – utility truck (amphibious); K: all wheel drive; W: tandem rear axles.
30 In other documents the whole of the Flight Deck is referred to as the Upper Vehicle Deck. Even this description implies that only the after helicopter spot was expected to be used on any permanent basis.
31 Amended from 'five'.
32 They were never carried operationally.
33 Amended from five.
34 Shortly to be COMAW and later COMATG.
35 Boilers by Babcock and Wilcox (550 psi; 850°F/454°C); Turbines by English Electric (22,000 hp/16.4 MW).
36 Not mentioned here is the 10 ton capacity, fresh water tank for supplying the troops ashore via a gas turbine, portable pump carried in the well deck.
37 The LCA Mk 2s were to be re-designated as LCVP Mk 2s (landing Craft Vehicle and Personnel) in 1966.
38 Its current title.
39 One was to overturn at Poole while approaching the beach with the loss of the driver of one of the two embarked tanks. The subsequent Board of Enquiry decided that this had not been a stability problem but a ballasting problem and the craft were allowed to continue carrying two tanks.
40 The Army's rolls were 150 feet long and dispensed from the back of a 3-ton lorry but those in the ABU had to be shorter to fit the spools carried by the fork-lift tractor.
41 Later: The Right Honourable the Lord Carrington, KG, GCMG, CH, MC, PC who had landed from an LST in northern Europe in June 1944 while serving with the Grenadier Guards.
42 Later: Lieutenant Commander, MBE.

43 To the order of the Ministry of Transport for the Ministry of Defence (Army): originally operated by the British India Steam Navigation Company they were transferred to the Royal Fleet Auxiliary on 3 January 1970.
44 Admiralty News Release N. 145/63.
45 Later, First Sea Lord.
46 First of three 13,900 ton (full load) LPDs: commissioned in September 1962. *La Salle* was sister ship.
47 Such as pre-lunch drinks before moving to the table.
48 Later Vice Admiral Sir Anthony Troup KCB, DSC* and the first Commanding Officer of *Intrepid* .
49 Later Vice Admiral Sir Patrick Bayly KBE, CB, DSC**.
50 First of two *Transports de chalands de debarquement*: 8,500 ton (full load). Commissioned January 1965.
51 Originally LCA Mk IIs – eventually renamed LCVP Mk IIs.
52 Known to his men as Oh Christ! Another Disaster. Later renamed 4th Assault Squadron.
53 Later to become a helicopter pilot and the senior Royal Marine on COMAW's staff during the Falklands campaign. Colonel, OBE.
54 Also an ocean racing skipper of considerable international success.
55 All was to change again in the early 1970s when the Amphibious Detachment became an all Royal Marines unit.
56 Later Colonel.
57 Letter to the author dated June 2004.
58 Later changed his name to Kendal.
59 Now deceased.
60 Such was his love of *Fearless* that years later, and in accordance with his wishes, he was committed to the deep from her.
61 The Dhofar War (1965–1975) was being fought by the Sultan's Armed Forces without outside help at this stage: even the war's existence remained classified until the discovery of Chinese dead on a battlefield on 11 January 1968.
62 The Commander was not a tall man: cruel tongues had it that the cause of his apparent breathlessness when speaking on the ship's tannoy was because he had to jump up and down to reach the microphone.
63 Belfast base.
64 Royal Navy shore base at Londonderry.
65 Eighth if a drifter under Royal Naval command is included.
66 Vice Admiral Sir Fitzroy Talbot, KBE, CB, DSO**.
67 FEARTEM 2/65 dated 16 November.
68 Major General A.M.W. Whistler, CBE.
69 Letter to the author dated 20 November 2004.
70 Royal Navy Commanders all with three gold stripes on their sleeves; this is a parody on the three gold chevrons worn by a Royal Marines' Sergeant.
71 Later Commander.
72 Now deceased.
73 The pennant numbers of the LCMs were *F1, F2, F3* and *F4* while those of the LCAs were *F5, F6, F7* and *F8*. A later version (an LCVP Mk 2 – *Foxtrot 7*) that took part in the Falklands campaign is displayed at the Royal Marines Museum at Eastney. *Foxtrot 4* was lost during the Falklands campaign, see Chapter 12.
74 He and seven fellow coxswains quickly became known, collectively, as 'Those magnificent men and their landing machines'.
75 Later Admiral Sir William Stavely, First Sea Lord: he was to command *Intrepid* from 1970 to 1972.
76 Ramped Powered Lighters. 100 tons fully laden.
77 Then stationed at Royal Marines Barracks, Stonehouse, Plymouth.
78 Cut short by two days for un-remembered reasons.
79 Then Commodore H.L. Lloyd, DSC, RN.
80 Headquarters Southern Command Press Release dated 18 April 1966.
81 Although, then, Captain C.D. Wareham RE of 36 Engineer Regiment recalls a 'horrified Number One watching heavy earth-moving equipment slipping and sliding up and down the internal ramps'. Dangerous though it may have looked and been, this type of evolution was to become very much *Fearless*'s business.
82 Such were the archaic 'rules' for qualifying.
83 Straight Street – a notorious run-ashore venue: Singapore's Bugis Street was close to being the Far East equivalent.
84 *Fearless* letter No. 4341/13 dated 11 November 1966.
85 Commander in Chief, Middle East.
86 GOC Middle East Land Forces.
87 AOC Middle East Air Force.
88 In the mid 1980s, the boffins of Bath, armed only with computers and the stability curves for a fast frigate decreed that the LCM/LCU was unstable with loads above six tons! Their advice was ignored by the users while they redesigned the sides of the LCUs so that extra buoyancy would come into play at an angle of heel that empirical experience had showed was beyond that that would have sunk the craft anyway. These high sides also gave the craft considerable extra windage and made the vessels less easy to manoeuvre and thus more dangerous to operate.
89 Command Post Exercise.
90 She was in a wheel chair.
91 Falaise is an area of Little Aden which includes good landing beaches.
92 Later Colonel Aylmer, DL.
93 Rubber, inflatable, assault craft powered by a 40 hp engine and able to carry about six fully-equipped troops.
94 Admiral Martin's Chief Staff Officer and a remarkable dinghy helmsman.

95 *The Micks. The Story of the Irish Guards* by Peter Verney. Pan Books, 1973.
96 Original is contained in C-in-C Middle East's Report of Proceedings 5530/36CINCME dated 13 December 1966.
97 It was non-existent. BR527 (Geographical Handbook for Western Arabia and the Red Sea) produced by Naval Intelligence was dated 1946 and did not mention Hauf although it did mention the neighbouring village of Jadhib; nor had there been any beach surveys as the area was considered to be of no strategic importance.
98 Minute A10/Q9 dated 31 October 1966.
99 HQ Joint Force Commander's Report in 24 Inf Bde letter 311G dated 11 November 1966.
100 As it should have been, for huge fans were fitted to blow out fumes when vehicle engines were running during maintenance periods or before a landing. These had been designed to change the air many times an hour.
101 See also Chapter 12 and replace 'jelly-fish' with 'krill'.
102 Modern charts are unchanged in this regard. Hauf is a pin-prick on a seventy nautical mile stretch of coast described in the Admiralty Pilot (No. 64) as 'almost straight with mountains rising abruptly behind it [with] occasional small patches of sandy coast'. During December strong north-easterly or northerly winds can kick up a considerable chop with no warning whatsoever and bring with them sand-laden air which restricts visibility. It is not unusual either at this time of the year for south-easterlies [on shore] to produce dangerous surf on the beaches.
103 At variance with CDS's report.
104 Hauf was to remain a danger to the Sultan's Armed Forces (SAF) as a DLF Headquarters, forward logistics base and training centre for the terrorists (including Chinese nationals) operating in the Oman. Later the DLF was to position 85 mm mortars at Hauf and later still even more threatening 120 mm and 130 mm guns which (according to John Akehurst in his book *We Won a War* – Michael Russell Publishing, 1982) pounded the Sultanate village of Sarfait 'incessantly and accurately'. The DLF was to change its name to the People's Front for the Liberation of the Arabian Gulf (PFLOAG) and would not be defeated by SAF until 1975.
105 In his book *The Micks*, Peter Verney says much the same thing: [The success was] *a clear demonstration of the fallacy behind the mystique which surrounds the supposed difficulties of an amphibious landing*. This was, though, a single ship, single unit, single flight-operation with a very limited, short-term aim and with no opposition. The difficulties arise when the battle has to be fought in the air, on the surface (and under it) before a foothold can be achieved ashore by numerous ships containing many and varied land formations each with a different task, area of operations and beach or landing zone.
106 Ex aircraft carrier of 17,000 tons (full load) carrying an earlier Mk of LCMs craned onto the flight deck and with spots for helicopters.
107 To commemorate the first anniversary of service life a number of statistics were published in the ship's onboard newsletter – others have been added:
Between November 1965 and December 1966 the ship has steamed 25,00 miles with, interestingly, 25 per cent of those miles in November 1966. The eight landing craft have, between them, steamed a staggering total of 21,000 miles while the flight deck has been landed on over 900 times by eight different types of aircraft. 4,200 troops and 400 vehicles have been embarked from 25 different Army and Royal Marines units. We have embarked 50 admirals and commodores, 66 generals and brigadiers, 14 air marshals and air commodores and 25 'distinguished' civilians while over 1,500 other officers and senior ratings and other ranks from all three services have been received for indoctrination visits.
108 RAF heavylift aircraft.
109 In fact the ship's arrival alongside was delayed by the absence of a suitable brow so while one was being sought the Captain 'left the ship by the slightly unusual method of being lowered by crane in his Land Rover to receive the call of the Commanding Officer of SAS *Bluff* (Commander van der Merwe) on the jetty'.
110 No 31/ME/BBM/20 dated 21st January 1967.
111 Later Brigadier.
112 Later, Major General, CB.
113 Written (hopefully) before that delightful word was hijacked by a less healthy milieu.
114 Jack Dusty – Supply Department.
115 The scene of a major US amphibious operation during the Korean War in which Royal Marines played a deception role.
116 Their definition had changed from LCA while in Singapore.
117 Three staff cars, 10 tractors, 63 Land Rovers, 5 one tonners, 45 three tonners, 1 Heavy Recovery Vehicle and 4 water bowsers. Vessels included 1 RPL, 1 harbour Launch and 1 'small boat'.
118 This time her cargo included 22 cars, 4 minibuses, 18 three tonners, 39 Land Rovers, 9 trailers, 4 tractors, 1 ten tonner, 1 heavy recovery vehicle, 1 fire engine, 1 ten ton crane, 1 coach, 3 one tonners, 1 steamroller, 1 cement mixer, 2 fuel bowsers and trailers, 1 sullage tanker, 1 RPL and numerous other assorted vehicles and crates.
119 Including a number of Royal Marines officers and SNCOs, on loan or secondment.
120 Commanded by Rear Admiral Edward Ashmore (FOF2) from the Far East who flew his flag in *Fearless* for a few days. Others ships included HMSs *Eagle*, *Albion*, *Phoebe*, *Appleton*, *London*, *Ajax*, *Minerva*, *Auriga*, *Barrosa* and several RFAs.
121 As an example of just how useful these ships were, HMS *Intrepid* was carrying nearly 1,000 bags of Christmas surface mail for all three services east of Suez. Labour troubles in London docks had prevented the loading of these bags into the designated merchant ship.
122 Commander Colin Robinson who had joined as the new MEO in Aden.
123 An inverted black cone.
124 Telephone conversation between the Rt. Hon Sir Michael Palliser, GCMG, PC and the author on 13 March 2003.
125 Sir Elwyn Jones.
126 MOD(N) signal 021807Z Oct.
127 Annex A to the Commanding Officer HMS *Fearless*' letter No. 231/47 dated 17 October 1968.
128 Paragraph 16 to Commanding Officer HMS *Fearless*' letter No. 231/47 dated 17 October 1968.

129 Later: Rear Admiral John Carlill OBE DL.
130 Captain R.P. Clayton was in temporary command due to Captain I.G. Raikes CBE DSC being ill.
131 Later: Sir Keith Speed RD DL. He had served for nine years as a regular seaman officer in the Royal Navy after Dartmouth and Greenwich before retiring and joining the RNR.
132 Letter to the author dated 25 February 2003.
133 *Fearless* letter 231/47 dated 17 October 1968: paragraph 7.
134 The Commanding Officer's cabin had been taken over by the Attorney General.
135 Later: CB.
136 Commanding Officer HMS *Fearless* letter No. 231/47 dated 17 October 1968.
137 Later to be *Fearless*'s Chaplain.
138 Exercise SWOP.
139 His private diaries. This version is corroborated in all but the most minor of details in other accounts.
140 Mr Gerald Kaufman, the Parliamentary Press Liaison Officer and later, a knighted socialist MP whose behaviour throughout the conference was considered the only sour note. One, repeatable (expurgated) quote: 'This man, alone, nearly scuppered any feeling of rapport the ship's company had established with the Delegates.'
141 Mrs Marcia Williams, then Harold Wilson's Personal Political Secretary, later Baroness Falkender, CBE. She was viewed in much the same light as Kaufman.
142 Mr Michael Halls, who died in 1970.
143 Letter to the author dated 4 June 2003.
144 Letter to the author dated 12 February 2003.
145 Letter to the author dated 9 April 2003.
146 DS5b's letter dated 27 November 1968.
147 18 October 1968.
148 In practice the largest to be held in western Europe since the war.
149 Brigadier J.M. Strawson: later Major General CB, OBE.
150 Brigadier H.D.G. Butler: later Major General CB, DL.
151 HQ 24 Inf Bde letter 626 G dated 5 December 1968
152 HMS *Fearless* letter No. 231/33 dated 12th November 1968.
153 *Fearless* letter No. 226/1 dated 8 January 1969.
154 Later Lieutenant General Sir John Richards, KCB, KCVO, Commandant General Royal Marines 1977 to 1981 and Marshal of the Diplomatic Corps 1982 to 1992. He died in 2004 while this chapter was being written.
155 See Annex Golf.
156 Later, Lieutenant Colonel Sir Seymour Gilbert-Denham, Crown Equerry.
157 National Archives ADM 53/170768.
158 *Fearless* letter No. 226/1(II) dated 6 April 1969.
159 DO 45RM 8/2/14(B) dated 28 January 1969.
160 Ibid.
161 CINCWF 131829Z March.
162 MOD(N) 141747Z March.
163 In truth, there were nine prospective bridegrooms, the rest were compassionate cases.
164 Letter to the author from Captain Ron Wheeler, RM, then the Embarked Military Force's Ship's Adjutant.
165 Sung to the Prime Minister by the ship's 'pop group' The Group – it was well and humorously received on the evening of Sunday, 30 March during an informal 'walk about' among junior ratings,
166 Miss R. Barton, Miss J. Colman, Miss A. Pring and Miss S. Tolton.
167 Group Captain Lord Cheshire, VC, OM, DSO**, DFC, RAF.
168 Commander Colin Robinson's diaries.
169 Later, Colonel.
170 E. Griffiths, MP for Bury St Edmunds.
171 Admiral Sir Terrance Lewin later Admiral of the Fleet Lord Lewin KG, GCB, LVO, DSC; Chief of the Defence Staff.
172 Out of a total of 95,500.
173 Dated 7th October 1969.
174 Recollections would appear to be hazy but it is believed that this was a replica of a London pub.
175 MBE, Royal Engineers.
176 Letter to the author dated 23 May 2003 plus official Report of the Visit of the Pipes and Drums.
177 Who died unexpectedly in September 2004 before he was able to offer his views on life in *Fearless*.
178 Later, Major. He had just relieved Major Douglas Mayhew: the post of OCAD and Beachmaster having now been combined and given to a Royal Marines Captain as originally complemented. Letter to the author dated 19 September 2004.
179 Including nine warships.
180 Commander Naval Forces Gulf's Report of Proceedings GNC 231/32 dated 28 May 1970.
181 As an example of a sample load that the ship might be expected to embark at any time, a look at a breakdown of the personnel for this occasion is interesting: 80 officers, 84 SNCOs and 611 'rank and file' were accommodated from the following headquarters and units (Appendix 2 to Annex C to the paper at footnote 180): HQ Naval Forces Gulf; HQ Land Forces Gulf; HQ Air Forces Gulf; A Sqn Life Guards; 1 Scots Guards; 4 Royal Anglian; 32 (Gulf Sqn) RE; G Sqn 22 SAS; 222 Sig Sqn; 255 Sig Sqn; 668 Sqn AAC; 2 Sqn RCT; 90 Sqn RCT; 73 Maritime Sqn RCT; 19 Field Ambulance Sqn RAMC; Ord Depot, Bahrain; 1 Inf Wksp REME; 261 PCCV; 1 Indep Coy RPC; 607 PFAC; 78 Sqn RAF; 84 Sqn RAF; JMS and elements of the PR Staff. One can only pity the poor souls appointed as Ship's Adjutant and OC Troops!

182 In the 1980s when the replacement LPDs were being considered the Procurement Specification called for the carriage of two, full-sized Mexeflotes. They were eventually removed from the design to save money.
183 *Fearless* letter no. 226/2 dated 23 June 1970.
184 The Commanding Office had been obliged to seek permission from FOCAS for his Senior Rates to do this.
185 Last night at sea celebrations.
186 For the statistically minded, during her second commission *Fearless* had steamed 76,350 nautical miles during which time her LCMs had conducted over 320 landings while her LCAs had landed troops just short of 200 times. She had carried 7,000 troops and 1,300 vehicles and her flight deck had safely managed 2,400 landings: the largest Embarked Force had been 902 during Exercise SEA HORSE. The Dental Officer filled 3,600 teeth and removed 350.
187 KCB, DSC, MC.
188 Then MP for Plymouth, Sutton and later Lord Owen.
189 Royal Marines file no. 7/10/57(9) dated 9 April 1970. Royal Marines archives.
190 It is interesting to note, too, that only the previous year, 1969, the Directorate of Naval Warfare and Captain Cassels (soon to be *Fearless*'s Commanding Officer) had begun to consider designs for a replacement LPD; with twenty or so more feet in length for extra fuel, accommodation and command spaces.
191 Due, of course, to the Government cutting manpower, and not through any professional inability on the part of the service itself.
192 Later Field Marshal Lord Carver and Chief of the Defence Staff 1973 to 1976.
193 Secret, UK Eyes Only, minutes dated 10 Feb 1970. Royal Marines archives.
194 Oral Reply on Thursday 26 November 1970.
195 Major, MC, VRD, Royal Marines, retired. Later Sir Patrick.
196 With little fuel the LPD cannot dock deep enough to float out the forward LCMs and if she is really low not even the after two LCMs will float.
197 Moss Pearson was one of the most experienced Landing Craft hands in the Royal Marines: LCM crewman, LCVP coxswain, 3 LSTs (*Messina* in the Pacific, *Reggio* and *Striker* in the Mediterranean) and two tours with a Commando in both *Albion* and *Bulwark*. Later: DSM of the Brigade Raiding Squadron and Branch Sergeant Major.
198 Headquarters Commando Forces.
199 Rear Admiral E.F. Gueritz CB, OBE, DSC*. Later: Admiral President of Greenwich.
200 Later, Admiral Sir John, KCB and C-in-C Fleet.
201 *Fearless* letter 231/66 dated 21 May 1971, FOCAS letter P.500/10 dated 3 June 1971 and HQ 24 Airportable Brigade's letter 367/8 W dated 22 May 1971.
202 Letter to the author dated 19 September 2004.
203 Ian Lamb believes that only the four-tonner got into difficulties.
204 Later Major General Kenneth Perkins CB, MBE, DFC.
205 Now Chief of Staff.
206 *Fearless* letter 225/41 dated 6 August 1971.
207 Vertical replenishment using one or more helicopters.
208 *Fearless* letter 226/3 dated 3 December 1971.
209 The former leader of EOKA.
210 His name can now be revealed: Sub Lieutenant H.S. Morgan.
211 Letter to the author from Ian Lamb dated 19 September 2004.
212 Bryan Straker was Commander British Forces Caribbean Area and Island Commander Bermuda, 1974–1976.
213 Colour Sergeant Mick Jones, a Drill Instructor and Detachment Quartermaster with a keen sense of humour.
214 Variations in drill centre around the Royal Marines not stamping their feet.
215 Ironically, just after all arctic clothing had been landed.
216 *Fearless* Report of Proceedings letter 226/3 dated 5 March 1972.
217 Who, as the senior officer involved, was to incur Their Lordships' displeasure.
218 *Fearless* Report of Proceedings letter 226/3 dated 5 March 1972.
219 Ibid.
220 Variation on the old saying that the Liverpool girls have hold of the tow rope when a ship makes a better speed than that planned for the homeward leg: usually helped by the engine room team adding a few 'homeward bounders' to the officially-set revolutions.
221 Letter to the author dated 18 September 2003.
222 Armoured Vehicles Royal Engineers: based on a Centurion main battle tank chassis they mounted both a demolition gun and a bulldozer blade.
223 *Fearless* letter 226/3 dated 1 May 1972.
224 Ibid.
225 Fertility and Wine.
226 John Devereux Treacher.
227 Letter to the author dated 29 March 2003.
228 FOCAS letter to C-in-C Fleet 226/6 dated 20 April 1972.
229 Whose name is known to the author but to save embarrassment …
230 Later, Lieutenant Colonel, OBE.
231 Since deceased.
232 In today's parlance, the Chief of Staff. See Annex Golf.
233 Later: Major General, OBE, MC.
234 Later: Major General, CB, OBE.

235 A long-running Royal Marines dream or fable. Larnaca can be inter-changed for any nearby city across the Globe.
236 Later, Admiral Sir Raymond Lygo, KCB.
237 Letter to author dated 29 March 2003. Whether or not the Admiral or his staff apologized is not recorded.
238 Later Admiral of the Fleet, GCB, DSC and Chief of the Defence Staff.
239 Letter to the author from Admiral Cassels dated 29 March 2003.
240 Letter to author dated 29 March 2003.
241 *Fearless* letter 226/3 dated 9 October 1972.
242 Originally an artistically and ornately galvanized iron bucket competed for by ships on the Beira Patrol to relieve boredom. Surgeon Commander Rick Jolly's book *Jackspeak* describes it thus: 'The sports involved were specified by the defending ship and "jungle" rules applied. The term is now used to describe any impromptu trophy played for by ship's in company and detached from home waters.'
243 The SACC Desk does exactly what its title implies. Representatives from all supporting arms , air, artillery, naval gunfire support, forward observation officers, engineers and so on man this desk in the centre of the Amphibious Operations Room and thus coordinate and de-conflict all support available to the land forces.
244 Tribal Class frigate of 2,700 tons.
245 An amalgamation of Captain Cassels' ROP 226/3 dated 2 August 1972 and a letter to the author dated 29 March 2003.
246 *Fearless*'s role in MOTORMAN was covered by Operation GLASSCUTTER.
247 Later, Major General Neil Carlier, CB, OBE and Commander British Forces, Falkland Islands 1987–1988.
248 Report of Proceedings: *Fearless* letter 226/3 dated 2 August 1972
249 For the naval historian, 40 Commando, already in Northern Ireland, was joined by 42 and 45 Commandos (41 Commando was in Malta) whose presence, along with other infantry battalions sent in from the mainland, helped to bring the British Army's total of battalions for this operation up to twenty-seven.
250 *Fearless*'s letter 226/3 dated 2 August 72.
251 1,017 ton (loaded) Army LCT Type 8.
252 *Fearless*'s letter 226/3 dated 2 August 72 and letter to the author dated 29 March 2003.
253 A 425 ton coastal minesweeper.
254 All landing craft officers and SNCOs are fully qualified in such journeys by blind-pilotage or visual reference.
255 To mark John Ainger's operational debut the OCAD fired two 9-mm rounds through his navigation note book and presented it back as a war trophy during the next wardroom party.
256 Later, Captain Keogh, Royal Marines.
257 Who had been the senior LCA coxswain of HMS *Anzio* as a corporal and who was much admired throughout the landing craft branch.
258 One of the most skilful of all LCM coxswains.
259 Royal Marines Captains under the Naval Discipline Act (and, in practice, on all occasions as pay and other privileges testified) were equal in rank to a Royal Navy Lieutenant Commander and thus an RAF Squadron Leader and an Army Major.
260 In Ken Robson's words.
261 19,600 ton Amphibious Command Ship.
262 One of many titles over the years: now Royal Marines Poole (Hamworthy). Currently, the Amphibious Trials and Training Unit, Royal Marines, is at Instow on the north Devon coast.
263 From NATO's point of view it was the largest such exercise ever: other UK ships included HMSs *Albion, Ark Royal, Blake, Fife* and *Juno* and the RFAs *Sir Geraint, Retainer, Lyness, Tidespring* and *Olwen*.
264 Leo Cooper, 1993.
265 Later Lieutenant General Sir Steuart Pringle Bt, KCB, Commandant General of the Royal Marines 1981–1984.
266 Captain William Staveley.
267 Later Brigadier and Commandant of the Commando Training Centre, Lympstone.
268 There was also a suggestion that it might not have been a submarine but the funnel from a known, underwater wreck on the side of the channel that had, over the years, rolled into the deeper part of the passage through which *Fearless* passed. It doesn't matter, she did not ground and everyone's reputation remained intact.
269 Largely due to *Fearless* replacing *Bulwark* as the latter was still in dockyard hands and industrial action was delaying the former's planned refit. The obvious solution was to run *Fearless* on but this had its problems as will be seen.
270 *Fearless* letter 226/3 dated 16 November 1972.
271 Not helped by one of the tugs suffering a similar engine failure at a critical moment.
272 Ibid.
273 Ibid.
274 Tragically he was to be killed during the Falklands campaign when his ship, HMS *Sheffield*, was sunk.
275 Later to lose an eye in Northern Ireland.
276 West Indies won by seven wickets despite strong support from *Fearless* at Queen's Park Oval.
277 Prime Minister of Canada.
278 Quote from the *Miami Herald* of Tuesday 26 February 1974 by Grace Wing Bohne a *Miami Herald* reporter: 'Like Commodore Horatio Hornblower, British Officers still carry telescopes as a badge of authority. Climax to the party was a retreat on the dock below, a throat-tightening spectacle with the lowering of the Union Jack and the ship's band marching past (drummer wearing a leopard skin) playing the evening hymn, both national anthems, and, as a spirited finale, "A Life on the Ocean Wave". (We had to ask the title, because J.P. Sousa didn't write it!)'
279 A naval version of the game of Ludo – but with various 'in-house' rules and variations. So cut-throat are the Uckers competitions that an Admiralty Fleet Order had to be promulgated laying down the 'official' rules.

280 Where, in Bridgetown, Barbados, Stirling Moss (later Sir Stirling) was taught to drive the Michigan tractor by Marine Lew May.
281 MOD (Navy) Press Release No. 62/75 dated 20 June 1975.
282 MPs, Defence and Navy officials from sixteen countries (including Argentina) plus the foreign press corps were invited to attend.
283 Expenditure Committee (HC 259, session 1974–75).
284 DN Plans 3/1 dated 1 April 1975.
285 Under Secretary of State for Defence (Navy).
286 Probably not much has changed over the years as far as the Government's attitude is concerned.
287 Who, earlier, had commanded the 45 Commando Battle Group with Captain Mark Kerr.
288 Killed in a motor accident in France after retiring from the Royal Marines.
289 Later Admiral Sir James, GCB; Commander in Chief Naval Home Command and Master of the Britannia Beagles.
290 *Fearless* was not the first Royal Navy ship to star in these films as HMS *Rothesay* (an anti-submarine frigate of some 2,800 tons) had sunk the villain's vessel off Key West in *Thunderball* in 1965.
291 It was rumoured that the cases had been packed before the fire and that *Fearless*'s presence and particularly her efficiency at fire fighting had not been wholly welcomed.
292 The Commanding Officer's share, three years later, was £1,400 before tax.
293 Caterer.
294 *Fearless*'s letter 226/1 dated 9 February 1976.
295 Two spots versus nine does not make for a speedy build up ashore by air but the four LCMs between them could, *in extremis*, land a whole Commando simultaneously, albeit rather untactically.
296 *Fearless*'s letter 226/1 dated 9 November 1976.
297 14 November 1976.
298 Commanded by Lieutenant Colonel K.N. Wilkins later, Commandant General Royal Marines.
299 Rear Admiral J.H.F. Eberle.
300 Sir Roger Moore's personal assistant. Letter to the author dated 4 September 2003.
301 Other awards were the Commander-in-Chief's Commendation to Cdr Tim Hayle (the XO), Lt Graeme Armstrong, FCOEA Michael Stephens, CMEM John Elder, LMEM Lee, LMEM 'Rowdy' Yates and MECH1 Michael Reed.
302 RPL 12 – HMAV *Medway*.
303 Unusually for these training cruises, one Wasp from 829 Naval Air Squadron, Portland, was embarked.
304 Embarked for the deployment from the Guards Depot.
305 *Fearless*'s letter 226/1 dated 16 March 1977.
306 *Fearless*'s letter 226/1 dated 24 August 1977.
307 Diverted from Saunton Sands, North Devon, due to excessive surf conditions.
308 *Fearless*'s letter 226/1 dated 24 August 1977.
309 Ibid.
310 Ibid.
311 *Fearless* letter 226/1 dated 16 December 1977.
312 Shore based training establishment at Rosyth, closed in 1985.
313 As a Lieutenant Commander, RNVR, Brooks Richards had won a DSC and Bar when serving with Coastal Forces between 1939–1944.
314 *Fearless*'s letter 226/1 dated 16 December 1977.
315 Personnel from all services were undertaking fire-fighting duties across the United Kingdom: the striking fire-fighters they replaced worked less hours for more money and were able to claim overtime and other bonuses including the right to strike for 'better' conditions.
316 Author's emphasis.
317 From sixteen different countries including, for example, Brunei, the Bahamas, Eire and Iran.
318 *The Daily Mail* and *The Daily Mirror* respectively.
319 *The Daily Telegraph, The Sun* and *The Daily Express*.
320 Later: Lieutenant Colonel.
321 A parody on a well-known naval song.
322 Later: Warrant Officer and the Landing Craft Branch Sergeant Major.
323 The crew was LMEM Dicky Dickens,, LS Dave Southworth, CEM Iain Pearson, Lt-Cdr Jerry Quinlan, NA Dave Houlden, MEM Martin Kinley, Colour-Sergeant Ken Murgatroyd, POEL Scouse Jones and Lieutenant Steve Goodwill, RM.
324 Later Captain and who died in 2004 before he could answer the author's plea for information.
325 MBE. Later, Commodore, OBE.
326 Later Sir John KCB, PC.
327 Leo Cooper, 1996.
328 Telephone conversation with the author, March 2003.
329 Later: CB. See his account in *Amphibious Assault Falklands*. Leo Cooper 1996.
330 OBE. See his account in *No Picnic*. Leo Cooper, 1985. Later: Major General CB.
331 Who had been HMS *Kent*'s Chaplain during the Gibraltar talks.
332 Hansard column 429.
333 Hansard column 453.
334 Then member of the Parliamentary Defence Study Group. Later: Sir Neville, Kt, JP, DL.
335 Later: Sir Philip, Kt.

336 Later: Lord, KCMG.
337 Later: Surgeon Captain.
338 The remnants of Hurricane Trevor.
339 A half-and-half mix of Guinness and champagne. The French consider this to be an insult to their 'national' drink, the Irish think likewise!
340 Taken from Michael Clapp's *Amphibious Assault Falklands*. Leo Cooper, 1996.
341 Later Admiral of the Fleet Sir Henry Leach GCB, DL; First Sea Lord. He had commanded HMS *Albion* in 1970.
342 *The Downing Street Years*. HarperCollins.
343 Second edition, Leo Cooper, 1992.
344 Conducted on board HMS *Hermes* by Admiral Fieldhouse and his Northwood staff.
345 *Intrepid*, the six LSLs, *Atlantic Conveyor*, *Canberra* and *Elk*.
346 Qualified Helicopter Instructor.
347 Commando pilots as opposed to 'pingers': anti-submarine warfare qualified aircrew.
348 Ewen Southby-Tailyour.
349 Mentioned in Despatches.
350 Precisely forty-five minutes late: H Hour had been planned for 0630 Z or 0230 local.
351 Who was to receive the DSC for his, and his crew's, actions that day and who was later to become First Sea Lord.
352 Undated letter to the author, 1983.
353 Later: Captain, DSC.
354 Who was to be awarded the DSM for his work this day and, later, after the LSLs *Sir Galahad* and *Sir Tristram* were bombed.
355 Undated letter to Martin Power.
356 Two of the four were AAB(M) Charlie Hill and AAB(M) Colin (Dolly) Grey.
357 Small crustaceans that swim in dense masses of about half a million to the cubic yard and well-known to like water cooling inlets.
358 Later Brigadier.
359 Later Colour Sergeant.
360 Later Major General, CB, DSO.
361 Royal Marine slang for a long cross-country march with a heavy load.
362 Who had commanded Naval Party 8901, the Royal Marines Falkland Islands Detachment, between 1978 and 1979.
363 Later: Sir Jeremy, KCB, MC*.
364 Commander, and the ship's MEO. Later, OBE.
365 Strips of metal foil launched by rocket to seduce an Exocet's radar away from the intended target.
366 Brian Johnston is quoted as saying: 'Bugger the orders. I've been frightened by a Royal Navy frigate when I was returning from Salvador Waters and I'm not going to risk that again in the dark. The Brigade needs these vehicles forward now. We'll sail.'
367 Normal crew is seven.
368 Then aged eighteen. Later: Warrant Officer 1 and RSM of 45 Commando and who has corroborated this version. Still serving.
369 This story has not been heard before by the author.
370 Radio (including radar emissions) silence.
371 Letter to the author dated 3 July 2003.
372 Later Commodore, DSC.
373 Tragically drowned in a boating accident in Cyprus in July 2003.
374 They were 'christened' VV and VC (the Squadron identifier letter is V for Victor). The original VC had been lost in Chile during the conflict. On returning home these were employed by the SAS at Hereford.
375 Letter to the author dated 17 May 2003.
376 Later, Lieutenant General Sir Martin, KCB, CMG, OBE; CGRM 1987–1990.
377 Usually a Midshipman informally appointed as a senior officer's assistant.
378 British Forces Lebanon.
379 *Fearless* letter 226/1 dated 20 January 1984.
380 *Fearless* mounted a number of exhibitions devoted to British Leyland and Jaguar cars: attracting considerable interest if not sales. This demonstrated how the unusual setting of an Assault Ship can be quite a draw to prospective customers.
381 1943–1946: including service with 41 Commando.
382 This has been considerably abridged.
383 A 160 ton Ford class Seaward Defence Boat.
384 In the manner of the day he was not allowed to retain the rank of Commodore into retirement.
385 Later, Rear Admiral Sir John, KCVO, CBE.
386 Later, Lieutenant General Sir Henry, KCB, OBE. CGRM 1990–1993.
387 Lieutenant Commander RNR. Later, Sir Robin.
388 Now deceased.
389 Director of Operational Requirements, Sea.
390 Ship's Life Extension Programme.
391 To be known eventually as Bay Class Landing Ships Dock (Auxiliary).
392 See Annex I.
393 A 121 ft Brooke Marine, Fast Patrol Boat.
394 From 651 Squadron Army Air Corps.

395 Later Major General, MBE. Still serving.
396 For which she had been refitted to accommodate both males and females at all ranks.
397 Later to leave the Royal Navy, obtain a degree in oceanography from Plymouth University and work in another male-oriented environment, oil exploration.
398 *Fearless* letter, dated 9 November 1991.
399 Letter to the author dated 13 February 2005.
400 Vice Admiral Sir Alan, KBE.
401 Sub Lieutenant Johanna Bollen surprised and delighted a number of Russian Second World War naval veterans by being appointed their conducting officer during their visit on board.
402 See Annex J.
403 An 8,500 ton (15,000 tons when docked-down) Landing Ship Dock.
404 See Chapter 25.
405 Flag Officer Scotland and Northern Ireland.
406 These forty-five foot craft were described in *Jane's Fighting Ships* two years earlier, as being of 'doubtful operational status'.
407 *Fearless* letter 226/1 dated 27 January 1994.
408 Kate Adie, OBE, in a letter to the author dated 11 February 2005.
409 *Fearless* letter 226/1 dated 7 November 1994.
410 Four Gazelles and two light hovercraft respectively.
411 *Fearless* letter 226/1 dated 7 November 1994.
412 Part of the citation was to read: 'The ship's involvement in the various projects made a very significant impression on the country and even attracted the praise of the country's President.'
413 Letter to the author dated 6 March 2005.
414 Conservative, under Harold Macmillan.
415 Report of Proceedings: *Fearless* letter 226/1 dated 7 November 1994.
416 Ibid.
417 Letter to Captain Tom Cunningham 23 March 2002.
418 Chief Boatswain's Mate.
419 Secretary of State for Defence.
420 Vickers Shipbuilding and Engineering Limited.
421 For the record, Nicola Cullen also wrote: 'We did away with the Women's Royal Naval Service in the early 1990s before I joined in 1994. I am still horrified when I am called a Wren Officer because I associate it with the blue lace, blue eye-shadow brigade and I joined the Royal Navy! Up until three years ago (2002) the females were still known as Wren Steward/Wren MEM and called that too. But to bring the girls in line the W was dropped and the only way you can identify if you have a female in your Division is by the service number. However, old habits die hard and you still find girls being called Leading Wren Smith!'
422 Letter to the author dated 18 March 2005.
423 Nicola Cullen was a Warfare Officer.
424 Officer in charge of nominating jobs and managing careers.
425 Later Major General, CBE; CGRM. 2004 – Still serving.
426 Commodore Paul Stone RN.
427 Translated as Exercise LOYAL FRIEND.
428 Major General David Pennefather CB, OBE. CGRM 1996–1998.
429 Undoubtedly, the most notable hotel in Singapore, despite (to be truthful, because of) its continuing, old-fashioned, colonial, status. Deservedly famous for its Tiffin Room, Long Room and Singapore Sling cocktails: now, alas, favoured more by Japanese tourists in shorts and festooned with digital video cameras around their necks than the British in cotton tropical suits and ties.
430 Later, Major General and CGRM 2002–2004.
431 Ex HMS *Intrepid*.
432 11,900 ton LSD launched in 1988.
433 Full Admiral equivalent.
434 Later Sir Alan, GCB, DSC: First Sea Lord.
435 Later Lieutenant General Sir Robert KCB, CBE: having been CGRM 2001–2002. Still serving.
436 Lately: the Brigade Air Squadron.
437 One of the jungle warfare instructors embarked in *Fearless* with 40 Commando was Sergeant Mick Harding.
438 *Navy News* July 1997.
439 Amphibious Assault Ship (LHD) of 40,650 tons.
440 One of three 7,665 ton San Giorgio class LPDs: *San Marco* was launched on Trafalgar Day(!) 1987.
441 Later Major General and CGRM 2004.
442 MBE. Later Major General.
443 Alderman Ted Agar Mayor of Scarborough 1996–1997 (with the rank of Admiral of the Coast from Haisburgh in the south to Nothland in the north) and for ten years Chairman of the Scarborough Harbour Authority wrote: *Chief Petty Officer 'Banjo' West was* Fearless's *head cook who did fantastic fundraising on behalf of the children at the local Friarage After School Kids Club.* Letter to author dated 18 November 2004.
444 Over 30,000 visitors.
445 19,000 visitors.
446 12,750 tons. Commissioned April 1998.

447 Enigmatically, this description had nothing to do with the weather.
448 Letter to Captain Fanshawe dated 5 November 1998.
449 *Press and Journal* 5 November 1998.
450 The first real test of the Amphibious Readiness Group in an operational Mediterranean deployment based around *Ocean* and *Fearless*.
451 Involving 73,000 troops with nearly 1,000 front-line (A Echelon) vehicles, fifty-three warships of which seventeen were Royal Navy and over 540 aircraft. Forces taking part were Egyptian, French, German, Greek, Italian, Jordanian, Kuwaiti, Dutch, UAE, UK and US.
452 Major General Rob Fulton CGRM. Later, Lieutenant General Sir Robert KBE.
453 See Chapter Sixteen.
454 Admiral Sir Nigel Essenhigh, KCB. Later First Sea Lord.
455 Taken from a draft document covering *Fearless*'s last commission and prepared on board the ship before the author was involved.
456 Lieutenant Commander Tom Joyce, Lieutenant Daniel Clarke and AEM Dan Ruszczyk.
457 Commander UK Maritime Force. Later Admiral Sir James, KCB, CBE, ADC: Second Sea Lord and Commander-in-Chief Fleet. Serving.
458 A mere £2m! or rather less than a mid-week lottery win.
459 Taken from a draft document covering her last commission and prepared on board *Fearless* before the author was involved.
460 Later: CBE, retired.
461 Taken from a draft document covering her last commission and prepared on board *Fearless* before the author was involved.
462 Back home, this was perceived by the press to be a muddle and one for which the Royal Marines Brigade Commander, Brigadier Roger Lane, was wrongly blamed by the Secretary of State for Defence.
463 Apart from, it is rumoured, some lively and accommodating, female, fighter pilots.
464 Letter to the author December 2003.
465 Bravo Zulu – Royal Naval expression of high praise.
466 See Annex C.
467 As she did so Commander Steve Farrington, QGM, her last MEO, allowed steam to pour from her funnels, like a coal-powered express train, just to emphasize her age!
468 518 feet long, just 2 feet shorter than the ship herself.
469 Minister of State for the Armed Forces.
470 CGRM 2002–2004.
471 Letters to the author 31 October 2004 and 6 March 2005.
472 http://www.hmsfearless.co.uk/home.htm
473 Lieutenant Commander Douglas Barlow in a letter to the author dated 30 July 2003: 'The Boatswain's lot was fast diminishing with the need for seamanship skills declining and the qualification began to be phased out in the 1960s. Those remaining would only be found in the big ships, on board minesweepers or ashore. My duties in *Fearless* were bound up in everything seamanship, for example RAS, anchors, cables, ropes, wires and associated equipment: ship's appearance, action stations, dock master, OOW, friendly Divisional Officer, jack of all trades, also good at cocktail parties and runs ashore. No genuine Bosuns remain but a ship's officer is designated if only for the paperwork for rigging warrants and so on! I was recently invited to dinner on board HMS *Illustrious* and my host took much pleasure in introducing me to the ship's Bosun; a charming lady Lieutenant!'
474 Plymouth: now, sadly, closed down.
475 COMATG. Later: Rear Admiral CBE.
476 Commander Brian Warren.
477 He was a Royal Marine!
478 The whole incident appeared on Spanish television the next day.
479 Flag Lieutenant or, in Army parlance, Aide de Camp.
480 Sergeant R.J. Rotherham.
481 Later Lieutenant Colonel MC.
482 Later: Major General, OBE. Commanded 40 Commando in the Falklands War.
483 4th Viscount Younger of Leckie.
484 Being the cheapest and far from the best design offered. They suffered considerable teething problems.

Index

Ranks are those held on first mention: subsequent promotions (if known) will be found in the text and in the notes. United Kingdom place names are in their own alphabetical order; others are under their country heading.